THE TRUTH WITHIN

The Truth Within

A History of Inwardness in Christianity, Hinduism, and Buddhism

GAVIN FLOOD

UNIVERSITY PRESS

Great Clarendon Street, Oxford, OX2 6DP,
United Kingdom

Oxford University Press is a department of the University of Oxford.
It furthers the University's objective of excellence in research, scholarship, and education by publishing worldwide. Oxford is a registered trade mark of Oxford University Press in the UK and in certain other countries

First published 2013
First published in paperback 2015

Published in the United States of America by Oxford University Press
198 Madison Avenue, New York, NY 10016, United States of America

British Library Cataloguing in Publication Data
Data available

Library of Congress Cataloging in Publication Data
Data available

ISBN 978–0–19–968456–4 (Hbk.)
ISBN 978–0–19–874521–1 (Pbk.)

In memory of my mother and father

Acknowledgements

I would like to thank the many people over the years who have contributed to my understanding of inwardness. I will not name them all, but particularly my teachers at Lancaster University, my colleagues at institutions where I have studied and taught, in Wales, Stirling, Virginia, and Oxford, and my friends. Most of this book was written under an Arts and Humanities Research Council (AHRC) fellowship that allowed me two terms away from teaching and administration, and I would like to thank both the AHRC and the three anonymous readers for their generous, and at times critical, comments. Similarly, the Oxford University Press readers offered insightful critique. I hope I have addressed their concerns, but even when I have disagreed I have taken their comments seriously and think the book is a better one for their assessment. Although his is a different kind of project to mine, I would like to thank Frank Clooney for conversation and for his prolific output on Hindu–Christian comparison. Thanks to Tom Perridge for encouraging me to submit the manuscript and guiding it through the publishing process. And finally, a deep and heartfelt thanks to my wife Emma Kwan for her love and support of this project, and indeed to my broader family.

I should like to thank Columbia University Press for permission to reprint a selected text from Julia Kristeva, *Hatred and Forgiveness*. 'Re-Statement of Romance' from The Collected Poems of Wallace Stevens by Wallace Stevens, © 1954 by Wallace Stevens and renewed 1982 by Holly Stevens. Used by permission of Alfred A. Knopf, an imprint of the Knopf Doubleday Publishing Groups, a division of Random House LLC. All rights reserved.

Contents

Preface xi

1. Introduction: The Mountains of the Mind 1

Part I History and Text

2. Prayer and Vision in the Middle Ages 29
3. Inwardness as Mystical Ascent 69
4. Inwardness and Visual Contemplation in Hinduism 103
5. A Hindu Philosophy of Inwardness 139
6. Inwardness Without Self 167

Part II Theory

7. A Theory of Religious Inwardness 193
8. The Phenomenology of Inwardness 221
9. The Historical Self and Comparative Religion 247

Epilogue 271

References 273
Index 299

Preface

'How then should one see the good life and the beauty it has? Go into yourself and look.'

Plotinus[1]

'Do not go out, return to yourself; truth dwells in the inner man.'

Augustine[2]

'Truth does not "inhabit" only the "inner man", or more accurately, there is no inner man, man is in the world, and only in the world does he know himself.'

Merleau-Ponty[3]

'Of all yogis, the one whose inner self has come to me, rich in faith, who worships me, he is regarded as most disciplined.'

Bhagavad-gītā 6.47[4]

'And she [Teresa] convinces herself not only that Jesus loves her but that this extraordinary "love object", as we would say, never leaves her, that He (Jesus) is always with her, that she is His wife, no less, and that her words are nothing but the words of her love object, Jesus, or God himself, words she is content in her humility to repeat.'

Kristeva[5]

'To thine own self be true.'

Shakespeare[6]

Although the roots of this book go back a long way into my past, the initial formulation began a few years ago in thinking about claims that a deeper truth than we encounter in the everyday world can be found within the self. The

[1] Plotinus, *The Enneads*, 1.6.9. Ricardus Volkamnn (ed.), *Plotini Enneades*, vol. 1 (Bibliotheca Scriptorum Graecorum et Romanorum Teunneriana, 1883), p. 95: *πως άν ούν ίδοις ψυχην άγαθην οίον το κάλλος έχει; άναγε έπι σαυτον και ίδέ.*

[2] Augustine, *De vera religione*, 39, n. 72: *Noli foras ire in te redi, in interiore homine habitat veritas.*

[3] Merleau-Ponty, M. *The Phenomenology of Perception*, trans. Colin Smith (London: Routledge, 1962), p. xii. *Phénoménologie de la perception* (Paris: Gallimard, 1945), p. 11: 'La vérité "n'habite" pas seulement "l'homme intérieur," ou plutôt il n'ya pas d'homme intérieur, l'homme est au monde, c'est dans le monde qu'il se connaît.'

[4] *Bhagavad-gītā* 6.47: *yoginām api sarveṣāṃ mad-gatenāntarātmanā | śraddhāvān bhajate yo māṃ sa me yuktatamo mataḥ.*

[5] Julia Kristeva, *Hatred and Forgiveness*, trans. J. Herman (Columbia University Press, 2010), p. 163.

[6] *Hamlet*, Act 1, scene 3, 78–82.

metaphor of interiority, and the attendant privileging of the inner over the outer, has been a claim, if not the central claim, of many religions throughout history. The idea that there is a truth within linked to the discovery of a deeper, more fundamental, more authentic self, has been a common theme and an idea that is still with us today. This interiority or inwardness unique to me as an essential feature of who I am has been an aspect of culture and even a defining characteristic of human beings; an authentic, private sphere to which we can retreat that is beyond the conflicts of the outer world. This inner world becomes more real than the outer, which is seen as but a pale reflection. Remarkably, the image of the truth within is found across cultures, and this book presents an account of this idea in the premodern history of Christianity, Hinduism, and Buddhism. In theistic religions, Christianity and some forms of Hinduism, the truth within is conflated with the idea of God within, and in all cases this inner truth is thought to be not only the heart of the person, but also the heart of the universe itself.

A story could be told of the foundations of the truth within in the earliest literary representations of the first millennium BC, the Upaniṣads, the Platonic dialogues, and the dialogues of the Buddha, and some sense of interiority is arguably present even in early cave art. A sense of inwardness in human evolution is closely connected with the stories we tell about ourselves, and the experiences we undergo both by ourselves and with others. The idea of an authentic, private realm unique to me, in which I compose poetry, fall in love, or contemplate my feelings, is probably a recent development; but a sense of a distinct self and the ability to express the sentiment 'I want' is presumably as old as the origins of language itself as we walked, or ran, out of Africa. The ability to reflect entailed by the sentiment 'I want' is integral, as we will see, to the idea of inwardness. Gazing at a plastic cast of the Turkana Boy in the Oxford University Museum of Natural History, we are in awe of this one and a half million year-old hominid; and if he had the ability to speak, perhaps even he had some sense of inwardness through the self-reflection that language allows.

This book does not attempt to trace a history of inwardness before written records began, but rather takes up the story at a relatively recent date, during a time when the boundary conditions around traditions were more stable—Christianity has creedal definition in East and West, and Brahmanical traditions such as the religions of Śiva and the Buddha have canons of revered texts and forms of spiritual practice taught through the generations. The book presents an account of inwardness in Christianity, Hinduism, and Buddhism, arguing that they share an understanding of truth within, not in terms of a private sphere, but in terms of a common imaginaire; and although there is an emphasis on the cultivation of subjectivity through spiritual practice, this subjectivity needs to be distinguished from the kind of private, romantic inwardness we are familiar with in late modernity.

The first epigraph above from Plotinus (third century AD) reflects a classical view derived from Plato—that there is a higher reality, a unitary truth, from which the proliferation and multiplicity of the world derives or emanates. This truth is found within the self and through contemplation; through turning away from the world, the person can realize the beauty of the truth within, which is the source and origin of us all. With Plotinus we need to turn to the self to perceive the unchanging, inner beauty of its truth. The journey of the alone to the alone is a journey inside ourselves, back to our real nature and authentic truth. Indeed, the outer world is even seen as an emanation or manifestation of this inner and higher truth for Plotinus. This monistic emanationism is virtually identical to some early forms of Hindu thinking such as we find in the Upaniṣads and in later traditions: the true self is found within the person through inner reflection or contemplation, and the journey back to the self is a journey into the self that is also a journey through the levels of the universe.

Christianity absorbs the Neoplatonism of Plotinus, and Augustine reflects it in his emphasis on interiority. For him, the turn inwards is a turn towards the self and simultaneously an upward movement towards God, who is found within the self. Augustine reads Plotinus along with the Bible to come up with the uniquely Christian vision of inner truth attained through grace. For Plotinus, there is an inner beauty that exists in a vast inner realm that, with later Neoplatonism, comes to be populated with a hierarchy of angelic beings—a hierarchy adopted by early Christianity, particularly Pseudo-Denys and Origen. Augustine inherits this model of cosmic interiority which is then adopted by the medieval theologians, some of whom we will encounter in the coming pages. With Augustine, we have the self as an inner space within which we find the truth, but a truth that is not unique to me but common to all, and a truth that is, furthermore, the truth of Christ.

It is the development of these ideas in the Middle Ages that this book traces, not only in sophisticated theology but also in more popular literature. Indeed, in both Europe and South Asia we have literary genres that are pre-philosophical in the sense that they are not clearly articulated arguments, but that nevertheless present strong accounts of the cosmos and the person's place within it. In Sanskrit we have an abundance of ritual and meditation texts that describe practices to realize the truth within and that display a cosmological inwardness. Similarly, in Christian Europe we have popular literature, both in Latin and the vernaculars, concerned with dying, with mysticism, and concerned with visions. These vision texts tell us a lot about medieval conceptions of the person and about an interiority that is crucial to our salvation. At the end of this period we have writers such as Teresa of Avila, who Kristeva refers to in our fifth epigraph, describing an interiority that is filled with transcendence in the form of Christ: an interiority in which Christ fills the self.

There are clearly analogues in these genres across civilizations; and while there are, of course, strong differences between the world views of medieval Europe and India—the emphasis on sin in Europe, for example, in contrast to the emphasis on rebirth in South Asia—they share a common conception of the person as being located within a cosmos (and so within a meaningful universe) and that the truth of the world can be found within the self. The cultivation of the inner self is, in theistic Hinduism, also the realization of God within the self, as we see in our fourth epigraph from the *Bhagavad-gītā*.

These popular world views about interiority find philosophical or theological articulation among the philosophers and theologians who offer arguments to support the idea that the truth is within, found through tracing a path back to the true self. Inwardness is here understood in terms of cosmology and enacted in ritual. Our interiority is given shape through participation in the practices of religion, which is a way in which the practitioner gains access to deeper resources of meaning within the self. This shared world view goes virtually unchallenged until the beginnings of the Renaissance where we witness a retreat of religion from cosmology and a de-emphasis on ritual participation in favour of individual conscience. The rise of humanism, and of the new science in particular, tend to put paid to cosmological inwardness in the West, with the cosmos being explained in mechanistic terms and the true self—the soul—being located outside of the mechanistic world and exercising freedom of will, as we find in Cartesian dualism. The non-material freedom of soul, on the one hand, in contrast to the material causation of the world, on the other, is a feature of this new world view. In place of a cosmological inwardness we have an individualism in which the person stands with her own power of autonomy and self-assertion. As signalled by Polonius' advice to his son Laertes in *Hamlet* (quoted on page xi) the new inwardness is no longer cosmological but individualistic and, above all, concerned with authenticity and being true to oneself—true to one's essential nature as a distinct and unique person with conscience and moral rectitude.

With the rise of science and the retreat of religion from cosmology as an explanation of the outer universe, subjectivity retreats to an inner realm. Inwardness becomes private and each of us comes to have her own, unique interiority linked to personal memory. Locke's individual mind is no longer a vast cosmos but a small dark room in which the self looks forlornly at images projected from the light coming in from the outside (an image that itself reflects in a diminished form the cosmological metaphor of Plato's cave). There is no inner light of truth here, but rather a space of individual subjectivity that has no real contact with others or the world other than through the light of the senses. This inner space is the place of individual consciousness, the *cogito*, which will itself be expunged from our thinking by an impressive range of philosophers from Hegel to Derrida in continental Europe, and from Hume to Ryle in the English-speaking world.

There was, then, a shift from the cosmic order of premodernity to Descartes' dualism of the *cogito* and matter—two distinct if interacting substances. But as we once no longer believed in the old cosmologies, so too we now mostly no longer believe in dualism and a strictly mechanistic universe. The very notion of the unified individual has been under attack for many years since Hume and Hegel, but particularly with Marx, who argued that our self-conceptions are the result of greater historical and economic forces beyond us. Continuing the theme of fragmentation, Nietzsche thought of inwardness as the space of the soul, which is the internalized and inverted distinction between the weak and the strong, identified with the good and the bad; for him, the creation of the soul is a result of the slave morality of Christianity that humanity needs to overcome. Freud, developing Nietzsche, argued that what we think and our sense of self is the result of greater unconscious powers exerting their influence over us. The unified self is shattered by conflicting unconscious desires. For Jung, such shattering was a prequel to a full integration of powers as an integrated individual; but for Freud, we moderns must simply live with the tensions and contradiction that we are unhappy because of repression—and yet repression is a necessary condition for civilization. Inwardness here is found in the swirling sea of unconscious forces that determine who we are, although rational, inner reflection can control these unconscious forces that seek to overwhelm us. Postmodernism takes up the idea of fragmentation: there is no such thing as 'man', which is simply the residue of a Western metaphysics left over from the days of empire; there is no depth any more, only surface.

But even this view is being left behind by the sweep of history. Science holds greater sway over the popular imagination in the West than at any point in the past. Quantum physics tells us that the world is much more mysterious than we once thought, and neuroscience tells us that subjectivity and objectivity are more closely integrated, especially in the light of Hebbs' law that states that 'neurons that fire together wire together'. The relevance of these contemporary developments on ideas of inwardness has yet to be determined, but, as has always been the case, contemporary discovery in the world affects our models in the humanities of who we are. We know that subjectivity cannot be understood except in relation to each other, and that a sense of inwardness is formed through interacting; our human sociality is hardwired, as is demonstrated by the mirror neuron and other systems in our brains.

The deconstruction of the privileged subject—the male, colonial, transcendental ego—by postmodernism and by critical thinking means that we can no longer intellectually return to the Augustinian, cosmological model, nor to the Cartesian model. But even so, our sense of inwardness persists. Having mapped the idea of inwardness in the histories of medieval Christianity, Hinduism, and Buddhism, and having set up a disjunction between the cosmological inwardness that is shared and the individualistic inwardness that is unique to each, I wish to make the issue more complex. In spite of the differences there are continuities between these different views of the self. Although Augustine inhabits a Neoplatonist influenced Christian world—so far away from our own world—nevertheless, when we read him, there is a resonance with the contemporary reader and we can recognize and identify with his thoughts and his struggles. We recognize something of our own life in his, even though in late modernity we have lost his deeply cosmological sense of the self. We no longer live in his world of angels and demons that inhabit the cosmos, and we no longer uncritically accept his cosmological Christianity. And yet we can see ourselves in him.

What is it that enables us to recognize a kindred spirit in Augustine and see continuity between his and our sense of inwardness? There is persistence to interiority that adapts and changes according to different circumstances, but that remains as a feature of a common humanity. This book is not an argument for a certain kind of religious interiority, but rather offers a historical argument about the nature of the religious self in premodern religions, contrasting these forms of subjectivity with those of modernity, while at the same time recognizing the continuity between ourselves and our forebears across continents. We glimpse a dimension of common humanity here. The book is also, therefore, an argument for comparative religion through a performance of it, and an argument for the importance of inwardness in shaping events in the world. Inwardness is clearly a form of knowledge that gives us understanding of who we are, and also a kind of poetry that expresses that understanding in the space of imagination. We can never again authentically inhabit the world of Bonaventure or Abhinavagupta, but arguably we have something to learn from their insistence on the truth within and our need to face the future drawing on human resources that reach into our pasts. The truth within is still existentially important for many millions of religious practitioners, a sense of self that is still important in many fields of human endeavour, from economics and politics to evolutionary biology. Understanding the foundations of contemporary religious world views is clearly important because kinds of religious inwardness continue to influence our political and legal reasoning, our ethics in recognizing human sanctity, and our interactions with others in the global, international arena.

READING GUIDELINES

A book such as this is wide-ranging and ventures into a number of specialist fields where I do not have first-hand knowledge and in which I have had to rely on the scholarship of others. A history of inwardness has necessitated a particularly interdisciplinary approach, one that assumes philological scholarship of Europe and South Asia but that hopes to go beyond the purely philological into philosophical and sociological speculation about the nature of inwardness in a cross-civilizational perspective. The epigraphs above foreshadow the journey of the book itself. The book moves from older accounts to more modern ones across civilizations. One of the features of the book is that in the readings I present I have tried to give the originals in the notes for readers with the requisite knowledge and interest. I have therefore tried to cater for two levels of reading: a specialist level for readers who wish to follow the Sanskrit or Latin texts, who will thereby be in a position to make judgements about the claims I make about them, and a non-specialist level. Indeed, specialists in some areas that the book touches on—philosophy, medieval history of ideas, philosophical Sanskrit—will not be specialist in other areas, and I hope to have written the book in such a way that the overarching argument guides the reader through the specialist readings. A reader with little interest in a particular religion could bypass those chapters as the general thesis that abstracts from those histories is found in Part II.

The introductory chapter offers a general orientation to the problem of inwardness, especially in the context of comparative religion. The following, Part I, contains four chapters on Christian and Hindu understandings of inwardness, and one on Buddhism. I have attempted here a parallelism in the Christian and Hindu material in describing firstly pre-philosophical genres of text and then philosophical or theological texts. With Buddhism, I have only written one chapter, as the main point is that Buddhism challenges the notion of an inner self that we need to address. I hope that this can be sufficiently completed in the readings I have offered.

Part II, Theory, then goes on to develop a comparison of the material we have seen in Part I. It develops a phenomenology of inwardness and outlines features that I argue are shared across traditions. Although I think that there are striking differences between the premodern religions I describe and a modern sense of inwardness, there are nevertheless also continuities that allow us to perceive those early forms *as* inwardness. The general theory of inwardness in Chapter 7 contrasts a participatory model in premodern religions where inwardness is a negation of individualism, with the affirmation of individualism in modernity. A collective subjectivity of the cosmic religions gives way to an individualistic subjectivity. Chapter 8 offers a general phenomenology of inwardness that draws out common features, not only of the shared subjectivity of the religions I have described, but of modernity too, such as self-reflection, reportability, and disclosure through signs. This leads to our last chapter, Chapter 9, which looks at the notion of the self in relation to comparative religion and offers an argument for comparative religion in the context of contemporary detractors. In particular, it begins to develop an account of inwardness in relation to world in terms of what I have called 'act theory' that presents an account of the relationship between inwardness and event producing action that in turn affects interiority.

A very different book could have been written through focusing wholly on poetry or other kinds of literature, or that looks exclusively at philosophy or art. I have not discussed philosophical notions of truth, nor attempted to adjudicate on the particular truth claims of the religions, although I have tried to articulate the truth of inwardness they assert. I have attempted to strike a balance between philosophical and non-philosophical genres of text and, although the range of material I cover is wide, hope that the overarching argument is coherent. I am, of course, responsible for any errors in my renderings of the texts. I have used standard transliteration for Sanskrit and have cited technical terms in the nominative beside the translation (thus *ātmā* rather than *ātman*, *karma* rather than *karman*, *cittam* rather than *citta*).

Gavin Flood

New Year's Day 2013
Oxford

1

Introduction: The Mountains of the Mind

Between 1885 and 1889, after his appointment as Professor of Classics in University College, Dublin, Gerard Manley Hopkins underwent a 'terrible pathos' during which he composed the poignant and bleak 'terrible sonnets' and in which he declared 'O the mind, mind has mountains . . .'[1] This sense of a vast, interior landscape is fundamental to human imagination and experience. Hopkins articulates both a modern sense of inwardness linked to alienation from himself, from his God, and from his fellow humans, a sense that becomes strongly thematized in the twentieth century, along with a traditional sense that it is within these inner depths that we encounter truth as transcendence or a sense of a power beyond the self. In Hopkins we find a kind of subjectivity or inwardness that both looks forward to the fragmentation of the human person in late modernity and back to a self-formation by tradition through the spiritual practices of Catholic Christianity. The purpose of this book is to examine how the idea of the truth within is formed in religions through spiritual practice, a formation of inwardness that can be contrasted with wholly secular understandings of the human person. In a sense the book traces a historical trajectory behind Hopkins' 'mountains of the mind' that is particularly formative in medieval Christianity and broadens out the inquiry to analogous ideas of interiority in South Asian religious history.

While the book intends to avoid reading back into past, distant cultures something that has developed only in more recent times, it does attempt to trace the development of inner truth or inwardness in the specific contexts in which it arose. Furthermore, the book is not simply a mapping of ideas about the truth within but is also an argument for the centrality of inwardness in scriptural religions, an argument that links text and spiritual practices to the formation of inwardness. We might even call this kind of inwardness, this search for inner truth, a shared subjectivity or 'corporate imagination'[2] in so

[1] Gerard Manley Hopkins, Sonnet 65, *Poems of Gerard Manley Hopkins* (London, New York, Toronto: Oxford University Press, 1948), p. 107.

[2] I take this phrase from Rowan Williams, *Dostoyevsky: Language, Faith and Fiction* (London and New York: Continuum, 2008), p. xi.

far as the subject of experience, the 'I', participates in a wider identity. This can be contrasted with a more recent sense of self that emphasizes individualism with inner depth, a sense that particularly derives from Romanticism. More specifically, the following pages unfold an argument that shows how the idea of the truth within is linked to genres of text along with liturgical and meditative or ascetic practices in the scriptural religions of Europe and South Asia. Hopkins knew such practices all too well and also experienced an unexpected inwardness in his mental turmoil and doubt. While Hopkins' interiority in the form of his dark despair might not have been produced in earlier centuries—although we have precursors in sixteenth-century melancholy—there is a sense in which we do recognize inwardness in the writings of earlier generations, but filled out with different content.

With Hopkins we see that inwardness is inseparable from religion, both in terms of his personal experience and in terms of his Duns Scotus influenced theory of inscape and instress, the particularity of each existence, and its communicative cohesion. Indeed, the history of religions has had an ambivalent attitude towards inwardness in the sense that thinkers who have expounded a view or experience of inwardness that stretched, challenged, or rejected the boundaries of tradition, have often been vilified, excommunicated, or even executed. One thinks of Eckhart's sailing close to the wind with Church orthodoxy, and Marguerte Porete who was burned at the stake for advocating a particular kind of interiority in which she became coterminous with her God: for Porete the truth within was God identical with the self.

The idea of the truth within can be captured in the image of the Tibetan Buddhist practitioner who meditates upon the external ritual diagram or *maṇḍala*, then closes her eyes and visualizes the diagram in the mind's eye. This eidetic image becomes the focus of practice and its intensification opens out an inner world where the realization of Buddhahood can be found. This kind of inwardness is closely linked to scriptural authority and the realization of the truth of tradition. For the Tibetan Buddhist the truth is within, and this truth is declared by the tradition and understood to have a timeless depth although conveyed through history. The same could be said of the Christian monk for whom God is within and who seeks him there through shared liturgy, private prayer, and sacred reading. It is certainly not my claim that the inner truth of the Buddha is the same as the Christian's God within, but there is clearly a parallel process of discernment and practice that we can identify. Furthermore, this inwardness is not so much concerned with developing individualism but rather with subsuming the sense of an 'I' within the tradition. The Cartesian *ego cogito* is subsumed by a collectivity greater than the individual, and the truth within is a truth that transcends the individual as such. Of course there are individual differences between people within traditions—we all have distinct, unrepeateable personalities and always have done—but religions create a shared imagination and shared narrative space within which people operate and within which they find an inner truth that is only articulated by the categories of the tradition they inhabit. The religious inwardness that seeks a depth of truth is concerned with conformity to the narrative of tradition and with the transformation of the personality: in medieval Christianity part of this is a resistance to diabolical influence; in Buddhism and Hinduism a transformation of the inner faults and patterns of erroneous perception. The seeker after inner truth wants to maintain a sense of presence, the being of the self, or the being of a transcendent power, along with the authority of tradition and text.

The formation of an inner space in the search for truth is also the formation of a moral space in which the person becomes open to the possibility of change and the promise of greater freedom through the restriction of ascetic and spiritual practice. Conforming to the pattern of tradition, to the narrative space of tradition, allows the practitioner to undergo a change—perhaps almost imperceptible over a lifetime—in which the complexity and conflictual nature of our personality is transcended. Such a transition or series of transitions from surface to depth (to use one traditional metaphor) is regarded as a moral good and indeed, the *summum bonum* of life. The transition from sinner to saint is an intensification of inwardness developed in tradition through spiritual practices (although the roles of sinner and saint are variable: one's man's sinner could be another's saint). This is often associated with an intensification of love: the Christian discipline is a structure that cultivates love of neighbour and love of God; the Buddhist develops compassion for all beings; and likewise, some Hindu traditions have focused on the love of God as the guiding metaphor of life.

But what do we mean by 'the truth within' or 'inner truth'? This is necessarily a vague term as although the religions under review share the metaphor of inwardness, the content of that inner truth varies according to tradition. There is an implicit contrast here between external and internal truth. The claims to internal truth are often at the expense of external truth that is regarded as being of lower order. Certain kinds of religious inwardness can be contrasted with the externalization of religion in dogma and especially in law. Indeed the idea of the truth within is sometimes (but not necessarily) associated with resistance to law and claims to a higher source of authority—the immediacy of self-experience or the apprehension of transcendence within the human person. If, as Derrida has observed, the other makes the law and the self has to be given up to it,[3] then inwardness is sometimes an implicit rejection of external law often in the belief that there is a higher law apprehended within the self. Mystical theology might be understood as the development of a certain kind of inwardness that makes epistemological claim over dogmatic theology and religious law. This is not to

[3] Jacques Derrida, 'Faith and Knowledge', p. 34, in Jacques Derrida and Gianni Vattimo (eds.), *Religion* (Stanford, CA: Stanford University Press, 1996), pp. 1–78.

say that many mystics were not also keen supporters of law (one thinks of the Jewish mystic and lawyer Isaac Kook, for example); but it is to register that inwardness can be marked by resistance to law and the externalization of religion. Indeed inwardness is counter to the Levinasian move to see religion purely in terms of the ethical relationship to the other. Inwardness posits a different centre of gravity—not necessarily the egological self, but a centre of gravity where language, coterminous with body, requires the formation of the human person through the other, rather than the subordination of the self to the injunctive demands of the other.

If the first resistance of inwardness is to law, perhaps a second resistance is to nature and the world. Seeking the truth within through spiritual practices such as prayer, fasting, and other kinds of asceticism might be seen as an attempt at inner flight and escape from the world of nature. There is clearly some truth in this in so far as practices that develop inwardness, both in Christianity and Brahmanical traditions, create (they would say discover) a rich, inner landscape, which becomes more intense than the outer world. But nevertheless we must not forget that inwardness can also be linked with a laudation of nature and seeing God in, or even as, nature. Hopkins, for example, saw God in nature—or rather God's glory reflected in nature as well as within the self.[4]

The relationship of inwardness to religion is therefore complex. The binary opposition that I am setting up between truth within and without, which is based on the metaphor of the container, is intended as a heuristic device through which to view a range of practices and ideas in religions. There is no pure interiority outside of the world, and even solitary hermits focused on developing an inner life are part of community and tradition. They are supported and part of a larger matrix in which their behaviour is meaningful. Even Kierkegaard's individualism cultivates inwardness through love of neighbour. The binary opposition between internal and external therefore operates within particular fields of meaning in scriptural religions, and in this book I am creating a space of comparison in which the binary distinction can operate and be abstracted from the particular traditions in which it is found. In a sense, the tradition-specific terms for the 'inner man' (*homo interior*) in Christianity, the 'inner self' (*antarātmā*) in Hinduism, and 'the truth of awakening through inwardness' (*pratyātmādhigamadharmaḥ*) in Buddhism are generalized into a concept of inwardness for the purposes of comparison. These terms are parallel, although the idea of inwardness is not restricted to their use within the traditions. In some ways this book is a reversal of common ways of approaching the philosophies of religions from a Christian perspective and then noting the differences and parallels with other religions, in so far as

[4] E.g. 'God's Grandeur' and 'Pied Beauty', *Poems of Gerard Manley Hopkins*, pp. 70, 74.

inwardness has been a central feature of Indian religions; and in beginning here we are, in a sense, reading Christianity through the lens of Indian traditions. This book is therefore a comparison of inwardness in European and South Asian religions that, although interesting in itself, raises questions of contemporary relevance about the importance of inwardness for understanding the human person and the place of inwardness in the contemporary world.

GENERAL ORIENTATION

The history of religions is replete with competing theories of the human person, from essentialist ideas (as in Hinduism) that the truth lies within as an innate essence that survives death, to constructivist views (as in Buddhism) that the inner truth is that the human person is empty of self, comprising analytically distinct parts. How we map the self across cultures is therefore one of the questions I seek to address. To answer this we will inevitably have made decisions about the nature of the person (that we may not even, or only vaguely, be aware of) prior to the inquiry.[5] Be that as it may, and with full acknowledgment of the Fichtean problematic of how a causally determined, objective world can give rise to a non-causally bound subjectivity, the general orientation of the present project assumes complexity, assumes a non-reductionist materialism, and argues that we can develop a comparative religion focused on the human person. This will entail some account of the connection between the person and macro-history.

Mapping the self across cultures is complex and needs to operate at different cultural levels, using categories of comparison that can be used outside of any particular culture. Text is one such fundamental category, and theories of the human person within religions are often based on arguments developed from, or supported by, textual revelations. But, above all, it is through spiritual practices that mediate between tradition and the human person that ideas about an inner truth are formed. Inwardness occurs in a particularly intense way in spiritual practices that seek to enthusiastically internalize the texts of tradition. This is not a crude claim that the text causes the self, but is an attempt to develop a more nuanced claim that text is an important element in a complex of cultural ('spiritual') practices that form the conception and

[5] The philosopher François Laruelle has claimed that a decision around which a philosophical system is based cannot be grasped philosophically as this entails the making of a further decision about it. The decisional structure of philosophy can only be grasped non-philosophically. See François Laruelle, *Philosophie et non-philosophie* (Liège: Pierre Mardaga, 1989), pp. 11–17. This non-philosophy can be understood as post-deconstructionist in its presupposition of the real (le réel) or the one (l'un), pp. 181–8.

experience of inwardness in the histories of religions in Europe and South Asia. While I do intend to engage with the philosophical dimensions of the claim, much of the current book will examine the ways in which text-based spiritual practice formed the idea of the truth within and the experience of inwardness at a time when Europe and South Asia were dominated by a linguistic 'cosmopolis' (to use Sheldon Pollock's term[6]) of Latin and Sanskrit respectively, which gave way to the dominance of vernacular languages in literature and polity at the beginnings of modernity.

Quite simply, premodern religions, spiritual practices, which are themselves suffused by text, are used to seek an inner truth—a truth that is found in interiority and a tradition-specific subjectivity. These forms of inwardness generate theories of the human person and contribute to broader cultural formation. Inwardness formed through such practices raises philosophical and theological questions about transcendence and raises the question of a common human nature. Questions of cultural history and theology/philosophy are linked such that we need to inquire into the ways in which spiritual practice relates to discourse, the ways in which cultures of self-cultivation relate to politics, and how the body is inscribed by religious and secular literatures. Such a project is, of course, potentially enormous and even hubristic, but I intend the enterprise to remain coherent through being controlled by the central thesis that the truth within traditional, premodern religions is formed by the cultivation of inwardness through spiritual practices. We might say that the kind of inwardness formed can be spoken of as a shared subjectivity that occurs through the cultivation of text-informed spiritual practices that overwhelm or supersede the *ego cogito*. We might contrast this shared subjectivity with the individualism that has developed from Romanticism through to modernity and the disenchantment with the world, but again I do not want the binary 'shared subjectivity' versus 'individualism' to be overdeterminate of the project. As with all binary oppositions, it has its usefulness in the domain of my project; but of course there are individualistic dimensions to the shared subjective as there are collective dimensions to modernist individualism.

Indeed, we might claim that the contents of inner truth are greatly variable but the process of inwardness is shared across times and cultures. Inwardness, I shall argue in Part II, has general features of self-reflection and narratability that we find not only in Śaiva or Buddhist literature, but in modernity as well. Hopkins' interiority is echoed as far as process is concerned in Rilke, whose 'heart work' involved a 'religious' vision of appearances in which 'a whole inner world was exhibited, as though an angel, in whom space was included,

[6] S. Pollock, *The Language of the Gods in the World of Men: Sanskrit, Culture and Power in Premodern India* (Chicago, IL: Chicago University Press, 2006). On Latin compared to Sanskrit, see pp. 259–80.

were blind and looking into himself. This world, regarded no longer from the human point of view, but as it is within the angel, is perhaps my real task...'[7] This kind of inwardness is not so far from the interiority of the mystical theologians we shall be discussing but perhaps with the proviso that the denotations of language are less literal: angels in the vision literature are external beings apprehended in interiority whereas Rilke's angels are part of the self.

I intend to orchestrate and develop these themes not only in concrete, historical instances in Part I of the book, but also at a level of philosophical and theological abstraction in Part II. Indeed, the philosophical or theological claim about inwardness needs to be distinguished from the phenomenological claim about the history of religions. On the one hand, I intend to offer a description of the truth within through selected readings from the histories of Christianity and Indian religions in which I am making a claim about the way in which inwardness is formed and performed through textual appropriation, through ritual, and through asceticism. On the other hand, such description arguably entails philosophical and, indeed, theological commitments about subjectivity or inwardness in religions. There are therefore two sides to my account. Firstly, it is a description (or first-level phenomenology) of tradition-specific subjectivity and inner truth formed through text-suffused practices. Secondly, such an account makes philosophical and weak theological claims about the relationship between self and world from a hermeneutical perspective. These two sides are connected, although one could arguably accept the phenomenological claim without agreeing with the hermeneutical claim; but it is my belief that the generation of first-level description of cultural and religious formation entails a further step necessitated by the pressures of such description.

It follows from my general account that the truth within experienced in inwardness or subjectivity is central to religions as meaning giving systems. Yet inwardness is not coterminous with individualism. Individualism is a sociological category linked to the rise of modernity out of Romanticism in the West and the development of the citizen, while inwardness, particularly the kinds of religious subjectivity I shall describe in the following pages, transcends individualism. Indeed, the goal of ascetic practice, as I have argued elsewhere, is the intensification of subjectivity at the expense of individuality, if by that we mean a monad or Cartesian consciousness that stands against the world.

The intensification of subjectivity in religious inwardness that we find in premodern, 'scholastic' religions, is different to modern ideas of inwardness that we have seen in the West since the Renaissance. In the history of

[7] Rainer Maria Rilke, *Duino Elegies*, trans. J. B. Leishmann and Stephen Spender (London: Hogarth Press, 1939), p. 10.

secularization subjectivity becomes linked with self-assertion and the self as possessor of liberty and rights. This identification of subjectivity with individualism is a hallmark of the secular West. We can understand this development in terms of the stripping of cosmology from subjectivity. In premodern religions—scholastic Christianity, for example—subjectivity is closely connected to a hierarchical cosmology, as we will see; but with secularization, cosmology is stripped away from subjectivity and we become persons outside of an inherently meaningful cosmos. Without cosmology, which connects the person's subjectivity to a broader community, a shared subjectivity becomes individual and privatized. This leads to characteristic features of the modern age, particularly alienation and fragmentation, and also to secular attempts, such as Communism, to heal alienation through an attempted eradication of the subjective. The discourse of human rights and the liberty of the individual have arisen in the context—or even due to—the eradication of the shared subjectivity we find in premodern, cosmological religion.

Inwardness—not individualism—develops in text-specific ways in premodern religion in order to realize the truth within. This argument is not simply an argument for social or cultural constructivism, but is also an argument for discovery. The language of inwardness is the disclosure of a world of experience and the opening out of a world for a practitioner or group of practitioners. It is a revealing of what lay hidden, of a truth that needs to be sought out and found within the self. The metaphor of an interior landscape experienced within the self, common in textual traditions, resists explanation purely in terms of the construction of the self; yet the metaphor is only accessible to others because of language. Inwardness is bound up with sociality and history and inseparable from language that links the human person to the world and text to the human person. The examples where inwardness exceeds language—as in music or the plastic arts—are exceptions, which rest, as it were, on top of the language of interiority. Indeed, as we will see, while the truth within might itself be ineffable, the process of finding it and the inwardness developed are reportable. Self-reflection and narratability are features of inwardness even where the inner truth itself is unutterable.

There are therefore three levels to my account: firstly, a presentation of the theory of the inner truth in terms of religious inwardness as a shared subjectivity or shared imaginative space; secondly, historical readings to substantiate the claim; and thirdly, the development of the implications of the thesis for the broader history of religions. Indeed, the book would not simply wish to offer a third order description but would wish to make a stronger claim about inwardness and meaning and its relation to transcendence that cuts across the historical trajectories of the traditions considered. The truths within are diverse, but the process of finding those truths is analogous in different religions. This is, therefore, an attempt to perform a hermeneutical phenomenology that takes seriously the critique of phenomenology over the last thirty years, and wishes to engage critically and constructively with the more recent philosophical and theological developments along with cultural or sociological, as well as semiotic, accounts. It is also to turn critical attention to the discourse of 'spirituality' and the somewhat, until very recently,[8] neglected and dated debates about mysticism and religious experience. Thus, on the one hand, this book is a description of the human person in the history of European and Indian religions; on the other, it is a claim about truth as inwardness in traditional religions. What we learn about the formation of the human person in the traditions provides material or evidence for the theoretical formulation about the centrality of subjectivity in religious life.

The aim of this book is therefore to examine the relation of the human person to religion through the narrower focus of inner truth and inwardness. Inwardness offers resistance to the exteriorization of religion that sees religion purely in terms of law and injunction; but, nevertheless, inwardness is formed through practices, through the habitus of tradition, and through the body. Indeed, the question of subjectivity and inwardness that the book deals with in some ways replaces the question of the body, on which so much has been written; but it is probably the same question viewed in a different way, as both body and inwardness are connected through the idea of text, and the very metaphor of inwardness entails the body as vessel that contains it. The human person and text, broadly understood, are intimately bound together. More specifically, the book presents a thesis that the human person in premodern religions is formed through textually embodied practices, and furthermore, this text-formed inwardness has been at the heart of important traditions as meaning-giving systems of thought and action. Indeed, 'inwardness' is a particularly appropriate term to describe narratives of identity that are specific to traditions while cutting across traditions in terms of the process of narrative construction. Inwardness as the truth within, as we shall see, is apposite in being an almost empty term that is filled out with tradition-specific and text-specific content.

While such a project might seem to be a straightforward historical mapping of the idea of inner truth and the text-self relationship in the history of Christian, Hindu, and Buddhist traditions, it also touches on a number of problems in philosophy, theology, and sociology. Perhaps one of the first problems to arise from the historical study is the way in which a historical mapping relates to the deeper problem of subjectivity in an objective world. To claim that a textually formed subjectivity or inwardness is central to religions is to give credence to an existential understanding of religions that goes against the grain of much contemporary critique of religion (and, one might add, the study of religion). While such an understanding is not uncritical of religion, it

[8] See, for example, Louise Nelstrop with Kevin Magill and Bradley B. Onishi, *Christian Mysticism: An Introduction to Contemporary Theoretical Approaches* (Aldershot: Ashgate, 2009).

is nevertheless sympathetic to the practices and concerns that have formed religious lives over centuries. The project intends to take seriously the claims of religious people about inner truth as claims about meaning and world, even though many of those claims, especially about cosmology, have been refuted by scientific development.

THE QUESTION OF METHOD

The 'method' of study is therefore integrally bound up with the 'object' of study. This inquiry is phenomenological because of the desire to allow what shows itself to be seen within religions, and it is hermeneutical because it recognizes the inescapably historical nature of inquiry. Such a hermeneutical phenomenology records or maps the integrity of appearances to human consciousness and locates both the 'object' of method and method itself within a historical trajectory. Such historical inquiry implicitly asks questions about meaning or the meaning of being, as Ricoeur has highlighted.[9] Yet there is an inevitable tension between these two strategies. On the one hand, the phenomenological account seeks description and has implied a problematic philosophy of consciousness—the observer—who describes what is seen from a privileged perspective of neutral objectivity or view from nowhere; on the other, the historical account seeks narration, a dialectical movement between process (historical method) and object (the chain of events) of historiography. Indeed, the historical implicitly critiques the phenomenological in claiming that, as all phenomena are not static but in motion through time, narration needs to trump description. As Jameson observes, something can never really be described because it is never static—it will not sit for its portrait.[10]

Yet, although the world will not sit for its portrait, change in the practices of old religions is slow, and the traditional practices of prayer, meditation, and asceticism are remarkably resilient to change. There is a sense in which we can offer thick description[11] of practices, allowing what shows itself to be seen through a phenomenological openness and reception. Yet such a phenomenology is always hermeneutical and historically located in recognizing the incompletion of description and the narrative thrust of events that form people's lives through the generations.

[9] Paul Ricoeur, 'Phénoménologie et Herméneutique', p. 61, in *Du texte à l'action: Essais d'herméneutique II* (Paris: Éditions du Seuil, 1986), pp. 43–81.

[10] Fredric Jameson, *Valences of the Dialectic* (London and New York: Verso, 2009), p. 30.

[11] It hardly needs to be said that this phrase is, of course, from Clifford Geertz.

Taking the term 'hermeneutic phenomenology' (*la phénoménologie herméneutique*) from Ricoeur,[12] I accept Ricoeur's critique of the Husserlian project. While it is beyond the scope of the present study to develop a critique of the phenomenology of religion,[13] we do need to say that hermeneutics has problematized phenomenology as developed by Husserl, specifically for its idealist and ego-logical orientation that, at least in one formulation, has downplayed intersubjectivity, the lifeworld, and history. But phenomenology is inescapably at the heart of hermeneutics as the allowing of appearances to show themselves, and is itself inevitably hermeneutical, as Ricoeur has pointed out, in that it is constituted in the *interpretation* of the ego—and such interpretation is inevitably historically and culturally bound; all self-understanding is mediated through signs, texts, and histories. The implications for the phenomenology of religion are that inquiry is dialogical, and object and method located within a particular history. There is an inevitable third place: the method or 'the how', the object or 'the what', and the subject or the 'for whom?'.

The method followed here, within the overarching idea of comparative religion, is phenomenological in allowing structures of tradition to show themselves through texts (mediated through philological method), and hermeneutical in highlighting the meaning of traditions and the meaning of being itself for practitioners, to those who have stood—and continue to stand—within the traditions that this study is concerned with. It is also hermeneutical in that what shows itself, only shows itself through signs that need to be interpreted and represented and which are material in nature.[14] The texts and practices of tradition are signs that allow us, standing outside of those texts and practices even if we do participate in them, to understand the kind of subjectivity to which they point. Furthermore, the material nature of the sign—the sign is always a material inscription—has implications that take the study towards an account of subjectivity in terms of material causation. Postmodernity taught us that in the sign, the signifier is divorced from the signified; we are floating in an ocean of signifiers without real reference. This moves towards a constructivist view of culture and religion that now needs to be questioned as signification is constrained

[12] Ricoeur, 'Phénoménologie Herméneutique', p. 61. For an account of the hermeneutic turn in phenomenology, see Andrzej Wiercinski (ed.), *Between Description and Interpretation: The Hermeneutic Turn in Phenomenology* (Toronto: Hermeneutic Press, 2005).

[13] See Gavin Flood, *Beyond Phenomenology: Rethinking the Study of Religion* (London and New York: Cassell, 1999), pp. 91–116.

[14] On the material nature of the sign, see V. N. Vološinov, *Marxism and the Philosophy of Language*, trans. L. Matejka and I. R. Titunik (Cambridge, MA: Harvard University Press, 1973), pp. 9–15. For the importance of this in contemporary theology, see Oliver Davies, 'Transformation Theology in its Historical Context' <www.transformationtheology.com/tt-in-its-historical-context.html> accessed 3 August 2012.

by forces outside of it, certainly economic and political, but arguably transcendent, although a transcendence which is inscribed within material causation. While this is not the main focus of this work, we need to square up to these consequences and to the implicit rejection of idealism in the kind of hermeneutical phenomenology I espouse. The two main problematics that emerge from our preliminary inquiry into method are therefore those of subjectivity and history. As such, the book needs to engage, to some extent, with sociology in a broad sense that has developed models of cross-cultural comparison, has been deeply concerned with the category of the person, and has performed not only analysis of how societies function, but prescription about how they should function.

The rationale for the choice of particular examples in the pages that follow is that they are good illustrations of the search for inner truth linked to inwardness. I have selected examples from two genres of text—pre-philosophical and philosophical—generally from a comparable time frame of the medieval period. I hope that the density of examples I provide will make the case about the importance of inwardness in the cosmological sense I have indicated. The Christian material on inner vision resonates with the Hindu material on visualization and the Buddhist material on inner transformation through meditation. There is a parallelism here that I hope to bring out in Part II.

While each of the chapters on Christianity, Hinduism, and Buddhism stands alone, so to speak, in presenting an account of inwardness in those traditions, the main purpose of presenting them is to pile up examples that bring home the point that the truth within is sought in interiority. I have used examples from within a comparable time frame on the grounds that in the Middle Ages there is a parallelism of technological, social, and political institutions. The West was not yet in advance of South Asia in medicine, science, war technologies, or political institutions. The religions of Europe and South Asia were parallel in both being dominated by a mode of scholarly discourse that used a single language for its communication (Latin and Sanskrit), a style of philosophical commentary that we might call scholastic, and these religions are above all cosmological. That is, Christianity and Indian Religions have a closed (although large) universe, which is hierarchically arranged and is linked to the structure of society. The meaning of life for those within these traditions is to locate themselves within this cosmos and, ultimately, to gain freedom from it.

The point of reading these materials together is, therefore, that they show how parallel these worlds are; and this parallelism in itself is interesting and in need of explanation, or at least acknowledgement. It is beyond the scope of this study to provide a world historical account of the development of religions that stretches beyond the Axial Age, but one might expect a parallelism of institutions across continents given particular technological restrictions of any society.[15] This study does not offer causal claims about this parallelism but simply observes it, and the cosmological inwardness we find in these traditions, apart from being inherently interesting, tells us something important about the nature of the human person in religions.

In one sense this whole book is a response to the question 'What is subjectivity or inwardness?' But before we trace any cross-cultural histories we need to gain some further clarity as to what the terms 'subjectivity' and 'inwardness' point to. Although restricted by a resistance to history, phenomenology has provided us with a language of inwardness and an approach that cannot be summarily dismissed. But in thematizing inwardness in the history of religions in the way that I intend to do, are we simply missing the point of a deeper analysis of self and religion that shows that inwardness is not foundational to human understanding? Heidegger's assessment of subjectivity as the founding principle of philosophy from Descartes to Nietzsche is clearly germane, along with his critique of egoistic philosophy that continues in postmodernity and post-foundational philosophy from Foucault to Kristeva. Indeed, the very notion of subjectivity has come under sustained philosophical attack from sociological and semiotic arenas for foundationalist pretensions and for ignoring culture, language, and history. With the development of the social sciences—particularly sociology in the nineteenth century—we see the rise of the idea that, rather than subjective consciousness, it is a shared consciousness that is important in understanding who we are. This theme developed from Compte to Durkheim, who saw religions in functionalist terms as collective representations expressing social effervescence, on the one hand, and in Marx, on the other, who saw religion as ideology or false consciousness. Weber, by contrast, perceived the importance of religion to lie in agency that expresses values that have historical effects (such as the effect of Protestantism on the rise of capitalism). To understand the human person in relation to religion we therefore need to take into account both phenomenological and sociological views.

Not only has sociology offered explanation of human persons in their interrelationality, but other disciplines have too, particularly psychoanalysis. Indeed, some might say that it is impossible to present an account of inwardness without psychoanalysis, whose very name indicates the inquiry into what is going on within a person's interiority. For psychoanalysis, the truth within is the truth of hidden motivations and desires. Psychoanalysis is primarily concerned with accessing these unconscious motivations through the symbolic analysis of the contents of consciousness. Partly coming out of psychoanalysis, semiotics seeks

[15] For a recent engaging attempt at such a history, see Robert Bellah, *Religion in Human Evolution* (Cambridge, MA: Belknap Press, Harvard University Press, 2012)—although he does not deal with the Middle Ages. The general perspective that religion is linked to human evolution is surely right.

to understand the person through the analysis of systems of signs within which we are embedded; Kristeva's work on abjection would be a good illustration of a combination of psychoanalysis with semiotics. This study does not directly engage with the work of Freud, Jung, Lacan, or Kristeva because its primary purpose is to present an account of the inner truth in a selected history of religions and to propose an account that does not seek psychoanalytic explanation, although such an account could be given.

Arguing for the centrality of inwardness in scriptural religions is not to de-historicize the subjective and uncritically accept a philosophy of consciousness. Indeed, without language, which is bound up with societies, cultures, and history and is itself a material inscription on the world, there is arguably no inwardness, even when that inwardness exceeds language as when absorbed in music, or absorbed in ritual or meditation. Even here, language performs an ostensive function and these events become narratable. Some German philosophers responding to Habermas, notably Manfred Frank and Dieter Henrich, and in a French context Alain Badiou, have argued that we need to revisit subjectivity as foundational, particularly on the grounds that subjectivity can exceed language. This is an important issue that we will return to. If subjectivity rests outside of language and is its precondition, then this is a philosophical justification for the phenomenon that inwardness is experienced in ways beyond language. It is in this sense that religion approaches art, particularly painting, in that subjectivity takes shape in the aesthetic moment of a collapse of temporality between the painting which objectifies the perception of the artist and the viewer, dislocated from the painting's source by time and location. Similarly, a religious subjectivity is formed in religions through textual practices, asceticism, liturgy, and prayer. This sense of self might be contrasted with a modernist subjectivity that is now more or less cut off from its cosmological roots. Taylor has characterized these as 'the porous self'—the premodern self whose boundaries allowed in cosmological forces such as angels and demons—in contrast to 'the buffered self' of modernity, armoured against the world,[16] for whom the gods are dead. As Taylor points out, with the porous self there was no clear demarcation between the 'natural' and the 'supernatural' that we find with modernity where the world becomes 'horizontal' with no 'vertical' or 'transcendent' dimension.[17] Our inquiry therefore entails the reading of texts concerned with the truth within and interpreting these texts through the lens of a hermeneutical phenomenology that will show us how the medieval religions of Europe and South Asia understood the self and what these religions share. In what remains of the introduction we

[16] Charles Taylor, *The Secular Age* (Cambridge, MA: The Belknap Press of Harvard University, 2007), pp. 35–43.

[17] Charles Taylor, 'What is Secularity?', in Kevin Vanhoover and Martin Warner (eds.), *Transcending Boundaries in Philosophy and Theology* (Aldershot: Ashgate, 2007), pp. 57–76.

therefore need to address the methodological question of the self in relation to history and the idea of comparative religion.

THE QUESTION OF HISTORY

In his lectures on the phenomenology of religious life, Heidegger sets out 'the historical' (*das Historische*) as the core phenomenon (*Kernphänomen*) of the phenomenology of religion.[18] The historical is a quality predicated of an object because it is temporally determined. For Heidegger in these early lectures phenomenology is intimately bound up with history. Thus, in his schema of phenomenological explication, he sets out particular stages in the development of a phenomenology of religious life. The first stage is the pre-phenomenological determination of phenomena 'object-historically', as a purely historical situation followed by gaining a picture of 'the phenomenal complex' from whence we can posit 'the study of origin'.[19] He then goes on to illustrate this method in a reading of Paul's First Letter to the Thessalonians written in the year AD 53, describing Paul in his object-historical complex, then going on to observe that we move on to seeing Paul outside of this complex when we perform the letter writing with him and ask fundamental questions such as 'How is the communal world given to him in the situation of writing the letter?'[20] We do so in order to understand the particularity of Paul writing his letter—in Heidegger's phrase, 'the originality of the absolute-historical in its absolute unrepeatability'.[21] To understand Paul's act we must first understand the object-historical situation in which Paul is located—first century Palestine; and secondly, we must shift from the object-historical to 'the enactment-historical situation' to perform a phenomenological inquiry.

Fundamental here is Heidegger's key, yet opaque, concept of the 'formal indication' (*die formale Anzeige*), which is at the heart of the phenomenological method for him. There has been much discussion about this; on the one hand, we have the view of Theodore Kisiel that the formal indication marks a radical break with Husserl, while on the other, Steven Crowe and Matthew

[18] Martin Heidegger, *The Phenomenology of Religious Life*, trans. Matthias Fritsch and Jennifer Anna Gosetti-Ferecei (Bloomington and Indianapolis, IN: Indiana University Press, 2004), p. 22. *Phänomenologie des Religiösen Lebens: Gesamtausgabe*, vol. 60 (Frankfurt: V. Klostermann, 1995), p. 31.

[19] Heidegger, *The Phenomenology of Religious Life*, p. 58.

[20] Heidegger, *The Phenomenology of Religious Life*, p. 61.

[21] Heidegger, *The Phenomenology of Religious Life*, p. 62. This idea of the unrepeatability of action is echoed in M. Bakhtin, *Towards a Philosophy of the Act*, trans. Vadim Liapunov (Austin, TX: University of Texas Press, 1995), pp. 2–3.

Burch argue for its continuities with the Husserlian method.[22] The formal indication is not so much a method, as bracketing might be so understood, but rather a general orientation to 'phenomena' that seeks to move from an account of contingency to essential features of what is being inquired into. For Heidegger, this means an indication of, or pointing to, a primordial sense of being. This primordial sense of being is the topic of philosophy and is the historical moment of the inquirer. Language, particularly indexicals such as 'I' and 'here', point to our historical situatedness as the presupposition of all phenomenological inquiry; it is the means whereby we undergo transformational understanding. The formal indication points to existence in the intertwining of meaning and fact, and all phenomenological inquiries are simply formal indications of the historical entities that we are. Formal indications are pathways of thought that lead to or indicate an essential realm characterized by structures such as care and temporality, and so doing to specify what makes an appearance the thing that it is.[23] A formal indicator is thus grounded in the structure of Dasein; 'mineness' would be an example of an appearance integral to my existence—without ownership there can be no understanding—and which indicates a fundamental structure of the world as a presupposition of all inquiry.

The formal indication is characterized only vaguely in Heidegger's text because it itself is void of content; it is necessarily empty and functions as a guide or constraint upon phenomenological experience and allows access to the (ontic) content of phenomena. Phenomenological practice needs to be one that formally indicates that appearances occur and thereby reveal what would have otherwise remained hidden; the formal indication reveals the invisible, and we might even say that it is the revealing of the invisible that phenomenology then records.

Almost by way of illustration, Heidegger turns the question of formal indication to phenomenology itself. To the question 'What is phenomenology?' he observes that the answer can be indicated only formally. Through the questions of the *what* of experience, the *how* in which something is experienced and the *how* in which 'the relational meaning is enacted',[24] phenomenology can be understood as the explication of these questions as a totality. The formal indication has nothing to say about content and through that avoids prejudgement. It is concerned with the relational, as Schalow and Denker observe—with the connection between the human situation as

[22] For a summary of the debate, see Matthew I. Burch 'The Existential Sources of Phenomenology: Heidegger on Formal Indication', *European Journal of Philosophy*, (2011), DOI: 10.1111/j.1468-0378.2010.00446.x. See also Arne Gron, 'Heidegger's Formal Indication', paper given at Christchurch College, Oxford, September 2007.

[23] Cameron McEwen, 'On Formal Indication: Discussion of the Genesis of Heidegger's "Being and Time"', pp. 231–2, *Research in Phenomenology*, 25/1 (1995), pp. 226–39.

[24] Heidegger, *The Phenomenology of Religious Life*, p. 43.

indicated by the indexicals 'I', 'here', and 'now'.[25] The formal indication is a sense that guides phenomenological explication and is grounded in life, grounded in the kind of being that we are, and invites us to repeatedly approach phenomena through the recognition of our own situation in time and the way in which we share in the being of the historical. That is, what is understood in phenomenological inquiry in McGrath's phrase is 'not an object for a subject but a lived experience for a living human being'.[26]

Here we have a striking difference between Heidegger and Husserl's phenomenological method. On the one hand, Husserl developed phenomenology as a first 'reduction' or bracketing (*epoché*) in which the question concerning the being behind appearances was suspended. On this view we have an observer (the *cogito*) who observes the stream of appearances to consciousness (the *cogitationes*) and through the *epoché* is open to what appears and can describe those appearances in this phenomenological attitude. By contrast, Heidegger's formal indication does not claim to suspend judgement about being but rather assumes human being and our location in time as a precondition for understanding. In contrast to the objectifying 'scientific' method of Husserl, Heidegger seems to be making a statement about the historically located nature of understanding and the necessarily formal indication of this as a guide to understanding the contents of any appearance, any phenomenon. As regards religion, the formal indication does not point to a suspension of judgement concerning the being behind appearances but rather to an inquiry that can raise ontological questions (and so is fundamentally phenomenological for Heidegger).

Heidegger's performance of his phenomenology in relation to Paul does not venture into theology, although it does require understanding and empathy (*Einfülung*) for Paul's situation. Although Heidegger makes the point that we cannot put ourselves in Paul's place, the shift from object-history to enactment situation is itself drawn from 'factical life experience'.[27] The enactment historical situation, such as the performance of Paul writing his letter, entails a

[25] Frank Schalow and Alfred Denker, *Historical Dictionary of Heidegger's Philosophy* (Lanham, MD: Scarecrow Press, 2010), pp. 115–16.

[26] S. J. McGrath, *The Phenomenology of Early Heidegger* (Washington, DC: Catholic University of America Press, 2006), p. 70. Although the formal indication is not mentioned in *Being and Time* it is a precursor for that work and represents the first part of the hermeneutic circle and the fore structures of understanding. There is a growing literature on the formal indication. See Daniel Dahlstrom, '"Heidegger" Method: Philosophical Concepts as Formal Indications', *Review of Metaphysics*, 47/7 (June 1994), pp. 775–95; Burch, 'The Existential Sources of Phenomenology: Heidegger on Formal Indication'; Theodore Kisiel, *Genesis of Heidegger's Being and Time* (Berkeley and Los Angeles, CA: University of California Press, 1993), p. 164; Hent de Vries, *Philosophy and the Turn to Religion* (Baltimore, MD and London: John Hopkins University Press, 1999), pp. 158–243. Also see Heidegger and Religion 1, Oxford University Research Archive <http://ora.ox.ac.uk>, Collection of Conference Papers, accessed 25 January 2012.

[27] Heidegger, *The Phenomenology of Religious Life*, p. 63.

phenomenological understanding of the self and its temporal reality that can only be made through a formal indication. Thus, although we cannot put ourselves in Paul's place, phenomenological inquiry entails some understanding of 'being like an I' (*Ichlichkeit*) which is unique to each historical situation. 'Being like an I' is a point of departure from which we can carry out an explication.[28] Heidegger goes on to develop this idea of pre-understanding and the forestructures of cognition in later work;[29] but what is important for us is that understanding entails more than an account of the object-historical—it involves an account of the situation-historical that entails some empathetic notion of an 'I'.

To understand the medieval sense of subjectivity we need the idea of 'something like an I'. But while this sense of the 'I' is fundamental for inquiry, the difficulties of positing 'something like an I' are considerable in so far as my sense of an 'I' has been formed in my own particular situation and we must perform a historicist caution about projecting modern notions of the self onto other times. Indeed, part of the argument of the current project is that we consistently misunderstand the notion of religious subjectivity through history and across cultures because of a reading of modern notions of the 'I' back into history. As we will see, traditional concepts of subjectivity are different to contemporary, late modern sensibilites.

Yet, on the other hand, we must not exaggerate the difference. There is still a sense in which when reading Augustine or Abhinavagupta we have an empathy, an understanding, that allows us to make Heidegger's judgement 'something like an I' as a precondition of our understanding. We can sympathize with Augustine's moral struggles; we can relate to Abhinavagupta's metaphors drawn from the human senses. So, although useful, the binary distinctions between porous self/buffered self, premodern/modern, or non-individual/individual are limited. We need to be cautious when reading texts from the past and from other traditions in other languages, but not so cautious that it inhibits our understanding. Indeed, in part we need to trace the boundaries that both restrict and allow continuity between a premodern and modern subjectivity. In the complex question of method we might therefore take from Heidegger the importance of understanding something in the specificity of its historical context and the importance of empathy understood as the cognition of 'something like an I', the recognition or pre-understanding of a continuity of human nature that is a necessary prerequisite for all historical and phenomenological inquiry. This is the presupposition entailed by hermeneutics.

[28] Heidegger, *The Phenomenology of Religious Life*, p. 64: 'being like an I belongs to each situation' (*Zu jeder Situation gehört Ichliches*).

[29] Martin Heidegger, *Being and Time*, trans. J. Macquarrie and E. Robinson (Oxford: Blackwell, 1962), pp. 192–5.

There are continuities here with the work of Merleau-Ponty, and to complement Heidegger's 'something like an I' we can add Merleau-Ponty's understanding of the lived body that entails the primacy of perception that brings us close to vitalism entailed in any understanding of the human. The focus on the body in social sciences, especially anthropology, largely derived from Merleau-Ponty's work, is well established and it is not necessary here to rehearse those arguments.[30] In speaking about subjectivity and inwardness we are inevitably speaking about the body and using the metaphor of inside and outside to discuss the human person. Merleau-Ponty speaks of how the body has the propensity to see as subject and be seen as object, both sensate and sensible, this reversibility being a key characteristic of perception.[31] There has been, partly stemming from this work, a tendency among some phenomenologists and cultural theorists to reject notions of interiority; we are all inscribed by culture; we are all surface with no depth since the signifier has been separated from the signified. We need simply to note here that by subjectivity we also mean body and, more specifically, the lived body within the lifeworld.

Our pre-understanding of subjectivity, the sense of 'I' or 'something like an I', being inextricably bound up with history (and temporality) therefore entails narrative and narratability. Indeed, narrative is fundamental to notions of the human person throughout history and across cultures because of the temporal nature of persons and because narrativity—the sequential unfolding of causally related events—is endemic. Not only is the self constituted through time, the self-identity that Ricouer calls *idem*—but the self is constituted as a life

[30] There is now a voluminous literature on the body and, by extension, gender. The anthropological discourse was particularly marked by John Blacking's (ed.), *The Anthropology of the Body* (London, New York, San Francisco: Scholars Press, 1977); also see Ted Polhemus' (ed.), *Social Aspects of the Human Body: A Reader of Key Texts* (London: Penguin, 1978). See also Thomas J. Csordas (ed.), *Embodiment and Experience; the Existential Ground of Culture and Self* (Cambridge: Cambridge University Press, 1994); F. E. Mascia-Lees (ed.), *A Companion to the Anthropology of the Body* (London: John Wiley, 2011). On the related field of experience, see J. C. Throop 'Minding Experience: An Exploration of the Concept of "Experience" in the Early French Anthropology of Durkheim, Lévy-Bruhl, and Lévi-Strauss', *Journal of the History of the Behavioural Sciences*, 39/4 (2003), pp. 365–82; Michael Jackson, *Existential Anthropology: Events, Exigencies and Effects* (Oxford: Berghahn, 2005); Hrvoje Cargonja, 'Ambiguous Experience: A Contribution to Understanding Experience as Discourse', *Studia Ethnogica Croatia*, 23/1 (2011), pp. 283–308. On the sociology of the body, see Brian Turner, 'The Body in Western Society: Social Theory and its Perspectives', in Sarah Coakley (ed.), *Religion and the Body* (Cambridge: Cambridge University Press, 1997), pp. 15–41; Brian Turner, 'What is the Sociology of the Body?', *Body and Society*, 3/1 (1997), pp. 103–7; P. A. Mellor and C. Shilling, *Re-forming the Body: Religion, Community and Modernity* (London: Sage, 1997). On religion and the body, see the edited volume by Coakley, Sarah Coakley (ed.), *Religion and the Body*. On cultural studies perspectives, see the three volumes edited by M. Feher et al., *Fragments for a History of the Human Body*, 3 vols (New York: Urzone, 1989). The phenomenology of the body was particularly initiated by Merleau-Ponty, although Gabriel Marcel was also important. On these developments see the still useful Richard M. Zaner, *The Problem of Embodiment: Some Contributions to a Phenomenology of the Body* (The Hague: Nijhoff, 1971).

[31] M. Merleau-Ponty, *Le Visible et l'invisible* (Paris: Gallimard, 1964), p. 178.

story—that Ricoeur calls *ipse*.[32] There is a narrative structure to life itself that gives rise to our sense of who we are as historically and culturally embedded beings.[33] The sense of 'the I' or 'something like an I' that is entailed in historical inquiry also tells us about the formation of history. Traces of the past remain in the present and that past is represented through memory and in the writing of history, as Ricoeur has meticulously argued in *Memory, History, Forgetting*. Shared memory, he writes, allows a group to have access to its past, and individual memory takes shape in the context of collective memory, which itself assumes individual memory of a person bearing testimony or being witness to an event. Witnessing event becomes testimony that in turn translates into history and historiography. Both history and historiography can support and correct collective memory.

On the one hand then, we have what we might call macro-history—the broad sweep of historical process through time that eclipses the particular event, as expressed by the Annales School;[34] on the other, we have persons who are subjects, living out their lives, making judgements, and performing acts of will within the constraints of their monetary, political, and religious economies. The relation between the micro-narrative of the human person and macro-history of a culture does not readily come into view. But we might say that subjectivity or inwardness impacts upon history in varying degrees through action (of course) and through record, through text—the testimonial that bears witness to event. The material nature of the sign means that intentional subjects or persons inevitably impact upon history as history impacts upon persons. While this may be a truism, it is nevertheless important for our study to raise the question of the relation between macro-history and subjectivity. We are the products of our age, and yet we can also influence specific outcomes that can be historically significant. Because we are beings with subjectivity and self-reflection, and because we are born with progenitors, into particular families, societies, and histories, there is a case for phenomenology, sociology, and semiotics as disciplinary engagements that have a stake in understanding subjectivity in relation to religion.

Lastly in this introductory section we need to turn less to the subject matter—the religious person—and more to the process of comparison. The current study is a work of comparative religion. In recent years this has been the subject of sustained critique from historicist, post-colonial, and feminist

[32] Paul Ricoeur, *Oneself as Another*, trans. K. Blamey (Chicago, IL: Chicago University Press, 1990), p. 116.

[33] The question of whether narrative is part of life itself, a narrative realist position, or whether narrative is pure cultural construction, cannot be gone into here. But see MacIntyre for a narrative realist position in contrast to Whyte for a constructivist position. Ricoeur is both a realist and a constructionist. See Flood, *Beyond Phenomenology*, pp. 126–37.

[34] See François Dosse, *History of Structuralism: The Rising Sign 1945 to 1966*, vol. 1, trans. D. Glassman (Minneapolis, MN: University of Minnesota Press, 1997), pp. 181–3.

discourse (see 'Comparative Religion', pp. 250–3). The general argument against comparative religion has run along the lines that if cultures are particular to place and history we need to understand people in their contexts, and comparing cultures or histories is of little value in understanding or explaining the particularity of social occurrence. Moreover, our histories are so embedded in power and a politics of representation that comparison often contains hidden or unconscious assumptions about the nature of the human and the social that are so deeply implicated in, for example, colonialism or the occlusion of women as to be without value in the contemporary context. Rather than comparison we need to deconstruct the conditions that give rise to particular historical discourses and power structures and where scholarship can serve a liberationist agenda that seeks to improve the human good. In the context of this significant critique of comparative religion, what is the justification for such an enterprise? Why compare?

THE QUESTION OF COMPARISON

MacIntyre was surely right in identifying accounts of rationality, morality, and justice as tradition-specific.[35] We are born into particular traditions of practice and educated to varying degrees in traditions of thinking that articulate and reflect on those social practices. MacIntyre himself identifies an Aristotelian tradition of moral inquiry that develops into medieval Catholicism through to the Scottish Enlightenment.[36] Rationality occurs within traditions of inquiry, and MacIntyre makes a good case for this, which we can corroborate through examining other traditions and thought worlds, such as those of India, over a comparable historical period. But if this is the case, what is the basis for comparison; and what is to be gained by comparison other than 'conversion' or the domination of one world view over another? We need to find a way of comparison that understands the tradition-specific nature of inquiry while at the same time acknowledging that inquiry transcends the traditions by which it is instantiated.

The general purpose of comparison is the furtherance of knowledge in the view that what one thing tells us can illuminate another. The human sciences have developed through comparison and now we have the subfields of comparative linguistics, comparative literature, comparative history, and so on. Comparative sociology tells us about social structures and institutions that all

[35] See, for example, Alastair MacIntyre, *Three Rival Versions of Moral Inquiry* (Notre Dame, IN: University of Notre Dame Press, 1990), pp. 127–9.

[36] Alastair MacIntyre, *Whose Justice? Which Rationality?* (Notre Dame, IN: University of Notre Dame Press, 1988), pp. 209–40.

humans inhabit; comparative linguistics shows us the similarities and differences between languages, how language functions, and the relationship of languages in history; and comparative history shows the parallel development in, for example, processes of rationality and institution.[37] Thus, through comparative linguistics we know that, and how, the Indo-European languages are related. Comparative religion developed in the nineteenth century within the context of colonialism and, as many erudite commentators have now highlighted, served to reinforce colonialist attitudes and to place 'the other' in a position of subordination.[38] Many of these studies are less an explicit critique of comparative religion; they are more a critique of the category 'religion' itself as a Western invention imposed upon the colonial other, usually in the service of a politically oppressive agenda.[39] The critique (and condemnation) of comparative religion has almost become a new orthodoxy. While I cannot engage with this extensive literature here, the present study is, in a sense, one response to the question of comparative religion through performing readings in the history of religions across traditions.

Reading across traditions is an enterprise that has something in common with comparative theology. This is a practice by theologians of reading other traditions in a spirit of openness and dialogue. The main practitioner of this practice, Francis Clooney, calls it 'deep learning across religious borders'.[40] Unlike an old-fashioned comparative religion, comparative theology does not

[37] Developing Weber, D'Avray has developed an interesting comparative history focusing on types of rationality in the medieval period: D. L. D'Avray, *Rationalities in History: A Weberian Essay in Comparison* (New York: Cambridge University Press, 2010), especially on the rationality of asceticism, pp. 123–34; D. L. D'Avray, *Medieval Religious Rationalities* (New York: Cambridge University Press, 2010), in relation to comparative law, pp. 126–36.

[38] Among the more important of these studies, see David Chidester, *Savage Systems: Colonialism and Comparative Religion in Southern Africa* (Charlottesville, VA: University Press of Virginia, 1996), which examines the development of comparative religion in an explicitly colonial context.

[39] There are many works on this theme, many coming to publication around the same time. Of particular importance, apart from Chidester cited above, are Talal Asad, *Genealogies of Religion: Discipline and Reasons of Power in Christianity and Islam* (Baltimore, MD and London: Johns Hopkins University Press, 1993); Timothy Fitzgerald's *The Ideology of Religious Studies* (New York: Oxford University Press, 2000) and his *Discourse on Civility and Barbarity: A Critical History of Religion and Related Categories* (Oxford and New York: Oxford University Press, 2007); Richard King, *Orientalism and Religion: Postcolonial Theory, India and 'The Mystic East'* (London: Routledge, 1999); Russell T. McCutcheon, *Manufacturing Religion: The Discourse on Sui Generis Religion and the Politics of Nostalgia* (New York and Oxford: Oxford University Press, 1997). A substantial and sustained argument about the invention of religion in relation to Sikhism is Arvind-Pal S. Mandair, *Religion and the Specter of the West: Sikhism, India, Postcoloniality, and the Politics of Translation* (New York: Columbia University Press, 2009); T. Masuzawa, *The Invention of World Religions or How European Universalism was Preserved in the Language of Pluralism* (Chicago, IL: Chicago University Press, 2005). On the defence of religion as an etic category, see my *The Importance of Religion* (Oxford: Wiley-Blackwell, 2012), pp. 14–15.

[40] This is, in fact, the subtitle of his book *Comparative Theology*.

claim to seek a neutral standpoint, nor to be a science of religion, but rather to stand within a specific theological tradition (as it happens, usually a Catholic one), from where it engages with another theological tradition. Comparative theology has some affinities with comparative religion but does not draw on social science or, particularly strongly, on history. Likewise, the present study has some affinities with Clooney's work in taking seriously the claims of traditions and in engaging with Christianity and Hinduism, although it does not stand within a theological tradition: it is not faith-seeking understanding. There is no explicit religious conviction that I seek to convey or explore, although I do wish to argue for a particular understanding of the truth within across traditions. What the present study does have in common with comparative theology is that it is a performance of reading across cultures in order to map the self and to present an account of subjectivity that holds up across traditions.

Such a reading occurs in a third space, as it were, of comparison. Comparison is necessarily an abstraction from different things, and the richness of one thing is inevitably lost in the process. The current project is an imaginative exercise in so far as it is a representation of three traditions and a way of discussing the inner truth of three traditions. This mode of comparison, or third space, has—to extend the metaphor—further layers or levels within it. Thus there could be a purely philological level of comparison for terms and their use, there could be a level of comparison focused on ritual or asceticism, or there could be an order of comparison for entire systems or institutions (of the kind that Weber made). There will be congruence between these layers or levels of discourse. Thus the term *antarātman*, inner self, which occurs at a philosophical level of abstraction, is congruent with the visualization of the self in prayerful interiority and in external behaviour or daily living. Such a term can be compared with *homo interior*, inner man, similarly operating at different levels. These layers of comparison are not unlike Charles Peirce's 'phemic sheet', which is a sheet of assertion where 'pheme' is a sentence within a particular realm of discourse.[41] A 'leaf' is a container of phemic sheets in a way here akin to the comparative study itself containing different types of comparison within the boundaries of particular kinds of discourse. I regard the comparative religion given here as akin to these phemic sheets in that the comparison is the creation of a mode of discourse. Rather than an absolute space, the comparison is a limited, bounded space in which we can create laws that govern the relationship between terms. For example, we might have a general rule that the terminology of inwardness is dependent upon broad metaphysical claims, or a rule that there is semantic variability of terms depending on level of discourse. Thus a comparative religion might comprise

[41] C. Peirce, 'Prolegomena to An Apology for Pragmatism', 4.538, *The Monist*, 16/4 (1906), pp. 492–546. Thanks to Peter Ochs for alerting me to the idea of phemic sheets.

several phemic sheets in which the meaning of terms varies depending upon which level it is operating at; yet, nevertheless, there is still a continuity of terms between levels or sheets. Thus the term 'body' might be used within one phemic sheet to refer to the lived body of everyday experience, while at another to refer to the society, and at another to the cosmos. Similarly, a Sanskrit term such as *nimitta* might be rendered as 'cause' in a purely philosophical discussion, but as an inner, eidetic sign in a discourse of Buddhist meditation.

CONCLUSION

The truth within has been a perennial idea in the history of human societies, but the idea of inwardness has not always been linked to our modern individualism. Indeed, the histories of Christianity, Hinduism, and Buddhism reveal something quite different; that inwardness is a shared imaginaire in which the structures or symbolic systems of the traditions show themselves. In fact, cultivating inwardness through spiritual practices seeks the erasure of limited desire in favour of tradition beyond the self. Although there are continuities with romantic ideas of inwardness in modernity, the inner truth of religions in history is not that which seeks well-being or authentic expression of inner states.[42] Rather we see in the traditional religions of the premodern period an intensification of inwardness—that there is a truth hidden within the self that is to be found and realized through the cultivation of spiritual practices in which the practitioner conforms to tradition, and in which life is imbued with meaning through the realization that the self is within a cosmos, within a trans-individual world order. Spiritual practices—prayer, meditation, asceticism—prepare the practitioner for death and going beyond the limitations of this life.

In making claims about the truth within in Christianity, Hinduism, and Buddhism, I am aware that I am using categories that are problematic. What is Christianity or Hinduism? What do we mean by premodern? What is an 'area' and what are the boundaries of Europe and South Asia? This argues that there is coherence to these categories in the sense that religions, it can be argued, are bounded cultural forms recapitulated through generations; and although the boundaries of both concepts and geographies in this field are not precise, it is nevertheless meaningful to speak of religions in this way in a global context.

[42] On spiritualities of well-being, see Paul Heelas, *Spiritualities of Life: New Age Romanticism and Consumptive Capitalism* (Malden, MA: Wiley-Blackwell, 2008), pp. 62–76, 177–9. See also Paul Heelas, 'Expressive Spirituality and Humanistic Expressivism: Sources of Significance Beyond Church and Chapel', in Steven Sutcliffe and Marion Bowman (eds.), *Beyond New Age* (Edinburgh: Edinburgh University Press, 2000), pp. 237–54.

We will return to these considerations in Part II, but have given sufficient background information to orientate the reader and set out the broad parameters of the project here undertaken. The inner truth is a theme found in Hinduism, Christianity, and Buddhism, which all developed methods of finding this truth through the cultivation of inwardness in spiritual disciplines. We can see this particularly in the medieval period. A hermeneutical phenomenology can bring out this parallelism at a sufficient level of generality that will enable us to see that inwardness is a constitutive feature of these religions that needs to be taken into account in any description or explanation. We will now begin a presentation of the historical material and texts before moving on to comparative reflection.

Part I

History and Text

At the heart of this study are three fundamental questions: Of who is there an inner truth? Of what does inner truth comprise? And how can we historically locate it?

In one sense the answer to the first question depends upon the answers to the other two. The idea of a truth within is the content of a person's inner life that is bound up with their location in historical time and in moral space. This study is particularly concerned with the idea of an inner truth in the history of religions or, more specifically, the histories of European Christianity and Hindu and Buddhist South Asia. It presents an account of the relationship between religion and the human person in which truth as inwardness or subjectivity is the ground of religious concern. The category of the human person can be associated with the idea that human beings have an inner life, a specific subjectivity, and that this inner life or inwardness is deeply implicated with the truth and meaning of life. This has been an important topic in human civilizations and religions: the cultivation of inwardness in the quest for truth through spiritual practices that connect human communities to transcendence is a common theme.

While our idea of the truth within has been formed by a particular historical trajectory in Western culture, the inner life is not exclusive to the West and forms a major component of South Asian and Chinese cultures and religions. This first part of the book seeks to examine ideas about inner truth in examples from medieval Christianity, Hinduism, and Buddhism and to trace a selective history of inwardness across these traditions. We will see in the following pages how the truth within is formed in different ways by different texts, different times, and different bodies. We will move from a 'what' and a 'where' in order to gain some sense of the 'who'. Thus, to offer an account of inner truth in comparative religion we will need to develop a phenomenology of history and text in the first instance.

In examining the idea of inner truth, which is also to examine the relationship between the human person and religion across a number of histories, the book develops a thesis that inwardness is formed in tradition-specific ways (and so the truths of inwardness are greatly variable) but the processes of cultivating inwardness are common across traditions. This has implications for a general theory of what it means to be religiously human. The phenomenology it presents (at a first level) is therefore complemented by a hermeneutical phenomenology (at a second level), which interprets the inner life in the context of history and develops a thesis that the quest for inner truth in premodernity is an intensification of inwardness that is collective. That is, although each individual cultivates and seeks the truth within him or herself, this quest and goal are forms of practice and thought beyond the individual in which he or she participates.

This shared subjectivity or inwardness as the cultivation of inner truth might be contrasted with the individualism of secular modernity. A premodern subjectivity is participatory in both a cosmological and legal sense in contrast to a modern subjectivity and the discourse of rights, which is abstracted from any cosmological context. In the following chapters we will present in some textual detail how the idea of the truth within is articulated in different genres of religious literature within a broadly compatible time frame. The rationale here is that during what we can call the medieval period popular genres of literature developed in Sanskrit and Latin, and later in vernacular languages, expressing popular views of the inner self alongside philosophical or theological discourse that is scholastic and commentarial in nature. Indeed, it is striking that we have popular texts in Latin and Sanskrit—and later, after about 1350, articulations of religious sentiment in vernacular languages—created at the same time, and a commentarial style of philosophy that is found in both Europe and South Asia during a period in which there is roughly parallel technological development and in which, as we see, social cohesion and authority is embedded within a cosmological world view. In Europe, the old cosmology is discarded in due course by mainstream philosophy and science (mostly in the seventeenth century) and South Asia begins to absorb new ways of thinking, although the cosmological world view persists into modernity at popular levels of culture in spite of colonization. As we will see, these traditions share a notion of the truth within that is connected to the cosmos within: the macrocosm is recapitulated in the microcosm.

2

Prayer and Vision in the Middle Ages

In William Golding's novel *The Spire*, the abbot Jocelyn is the mastermind behind the tallest spire stretching to heaven ever yet built. He tells his tormented master builder, Roger, who wishes to stop building on the grounds that the foundations are not deep enough and the spire will fall, that they have no choice but to go on. The building is not simply a stone structure; it is in fact 'a diagram of prayer; and our spire will be a diagram of the highest prayer of all'.[1] Moreover, God himself granted this vision to Jocelyn, and since they were both chosen, they have no choice but to go on. Jocelyn is aware of three of them speaking high up on the half-built spire, the third presence being his guardian angel. Golding conveys something important about the medieval world view and how the notion of the human person is conceived. We are all part of a much bigger picture, part of a cosmos, and can be instruments of a cosmic, divine will. This divine will works through us, and Jocelyn's tower is an expression of the divine will working through the human. The purpose of Jocelyn's life is to see the completion of the spire, to do what is not reasonable, to respond to the command 'out of some deep place', 'to do what makes no sense at all', so that 'if men have faith, a new thing comes'.[2] The new things come when the human person becomes a vehicle for divine will, and while on one reading the spire is the expression of Jocelyn's individual drive and ambition, on another reading it is the expression of divine intention. Although this is a work of fiction, in the figure of Jocelyn, Golding captures the medieval understanding that we are contained within a sacred canopy, that the human will can be aligned to divine will, and that this transcendence of the individual is the highest fulfilment of earthly life.

The human person has always been a central theme in the history of Christianity. Inheriting a collectivist, world affirming ethos, with its emphasis on family and community from what became Judaism, as well as a monastic, world negating ethos from Greek philosophy and Neoplatonism, Christianity developed a keen interest in the human person as the locus of competing needs

[1] William Golding, *The Spire* (London: Faber, 1964), p. 120.
[2] Golding, *The Spire*, p. 121.

and locus of working out virtue in concrete historical situations. These competing values were focused on the body and, as de Cereau reminds us, the loss of a body—that of Jesus Christ—was a foundational event to be replaced by the institution of the Church and Christian discourse.[3]

By the early Christian centuries we have the competing values of monastic renunciation along with the affirmation of family and individuality as human goods, themes that develop through the High Middle Ages. Charlemagne, in 811, asked his bishops and abbots what it meant to leave the world, and whether either alms bearing or public marriage was the only difference between 'those who left the world and those who cleaved to it'.[4] Social distinctions were important, and monks were marked out from nobles by tonsure, clothing, and food. Knowing one's place, the boundaries between the social orders, was crucial for the smooth running of society. With Protestantism, as Weber has shown, we have the affirmation of both world affirmation and renuciation in non-renunciate asceticism; true detachment is being in the world, but not of the world. Alongside the rise and fall of these different value affirmations we have an emphasis on salvation, both through God's saving grace and through human effort, with varying emphasis on one or the other in different Churches and different periods. If we lead an upright and moral life we will be saved through grace. These different orientations have lead to different conceptions of the human person throughout history, which have arguably had serious consequences, if Weber is right, for macro-historical processes and economics.

Our purpose here, in this and the next chapter, is to glean an understanding of Christian ideas of the truth within, and how the theme and experience of inwardness develops within the tradition. We have an elaborate symbolic system integrated into and expressing a Christian cosmology that is mapped onto the body and mapped onto subjectivity (which are two ways of saying the same thing). The focus on inwardness in Christian discourse is also a discovery of the way in which the subject recapitulates the broader cosmological structure within the self. Inwardness is not secret in the early Christian tradition through the Middle Ages; but the journey within, which is a journey to discover God, is available to all. There is a transparency of the self in medieval literature that is to disappear in the later tradition. The symbolic, cosmological world of the Middle Ages disintegrates at the end of the period[5] and gives way to a different kind of inwardness that has retreated from cosmology, now claimed by an objectivist, scientific discourse. A symbolic

[3] Michel de Certeau, *The Mystic Fable*, vol. 1: *The Sixteenth and Seventeenth Centuries*, trans. M. B. Smith (Chicago, IL: Chicago University Press, 1992), p. 81.

[4] Giles Constable, *Three Studies in Medieval Religious and Social Thought* (Cambridge: Cambridge University Press, 1995), p. 262.

[5] De Certeau, *The Mystic Fable*, p. 91.

world view gives way to a mechanistic world view; a cosmic order gives way to a cogito and to a corresponding shift in understanding the human person. Within the medieval symbolic universe, the nature of the human person and inwardness in particular were articulated in different literary genres. We need to interrogate primarily two kinds of literature here: on the one hand, popular treatises—our examples in the following pages will be primarily from text in Middle English; on the other, theological writing (dealt with in the next chapter) that would have been restricted to an educated elite.

In many ways the main focus of religion in the premodern world is on exterior forms rather than on inwardness: on the daily performance of the liturgy, on rites of passage, on pilgrimage, and on knowing one's place within the social body. Yet the theme of inwardness plays a crucial part in even apparently exterior forms of religion in that underlying these forms is a world view in which the human person is integrated into a broader cosmos and subjectivity pervaded by forces beyond the self. The practices of liturgy (or external prayer), inner prayer, and vision all assume a world view in which the person is integrated within a society with highly defined roles which, in turn, is understood in cosmological terms as part of a hierarchical, cosmic structure. Externalization that in some ways characterizes medieval religious forms itself is never purely external but a sign that points to a kind of inwardness that is integrated into a total cosmic picture. This total cosmos is a symbolic world that medieval persons inhabited with varying degrees of intensity; thus, monastics were attempting to find God through acetic and contemplative practices, whereas the knighthood, although still participating in the same symbolic world order, was more concerned with explicit political power. The rhetoric of the knighthood—those who fight—and of the clergy—those who pray—was integrated within a shared world view and a shared narrative of salvation and alliances with God. Inwardness must be seen as a particular kind of participation in this world view and an intensification of a vertical link to transcendence.

Two genres of literature that relate to the pietistic realm and the theoretical or theological realm can be related to the two human faculties of imagination and reason. This distinction can provide us with a principle for organizing the mass of textual material available. On the one hand, there is a wealth of texts in Latin—and later in vernacular languages—that are concerned with popular piety. This literature is focused on the liturgy, moral exhortation, penance, prayer, the art of dying, types of sin, the paternoster, and with vision. In all of these texts, we have rhetoric of a symbolic order in which human imagination as a creative faculty plays a central role. On the other hand, there is a sophisticated language of philosophy focused on reason that reflects upon the imaginative and is expressed through learned commentaries as well as systematic theology. What we might call the literature of imagination or popular piety—particularly the vision texts that we will be discussing below—is a pre-philosophical articulation of themes that the literature of reason reflects on. If Aquinas understood the human being as a rational animal, we might add that this period shows the human to be an imaginative animal as well. We will need to examine some of this pietistic literature of imagination in the current chapter and focus on the literature of reason in the next. This 'lower' genre of literature is just as much an index of notions of inner truth as the theological and philosophical genre.[6] In the current chapter, after some general reflections, we will examine this cosmological understanding of the truth within as illustrated in pre-philosophical, pietistic literature in Middle English, paying particular attention to vision texts. Towards the end of the Middle Ages we have a shift from the use of Latin, which had formed a common language of the educated elites, to vernacular languages, and a corresponding broadening of the field of reception.

THE HIGH MIDDLE AGES

By the High Middle Ages (*c.*1000–1300) some of the major theological controversies that had plagued the early Christian centuries had largely been settled by the various councils during the first millennium, and the Eastern and Western Churches had parted company with the East–West schism of 1054 when the Roman Catholic, Latin tradition parted from the Orthodox, Greek tradition. Other theological controversies emerged, over icons in the East, over the response to Aristotle and reason, and over universals and particulars in the West. Latin became the lingua franca of the educated elites in the West, and the language of theology. During the twelfth century in particular we have a new orientation towards the person expressed in various genres of literature such as a renewal of religious autobiography, the development of romances, and courtly love poetry, alongside the development of new social institutions, especially new monastic orders. We also have a more clearly demarcated distinction between the sacred and the profane with a professional clergy and the emergence of a distinct chivalric order. During the twelfth century and into the thirteenth, this separation of the sacred from the profane is reflected in law with the gradual demise of the ordeal as a method of trial.[7]

[6] William I. Miller makes the point that more popular sources, such as the saga, contain a wealth of information about the everyday understanding of the self, particularly the idea of honour. William I. Miller, 'Deep Inner Lives, Individualism and the People of Honour', pp. 192–3, *History of Political Thought*, 16/2 (1995), pp. 190–207.

[7] Peter Brown, 'Society and the Supernatural: A Medieval Change', *Daedalus*, 104/2 (1975), pp. 133–51. Brown observes that the ordeal depended upon supernatural intervention—the curing of blisters from holding a red hot iron to prove innocence for example—which the Church came to reject by 1215 at the Lateran Council: 'To invoke a controlled miracle by

From the late tenth century European society becomes less violent with the development of more stable social institutions. Thus, for example, in France, the 'Peace of God' movement initiated by Bishop Guy of Le Puy in 975 was instigated to restrain secular lords and knights from pillaging churches and attacking local populations: he made the knights swear an oath to maintain peace on threat of excommunication.[8]

Along with the development of more stable social conditions, a general recognition of the value of learning and an investment in education takes place during this period. Along with philosophical and theological texts we have the development of a literary tradition that sees the revival of classical learning as in the humanistic scholar John of Salisbury, secretary to Archbishop Thomas Becket.[9] During this time we have the rediscovery of the Classical world of learning with the translation into Latin of Greek and Arabic texts on science, medicine, and philosophy—particularly the translation and study of Aristotelian logic.[10] While there is much more centralized control in Christianity over doctrine and belief than, as we shall see, in Hinduism, nevertheless there was a burgeoning mystical and homiletic literature that was not particularly concerned with precise doctrine (and sometimes authors of such literature found themselves in trouble with Church authorities, especially women who had no other voice). This more popular literature was produced in a time of great religious energy, with monastic communities of men and women developing at a time of population expansion, population settlement with fewer mass migrations (as had happened with the Vikings in England) and, along with the growing population, the development of strong economies based on trade.

The population increase and economic boom of this period were due to a shift in the ways in which power and wealth were acquired and maintained. In the earlier medieval period, European Kings had obtained wealth through warfare and plunder; but from the tenth century we have, as MacCulloch documents, 'the purposeful creation of networks of new village settlements,

the ordeal in the course of a secular law suit was to "tempt God"' (p. 136). See also R. Bartlett, *Trial by Fire and Water: The Medieval Judicial Ordeal* (New York: Oxford University Press, 1986).

8 Kathleen G. Cushing, *Reform and the Papacy in the Eleventh Century: Spirituality and Social Change* (Manchester: Manchester University Press, 2005), pp. 39–54.

9 On the educational developments and rediscovery of the Aristotelian sources along with Arab commentaries, see R. F. Swanson, *The Twelfth Century Renaissance* (Manchester: Manchester University Press, 1999), pp. 103–4. On the changes from the mid-tenth to thirteenth centuries brought about by the discovery of the classical age, especially Aristotelian logic, see R. R. Bologar, *The Classical Heritage and its Beneficiaries* (Cambridge: Cambridge University Press, 1958), pp. 149–62; J. W. H. Atkins, *English Literary Criticism: The Medieval Phase* (Cambridge: Cambridge University Press, 1934), pp. 65–6; J. W. Baldwin, *The Scholastic Culture of the Middle Ages* (Lexington, MA: Heath, 1971), pp. 39, 59, 62–5.

10 Bologar, *The Classical Heritage and its Beneficiaries*, pp. 162–200.

with many more legal obligations on their newly gathered inhabitants'.[11] This process of expansion resulted in higher agricultural yields, more stable social conditions—which solidified into the feudal system in which farmers became serfs to their overlords—and the expansion of trade with neighbouring areas. Social locations became more solidified, with a concern for social classification, such as into those who preach, those who fight, and those who labour, and the emergence in the eleventh century of the class of feudal knights.[12] The expansion of trade was also accompanied by the expansion of Christianity into in the East (what is now Poland, Hungary, and the Czech Republic) and in the North (Scandinavia).[13] The Church responded constructively to the new situation, organizing the land such that each of the new villages had a Church within a territorial unit of a parish.[14]

Within this new political and social situation in the twelfth century—this first European revolution or renaissance—[15] the Western Church expanded its power over the minds and hearts of the populace, often defending the rights of the poor against tyrannical oppression, and consolidating its power over European monarchies. In such an environment monasticism prospered, becoming the powerhouse of religious ideas and a source of piety and inspiration for the broader population. Men and women were caught up in the religious passion of pilgrimage, alongside more sober monastic reflection and regular practices of prayer and asceticism. Devotional practice spread throughout society. Pilgrimage centres flourished (such as Canterbury and Ely in England, and Santiago de Compostela in Spain)[16] and great monastic churches, such as at Cluny, grew in importance and expanded in size.[17] Monastic centres spread

[11] Diarmaid MacCulloch, *A History of Christianity* (London: Penguin, 2009), p. 368.

[12] G. Duby, 'Les origines de la chevalerie', *Settimane di studio sull'alto medioevo*, 15/2 (Spoleto, 1968), pp. 739–61.

[13] Robert Barless, 'From Paganism to Christianity in Medieval Europe', in Nora Berend (ed.), *Christianization and the Rise of Christian Monarchy: Scandanavia, Central Europe and Russia c. 900–1200* (Cambridge and New York: Cambridge University Press, 2007), pp. 47–72. This volume also contains essays on each of these countries. Also see MacCulloch, *A History of Christianity*, p. 368; Richard Fletcher, *The Conversion of Europe, from Paganism to Christianity 371–1386* AD (London: Fontana, 1998), chapters 7 and 11.

[14] MacCulloch, *A History of Christianity*, p. 369.

[15] See R. I. Moore, *The First European Revolution, c. 970–1215* (Oxford and Malden, MA: Blackwell, 2000); D. E. Luscombe, and G. R. Evans, 'The Twelfth-Century Renaissance', in J. H. Burns (ed.), *The Cambridge History of Medieval Political Thought c.350–c.1450* (Cambridge, New York, Melbourne: Cambridge University Press, 1988), Cambridge Histories Online, accessed 7 December 2012, DOI:10.1017/CHOL9780521243247.014; R. L. Benson, and G. Constable with C. D. Lanham (eds.), *Renaissance and Renewal in the Twelfth Century* (Oxford: Clarendon Press, 1982; 2nd edn, London and Toronto: University of Toronto Press, 1991); C. N. L. Brooke, *The Twelfth-Century Renaissance* (London: Thames & Hudson, 1969). Also Edward Grant, *God and Reason in the Middle Ages* (Cambridge: Cambridge University Press, 2001), chapter 1.

[16] D. Webb, *Medieval European Pilgrimage, c.700–c.1500* (Basingstoke: Ashgate, 2002).

[17] MacCulloch, *A History of Christianity*, p. 366.

their influence and established monasteries far from their place of origin (the Cluniac priory at Lewes in Sussex, founded in 1088, is a good example).

With the springing up of parish churches and the continued growth of the cathedrals, ritual became the main focus of religion—the collective recollection each day of the Christian narrative of the death and Resurrection, as well as the commemoration of lesser saints.[18] The liturgy was performed each day to the accompaniment of plainsong in the great cathedrals, which developed into the soaring polyphony of the Renaissance. These liturgical procedures were recorded in beautifully illustrated works that contained both the text of the liturgy and the accompanying musical notation. Along with the prayers of the Eucharist collected in *sacramentarium*, we have the divine office (*officium divinum*), or liturgy of the hours, developed for use both in cathedral and home.[19] The cathedral became a centre of prayer, the repetition of a ritual pattern through the generations that was more important in sustaining the tradition than theology and gave more nourishment to the populace than learned texts. While there was great emphasis on the liturgy, particularly in monastic settings, along with a sophisticated theology of the sacraments, there was also an emphasis on devotion and the cultivation of inner sanctity through prayer and virtue. Ritual and reading helped cultivate the 'inner man' (*homo interior*) and the journey to God. Within this transformed environment, an understanding of the human person developed that maintained the potential sanctity of the person amidst a social and political situation that was oppressive for the majority of the population, and often cruel by modern standards; indeed, serfs were completely controlled by their overlords, a situation that persisted in rural Russia up to the revolution.

Our primary sources for understanding the concept of the human person during this time are the works of theologians from Anselm to Aquinas, along with works of popular piety, vision, and, in the later period, the development of personal books of prayer used in private devotions. Within this climate of an expanding economy, particularly in the twelfth century, we have the growth of experiential religion that focused on the cultivation of inwardness where the person met God (the truth within was divine) which became intellectually

[18] On medieval liturgy, see Éric Palazzo, *Le Moyen Âge: Des origines au XIII siècle* (Paris: Beauchesne, 1993); on the medieval books of the mass, the Sacramentaires, pp. 47–83; E. Rose, *Ritual Memory: The Apocryphal Acts and Liturgical Commemoration in the Early Medieval West (c. 500–1215)* (Leiden: Brill, 2009)—on the liturgy and the hours, pp. 6–10, and on the commemoration of lesser Saints such as St Bartholomew, pp. 79–123; M. Metzger *Les Sacramentaires* (Brepolis: Turnhout, 1994), pp. 29–32, 34–6; C. Vogel, *Medieval Liturgy: An Introduction to the Sources*, trans. W. G. Storey and N. K. Rasmussen (Washington, DC: Pastoral Press, 1986), p. 64.

[19] Rose, *Ritual Memory*, p. 10; J. Harper, *The Forms and Order of Western Liturgy from the Tenth to Eighteenth Century* (Oxford and New York: Oxford University Press, 1991), pp. 73–108. On the liturgy of the hours, see Eamon Duffy, *Marking the Hours: English People and their Prayers 1240–1570* (New Haven, CT and London: Yale University Press, 2006), pp. 3–22.

articulated as mystical theology. Various literary genres contribute to our understanding of the truth within, including manuals of meditation and devotion, articulate theologies, letters, poems, romances, and autobiographical works. Most of these genres developed after the eleventh century, although there are precursors from an early period in Christian writing. Augustine's *Confessions* lays the foundations for future autobiographical work in Abelard and Nogent, and the writings of an obscure sixth-century Syrian mystic, Dionysius the Pseudo-Areopagite—or the Pseudo-Denys, as he came to be called—laid the foundations for mystical theology, positing a relationship between the vision of the heavenly realms and the ecclesiastical hierarchy.[20]

The eleventh century marked the beginnings of a social and cultural change that fully developed in the twelfth. The monastery, which had been the centre of cultural life, came to be replaced, after 1130, by the cathedral; and by the early thirteenth century, the Church had a fully fledged cult of relics—such as pieces of the true cross, Christ's blood, and even the crown of thorns at Notre Dame—many of which had been plundered from the east by the Frankish knights who captured Constantinople in 1204.[21] This growth of popular religiosity also meant a proliferation of kinds of devotional practice that were outside of the control of the Church, of particular importance being kinds of personal religious experience—forms of mysticism and vision—often practised by the socially marginalized, particularly women. While there were highly respectable forms of mystical theology, the Church was generally suspicious of personal religious experience, and 'mysticism' came to exceed the boundaries of control by the institution of the Church. The Church wanted to bridge the gap, that it perceived to be an evil, between the institution and popular practice.[22]

Amidst this social and religious change, the twelfth century witnessed a significant shift in the concept of the person; a period in which we find the roots of the notion of the individual in a sense that modernity would recognize, as a self-motivated agent with open-ended projects. In order to understand the idea of the inner truth during this period we need to examine the notion of the individual and the person's location in the cosmos.

[20] Denys Turner, *The Darkness of God: Negativity in Christian Mysticism* (Cambridge: Cambridge University Press, 1995), pp. 19–49.

[21] Georges Duby, *Le temps des cathedrals: L'art et la société 980–1420* (Paris: Gallimard, 1976), pp. 153, 190.

[22] De Certeau, *The Mystic Fable*, p. 86: 'This proliferation of private experiences, which was tied to the individualization of practice (from the development of auricular confession to personal devotions), appeared dangerous. "*Mystical*" *came to designate what had become separate from the institution.*'

THE IDEA OF THE INDIVIDUAL

The question of what constitutes an 'individual' and where we find precursors to the modern notion of the individual have been much discussed. Can liberal notions of the individual as a self-regulating, autonomous agent, the possessor of human rights, be traced back to the Middle Ages? There is a vast literature on individualism, but let us begin with the classic 1917 account by Georg Simmel as he highlights here certain features that we associate with the term. He begins his article 'Individualism' with an Italian chronicler saying how, in Florence, every man chose to dress 'in his own unique manner', which indicates a liberation from medieval forms of community and the emergence of 'character, distinction, and independence'.[23] Simmel does not offer a precise definition, but discusses individualism (*individualismus*) in general terms as 'a state of being, a sensibility, or as an aspiration' which expresses a behavioural quality that cannot be reduced to any more primordial instinct.[24] There are two aspects to this sensibility: on the one hand, individuals 'rest within themselves... as unities with a certain intrinsic being, meaning or purpose of their own'; yet they are also 'parts of one or many wholes that exist outside of them as an encompassing totality towering above them'. He goes on: 'individuality is what we call the form in which an attempt is made to unify these dual poles of human existence'.[25] Simmel distinguishes between individualism as it is worked out in Romantic cultures in contrast to Germanic individualism, which is quite different. The former, as illustrated by the Florentine fashion code, understands individualism to be the aspiration towards a general type. The desire for separation, autarchy, and self-reliance is directed towards a human type as such, in contrast to Germanic individualism that is concerned with singular value and the inner moral conscience of the personality, such as we find in Kant. It is the former that has had a broader appeal and greater impact on history, says Simmel.[26]

For Simmel then, individualism is an ideal type as well as a sociological reality of human persons that has developed since the Renaissance. The ideal type lays emphasis on self-reliance, uniqueness, creativity, and the expression of will in the performance of unrepeatable action in the world. For Kant, such assertions of autonomy need to be governed by the inner moral law. When and where such a concept—whether as a shared ideal or particular human instance—began is the question that has concerned many scholars, as it highlights the path to modernity. Where did such an idea begin?

[23] Georg Simmel, 'Individualism', *Theory, Culture and Society*, 24/7–8 (2007), pp. 66–71; also in Klaus Latzel (ed.), *Georg Simmel Gesamtausgabe*, vol. 13, trans. Austin Harrington (Frankfurt: Suhrkamp, 2000), pp. 299–306. Online version at: <http://tcs.sagepub.com/content/24/7-8/66.citation> (accessed 4 April 2012).

[24] Simmel, 'Individualism', p. 67.

[25] Simmel, 'Individualism', p. 67.

[26] Simmel, 'Individualism', pp. 68–9.

In contrast to nineteenth-century scholars who located the rise of the individual in the Renaissance (particularly Jacob Burckhardt),[27] a number of scholars have identified the twelfth century, in particular, as a time in which we can locate the origins of the modern notion of the individual. We can see the individual emerging in terms of a psychological self-examination and as expressed in literature, particularly romances, and in the autobiographies of Peter Abelard (1079–1142), Guibert de Nogent (1055–1124) and, later, Beatrice of Nazareth (d.1268). Ullman has charted the emergence of the political individual from the subject to citizen,[28] Peter Dronke[29] and Robert Hanning[30] have written about a new sense of individualism in lyric poetry, and John Benton,[31] Colin Morris,[32] and Richard Southern[33] have developed the philosophical and psychological dimensions of this immergence. The anthropologist Alan Macfarlane has proposed that the roots of individualism lie in thirteenth-century England, arguing through extensive comparison that the nature of English society was not the kind of peasant society found in other European locations.[34] Steven Lukes has traced the semantic history of 'individualism', locating its origin in the nineteenth century, particularly the term 'individualisme' in the work of Joseph de Maistre, who, in 1820, referred to the social order being 'shattered to its foundations' because of liberty, the lack of religion, and the growth of individual opinion that was a kind of 'political Protestantism carried to the most absolute individualism'.[35] This idea was

[27] Jacob Burckhardt, *The Civilization of Renaissance Italy*, trans. S. Middlemore (London: Penguin, 1990), pp. 87–110.

[28] Walter Ullman, *Individual and Society in the Middle Ages* (London: Methuen, 1967); *Medieval Foundations of Renaissance Humanism* (London: Elek, 1977). See also Aaron Gurevish, *The Origins of European Individualism*, trans. Katharina Judelson (Oxford: Blackwell, 1995). On traces of individualism as far back as Iceland epics, see Miller, 'Deep Inner Lives: Individualism and People of Honour'. On the modern ideology of individualism, see Louis Dumont, *Essays on Individualism: Modern Ideology in Anthropological Perspective* (Chicago, IL: University of Chicago Press, 1986), on its Christian origins pp. 23–59.

[29] Peter Dronke, *Poetic Individuality in the Middle Ages 1000–1150* (Oxford: Clarendon Press, 1970), especially pp. 1–32; see also his *Medieval Latin and the Rise of the European Love Lyric*, 2 vols (Oxford: Clarendon Press, 1966–7).

[30] Robert W. Hanning, *The Individual in Twelfth-Century Romance* (New Haven, CT: Yale University Press, 1977).

[31] John Benton, *Self and Society in Medieval France: The Memoirs of Abbor Guibert of Nogent* (Toronto: University of Toronto Press, 1984); 'Individualism and Conformity in Medieval Western Europe', in Amin Banani and Speros Vryonis (eds.), *Individualism and Conformity in Classical Islam* (Wiesbaden: Harrassowitz, 1977), pp. 145–58.

[32] Colin Morris, *The Discovery of the Individual 1050–1200* (Cambridge, MA: Medieval Academy of America, 1972), especially pp. 64–95, 139–57.

[33] Richard W. Southern, *Medieval Humanism and Other Studies* (Oxford: Blackwell, 1970)—on medieval humanism, pp. 29–60. Southern also links the individual with the rise of the concept of property after the twelfth century, pp. 53–5. On property rights, also see Alan Macfarlane, *The Origins of English Individualism: Family, Property and Social Transition* (Oxford: Blackwell, 1979), pp. 131–64. See also Brown, 'Society and the Supernatural: A Medieval Change'.

[34] Macfarlane, *The Origins of English Individualism*, pp. 9–10, 34–48, 152–63, 165.

[35] Steven Lukes, *Individualism* (2nd edn, Colchester: ECPR Press, 2006), p. 21.

reflected in later counter-revolutionaries, the Saint-Simonians, who followed Claude Henri de Saint-Simon's critique of the Enlightenment's promotion of the individual as destroying the idea of obedience and duty, thereby destroying power and law, the essential pillars of good social order.[36]

In contrast to this general thrust of scholarship finding the roots of individualism in the twelfth century, Bynum has been a moderating voice, claiming that the evidence for individuality has been somewhat exaggerated. Indeed, if the implication has been that discovery of the individual expressed as self-scrutiny, as we see in the autobiographies, entails a loss of community, then this clearly is not the case. Twelfth-century religion, says Bynum, 'did not emphasize the individual personality at the expense of corporate awareness'.[37]

This is a crucially important point. While we can recognize something of modern individualism in the letters and autobiographies of some writers, it is not Simmel's ideal type of Romantic individualism, nor the autonomy of Germanic individualism, nor the classical liberal notion of the individual as one with the capacity to govern his or her life through an individual thought process.[38] Bynum characterizes it rather as a search for 'the self', and we are in territory much closer to other cosmological religions—in India particularly, as we will see—than to Western modernity. What monastics and theologians believed they had discovered was not so much the individual (indeed the term *individuum* was used only in relation to the dialect in philosophy) but the soul (*anima*) or the 'inner man' (*homo interior*). This inner man was not the individual, but the self (*seipsum*) made in the image of God—the *imago dei* that is identical in all human beings.[39] There is no search for satisfaction or individual self-expression in this, but rather the religious life was seen as a journey towards God done in conformity to the Church, to the spiritual master, and to the spiritual exercises of prayer, fasting, and contemplation. Even outside the religious sphere the idea that individuality develops in the twelfth century needs to be treated with caution. As John Benton observes, one of the notable features of medieval society is the lack of acceptance of difference and the antipathy towards deviation of belief and behaviour.[40] Morris responded to Bynum's point that the claim about the origins of individualism in the twelfth century is not so much of cultural identity with

[36] Lukes, *Individualism*, p. 22.

[37] Caroline Walker Bynum, *Jesus as Mother: Studies in the Spirituality of the High Middle Ages* (Berkeley and Los Angeles, CA: University of California Press, 1982), p. 85.

[38] Tibor M. Machan, *Classical Individualism: The Supreme Importance of Each Human Being* (London: Routledge, 1998), pp. 1–16.

[39] Bynum, *Jesus as Mother*, p. 87.

[40] Benton, 'Individualism and Conformity in Medieval Western Europe', pp. 151–3. On the persecution of minority beliefs, see Michael Frassetto (ed.), *Heresy and the Persecuting Society in the Middle Ages: Essays on the Work of R. I. Moore* (Leiden: Brill, 2006). See also the seminal work of R. I. Moore, *The Origins of European Dissent* (New York: St Martin's Press, 1977)—on the reception of the new Cathar heresy, pp. 168–96.

modernity—clearly this is not the case—but rather that during this time we can discern respect for humanity, reason, and individuality 'which were largely lacking in the preceding five hundred years and which were to have a lasting impact on the growth of Western culture'.[41] This general concern for humanity we might not wish to restrict to twelfth-century Europe, as clearly it is present in ancient Judaism, and in early Buddhism, with its emphasis on compassion.

While there undoubtedly are texts—especially letters and autobiographies—in which we can recognize something of the modern notion of the individual as self-expression, creativity, and uniqueness, we must not forget that conformity was an important dimension of medieval understandings of the human person. In a monastic setting—or rather, in the realm of spiritual practices—this conformity was in relation to the development of inwardness. Through spiritual exercises—reading, asceticism, lay piety, and contemplation—the person tried to develop an inner transformation as laid down within the structures of tradition. Indeed, the inner transformation was dependent upon this degree of conformity. The monk or nun in a monastic setting in one sense eradicated his or her distinctiveness by wearing the same clothing as everyone else, by taking on a new name, by living in accordance with a regulated life, and by subjecting themselves to a regime of spiritual practice. We might even see this as the eradication of autonomy or, more accurately, describe it as an intensification of subjectivity and inwardness. Through an outer conformity, the monk or nun developed an interiority whose end goal was redemption and sanctification. The individual as expressivist was antithetical to this goal and practice, but the human person as subjectivity and inwardness in which to cultivate the quest for the truth within is the very heart of the spiritual transformation envisaged by these monks and nuns. Individualism must be distinguished from subjectivity because of the conformity of the person to institution and tradition.

Yet we nevertheless need some language that describes the shift in emphasis from communal identity and communal experience towards a different kind of subjectivity that we might even call personalism. With stable social institutions—particularly the Church—we see, during this period, a concern for the person as reflected in certain genres of literature such as courtly love poetry, letters, and autobiography.[42] Clearly there is a sense of the person in

[41] Colin Morris, 'Individualism in Twelfth-Century Religion. Some Further Reflections', in *The Journal of Ecclesiastical History*, 31/2 (1980), pp. 195–206.

[42] See the interesting book by Sarah Spence, *Texts and the Self in the Twelfth Century* (Cambridge, New York, Melbourne: Cambridge University Press, 1996), which argues for a correlation between body and text in medieval authors, particularly the autobiographical letter of Abelard and Guibert of Nogent's autobiography that draws on Augustine's *Confessions*. Also, J. Huizinga, *The Waning of the Middle Ages*, trans. F. Hopman (London: Penguin, 2001 (first published 1924)), on love and letters pp. 116–23. There is a shift in the later period to a bucolic, pastoral vision of the idyllic life, pp. 124–33.

this literature that was not there in, say, the second century. Romantic love, from the troubadours through to chivalric courtly love, is another indication of a shift of emphasis towards personalism—although romantic love is not exclusive to this period in the West (we simply need to read Sanskrit poetry to see this). But we should not exaggerate the roots of modernity in this literature and need to be cautious about claiming that in the twelfth century we find an individualism that Simmel would recognize.

In relation to this, some have argued that a discourse of rights begins to emerge in the twelfth century with the idea of justice or *ius*. While most scholars located the origins of a rights discourse to the sixteenth century—or perhaps earlier in the thirteenth century, with William of Ockam who argued for the competing claims of individuals in the notion of justice against the Thomist idea of ordered justice—others have seen this rights discourse as originating in the earlier medieval period in Roman law. Brian Tierney has argued that the meaning of the Latin term *ius* shifted from right order or law with medieval jurists and ecclesiastics, to the claims of individual persons. Rufinus, for example, claims Tierney, begins not with the objectivity of what is 'just', but rather with the human personality; natural *ius* is the power by which a man can discern good from evil, and is only secondarily objective law.[43] In contrast, others have emphasized discontinuity in the discourse of rights—such as Leo Strauss, who argues that objective *ius* is only replaced with an emphasis on subjectivity with Hobbes, and Michel Villey argues persuasively that the person was understood not as self-sufficient, but as being constituted within a series of relationships.[44] Milbank has supported this perspective, arguing 'against human rights' as a recent liberal discourse that misunderstands the sacral nature of the human person that was recognized by the original conception of *ius*.[45] The broader point is that with the medieval world view we have a participatory model of personhood in which the person

[43] Brian Tierney, *The Idea of Natural Rights: Studies on Natural Rights, Natural Law and Church Law 1150–1625* (Atlanta, GA: Scholars Press, 1997); 'Historical Roots of Modern Rights: Before Locke and After', Ave Maria Law Review, 3/1 (2005), pp. 23–43, 25. 'Natural Law and Natural Rights: Old Problems and Recent Approaches', *The Review of Politics*, 64/3 (2002), pp. 389–406. For a good summary of the discussion, see Charles J. Reid, *Power over the Body, Equity in the Family: Rights and Domestic Relations in Medieval Canon Law* (Grand Rapids, MI and Cambridge: Eerdmans, 2004), pp. 18–24 and S. Adam Seagrave, 'How Old are Modern Rights? On the Lockean Roots of Contemporary Human Rights Discourse', Journal of the History of Ideas, 72/2 (April 2011), pp. 305–27; and Francis Oakley, *Natural Law, Laws of Nature, Natural Rights: Continuity and Discontinuity in the History of Ideas* (London: Continuum, 2005), pp. 87–109.

[44] Leo Strauss, *Natural Right and History* (Chicago, IL: University of Chicago Press, 1953), pp. 202–51. Michel Villey, *La formation de la pensée juridique moderne: Cours d'histoire de la philosophie du droit* (4th edn, Paris: Montchrestien, 1975), pp. 236–9, 541–47.

[45] John Milbank, Against Human Rights [document], Centre for Philosophy and Theology, University of Nottingham, <http://www.theologyphilosophycentre.co.uk/papers/Milbank_Against HumanRights.pdf> (accessed 3 August 2012).

participates in the objective order of justice that is distinctive in not being a discourse of rights based on the autonomy of the individual and a model of inherent rights.

We need then to distinguish between individualism as a characteristic of modernity, and individuality as a feature of human persons that refers to the particularity and unrepeatability of each. It would not be correct to describe such cultivation of inwardness as individualism, for although we have an emphasis on the individual human person, the form of inwardness is specific to the tradition and the internalization of the goal of redemption. Indeed, in many ways the cultivation of an intense inwardness through spiritual practices, such as we find in the Christianity of the High Middle Ages, is anti-individualist. While the person is particular (and so displays individuality), the person needs to be made as pure as possible so as to approach God—and this means, for the monk or nun, the eradication of lower desires and the cultivation of virtue. There is a pre-established pattern of holiness that the religious person aspires to. It is this cultivation of holiness, mostly, although not exclusively, in a monastic setting, where we see the transformational possibilities of the human person. Such cultivation was understood as movement—a movement within, deeper into the self, which was simultaneously to move deeper (and higher) into the cosmos and closer to God.

INWARDNESS AND COSMOLOGY

As C. S. Lewis marvellously showed, the medieval world had a model of the universe within which human beings were located. This model—partly derived from biblical accounts, partly derived from classical accounts—was of a vast, but closed, universe in which each part was linked to other parts in a hierarchical sequence. Thus, Lewis opens *The Discarded Image* with an account of a poem called *Brut*, written by an English priest, Lazamon (between 1160 and 1207), in which he described the air being filled with good and malevolent beings—aerial daemons—an idea that he received from a Norman poet Mace (*c.*1155) who took it from Geoffrey of Monmouth (before 1139), who in turn had taken it from Apuleius (second century CE), who took it from Plato. Plato was inheriting a cosmology he had himself received.[46] In Apuleius' cosmos the human realm is separated from the gods by the innumerable daemons, some of whom were once human and some never human but possessed qualities that affect the human world such as sleep and love.[47]

[46] C. S. Lewis, *The Discarded Image: An Introduction to Medieval and Renaissance Literature* (Cambridge: Cambridge University Press, 1964), p. 2.

[47] Lewis, *The Discarded Image*, p. 42.

Lewis makes the important point that, in spite of various disagreements over intellectual matters—such as realism versus nominalism, effort versus grace—the contained, hierarchical model of the cosmos remained the backdrop of such disputes and lasted well into the seventeenth century.[48] What is striking is that the vast hierarchy outside the human person is also found within the person as a microcosm that recapitulates the macrocosm.[49]

Pseudo-Denys is the most important figure in establishing this cosmology. It is his angelic hierarchy that comes to be accepted by the Church and which is crucial in understanding the divine–human relationship. The celestial hierarchy comprises three tiers above the human, the first tier itself comprising three species—the seraphim, cherubim, and thrones; the second tier comprises dominations, potestates, and virtues; and the third tier comprises principalities, archangels, and angels. Only the lowest sphere is directed towards the human and, through them, God interacts with humanity. Indeed, the Annunciation was declared by an angel, and Aquinas cites Denys on this matter that the mediation of angels—even in this important matter—remains unbroken.[50] The hierarchy of beings is also associated with the elements. Indeed, the human person is the microcosm containing the four elements—earth, water, air, and fire—which corresponding to the flesh, blood, breath, and heat of the body,[51] and beings comprise different kinds of elements and are driven by different forces. The kind of body a being has depends upon the balance of the four elements within it. Thus Evagrius (*c.*345–99), following Origen, can say that with the angels there is a predominance of intellect (*nous*) and fire, with humans a predominance of concupiscence (*epithumia*) and earth, and with demons a predominance of anger (*thumos*) and air.[52] An important source of this general hierarchy is Neoplatonism and the doctrine of Plotinus (CE 205–70), which comes into Christianity through Macrobius' fifth-century Latin abridgement of the doctrine of the scale of being. Macrobius (and Plotinus) has Mind (*nous*) arising from the supreme God (the one) and

[48] Lewis, *The Discarded Image*, p. 13.

[49] Arnold Angenendt, *Geschichte der Religiosität im Mittelalter* (Darmstadt: Wissenschaftliche Buchgesellschaft, 1997), pp. 203–12.

[50] Lewis, *The Discarded Image*, p. 73. Lewis quotes the *Summa Theologica* III Quest. XXX Art. 2, which reads in response to the question why an angel should announce the Incarnation: *primo quidem, ut in hoc etiam sevareturdivina ordinatio, secundum quam mediantibus angelis divina ad homines perveniunt*... 'that even in so great a matter (*in hoc etiam*) the system (or pattern, *ordinatio*) whereby divine things reach us through the mediation of angels might be unbroken' (p. 73).

[51] Jacques Le Goff, *Medieval Civilization 400–1500*, trans. Julia Barrow (Oxford: Blackwell, 1988), p. 138.

[52] A. Guillaumont (ed.), *Les Six Centuries des 'Kephalaia Gnostica' d'Evagre le Pontique. Edition critique de la version syriaque commune et édition d'une novelle version syriaque, intégrale, avec une double traduction française*. Patrologia Orientalis, vol. XXVIII, fasc. 1 (Paris: Frimin Didot, 1958), p. 121. I quote this in *The Ascetic Self: Subjectivity, Memory and Tradition* (Cambridge: Cambridge University Press, 2004), p. 151.

from Mind arises the Soul (*psuche*), from which all other things arise and which reflect it. Macrobius writes in a passage quoted by Lovejoy:

> Since, from the Supreme God Mind arises, and from Mind, Soul, and since this in turn creates all subsequent things and fills them all with life, and since this single radiance illumines all and is reflected in each, as a single face might be reflected in many mirrors placed in a series; and since all things follow in continuous succession, degenerating in sequence to the very bottom of the series, the attentive observer will discover a connection of parts, from the Supreme God down to the last dregs of things, mutually linked together without a break.[53]

This passage is a good illustration of the idea of a hierarchical cosmos that emanates down from higher, purer forms to lower, more impure forms, such that the lower reflect the higher. The lower forms stream forth from the higher in a continuous succession and recapitulate, in a more impure and restricted way, those higher forms. While Christian writers did not accept emanationism because of the doctrine of creation *ex nihilo*—although we still find echoes of emanationism in some writings of Denys—they did accept the general principle of a system or divine order (*ordinatio divina*) in the cosmos; this divine order was a hierarchy of being, with God at the top, through the mediations of angels and other supernatural beings, to humanity and, in due course, below this to demonic hell-realms. This essentially Neoplatonic cosmology is grafted onto a Christian world view of salvation through Christ, and final redemption or condemnation at the Last Judgement, with souls being weighed by St Michael, as we see depicted in so many medieval churches and cathedrals, from the twelfth-century wall paintings in local parish churches—such as South Leigh in Oxfordshire—to the great façade depicting the Last Judgement at Notre Dame de Paris. The idea of a cosmic hierarchy, derived from Neoplatonism, is broadly incorporated into a Christian world view, as we see in the writings not only of Denys, but Augustine too, through to Aquinas and even Dante. This world order was not replaced until religion retreated from cosmology, which became the purview of science by the seventeenth century.[54]

Alongside the chain of being in an ordered cosmos we have the Christian narrative of the Fall of Man, the necessity of salvation, the Incarnation and redemption, and the Last Judgement. The medieval concept of the human person therefore necessitated understanding the place of humanity in the divine order, spatially below the angels and temporally in a post-Fall state anticipating the second coming of Christ. The hierarchical, cosmological

[53] Macrobius, *Commentary in Somnium Scipionis*, I, 14, 15. Quoted in Arthur O. Lovejoy, *The Great Chain of Being* (Cambridge, MA: Harvard University Press, 1936), p. 63.

[54] On the retreat of religion from cosmology, see Oliver Davies, *The Creativity of God: World, Eucharist, Reason* (Cambridge: Cambridge University Press, 2004), pp. 17–28.

symbolism is inscribed within a chronology of 'before' and 'after':[55] before The Fall, after The Fall; before Christ with the Old Testament, after Christ with the New; before the Second Coming, after Judgement. Before final Judgement, in the meantime, the Church Militant (*Ecclesia Militans*)—the temporal Church on earth—fights against sin, while the Church Triumphant (*Ecclesia Triumphans*) rests in heaven with the Church Expectant (*Eccesia Expectans*) comprising all souls in purgatory awaiting their final entry into heaven. This doctrine of purgatory had developed by the 1170s—a place for souls whose sins were not so great as to earn everlasting damnation, but who needed further purification before entering heaven.[56] It was within this time frame and cosmological structure that people in the High Middle Ages saw themselves, and into which they fitted all new knowledge. Indeed, all of human history was understood in Christian historiography within a single paradigm as the history of salvation.[57] Even spatial geography was understood in the light of this narrative, with Jerusalem as the centre of the earth, the original earthly paradise, Eden, to the east, and outlandish creatures dwelling on the periphery—particularly India—which contained many strange types of creature that captured the medieval imagination. The human person in this cosmology was constantly subject to external forces that are, in effect, moral forces in the form of angels and demons. All good actions come from the Lord, and all evil acts come from God's fallen angel, the Devil, who can appear in various guises and who people need to be on their guard against.[58] The purpose of life in this world view is the progressive development of the soul and the return of the person to God. This return is through the cosmos, through the world of angels who manifest in symbols: the illuminative divine light descends to the human world in revelations and 'the mystical narration of sacred language' and so fills our intelligence and allows our participation and we ascend to the presence of God.[59]

[55] De Certeau, The *Mystic Fable*, pp. 92–3.

[56] J. Le Goff, *The Birth of Purgatory*, trans. A. Goldhammer (Chicago, IL: Chicago University Press, 1986), pp. 133–4.

[57] Arno Borst, *Medieval Worlds: Barbarians, Heretics and Artists in the Middle Ages*, trans. Eric Hansen (Cambridge: Polity Press, 1991 (first published 1988)), p. 63.

[58] Le Goff, *Medieval Civilization*, p. 160–2. This phenomenon persists into early modernity. See the case of Christoph Haizmann, reported by Freud and commented on by Michel de Certeau in *The Writing of History*, trans. Tom Conley (New York: Columbia University Press, 1988), pp. 287–307. On the Devil and angels, see Angenendt, *Geschichte der Religiosität im Mittelalter*, pp. 151–9. Angenendt gives the example of the Devil appearing to Hildegaard of Bingen as a long 'worm'.

[59] Robert Javelet, *Image et Resemblance au Douzieme Siècle de Saint Anselme à Alain de Lile* (Paris: Editions Letopuizey et Ané, 1967), vol. 1, p. 165, citing Hugh of St Viktor. On participation in early Christianity, see Torstein Theodor Tollefsen, *Activity and Participation in Late Antique and Early Christian Thought* (Oxford and New York: Oxford University Press, 2012), p. 161: 'The central idea of participation can be defined thus: it is a movement of the divine towards the human, and of the human towards the divine.'

INWARDNESS IN RITUAL AND MYSTICISM

This understanding of the human person as being subject to external powers—not only political and social forces that control their economic position and status, but supernatural forces too that influence their moral being—might in some ways be seen as antithetical to the idea of inwardness. But this is not the case, for the concept of the human person, at all social levels, was not of a monadic ego cut off from others and from the world, but rather a person was constituted by a culturally mediated relationality, not only with fellow human beings, but with the broader cosmos and the beings it contains, both natural and supernatural. Through the repeated, daily act of liturgy the person became wholly integrated into the collective body of the society and, so it was believed, into the collective body that is the Church and Christ. The liturgy in monastery, cathedral, and parish church provided a Durkheimian social cohesion and allowed participants to dwell within a coherent and meaningful frame of reference. Generally this frame of reference went unchallenged, and there was a high degree of conformity; and where the liturgical pattern and world view behind it was challenged—as we see in various heresies such as the broad-based movement termed the Free Spirit—this was not by some individualistic notion of the self, but rather by a different kind of conformity to a different collectivity.[60]

Yet alongside this ritual understanding of the person, we find in medieval Christianity a growing sense of inwardness as being integral to the human person in his or her religious orientation. Alongside the belief in angels, demons, and God's providence, a strong mystical theology developed at various cultural levels from complex philosophical accounts of the self, to personal accounts of mystical experience, particularly in the late Middle Ages (after 1300). The whole orientation of spiritual practices, mostly (but not only) in monastic life, was towards developing and intensifying inner life, which was understood as the soul's or mind's journey towards God—to borrow the title of Bonaventure's text (see 'Bonaventure's Journey of the Soul', pp. 73–80). As there is an outer pilgrimage in which the devout travel to a sacred place to celebrate a saint's day or perform a penance, so there is an inner pilgrimage towards God. This inner pilgrimage was cultivated in monastic circles where an intense sense of subjectivity developed within the monastic order of the liturgy. Asceticism and prayer forged an inwardness that was understood in terms of both ascent towards God, and moving deeper into the self: the metaphors of depth and height are conflated in contemplation. In all of these senses, in liturgy and mysticism, participation in the cosmological process is a key to understanding here. The person is not an autonomous individual but is transformed through

[60] On the Free Spirit heresy, see Robert E. Lerner, *The Heresy of the Free Spirit in the Later Middle Ages* (Berkeley and Los Angeles, CA: University of California Press, 1972).

participation in the structures of the Church that are integrated into the structure of the very cosmos: complete or final participation, which is human destiny, being fuller than participation at the beginning of the process.[61]

We need to understand religious inwardness at different levels of social being: among the broad laity, among the monastics, and among the lay religious (i.e. the laity who perform more intense devotional service, such as mystics in the later Middle Ages). Spiritual practices existed among all of these groups in varying degrees of intensity. We can identify three principle practices that are addressed by distinct genres of literature: liturgy, prayer, and vision.

Liturgy

The liturgy was the heart of religious practice, celebrated daily in the great monastic churches and later in the cathedrals. The Eucharist was (and arguably still is) the supreme act of worship in Christianity that we might say exists in terms of practice and enacted symbolism affecting participants—even though they may not be aware of its meaning; it also exists as a key theme of theology. The Eucharist combined ideas of sacrifice and commemoration, with the abolishing of violent sacrifice and its replacement by memory. In certain prayers of the mass, observes Palazzo, the emphasis is on the sacrifice of Christ in the memorial act of the rite, which is theology *on* the Eucharist; whereas other prayers emphasize the transformation of bread and wine into the body and blood of the Lord at the moment of consecration, which is theology *from* the Eucharist.[62] The violent, literal sacrifice has been transformed into the sacrifice of Christ commemorated in the mass; sacrifice has become internal to the ritual. Similarly, the bread and the wine transformed into the body and blood, through their consumption, become internal to the devotee. Through the Eucharist the practitioner shares in the saving work of Christ 'that is analogous to bodily nourishment'.[63] More than this, the Eucharist is a sign for a deeper union with Christ: Christ is the spiritual food, according to Aquinas, that is prior to the sacrament itself, which is therefore

[61] Javelet, *Image et Ressemblance*, vol. 1, p. 145. Javelet writes: 'La participation finale est supérieure à la participation initiale—temporelle—mais correspond à l'éternelle prédestination de l'homme, applelé à être dieu par et avec Dieu.'

[62] Éric Palazzo, *Liturgie et société au Moyen Age* (Paris: Aubier, 2000), p. 21. For a thorough account of liturgical literature, the *sacramentarium*, see Palazzo, *Le Moyen Age*, pp. 47–83. For a stemma of families of sacramental texts, see p. 59. On the sacramentaries also see Vogel, *Medieval Liturgy*, pp. 61–106.

[63] P. J. Fitzpatrick, *In Breaking of Bread: The Eucharist and Ritual* (Cambridge: Cambridge University Press, 1993), p. 197.

a sign.[64] This came to be the standard theological view, and Peter Lombard subsumes all sacraments under the category of the sign.[65] In this sign we see the collapse of past and future into the present moment,[66] a combination in which the voice from the past comes alive in the present in anticipation of the future.

The practice of the sacraments was theorized to a sophisticated degree by the medieval theologians, particularly Aquinas, linking them in with human nature. The sacraments as sensible signs of immaterial things, or 'visible forms of invisible grace',[67] were integral to giving fallen human beings access to God through material reality. As human beings, according to the medieval theologians, we are embodied souls who have the cognitive capacity to come to know spiritual truth through sensible reality. Angels as bodiless intellects have direct knowledge of the spiritual world without the mediation of the senses, whereas non-rational animals have no cognition of immaterial things. It is only the human that can, or must, perceive spiritual reality through the material senses and the material sign, and this perception is for their benefit and enhancement. Adams cites Hugh of St Victor in answering the question as to why God placed human souls in bodies—that God's self-diffusing goodness in such creation 'opens the opportunity for the human soul to become more Godlike still by imitating God in the exercise of providence'.[68] The Eucharist, above all the sacraments, is integral to the Christian life, and its practice undertaken in action at a pre-philosophical level. The liturgy takes place in a church or the great cathedrals, which become a physical articulation of theology exemplified in Abbot Suger's stone 'theology' of the Gothic cathedral of St Denis, north of Paris. Here, in response to a need to expand the space of worship, Abbot Suger designed an architecture to reflect God's light and focus the mind on worship.[69] Thus, although the liturgy appears external in the sense that it involves a sequence of human actions such as recitation, movement of the body, and consumption, it only makes sense because of subjectivity: that the very structure of the human—human nature itself—allows for interaction of the

[64] Quoted and discussed by Fitzpatrick, *In Breaking of Bread*, pp. 197–8.

[65] For a clear account, see M. M. Adams, *Some Later Medieval Theories of the Eucharist* (Oxford: Oxford University Press, 2010), pp. 33–5.

[66] Palazzo, *Liturgie et société*, p. 22.

[67] Peter Lombard, *Sentences* IV. D. 1. C. 2. Cited by Adams, *Some Later Medieval Theories of the Eucharist*, p. 34.

[68] Adams, *Some Later Medieval Theories of the Eucharist*, p. 37. For a lucid overview of different medieval theologians' understandings of the liturgy in relation to human nature, see Adams, pp. 33–50.

[69] The classic study is E. Panofsky, *Abbot Suger on the Abbey Church of Saint Denis and its Art Treasures* (2nd edn, Princeton, NJ: Princeton University Press, 1979 (first published 1946)). A. W. Robertson, *The Service Books of the Royal Abbey of Saint Denis: Images of Ritual and Music in the Middle Ages* (Oxford: Oxford University Press, 1991), pp. 46–9; on the integration of architectural theory and liturgy, pp. 235–48.

material world with the spiritual world in the sacrament. Through participating in the liturgy the person is participating in a collective subjectivity that, in the Christian world view, brings the person closer to God (and, in the case of orthodoxy, sets the conditions for becoming divine—for *theosis*). Peter Damian's monks ask him why they need to repeat the psalter and the cycle of monastic prayers while in the isolation of their own cells when nobody is present. Damian replies that, even though there are no other human beings there, the whole Church is present.[70] Through participation in the material form of the liturgy we find a transformation of subjectivity such that the boundaries of the person are stretched to embrace the Church, that in turn is an expression of divine grace. There is no private liturgy, nor indeed a private subjectivity, in the performance of Christian ritual. In a similar way, in vision literature we find an intensification of subjectivity in the sense that visions occur to a particular person within themselves, yet this subjectivity is participatory in the broader cultural and political arena.

Prayer

Prayer was also at the heart of religious practice, and while the liturgy itself can be seen as an extended prayer, there were also practices of inner or private prayer, and manuals of prayer were produced as guides and encouragement for the practice. Using a prayer book guided monks to awareness of sin and repentance before the adoration of the saints and God.[71] A number of texts were produced, particularly in the later Middle Ages, ranging from manuals of prayer to works of mystical theology, that can also be read as practical manuals—for instance, *The Cloud of Unknowing*. Works in Middle English are particularly interesting as practical manuals. For example, the *Contemplations of the Dread and Love of God* was composed in the south-west Midlands some time during the last quarter of the fourteenth century and the first quarter of the fifteenth. It is a manual of prayer intended for men and women, both lay and monastic, that describes how to pray, and ends with a meditation or visualization of Christ's sufferings, thereby looking forward to Ignatius' *Spiritual Exercises*. The text is also indicative of attitudes in that it offers basic moral teachings and reflection on fundamental Christian values, such as charity and love of God and world.

[70] I cite this in *The Ascetic Self*, p. 190: 'If, therefore, those who believe in Christ are one, then whenever we find a member according to outward appearances, there, by the mystery of the sacrament, the whole body is present.' *Si ergo credentes unum est ubicunque videatur esse per corporalem speciem membrum, ibi etiam per sacramenti msterium totum est corpus.*

[71] John Hirsch, *The Boundaries of Faith: The Development and Transmission of Medieval Spirituality* (Leiden: Brill, 1996), pp. 11–22.

The text begins with general statements that men and women should desire to love God, and how they were sometimes visited with a spiritual (*gostliche*) sweetness in the lover of God.[72] Dread is the beginning of wisdom that leads to charity, which is love of God and neighbour that we should cultivate in adversity and in prosperity. There are various degrees of love: the first degree is made up of the love of the body, such that the body might be sustained, love of neighbour, friend, and enemy; the second degree is 'clean love', comprising love of virtue and rejection of vice, the despising of all evil custom, the rejection of even small or venial sin; the third degree is 'steadfast love' with all one's desire, thinking constantly upon God, and resisting temptation. 'Perfect love' is the fourth degree, a love in which a man 'is ready to die gladly for his brother'.[73] To achieve these degrees of love, along with good living one must learn to pray. Indeed, prayer is the way in which the troubled soul can communicate with God; but to do this we need to control desire—as Saint Gregory has said, 'the more we are troubled with thoughts of fleshly desire, the more need we have to stand in fervent prayer'.[74] And, in prayer, we should not ask for things for ourselves, but only that God's will be done. Here the text gives advice about how to pray,[75] not to fall asleep, and to put away 'wicked thoughts and perilous imagination', which is in fact the 'wicked angel'. Prayer should be practised in a quiet place without disturbance,[76] and the text culminates in a visualization that the devotee can practise; a short meditation on the passion.

Reading 1

You may imagine in your heart, your Lord entrusted to his enemies with many slanders and insults, brought before a judge and falsely accused by many wicked men. He answered nothing but endured their words. They would have him dead of necessity, but first they would have him endure pain. Behold the good Lord

[72] Margaret Connolly (ed.), *Contemplations of the Dread and Love of God* (Oxford: Oxford University Press for EETS, 1993), p. 7, lines 26–43, p. 6.

[73] Connolly, *Contemplations*, p. 23.

[74] Connolly, *Contemplations*, p. 29: *the more we be trauailled with thoughtis of flescheliche desires, the more nede we haue to stonde bisiliche in preiers.*

[75] Connolly, *Contemplations*, p. 31: 'And when you shall pray you must pray with full heart and put away from all vanities of the world, all imagination and idle thoughts. To this accord a holy scholar said: "when we stand to pray, we must avoid all fleshly and worldly thoughts and not allow our heart to be occupied otherwise than with our prayer".'

Also whan thou schalt preie thou must preie with ful herte and putte awey fro the alle vanities of the world, alle ymaginacions and yudul thoghtes. To this acordeth an holi clerk and seith: 'Whan we stonde to preie, we moste voide all flescheliche and worldeliche thoughtes, and suffre no oure herte otherwise be occupied than aboute oure preiour.

[76] Connolly, *Contemplations*, p. 41: 'When you prepare yourself for prayer or have devotion, seek a private place from all kinds of noise and have time to rest without any interruption. Sit there or kneel as is easiest for you.'

Whan thouh schappest the to preie or haue eny diuocion, fond to haue a priue place from alle maner noise, and time of reste withoute eny letting. Sitte ther or knele as is thi moste eise.

> shivering and quaking, his body naked, bound to a pillar, wicked men standing about him and scourging that blessed body without pity for no reason . . . In such a way you should pray in the beginning; and when you have really entered into devotion, you shall have perhaps better feeling in prayer and holy meditations, otherwise than I can show.[77]

This visualization of Christ's suffering is the climax of the text, but also a suggestion that this is simply the beginning of prayer. Christ is the truth within. The image of Christ is very vivid, and the text is clear that the practitioner should imagine—that is, visualize—the scene within his own heart. The text gives the image of Christ's suffering at the hands of his torturers and his crucifixion until his head hangs down and his heart is pierced through his side. A number of things are striking about this text. Firstly, the overall structure of the entire text moves from the development of morality to instructions on prayer itself, and ends with this cultivated vision or visualization of the passion. Secondly, the strong visual element of the prayer is a meditation combined with tearful devotion. This is a meditational devotion that is to be cultivated by the practitioner in a way that his or her subjectivity becomes overwhelmed by the text—or rather by the image that the text carries. Although the term imagination is used, it does not denote 'mere imagination' or 'unreality', but points to a participation of the practitioner in a narrative structure whose origin is historical—the crucifixion—but whose meaning is ever present and real. The event from the past at the heart of the Christian narrative is brought to life in the present through visual prayer. The narrative story of the New Testament is retold here in the text, and thereby retold in the imaginations of each reader who puts this into practice. Through this visualization the practitioner erodes his individuality and participates in a larger, shared subjectivity. Indeed, the text exhorts the devotee to jettison his own will so that the Lord's will replace his own: 'As often as you pray, whatever you pray, put your entire will into God's will and at the end of prayer, always desire in each asking that his will to be fulfilled and not your will.'[78] Through reading the book and putting it into practice, the devotee's inwardness is intensified and his individuality eroded. Through participation in the text the practitioner becomes part of the broader cosmos and Christian history.

[77] Connolly, *Contemplations*, p. 44: *Thou maist ther ymagine in thin herte, as thou sey thi Lord take of his enemys with mony repreues and dispites, broght bifore a juge, falsliche ther accused of mony wicked men. He anwereth right noght but mekeliche suffred here wordis. Thei wolde haue him nedes ded, but ferst to suffre peynes. Bihold than that goode Lord chiuering and quaking, al his bodi naked, bounde to a piler, aboute him stonding wicked men withouten eny resoun sore skorging that blessed bodi withoute eny pitee.... In such a maner thou maist preie in thi bigynning; and whan thou art wiel entred into deuocion, thou schalt haue percas better feling in preiere and holi meitacions, otherwise than y can schewe.*

[78] Connolly, *Contemplations*, p. 30: *As ofte as thou preiest, whateuer thou preiest, put al thi wil into Godis wil in the ende of þi preier, desiring euermore in eche asking his wil to be fulfillud and nothing thi wil.*

Vision

We can make a distinction between high or academic theology, that began in the monasteries and became a defining feature of the medieval university, and more popular religious texts written for a literate, although not university educated, populace. This literature includes religious handbooks (such as the Middle English *Pricke of Conscience*), 'Craft of Dying' or Ars Moriendi, didactic poems such as the thirteenth-century 'Death' and 'Sinner Beware', and vision literature.[79] Didactic poetry in Middle English offers warnings against sin, the shortness of life, and the need to face death with impunity. 'Sinners Beware' is a text that seeks protection from the devils who seek to ensnare us and exhorts us to shun sin in fear of the pains of hell.[80] 'Death' provides a graphic reminder in verse of bodily decay in the grave, how all friends have abandoned the dead man, and, speaking in the first person, how 'there never, no, cometh light, there I shall meet many and awful whyte [ghost]'.[81] While, in the earlier period, vision texts were composed in Latin, towards the end of the Middle Ages they were composed in vernacular languages, and some of the Latin texts translated into the vernaculars. The 'Craft of Dying' literature about the fate of the soul after death, and on how to die a good death in Christ, were compiled mostly in the fifteenth century and based on two Latin texts entitled *Ars Moriendi*.[82] The moment of death was crucial for the fate of the soul, when demons awaited to take the person if they could.[83] Ritual preparation for death was very important, and these books were practical guides.[84] We might add to this literature the increasing

[79] On the history of this broad-based religious literature, see Peter Dinzelbacher, *Vision und visionsliteratur im Mittelalter* (Stuttgart: Anton Hiersemann, 1981); particularly useful is the chronological table, pp. 24–8. On the visionary and persons in the other world, see pp. 146–68.

[80] 'Sinners Beware' in Richard Morris (ed.), *An Old English Miscellany* (London: Early English Text Society, 1872), pp. 72–83.

[81] 'Death', p. 181, Morris, *An Old English Miscellany*, pp. 168–84. See also the sobering 'Signs of Death', p. 101 in the same volume.

[82] The Latin texts are dated fifteenth century, but a large literature developed. Perhaps the most well known is that published by William Caxton, *Here Begynneth a Lityll Treatyse Short and Abrydgyd Spekynge of the Art and Crafte to Knowe Well to Dye* (London: Emprynted by Richarde Pynson, 1495), p. 2: 'Bodily death is the most fearful thing of all other things. It is the death of the soul as much more terrible and reproachable. As the soul is more noble and more precious than the body and the death of sinners is right cursed and evil, but the death of just and true people is precious unto God. For the dead men be well happy that die in our Lord. To this purpose, Plato says that continuous remembrance of death is sovereign wisdom. Also for truth, the bodily death of good people always is non other thing but the issue or going out of prison and of evil and discharging of a right grevious burden.'

[83] Philippe Ariès, *The Hour of Our Death*, trans. Helen Weaver (Oxford: Oxford University Press, 1991 (first published 1981)), p. 109; Eamon Duffy, *The Stripping of the Altars: Traditional Religion in England 1400–1580* (New Haven, CT and London: Yale University Press, 1992), pp. 313–27.

[84] There is a large literature on death and dying in the Middle Ages and Renaissance. The classic study is Ariès (see note 83), but also see Michel Vovelle, *La mort et l'Occident de 1300 à*

popularity of personal prayer books, the books of hours. While the majority of the population were probably illiterate, there was a growing literate populace who were also devout but not monastics; for them this literature provided spiritual nourishment.

A particularly interesting genre of medieval literature that illuminates the medieval Christian understanding of the person and inwardness is the vision literature (*visio*). This is mostly composed in Latin, although there are vernacular translations, particularly in Middle English. The literature articulates the imagination of the society that produced it; and in many ways, through examining this literature, we go to the heart of the medieval understanding of the human person. This genre presents an account of the soul's journey to the other world and reflects older classical narratives of Orpheus, Hercules, Theseus, and even Odysseus' journey to the underworld, moulded on to a Christian vision and cosmology. Generally the vision literature tells of a visionary who has had some sort of collapse due to illness, and describes the journey of his soul during this time to another world, his experiences there in hell and/or purgatory and heaven, and his return to the body where he recounts the tale and draws moral lessons from it. This is Dante's vision before Dante. The standard scholarship here is Carozzi's *Le Voyage de l'âme dans l'au-delà, d'après la literature latine (Ve-VIIe siècle)*, which charts the development of the narrative from classical sources through the Christian theologians and anonymous visionary literature.[85] These texts were part of a much larger body recounting visionary experiences of Christ or the Virgin,[86] and must also be seen as part of the broader literary genre of religious handbooks such as the 'Art of Dying' literature.[87] People were encouraged to reflect on their mortality

nos jours (Paris: Gallimard, 2001 (first published 1983)); Nancy Lee Beaty, *The Craft of Dying: A Study in the Literary Tradition of the Ars Moriendi in England* (New Haven, CT: Harvard University Press, 1970), on the ars moriendi texts p. 53, on Thomas Lupset's *The Waye of Dyeng Well* (1534), pp. 54–107; Paul Binski, *Medieval Death: Ritual and Representation* (Ithaca, NY: Cornell University Press, 1996), on the good death pp. 33–47; Carlos M. N. Eire, *From Madrid to Purgatory: The Art and Craft of Dying in Sixteenth-Century Spain* (Cambridge: Cambridge University Press, 2002), pp. 24–33, meditation on death and judgement, pp. 73–8; Ralph Houlbrook, *Death, Religion and the Family in England 1480–1750* (Oxford: Clarendon Press, 1998); Craig M. Koslofsky, *Reformation of the Dead: Death and Ritual in Early Modern Germany 1450–1700* (New York: St Martin's Press, 2000), pp. 22–3; Austra Reinis, *Reforming the Art of Dying: The Ars Moriendi in the German Reformation (1519–1528)* (Aldershot: Ashgate, 2007), on the later period pp. 17–46, 143–92; Huizinga, *The Waning of the Middle Ages*, pp. 134–46.

[85] Claude Carozzi, *Le Voyage de l'âme dans l'au-delà, d'après la literature latine (Ve-XIIe siècle)*, Collection de École Français de Rome (Paris: de Boccard, 1994).

[86] Robert Easting, *Annotated Bibliography of Old and Middle English Literature*, vol. III: *Visions of the Other World in Middle English* (New York: D. S. Brewer, 1997), p. 3. On visualization in relation to instrumental rationality, see D. L. D'Avray, *Rationalities in History: A Weberian Essay in Comparison* (New York: Cambridge University Press, 2010), pp. 134–7.

[87] W. F. Nijenhuis (ed.), *The Vision of Edmund Leversedge: A Fifteenth Century Account of a Visit to the Other World edited from BL MS Additional 34, 193 with an Introduction, Commentary and Glossary* (Nijmegen: Katholieke Uniersiteit te Nijmegen, 1990), pp. 16–17.

and to meditate upon what awaits them beyond the grave, and the vision literature serves to encourage this purpose. Indeed, the manuscript collections often contain several visions that were intended to be read together.[88] Although the earlier texts were composed exclusively by men, the genre of vision was attractive to women who were excluded from the universities and Latin learning and who, in the later Middle Ages, composed treatises in vernacular languages. Of particular importance here are the Beguines, such as Mechthild of Magdeburg (*c.*1212–82) and the multiskilled Hildegard of Bingen (1098–1179).

There were three sets of sources for the vision literature: from classical antiquity we have the myth of Er in Plato's Republic (10.613b–621d), who goes into the other world and recounts his experiences upon returning to the body, and stories from Plutarch, from Jewish and early Christian apocrypha and apocalyptic traditions, particularly the *Apocalypse of Paul (Visio Sancti Paulus)*, and from Celtic, particularly Irish sources recounting visions (*fis*) and voyages (*immram*) of the soul.[89] A large amount of vision material survives in manuscripts and inserted into other narrative accounts, such as Bede's *Ecclesiastical History* and Gregory of Tours' *History of the Franks*. The volume of manuscript evidence bears witness to the popularity and importance of this literature, and manuscripts continue to be faithfully copied into the sixteenth century.[90] Although we have some texts from the ninth century, such as the visions of Wetti, most vision texts were composed in Latin during the twelfth and early thirteenth century, many of which were translated into vernacular languages, particularly Middle English, although there are some texts from the fifteenth century. This literature was widely disseminated, and monks and nuns in England would have been aware of the visions of Dryhthelm accounted for in Bede (d.735), which describes Dryhthelm being led by a being with a shining face and a bright garment to witness the pains and joys of the other world ('the joyful mansions of the soul'),[91] Wetti's vision, Tundale's vision, the monk of Wenlock, the monk of Orm, Henry of Sawtry's *Tractatus de Purgatorio Sancti Patricii*, and others.[92] One of the most important late twelfth-century texts that has come down to us is the *Visio Monachi De*

[88] Easting, *Annotated Bibliography*, p. 8.

[89] Easting, *Annotated Bibliography*, p. 9.

[90] Easting, *Annotated Bibliography*, p. 10.

[91] Bede, *Historia Ecclesiastica* 5.12, in James Campbell (ed.), *Bede: The Ecclesiastical History of the English People and Other Selections* (New York: Washington Square Press, 1968), pp. 268–74. Bede tells us that Dryhthelm had died and rose from the dead, divided his property, and went to live in a monastery by the Tweed where he had his vision and practiced asceticism, such as standing up to his waist or neck in the water. This vision is also mentioned in the Anglo-Saxon Chronicle for the year 693. G. M. Garmonsway (trans.), *The Anglo-Saxon Chronicle* (London: Dent and Sons, 1953), p. 41.

[92] Robert Easting (ed.), *The Revelation of the Monk of Eynsham* (Oxford: Oxford University Press for the Early English Text Society, 2002), p. lxxviii. For a popular edition, see Eileen Gardiner (ed.), *Visions of Heaven and Hell Before Dante* (New York: Ithaca Press, 1989).

Eynsham, the *Revelation of the Monk of Eynsham*, composed in 1196 or 97 and translated into Middle English, and also into Dutch and German, probably in the fifteenth century.[93]

The Eynsham text is especially interesting as it tells the story of a monk whose visions occur in an ecstatic contemplation. The visionary is named Edmund, and the text written by his brother Adam who was sub-prior of the Benedictine monastery at Eynsham, five and a half miles west of Oxford. Adam went on to become chaplain to Hugh, the Bishop of Lincoln, and his biographer (1197 to 1200) composing the *Life of Saint Hugh, Magna Vita Sancti Hugonis*.[94] The *Visio Monachi de Eynsham*' describing his brother's visions that occurred during the period of a two-day trance, became very influential and was translated, not only into Middle English, but also into French verse and German prose. Thirty-three manuscripts survive bearing witness to its significance. The *Visio* was written at a time of a legal dispute about jurisdiction over the Eynsham monastery; whether it should be controlled by the crown (King Richard I claimed patronage) or by the Bishop of Lincoln, and the text reflects this in using biblical quotations about good kingship and the responsibilities of the powerful.[95] Adam recounts various details surrounding his brother's vision, notably that at Christmas 1194 Edmund was sick with quinsy in Oxford; he then entered the monastery at Eynsham where he was ill most of the time for over a year. His condition worsened before Lent 1196 when he prayed for a vision of the other world. He partly recovers, but falls unconscious on Good Friday and is found by his fellow monks in the Church. He only regains consciousness on the evening of Easter Saturday, begins to speak of his visions, and he attends matins and the Easter Resurrection enactment on Easter Sunday, fully recovered from his illness.

Edmund's vision, reported by Adam, does not recount hell, but rather purgatory; and the paradise he experiences is not the highest heaven, but may be the original earthly paradise. Purgatory is divided into three places, with souls suffering varying degrees of torment depending upon their sin, which Edmund recounts and illustrates with particular stories of people who he had personally known. The first place contains souls bound together and flogged, although they have hope of their eventual salvation. Here he encounters various churchmen, including Godfrey of Eynsham, who was abbot for

[93] Easting, *The Revelation of the Monk of Eynsham*. This edition contains the Latin text from manuscript sources and the Middle English parallel translation from the two printed copies of 1483 (no manuscript sources survive).

[94] Decima L. Douie and Dom Hugh Farmer (eds.), *Magna Vita Sancti Hugonis: The Life of St Hugh of Lincoln*, 2 vols (reprinted with corrections, Oxford: Oxford Medieval Texts, 1985). Eynsham was evidently an important monastery as we also have extra-liturgical Latin hymns from the same period, mostly addressed to angels. Dom A. Wilmart, *Auteurs Spirituels et textes dévots du Moyen Age latin* (Paris: Librarie Bloud et Gay, 1932), p. 551.

[95] Easting, *The Revelation of the Monk of Eynsham*, 'Introduction', pp. xxxvi–xxxvii.

forty-four years, being punished for nepotism and negligence, Joscelin, Bishop of Salisbury (Golding's inspiration?), suffering because of sexual immorality, and Baldwin, Archbishop of Canterbury, criticized for his dealings with monks, who died on crusade at Acre. The second place contains a foul pond, and further on a hill with one side burning with fire and the other freezing cold: innumerable souls ('like a hive swarming with bees') rotate from one location to the other. Here Edmund meets people he knew in life, such as an alcoholic, Goldsmith from Osney, who, although devoted to St Nicholas, is suffering as a consequence of his drinking and temptation by devils. The third realm is a place of snakes and demons and set aside for homosexuals, among whom Edmund meets a lawyer that he knew who will suffer there till the Last Judgement. In all of these encounters Edmund criticizes Church corruption, monastic homosexuality,[96] and unchaste priests dispensing the sacrament. The vision can even be understood as an eschatological interpretation of history and a social perception that offers a critique of contemporary society.[97]

The body of the vision occurs over forty-three short chapters (14–57). Edmund describes how on Good Friday he became unconscious on the floor of the chapter house, and how he was guided by St Nicholas through the regions of purgatory. St Nicholas was the patron saint of the abbey at Osney Lane near Oxford, where Edmund had grown up. The text is written in a direct style that is very vivid in its descriptions of the pains of purgatory. For example, near the beginning of the vision we read:

Reading 2

Infinite kind and diversities of pains were there that I saw. Some of them [the souls] were roasted at the fire. Some were fried in a pan. Some were slashed to pieces with fiery nails unto the bones and to the losing of their joints. Some were submerged in baths of pitch and brimstone with a horrible stench and other things melted by heat, such as lead, brass, and other diverse metals. And some were gnawed with venomous teeth of awesome snakes. Some also were caste down thick in a row, some were smitten with sharp stakes and poles whose ends were all fire. And while some were hanging on gallows, others were pulled apart with hooks, and some were beaten sore with scouges, and so in hard punishment they were all mutilated. Truly, among those persons many were bishops and abbots and others were dignitaries. Truly, some flourished in prosperity in

[96] For an analysis of the invective against sodomy, see Sven Limbeck, '"Turpitudo antique passionis"—Sodomie in mittelalterlicher Visionsliteratur', in Thomas Ehlen, Johannes Mangei, and Elisabeth Stein (eds.), *Visio Edmundi monachi de Eynsham: Interdisziplinäre Studien zur mittelalterlichen Visionsliteratur* (Tübingen: Gunter Narr Verlag, 1998), pp. 39–58. This reflects Peter Damian's invective in his *Book of Gomorrah* (*Liber Gomorrhianus*) trans. P. J. Payer, *The Book of Gomorrah: An Eleventh-Century Treatise against Clerical Homosexual Practices* (Ontario: Wilfred Laurier University Press, 1982).

[97] This is the angle that Thomas Kreuzer develops on the text in 'Jesneits und Gesellschaft. Zur Soziologie der "Visio Edmundi Monachi de Eynsham"', pp. 44–53, in Ehlen et al. (eds.), *Visio Edmundi*, pp. 39–58.

spirituality, some in temporality, and some in religion, who were punished in double sorrow above other persons. For I saw them that were clerks, monks, nuns, laymen and laywomen, much less punished and put to pains, (depending on) how much less they had before of worldly dignity and prosperity. In truth I saw them injured in a more special bitterness of pain above others, who I knew in my time were judges, prelates and others . . .[98]

The text is replete with this kind of graphic detail for all three regions of purgatory the text describes. What is notable is the pervasive use of the first person—this is clearly a personal vision—and that this account, based on experience, has authority. It is also clear that the account is linked to a moral vision and that he perceived the inverse in the next world of what might be expected. The highly honoured and successful in this world suffer more than the humble, be they churchmen or in secular professions. On his journey through the three regions of purgatory, Edmund speaks with different tormented souls; the prior of the abbey (Godfrey), who he had known, suffering for personal sin ('carnal affection and love that I had to my friends') and for the sins of his flock committed because of his own ineptitude and mismanagement.[99]

Moving on through these regions, St Nicholas and Edmund at last come to paradise. Here they first come upon a massive wall of crystal with an open gate in it:

Reading 3

Now moreover, when we were passed all these places and aforesaid sights, and had gone a good space more inward, and ever grew to us more and more joy and fairness of place also, at last we saw at a distance a very glorious wall of crystal whose height no man might see, and length no man might consider. And when we came there, I saw within a very fair, bright, shining gate that stood open, surmounted by a cross. Truly there came in groups the multitude of those blessed souls that were next to it, and would come in at that fiery gate. The cross was set

[98] Easting, *The Revelation of the Monk of Eynsham*, pp. 45–7: *Infynite kyndes and diuersytees of peynys where there that Y sawe. Some of hem were rostyd at the fyre. Some were fryed in a panne. Some were al to-rasyd with Fyry naylys vnto the bonys and to the lowsing of her ioyntys. Some were soden in bathis of pyche and brymstonne with an horabul stenche and other things melted by hete, as ledde, brasse, and other dyuers metellys. And some were gnawyn with the venummys teth of wondyrfull wormys. Some also were caste done thicke on a rowe and smyt throw with sharpe stakys and palys who-ys endys were alle fyre. And whyle some were hangyn on gallows, odyr were al to-drawyn with hokys, and some were betyn sore with scurgys, and so in hard example they were al to-toryn. Trewly, of tho persons mony were bisshoppis and abbotys and other were of other dignitees. Sothely, some flowryd in prosperitie in the spyrytualite, some in the temporalite, and some in relygyon, the whiche were syen ponisht in dowbulle sorowe aboue other persons. For Y saw them that were clerkys, monkys, noonys, lay-men and lay-wemen, so mekyl lesse ordended and put to peynys, howe mekyl the lesse they had before of worldely dygyte and prosperyte. In trowthe Y sawe hem greuyd in a more specyal bitternesse of peynys aboue other, the whyche Y knewe in my tyme were iugys and prelatys of other* . . . (My rendering into modern English.)

[99] Easting, *The Revelation of the Monk of Eynsham*, pp. 91–7.

> in the middle of the gate and now she was lifted up aloft and so gave to them that came there, clear and free entrance, and afterward she was let down again and so shut out others that would have come in. But how joyful they were that went in and how reverently they waited and stood outside for the lifting up of the cross again, I cannot tell by any words. Truly, here Saint Nicholas and I stood still together, and the lifting up of the cross and letting it down again, whereby some went in and some awaited outside, I behind a long time in great wonder.[100]

Going with St Nicholas further into this heaven, Edmund perceives a vision of Christ on the throne that he perceives for a short period of time before his guide brings him back into the world.

> **Reading 4**
> And inwardly [there was] nothing I might see but light and the wall of crystal through which we came in. And also, from the ground up to the top of that wall were steps arranged and ordered fair and marvellously, by which the joyful company that had come in at the aforesaid gate, gladly ascended up. There was no labour, there was no difficulty, there was no waiting in the ascent, and the higher they went, the gladder they were. Truly, I stood beneath on the ground, and I was and beheld for a long time how they that came in by the gate ascended up by the same steps. And at last, as I looked up higher, I saw our Lord and Saviour, Jesus Christ, in the likeness of a man, sitting on a throne of joy, and about him, it seemed to me, were five hundred souls which had stepped up to that glorious throne, and so they came to our Lord and worshipped him and thanked him for his great mercy and grace showed and done to them. And some were seen on the upper part of the wall as they had walked hither and thither. Truly, I knew for certain that this place where I saw our Lord sitting on a throne, was not the high heaven of heavens where the blessed spirits of angels and the holy souls of righteous men rejoice in the sight of God, seeing Him in His majesty as He is, where also innumerable thousands of holy spirits and angels serve Him and assist Him. But that from there, without any difficulty or delay, they ascend up to the high heaven, where they are blessed with the sight of the everlasting Godhead, where only the holy angels and souls of righteous men that have the perfection of angels, see the invisible and immortal King of all worlds face to face. They have

[100] Easting, *The Revelation of the Monk of Eynsham*, p. 161–3: *Forthermore nowe, whenne we were paste al theses placys and sightys aforeseyde, and had gonne a good space more inward, and euer grew to vs more and more ioye and feyernes of placys also, at the laste we sawe a aferre a ful glorious walle of crystal, hoys heythe no man might see, and lenthe no man might consider. And when we came thedyr Y sawe within-forthe a ful feyre, brighte, schynyng gate and stode opyn, saue hit was signed and leide ouer with a crosse. Truly, theder came flockemele the multitude of tho blessyd sowlys that were next to hyt, and wolde cum in at that feyre gate. The crosse was set in the myddys of that gate, and nowe sche was lyfte vppe an hye and so gaue to hem that came thedyr an opyn and a fre entrying, and afterward sche was lettyn done ageyne, and so sparyd other oute that wuld haue commyn in. But howe ioyful they were that wente in, and how reuerently they taryde that stode withoute abydying the lyftyng vppe of the corss ageyne, Y cannot telle by no wordys. Sothely, here Sent Nycholas an Y stode stille to-geder, and lyftyngs vppe of the cross and the lettyngs done ageyne, wherby somme wente in some taryde withoute, I behilde long tyme in grete wonder.*

immortality and dwell in the light that is inaccessible, for no man may come to it which no mortal man sees nor may see. Truly, He is seen only by holy spirits that are pure and clean, which are not pained by corruption of body nor of soul. And in this vision that I saw, I experienced so much joy and gladness in my soul that whatsoever may be said of it by many mouths, so little it is, and insufficient to express the joy of my heart that I had there.[101]

This is a remarkable vision that clearly articulates the cosmological vision of the medieval Christian world view. We are in a symbolic universe here,[102] where we have the idea of a chain of being, a graded hierarchy of levels represented in the steps, the idea of perfected beings, the angels, who had never experienced corruption, and the idea of perfected beings, the souls, that had been human but have achieved perfection akin to the angels. In this vision Christ is seated on a throne worshipped by righteous souls. But this is not the very highest heaven and from here the righteous can ascend even higher to 'the heaven of heavens' where they have the vision of the supreme Godhead, which is normally invisible but beheld by those souls with sufficient purity. Edmund is presumably not sufficiently pure—and also still connected to his body—to experience the very highest heaven. The heavenly hierarchy is thus connected to the purity of perception, and purity of perception means moral

[101] Easting, The *Revelation of the Monk of Eynsham*, pp. 163–5: *And wyth-ynforthe, no-thyng Y myght see but lighte and the walle of crystalle throw the whyche we came yn. And also, fro the gronde vppe to toppe of that walle were grycis, ordende and dysposyd feyre and meruelusly, by the whyche the ioyful company that was cum yn at the forseyde gate gladly ascended vppe. Ther was no labur, ther was no difficulte, ther was no taryng yn her ascednyng, and the hier they wente, the gladder they were. Sothely, Y stode benethe on the grunde, and longe tyme Y saw and behyde how they that came yn at the gate ascended vppe by the same grycis. And at the laste, as Y lokyd vppe hier, Y saw yn a trone of ioy sittying owre blessyd Lord and Sauyur, Ihesus Criste, yn lykenes of man, and abowte Hym, as hyt semyd to me, were a fyue hondred sowlys, the whyche late had styed vppe to that glorius trone, and so they came to owre Lorde and worschipte Hym and thankyde Hym for Hys grete mercy and grace schewyd and done to hem. And some were seyne on the vppur partys of the walle as they had walkyd hethyr and dedyr. Trewly, Y knew for certen that thys place, were Y saw oure Lorde syttying yn a trone, was not the hye heuyn of heuyns, where the blessed spiritis of angels and the holy sowlys of ryghtwys men ioyin yn the seyghte of God, seyng Hym yn Hys mageste as He ys, where also innumerable thowsondis of holy spiritys and angels serue Hym and assiste Hym. But than fro thens, wythowten any hardnes or tarrying, they ascende vppe to the hey heuin, the whyche ys blessyd of the syghte of the euerlastyng Godhed, where al only the holy angels and sowlys of ryghtwes men, that byn of angels perfeccion, seyn the ynuisible and inmortalle Kynge of al worldys face to face, the whyche hathe only inmortalite, and dwellyth yn lyghte that ys inaccessible; for no man may cumme to hyt, the whyche no mortalle man seithe, nethyr may see. Sothely, He ys seyne only of holy spiritys that byn pure and clene, the whyche be no greuyd by no corrupcion of body, nethir of sowle. And in this vision that Y saw, so mekylle Y conceuyd yn my sowle of ioy and gladness, that wat-sum-euer may be seyde of hyt by mannys mowthe, ful lytyl hyt ys, and onsufficient to expresse the ioy of myne herte, that y had there.*

[102] See M. D. Chenu, 'The Symbolist Mentality', in *Nature, Man and Society in the Twelfth Century: Essays on New Theological Perspectives in the Latin West*, trans. Jerome Taylor and Lester K. Little (Chicago, IL: Chicago University Press, 1968 (first published 1957)), pp. 99–145 (pp. 141–4); Marie-Thérèse d'Alverny, *Études sur le symbolisme de la sagesse et sur l'iconographie*, ed. Charles Burnett (Aldershot: Variorum, 1993).

purity. Only the souls pure in spirit—which means only souls who do not have worldly attachments and desires for pleasures of the senses—can attain to the highest vision of God. The quality of perception that the souls have, which is controlled by their nature and the degree of sin they contain, determines the world of their experience and perception. Thus the souls in purgatory cannot perceive the highest Godhead, nor even the lower vision of Jesus on the throne, because they are weighed down with sin that they need to be released from through its purgation to attain to the highest vision. The sufferings of purgatory can be understood in this cosmology as a purification of perception. The experience of heaven itself, which is actually the vision of God, firstly in the human form of Christ as King and secondly as Godhead, is joyful and ineffable, a characteristic of mystical experience noted by many other visionaries. Edmund is overwhelmed and cannot sufficiently articulate 'so much joy and gladness'. St Nicholas brings Edmund back through the same gate and he returns to the body with an exhortation from the saint:

> **Reading 5**
> And greatly he exhorted me how I should dispose of myself, to await the day of my calling out of my body in cleanness of heart and body, and meekness of spirit with diligent keeping of my religion.[103]

This vision is typical of the genre. The narrative structure of the Eynsham text and its themes are found in other vision texts, notably an illness or approach to death, the guide to the other world (here St Nicholas), the torments of souls in purgatory, the joys and vision of heaven, and the return to the world with a salutary lesson from the vision. The much later *Vision of the Edmund Leversedge*, for example, composed in Latin in 1465 and translated into Middle English, contains many of the themes of *Eynsham*.

Edmund Leversedge is a young man in Somerset who falls ill with the plague. He is tempted by horribly deformed devils; his soul leaves his body through his mouth and comes to a green close, like a churchyard, where he meets his guardian angel who takes him to a twilight world. Leversedge is tortured and tempted by devils that if he goes with them, they will make him a lord among them. He overcomes them by calling on Christ's name. A second group of devils come along and torture and tempt him. Just in time his angel, who for some reason had gone away, returns, and the devils flee. The angel takes Leversedge's soul to the top of a hill that the devils cannot ascend where a ladder made of crystal stretches into the sky. The soul climbs the ladder to a place of light and joy. From there the angel leads the soul to an even higher

[103] Easting, *The Revelation of the Monk of Eynsham*, p. 167: *And gretely he exhortyd me how Y schulde dispose me, to abyde the day of my callyng oute of my body yn clennes of herte and body, and mekenes of spirite with dylygent kepying of my religyon.* Note the early use of the category 'religion', long before the seventeenth-century development of the secular.

place by another ladder where the soul, blinded by the light, falls on his knees and asks for mercy. The devils cry out his sins—that he has worn too many fashionable clothes—and other voices defend him. Suddenly the soul finds himself on top of the hill once more where a lady comes and rebukes him not to sin and to change his ways, which he agrees to. She tells him that he should not wear fashionable clothes, should not kiss women, should not visit the 'washerwoman', and should go to study theology in Oxford for eight years under an alias. The woman vanishes and the angel brings the soul to the parish church at Frome in Somerset and shows him the road to Oxford. There is some discussion with the vicar of Westbury and three priests of Frome, and Leversedge thanks God for his deliverance and tells us that his friend, a monk of Witham, rendered his vision into Latin.[104]

This text is written almost three hundred years after the Eynsham vision yet contains many motives found there and in other vision literature. Like the Eynsham text, Leversedge has a guide through the other world—albeit one who seems to abandon him from time to time—vivid descriptions of devils, and a description of heaven that echoes the Eynsham vision. The topography of the other world is also similar. The angel brings the soul to a high hill where the soul sees beneath him the devils who have no power to ascend. From the top of the hill a ladder made of crystal appears which brings the soul into great light and joy. Beyond this there is a second place, even brighter, that the soul could not apprehend.[105] Crystal walls and ladders are a theme, the two levels of heaven beyond the top of the hill, and the ineffable joy of the vision. Edmund in the Eynsham text speaks of the delightful peal and melody of

[104] Nijenhuis, *The Vision of Edmund Leversedge*, summary of narrative, pp. 9–12. For a history of Leversedge, and how he married into a wealthy family of Frome, see p. 70. There is no evidence that he ever studied at Oxford.

[105] Nijenhuis, *The Vision of Edmund Leversedge*, lines 240–72: '*And when the good angel had brought my soul to the top of the hill, my soul looked down and at the foot of the hill beneath to the four or five devils, none of them having power to ascend to the top of the hill. And my soul looked beside him and there appeared from the top of the hill stretching into the sky, a ladder with flat staves, broader than a man's hand, appearing as white as crystal, upon which ladder suddenly my good angel led me and put me upon. And when my soul was at the highest point of the ladder, the firmament opened and my soul was brought into a very great light and joy. Within was certain people, but from that place I was presently led by my good angel up into another place of greater brightness, which was brighter and lighter than the first. And that second place was so bright and so clear that what time my soul was entered in the door, with the reflection of the light and brightness with the place, the vision of my ghostly soul was taken from it.*' My rendering into modern English. On comparison with other visions, see Nijenhuis, p. ii. The theme of heaven made of gold, crystal, and precious stones is found in other vision texts, such as Wetti's vision where the high mountains of heaven are made of marble (Gardiner, *Visions*, p. 68). On Wetti's vision, see Mary Carruthers, *The Craft of Thought: Meditation, Rhetoric and the Making of Images, 400–1200* (Cambridge: Cambridge University Press, 1998), pp. 179–83. Tundale's vision too (1149) describes the three walls of heaven comprising silver, gold, and precious stones. Jean-Michel Picard, *The Vision of Tnugdal* (Dublin: Four Courts Press, 1989), p. 109.

bells that he heard just before his return to the body where the joyful sound was replaced by the sound of his brethren's voices.[106]

What is striking about these vision texts is how place-specific they are in their origin—Eynsham and Frome—and how the narrative structure of the journey into the other world with a guide, and safe return, involves the visionary engaging souls in conversation who he had known in life. This theme is also taken up by Dante, that the everyday is intertwined with cosmology and eschatological history.

Lastly we need to make an observation about gender in relation to the vision literature. Religious structures were orientated towards men, political power was generally, although not exclusively, held by men, and theological texts were generally only written by men, in Latin. Women were generally, although again not wholly, excluded from a high level of education. Yet through the Middle Ages there is a burgeoning mystical literature composed by women. Women's visionary literature is particularly interesting in this regard. Although the earlier vision literature in Latin was exclusively written by men, the later period witnessed the growth of women's spirituality, especially in well-endowed women's houses where they practised a collective life of prayer and work. These women's communities, that developed especially in continental Europe, were known as Beguinage, and the women who lived in them as Beguines. There are many Beguine visionaries, such as Mechthild of Magdeberg (*c.*1212–82), who composed a visionary text *The Flowering Light of the Godhead* (*Das fliessende Licht de Gottheit*)[107] and Marguerite Porete's *Mirror of Simple Souls* (*Miroir des simples âmes*) that cost her her life in 1310, and they bear witness to a mystical literature that is more theologically sophisticated than the earlier vision texts we have looked at.[108]

What then, can we glean from this literature about the nature of the human person? Firstly, we might say that the vision texts promote inwardness—the visions are seen by the inner eye when the visionary is apparently unconscious and dead to the world. This inwardness is an intensification of subjectivity that in one sense is unique to the visionary, yet in another shows how the visionary is conforming to a collective identity. The narrative of the visionary's life is seen to conform to the narrative of the otherworldly journey. Secondly, we can

[106] Easting, *The Revelation of the Monk of Eynsham*, p. 167.

[107] Mechthild of Magdeburg, *Das fliessende Licht der Gottheit*, ed. Gisela Vollmann (Frankfurt am Main: Deutscher Klassiker Verlag, 2003); trans. Lucie Menzies as *The Revelations of Mechthild of Magdeburg (1210–1297) or The Flowering Light of the Godhead* (London: Longmans Green, 1953).

[108] There is quite a large literature on this. See, for example, Amy Hollywood, *The Soul as Virgin Wife: Mechthild of Magdeburg, Margueritte Porete, and Meister Eckhardt* (Notre Dame, IN: University of Notre Dame Press, 1995); Grace Janzen, *Power, Gender and Christian Mysticism* (Cambridge: Cambridge University Press, 1995); Bernard McGinn, *The Flowering of Mysticism: Men and Women in the New Mysticism, 1200–1350* (New York: Crossroad Publishing, 1998), pp. 153–265.

say that these texts evince a strong moral vision and promotion of Christian values. Indeed, they function as social critique and give voice to concerns that it might otherwise have been difficult to raise about institutional moral failings. Indeed, Middle English literature marks an increased concern with morality, and in a pre-Protestant era many texts advocate the examination of conscience, the critique of sin, and the development of virtues that tend to be associated with a later kind of piety. Thus, around 1440 we have *Jacob's Well*, a treatise on cleaning a man's conscience; and earlier, Robert of Brunne's *Handlying Sinne*, concerned with 'sins' from gluttony and sexual immorality of the clergy, to wearing fashionable clothes (a sin that Edmund Leversedge was also prone to).[109] The political as well as personal nature of these texts is striking. The private vision is not really private, although it occurs in the interiority of the mind, but is more of a collective subjectivity in which the visionary's inwardness conforms to a traditional pattern while using that pattern as a vehicle for a moral vision that is a corrective to received practice. Thirdly, although the texts are still within the cosmological world view, they express an idea of the person as morally responsible who undergoes a personal Judgement at their own death. Rather than waiting in the grave for the final Judgement when the graves will be opened and the deeds of each laid bare, we have a Judgement that occurs upon death, and an ensuring punishment—which is also a purification—in purgatory.

FROM PARTICIPATION TO CONSCIENCE

At the end of Edmund's vision, as we have seen, St Nicholas exhorts him to live a good life and to keep his religion. This moral injunction is important and presages what is to become far more central in later centuries with the Renaissance and the Reformation. Gradually at first, along with the retreat of religion from cosmology with the rise of science, we have the centrality of cosmological participation becoming replaced with an emphasis on belief, self-scrutiny, and moral conscience.[110] The textual material so far discussed places the human person within a cosmos, and part of leading a right and virtuous

[109] See R. Furnivall (ed.), *Robert of Brunne's Handlying Sinne AD 1303 with those Parts of the Anglo-French Treatise on which it was Founded* (Oxford: Early English Text Society, 1901). We also find this sin in 'Sinners Beware' 94.

[110] See M. D. Chenu, *L'eveil de la conscience* (Montreal: Insitut d'Études Medievale; Paris: Libraire Philosophique, Vrin, 1969). Chenu traces the experience of interiority (*l'intériorité*) to the twelfth century linked to courtly love (*l'amour courtois*), especially Abelard who gave the subtitle to his *Ethics* the ancient formula 'know yourself' (*gnôthi seauton*), p. 45. The education of conscience is an exercise of prudence that lies between the objective universal order and subjectivity, pp. 57–8. Chenu regards Abelard as the first modern man, pp. 17–32.

life is knowing where and how we are placed within it. The ecstatic visions described in the vision literature present the person in relation to the hierarchical cosmology and link this hierarchy to a morality in so far as the good, pure soul can have a vision of heaven and come into God's presence, whereas the soul weighed down with sin cannot, but must suffer the torments of purgatory until purified. Other souls, of course, are condemned never to have that highest vision but to remain in a place of torment. Here, the ontological condition of the soul is related to what it can know and what can be perceived, an idea that becomes theorized in theological literature, as we will see in the next chapter. In this world the cosmos is morally structured and the person's perception and place is related to their moral being.

So far we have emphasized the participatory model of human existence espoused in the medieval world. We participate in the cosmos, in God's creation, as agents, and accept salvation through the cosmic Christ who is mediated through the structures of the Church, which is the bride of Christ and also Christ's body.[111] We gain access to the mystery of Christ's saving work through participation in the liturgy and through inner practices of asceticism, prayer, and contemplation. In this medieval world it is not enough simply to believe in the saving grace of Christ; we need to participate in the practices handed down through the Church; we need to belong to a community and share its liturgical practices. The ecstatic vision of the few recorded in the vision literature is simply one extreme or possibility within a coherent world view that assumes the daily ritual behaviour of ordinary people. All share in this world, from peasant, to knight, to cleric.

Alongside the vision literature, which expresses this participatory world view, are many other treatises, some already mentioned, in vernacular languages, that are generally exhortations to virtuous living. While I would not wish to exaggerate the distinction, there is a change from a participatory model to an emphasis on conscience and personal morality as the centuries move towards the Reformation. There is, of course, exhortation to good behaviour in the vision literature—as we have seen in the Eynsham text—but, as the period develops, we can see an increasing emphasis on moral conscience, particularly by the fifteenth century. This is what we would expect as we move towards the Reformation with its emphasis on individual moral conscience. To take examples from the prolific Middle English literature—while they deal with cosmological themes (the fate of the soul after death) they also focus on moral development. Among the earlier texts we have didactic poems, already mentioned, such as 'Death' and 'Soul Beware' that can be dated to the twelfth century. In 1303 we have Robert of Brunne's *Handlying Synne*, which is a Middle English translation of a French text concerned with sins

[111] For this model of the Church (and others) see A. Dulles, *Models of the Church* (Dublin: Gill and Macmillan, 1976), pp. 50–62, 137, 139–40.

such as gluttony, lechery, the following of new fashions, the evils of kissing, and the problem of priestly sexual immorality—when priests marry or take mistresses. The text is condemnatory of women who 'sin with priests', and tells a tale of a priest's concubine who dies and her body is carried away by demons.[112]

Likewise, the *Pilgrimage of Human Life*, anonymously translated into Middle English in the fifteenth century from the French poem of Guillaume de Deguilleville, a monk of the Cistercian abbey of Chaalis in 1331, is another excellent example of the exhortation to moral uprightness.[113] This text seems to be a precursor of Bunyan's *Pilgrim's Progress* with a monk as the pilgrim whose goal is the New Jerusalem in the next world. The text seems to lack a certain narrative coherence, at least to the modern reader, and the plot is somewhat complex; but in four books it describes Pilgrim's journey to the gate of the New Jerusalem guided by Grace Dieu, the personification of grace. He is given the sacraments, the armour of the virtues, the staff of hope, the satchel of faith, and Memory. Of the two paths—idleness and occupation—he chooses the wrong one, and succumbs to the sin of Sloth, the Devil's wife, followed by Pride, Envy, and Anger. Book four contrasts the turmoil of the world with the peace of the cloister and calls the monastic life 'the ship of religion' to take the pilgrim across the sea of the world. The mast of the ship is Christ, the wind is the Holy Spirit, and the monastic virtues of the monastic houses of Cluny and Citeaux are available for the Pilgrim to use. This ship binds back 'the dissolute and defouled soul', and so long as the 'good religious' keep the rites the ship will not fail. Grace Dieu leads Pilgrim into the ship. Finally, Death approaches and Grace Dieu comforts the Pilgrim with the promise of resurrection. Pilgrim finds himself at a gate where he must promise to do penance and pay for his remaining debt of sin in purgatory. Death scythes him and he wakes terrified.[114]

Finally, from the early fifteenth century we have *Jacob's Well: An English Treatise on the Cleansing of Man's Conscience*[115] which is a good illustration of the shift from and emphasis on liturgical participation, to an emphasis on moral conscience in pre-philosophical literature. Jacob's well is a pit of foul water representing the human body. The well is to be cleaned by well cleaners until it is fit for the grace of God. With the removal of dirty water the cleaner finds the mire of sin which must be removed with 'skeet and skavel, shovel and spade, and pickaxe' until we stand on the firm ground of seven virtues. To prevent sin re-entering the well, five water gates—that is, the senses—must be

[112] Furnivall, *Robert of Brunne's Handlyng Synne*, pp. 253–6.

[113] Henry Avril, *The Pilgrimage of the Lyfe of the Manhode, Translated Anonymously into Prose from the First Recension of Guillaume de Deguilevile's poem Le Pèlerinage de la Vie Humaine* (Oxford: Early English Text Society, Oxford University Press, 1988).

[114] Avril, *The Pilgrimage of the Lyfe of the Manhode*, beginning line 6719, p. 161.

[115] Arthur Brandeis, *Jacob's Well: An English Treatise on the Cleansing of Man's Conscience Edited from the unique MA about 1440 in Salisbury Cathedral* (London: EETS, 1900).

shut against temptation, and the well lined with the stones of faith. Only then will Christ rest at the well and be refreshed by water given by the Samaritan woman, that is the soul. After death the soul will climb up the ladder of charity to heaven.[116]

There begins to be a shift from participation to an emphasis on conscience and a need to purify conscience through being transparent and confessing.[117] The 'private' experience of sin was to become public through confession, within monastic orders such as the Dominicans. But even now, with the development of confession, the person is part of the collective body. He has no individual privacy but rather has an inwardness that all share in: the collective body is recapitulated in the personal. The shift is also seen in the idea of Judgement. In the earlier Christian eschatology the Last Judgement will come and the resurrected bodies from the graves will be judged accordingly. In the vision literature we have the idea that there is a pre-judgement—judgement in the sense that the soul at death goes to purgatory (and so is judged) before its sins are so cleansed that it can enter heaven. We see a shift here from a communal Judgement at the end of time to an individual Judgement at death, which is in accord with the general orientation towards personal moral choice. By the time of the Reformation a complete shift has occurred, and the connection that existed in the medieval world between the living and the dead has been largely broken; with Luther's abolition of purgatory, the dead have been placed beyond the living.[118] Yet while this is a shift of emphasis, the moral choice made is still within a collectivity; we are not yet at a point of modernity and the establishing of individuality against the collective, but we can see glimpses here of what is to come.

CONCLUSION

So far we have expounded the participatory model of the human person found in the High Middle Ages with its emphasis on conformity, along with an emphasis on the truth within as inwardness, or subjectivity, that is non-individual. This inwardness is set within a symbolic framework or world view that is a closed system—synchronically hierarchical in structure, and diachronically contained within a Christian narrative of the Fall and Judgement. In many ways, this period is future orientated in its anticipation of final Judgement and its desire for a better future. As the period moves on we find more emphasis on moral conscience and the necessity of each person to expiate sin through developing virtue, although we are still, even here, within

[116] Brandeis, *Jacob's Well.* [117] De Certeau, The *Mystic Fable*, p. 88.
[118] Koslofsky, *Reformation of the Dead*, pp. 19–21.

a participatory model of religion in which the self is transparent with no secrecy. This is reflected in medieval ritual life and in what we might call pre-reflexive or pre-philosophical literature, especially the vision texts. Participation in the liturgy, and thereby in the body of Christ, contemplative prayer, and occasionally ecstatic vision, are the main features of the religious life during the long Middle Ages. William Golding's Jocelyn has created a new architecture in the spire unsupported by buttresses and based on shallow foundations, yet an architecture that still assumes the participation of the human person in the cosmic drama. The angels and demons still surround us and interact with us. Jocelyn is aware of his guardian angel at his back, yet we know as late modern readers that this sensation is, in fact, no angel, but tuberculosis signalling his demise; no angel, but a disease signalling the disenchantment with the world. But it will be long centuries before the complete demise of the symbolic world that Jocelyn inhabits with the loss that entails (no certainty in old truths) and with all its gains (the cure of Jocelyn's disease).

The literature we have examined is now simply a trace of the life of the Christian community that saw inwardness as integral to the nature of human beings and to their salvation. Through inwardness we gain access to inner truth that is also transcendence, and through inwardness we gain knowledge of the true nature of the human person—where and how we stand in relation to the economy of salvation. This relationship between inwardness and transcendence, between the human person and God, is mediated through the forms of religious practice we have seen—liturgy, prayer, and vision—but is also theorized to a sophisticated degree throughout Christian history. It is to the way in which the pre-philosophical understanding of the person that we have examined is articulated in rational theology that we now need to turn.

3

Inwardness as Mystical Ascent

We have seen in the genre of vision texts how the human person was understood as being within a closed, symbolic universe, and how an intensification of inwardness or subjectivity through inner vision was linked to the experience of an objective cosmic and social order. While this literature expresses a broad cultural consensus about the nature of the person, during this period there also develop sophisticated anthropologies that theorize more popular understandings of the self, and in turn influence those popular genres of text. The High Middle Ages sees the rise of scholasticism and reflection on the nature of self and experience. The scholastic account of the person is well illustrated through mystical theology that presents a view of God within the self who could be found through introspection by following the inner practices of contemplation, asceticism, and religious reading. The Delphic motto 'Know yourself' became a recurring theme in the twelfth century.[1] We also have the beginnings of a 'rights' discourse and questions raised about the relation of the person to the state, the obligations of kings and commoners, and about justice. During this time we witness the foundations of the modern state and the seeds of modern democracy, particularly in England with the Magna Carta (1215), the secularization of law, its being established on a rational basis rather than the supernatural agency of the ordeal, and the development of the idea of the citizen with rights and obligations.

Towards the end of the Middle Ages we increasingly find an emphasis on subjectivity as individuality which accompanies an increasing secularization until, by the time of Hobbes and others in the seventeenth century, subjectivity has been stripped of cosmology and any sense of subjectivity as imbued with sacrality has been largely lost, with the exception of some pietistic movements that try to recapture the sacred sense of the self. In this chapter we need to focus on the medieval, scholastic understanding of the sacrality of the

[1] Spijker p. 1 notes that it is used by Abelard at the beginning of his *Ethica* and by Hugh of St Victor in the *Didascalion*. Spijker has written an interesting study of the inner life in the medieval period. Ineke van Spijker, *Fictions of the Inner Life: Religious Literature and Formation of the Self in the Eleventh and Twelfth Centuries* (Turnhout: Brepols, 2004).

person—even that God is within the self—that develops from Neoplatonism, through Augustine, Anselm, and Aquinas to later mystical theologians.

Although the secular state moves away from the collective subjectivity of the medieval world, that subjectivity nevertheless forms the basis of the privatized subjectivity of modernity with its emphasis on the civil obligation of the citizen in the emerging state. The sacrality of the person articulated in scholastic theology is a precondition for an ordering of objective rights expressed in law, part of which entails the obligation of the self to the state. The medieval scholastics understood the person to be characterized by a subjectivity that is collective and not individual; the person participates in a cosmos expressed through the hierarchical structures of Church and State, and the inner journey to God—a journey through the layers of an internalized cosmos that we might call a cosmological psychology—is different to the privatized subjectivity of later eras in which cosmology is erased from subjectivity. The alienation and fragmentation of the modern self is linked to the development of the secular state and the individualization of subjectivity away from any collective imagination and shared sense of inwardness.

Before the secular state, law and inwardness are two dimensions of understanding the person that come to be theologically articulated during the scholastic period. On the one hand we have what might be called the ordering of the soul through legal obligation and responsibility; on the other we have the ordering of the soul through its conformity to an inner cosmological structure that, although discovered in interiority, is nevertheless an objective order. Sometimes these two orders were in conflict when inwardness did not conform to canon law, as we see with various accusations of heresy (in the case of Eckhart or Porete for example). But many mystical theologians were keen for their inner experience to confirm the doctrines of the Church. We therefore need to examine the discourse of interiority that is concerned with mystical ascent or vision, and the discourse of exteriority where the person is subject to law. How are these connected? Both mysticism and law are within the same symbolic world view or frame of reference that sees the person integrated into a broader realm of existence: cognition, perception, and inwardness are united in the person's participation in the broader cosmic picture, which has expression through legal, ecclesiastical, and social structures. This is what is meant by the sacrality of the person. The idea of inwardness being constitutive of the human person, which is nevertheless an objective inwardness, is part of the broad scholastic account which, in turn, has its roots in Classical thinking, Neoplatonism, and particularly in Augustine. We need to focus on the scholastic perspective as exemplified in the writings of Bonaventure, who introduces a sophisticated discourse of interiority, and Richard of St Victor, who presents an early account of inner vision through an allegorical exegesis of Genesis. Indeed, Richard's texts on contemplation were to have a strong influence on later thinkers from

Bonaventure, to Dante, and even Ezra Pound.[2] But first we need to say something of the general intellectual climate.

SCHOLASTICISM

The intellectual centres of Europe shifted from the monasteries to the new, Islam inspired universities beginning at Paris, Oxford, and Cambridge during the twelfth century.[3] This was a time of great intellectual ferment marked above all by the introduction of Aristotle into the European world via his Arabic translators. Indeed, so great was the intellectual shock that the study of Aristotle was periodically forbidden by the Church authorities until about 1255. The question about the importance of reason in relation to revelation was a central issue. If all knowledge about the universe, and even about God, could be acquired by reason alone, what need is there of religion as revelation? According to Thomas Aquinas, the purpose of scripture is to convey the truth so that humans might be saved, and Thomas regarded this revelation as being compatible with reason, which allows us to interpret the scriptures and make them relevant.[4] The works of Aristotle were a challenge, but also an opportunity that the great thinkers of the age took on board, above all Thomas Aquinas who achieved a synthesis of Aristotle's intellectual system with Christian theology, rethinking Aristotle's philosophy in the light of what he perceived to be Christian truth.[5]

[2] Dick Barnes (trans.), *Richard of St Victor's Treatise of the Study of Wisdom that Men Call Benjamin: As Adapted in Middle English by the Author of the Cloud of Unknowing* (Lewiston, Queenston, Lampeter: Edwin Mellen Press, 1990), p. 11.

[3] George Makdisi, *The Rise of Humanism in Classical Islam and the Christian West: With Special Reference to Scholasticism* (Edinburgh: Edinburgh University Press, 1990), pp. 309–17. Makdisi shows how the Islamic practice of disputation or defending a thesis, after which a student had a licence to teach, developed in Islam and only after in Christianity; 'Classical Islam produced an intellectual culture that influenced the Christian West in university scholarship. It furnished the factor that gave rise to the university, namely, the scholastic method, with its concomitants the doctorate and academic freedom' (p. 37). See also James H. Overfield, *Humanism and Scholasticism in Late Medieval Germany* (Princeton, NJ: Princeton University Press, 1984), pp. 3–60 on the history of the German university system.

We might add that scholastic disputation was also a feature of Indic (Buddhist, Hindu, Jain) culture in earlier centuries. See the volume of papers edited by José Cabezón, *Scholasticism: Cross-Cultural and Comparative Perspectives* (Albany, NY: SUNY Press, 1998). Cabezón develops Masson-Oursel's interest in scholasticism as an important category for comparative philosophy, p. 4, 'Introduction', pp. 1–17. See especially the essay by F. Clooney, 'Scholasticisms in Encounter: Working Through a Hindu Example', p. 177.

[4] Per Erik Persson, *Sacra Doctrina: Reason and Revelation in Aquinas*, trans. Ross Mackenzie (Oxford: Basil Blackwell, 1970 (first published 1957)), p. 53.

[5] F. Copleston, *A History of Philosophy*, vol. 2: *Medieval Philosophy* (London: Continuum, 1999 (first published 1950)), pp. 423–34. The bibliography for Aquinas is, of course, vast. But on his theology in general, see Perrson, *Sacra Doctrina*.

Deeply influenced by Aristotle's *De Anima*, Aquinas regarded the person as a complete entity comprising body and soul. The great Dominican is no dualist, and for him the person is an ensouled body, which means that we are not simply bodies without intellect and will (as animals) but bodies enlivened by intellect and will which makes us human. In the vision literature we have looked at, the person *is* the soul that survives the death of the body and goes to its just reward; the soul is the essential person, but for Aquinas this cannot be so. The human soul is the form of the body, but I am not my soul.[6] When we die the soul leaves the body, but the person does not survive, although Aquinas accepts that the soul will be reunited to the body in the future with the resurrection of the dead (as promised in Christian revelation). But because the soul is the intellect and animating principle of the body, it cannot alone constitute the whole person. We are not disembodied souls but persons with emotions (*passiones animae*) and desires. We have the ability to act as agents, and so have moral responsibility, and our actions are driven by our dispositions (*habitus*). For Aquinas, the human person is not the disembodied entity of Neoplatonism, but is created and sacred in itself as body and soul: it is the complete person that reflects the image of God, not the soul alone.[7]

It is not that all scholastic theologians had the same views about the person; of course not. But they all operated within the same symbolic universe and through the mode of commentary upon text—particularly Peter Lombard's *Sentences*—and engaged with the same philosophical and theological problems, such as the relation between essence (*essentia*) and existence (*existentia*) generated by the new philosophy. The Aristotelian avenue opened up new pathways of thought, but also brought into question previously held truths, in particular the question as to which should predominate—reason, or faith in revelation? And what is the status of theological science in relation to the new science of reason? Aquinas forms a coherent synthesis and establishes Christian theology on a firm basis of rational, systematic thinking.

A contemporary of the Dominican was the Franciscan Bonaventure. Both Thomas and the Bonaventure (who became affectionately known as the Angelic and Sepharic doctors respectively) were in Paris, and both were theologians engaged with the most recent philosophical developments. Of the two, Bonaventure is sometimes regarded as the more conservative thinker in the sense that he resists the new Aristotelianism in favour of a more traditional Augustinianism (and therefore Platonism), but it is to Bonaventure

[6] Thomas Aquinas, *Summa Theologica*, 1 Q.76 Art. 8 (Rome: Barri-Duccis, 1877), pp. 30–1; trans. Fathers of the English Dominican Province as *The Summa Theologica of St Thomas Aquinas*, part 2 (London: Burns, Oates and Washbourne, 1920).

[7] Thomas Aquinas, *Questions on the Soul (Questiones de Anima)*, trans. J. H. Robb (Milwaukee: Marquette University Press, 1984), pp. 42–51.

that we must turn for an account of the human person in relation to a cosmological inwardness, and for whom an intensification of subjectivity is linked to an objective structure of the cosmos. Bonaventure's theology of the person is no individualistic or romantic account of the self, but a kind of objective phenomenology of the Platonic–Christian ascent to God.

BONAVENTURE'S JOURNEY OF THE SOUL

Bonaventure (*c.*1217–74) became a Master of Arts in Paris in 1235 and joined the Franciscan order. Throughout his life he worked to unify the order and became the Minister General of the Franciscans. He codified the statutes of the order (Constitutions of Narbonne, 1260), wrote a biography of St Francis (1263), and along with his administrative work composed a number of treatises on theology, such as his commentary on Peter Lombard's *Sentences*, as well as mystical and devotional works.[8] Along with Bernard of Clairvaux he has been described as the premier mystical teacher of the medieval West.[9]

Although the Franciscan order had an ambiguous relationship with Church authority—later Franciscan spirituals even being burned at the stake for heretically rejecting a papal bull that obedience to authority should take precedence over poverty—Bonaventure was a highly respected and orthodox figure. Deeply devoted to St Francis, who passed away when Bonaventure was still a boy, he envisaged the mystical ecstasy of his master as the *summum bonum* of human life. In 1259, thirty-two years after his master's death, Bonaventure composed his masterpiece *The Journey of the Mind into God* (*Itinerarium mentis in Deum*), which describes the journey of the soul/mind (*mens*) into God, as Francis had experienced, and maps onto this path his complex metaphysical system. The term *itinerarium* designates not so much an actual journey as the route or plan of the journey—an itinerary. Indeed, this is not simply an account of a mystical journey based on experience or imagination, but is a collocation of a number of influences. In particular, as Denys Turner has pointed out, Bonaventure can be seen as a theologian who inherits two traditions of Augustine and the Pseudo-Dionysius, which are balanced in his distinctive work.[10] On the one hand we have the objective, cosmical hierarchy of Dionysius with its three orders of

[8] On Bonaventure's life, see Ewart Cousins, 'Introduction', pp. 2–8, *Bonaventure*, trans. Ewart Cousins, Classics of Western Spirituality (New York: Paulist Press, 1978), pp. 1–48.

[9] Bernard McGinn, *The Flowering of Mysticism: Men and Women in the New Mysticism, 1200–1350* (New York: Crossroad Publishing, 1998), p. 87.

[10] Denys Turner, *The Darkness of God: Negativity in Christian Mysticism* (Cambridge: Cambridge University Press, 1995), pp. 102–3.

angelic beings,[11] while on the other we have an interiority stressed by Augustine. Both are brought together, as Turner discusses, in Bonaventure, and his work could be said to form an 'interiorized hierarchy',[12] although the interiorization of the cosmical hierarchy did not originate with Bonaventure and can be found in earlier theologians such as Clement of Alexandria.[13] Bonaventure was an almost systematic theologian who inherited these traditions; from within the Augustinian tradition, a Platonism or Neoplatonism, rather than the Aristotelianism of his learned contemporary, Thomas. Let us begin our account with a description and reading of the text in order to bring out Bonaventure's anthropology so that we might see it within the broader historical context of his time.

Bonaventure lived within the symbolic universe we have described in the last chapter. He, of course, accepted the Christian narrative and accepted the world to be symbol or image that reflects the higher truth of God. We will be judged, and some redeemed at the end of time when Christ returns; but, in the meantime, some blessed people can journey to God within themselves and experience a vision of the Lord that is a precursor of what is to come. The *Itinerarium* is a work that seeks to articulate a narrative of a journey within which is also a journey through cosmical regions back to God. While it can be read almost in a naïve way, its simplicity is deceptive as it carries within it a structural hierarchy in which different levels are homologous.

The text begins with the prologue, auspicious verses (akin to the *maṅgala* verse of a Sanskrit text) calling upon God, the source of all illumination, and praising St Francis. Thirty-three years after the master's death, Bonaventure tells us that he withdrew to Mount La Verna to seek peace (*pacem*), the very place where St Francis had experienced his ecstatic vision. While reflecting on the way the soul ascends into God he thought of Francis' vision of the six-winged seraph in the form of a crucifixion, after which Francis carried the stigmata until his death two years later. Bonaventure understood that the seraph represented the rapture of the saint and the road by which it can be attained. Bonaventure then goes on to describe the six wings as six levels of illumination by which the soul ascends to peace 'through ecstatic elevations of Christian wisdom' (*sapientiae christianae*).[14] The six wings symbolize the six steps from creature to God. In seven chapters that the author insists must be mulled over with great care, we are presented with the stages of ascent into God and the journey from the external senses inward to the contemplation of

[11] *De caelestia hierarchia* 6 and 7. Dionysius the Pseudo-Areopagite, *Mystical Theology and the Celestial Hierarchies*, trans. The editors of the Shrine of Wisdom (Godalming: Shrine of Wisdom, 1949), pp. 37–8.

[12] Turner, *The Darkness of God*, p. 103.

[13] Bogdan Gabriel Bucur, *Angelomorphic Pneumatology: Clement of Alexandria and Other Early Christian Witnesses* (Leiden: Brill, 2009), p. 49.

[14] Bonaventure, *Itinerarum mentis in deum*, 3, Cousins' translation p. 34.

the image of God in the imagination, through to the intellect and culminating in mystical ecstasy. The first two chapters deal with the general project and contemplating God in the sensory world, chapters three to four on introspective contemplation, and chapters five to seven on the intellect and God as its object. Let us take a reading from the first chapter:

Reading 6

By praying in this way, we receive light to discern the steps of the ascent into God. In relation to our position in creation, the universe itself is a ladder by which we can ascend into God. Some created things are vestiges, others images; some are material, others spiritual; some are temporal, others everlasting some are outside us, others within us. In order to contemplate the First Principle, who is most spiritual, eternal and above us, we must pass through the vestige which is material, temporal and outside us. This means to be led in the path of God. We must also enter into (*intare*) our soul, which is God's image, everlasting, spiritual, and within us. This means to enter in the truth of God. We must go beyond to what is eternal, most spiritual and above us, by gazing upon the First Principle. This means to rejoice in the knowledge of God and in reverent fear of his majesty (cf. Ps 85.11).[15]

The first thing that strikes us is the clear statement that the universe is a ladder (*scala*), an ancient image for the hierarchical cosmos partly stemming from the biblical image of Jacob's ladder.[16] The creation is itself a means of achieving the highest beatitude and has been created to facilitate the human encounter with God. The world is created to help people know and love God. Indeed, if it were not for the Fall, the universe would be a perfect reflection of the divine image; but the image is broken and shattered because of that cataclysmic event that introduced death into the world. Thus the cosmos, which entraps the soul through temptation, is also the means or the path of its salvation and restoration to purity. The term 'ladder' implies the cosmical hierarchy or scale of

[15] Bonaventure, *Itinerarum* 1.2 (5:297a): *In hac oratione orando illuminatur ad cognoscendum divinae ascensionis gradus. Cum enim secundum statum conditionis nostrae ipsa rerum universitas sit scala ad ascendendum in Deum; et in rebus quaedam sint vestigium, quaedam imago, quedam corporalia, quaedam spiritualia, quaedam temporalia, quaedam aeviterna, ac per hoc quaedam extra nos, quaedam intra nos; ad hoc quod perveniamus as primum principium considerandum, quod est spiritualissimum et aeternum et supra nos, oportet nos transire per vestigium, quod est corporale et temoprale et extra nos, et hoc est deduci in via Dei; oportet, nos intrare ad mentem nostram, quae est imago Dei aeviterna, spiritualis et intra nos, et hoc est ingredi in veritate Dei; oportet nos transcendere ad aeternum, spiritualissimum, et supra nos, aspiciendo ad primum principium, et hoc est laetari in Dei notitia et reverentia Maiestatis.*

[16] The idea of the cosmos as a ladder has earlier reference, especially the idea of the cosmic ladder as an image of interior transformation. See Bucur, *Angelomorphic Pneumatology*, pp. 42–51. Clement refers to the Gnostic soul that surpasses the greatness of contemplation, moving to higher and higher spheres depending on purity of heart. This idea has its sources in biblical and other traditions of transformation from the human into the angelic realm. This transformation into angels is eliminated from the Christian tradition, but retained in Judaism (p. 46).

being that we have discussed (see 'Inwardness and Cosmology', pp. 42–5). Bonaventure explicitly refers to Jacob's ladder that we must ascend; placing our foot on the first rung we behold the material world as a mirror through which we must pass over into God as the Hebrews passed over from Egypt and Christ into the realm of the Father.[17] Being, as McMahon points out, is the same throughout the hierarchy, but there are different degrees of capacity, with higher levels having the capacities of the lower, but realized in a more complex way,[18] and the higher levels encompassing the lower. Thus, at higher levels, beings are aware of—and can even influence or control—levels below them in the hierarchy. This was a popular view, as we have seen, and pervades medieval literary genres. With Bonaventure we see not simply the acceptance of the 'Christian–Platonist' ascent, but also the insistence on the interiority of the ascent. Along with Augustine, Bonaventure thinks that God is 'more inward than my innermost and higher than my uppermost' (*interior intimo meo et superior summo meo*).[19] To journey to God is to ascend the ladder of being, which is simultaneously a journey to the interior of the self: the deepest and innermost ground of our being. The journey to God is a journey and return to oneself.

Developing the idea, Bonaventure makes three distinctions in the above passage between vestige and image, material and spiritual, and temporal and everlasting. The temporal, material world, in true Platonic form, is a vestige of the everlasting spiritual world; a simulacrum of a purer image that itself is a reflection of God. This threefold movement, Bonaventure tells us, corresponds to the three day's journey into the wilderness, the threefold intensity of light of evening, morning, and noon, and the existence of things as matter, in the mind and in the 'Eternal Art' (*arte aeterna*) that refers to Christ.[20] The movement from vestige to image is a movement from externality to internality and ultimately to the vision of God. Both humans and angels are images of God because they have intellects, whereas other creatures who only have bodies are vestiges. Bonaventure makes this simple scheme more complex in so far as there are three broad realms (themselves subdivided) that the six stages map onto. The outer realm (*extra nos*) of vestiges is accessed through the senses (*sensualitas*) whose object is the corporeal realm (*corporalia*), whereas the inner realm (*intra nos*) of the spirit (*spiritualis*) has as its object the spiritual

[17] Bonaventure, *Itinerarum* 1.9. The image of the mirror is of note. Nédoncelle makes the point that external reality reflects internal reality as is suggested by the title 'Mirror' for many medieval treatises on spirituality. Maurice Nédoncelle, 'Intériorité', p. 1899, *Dictionnaire de Spiritualité: Ascétique et mystique doctrine et histoire*, eds. M. Viller, F. Cavallera, and J. de Guibert (Paris: Beauchesne, 1971), vol. 7, pp. 1878–1903.

[18] Robert McMahon, *Understanding the Medieval Meditative Ascent: Augustine, Anselm, Boethius, and Dante* (Washington, DC: Catholic University of America Press, 2006), pp. 14–15.

[19] Augustine *Confessions* 3.6.11, quoted in McMahon *Understanding the Medieval Meditative Ascent*, pp. 10–11.

[20] Bonaventure, *Itinerarium* 1.3–4.

realm (*spiritualia*). Beyond this is the mind (*mens*) in itself, whose object is God above, the most spiritual entity (*ens spiritualissimus*) who is beyond us (*supra nos*), wholly transcendent, and yet within us.[21]

We approach God as a journey from outside to inside and above. Outside we approach God through the vestige, inside through the image, and above, which is also within, by the light of God shining upon the mind.[22] Each of these three stages is subdivided into two, thereby making the six stages of ascent that correspond to particular chapters of the *Itinerarium*. The senses can contemplate God 'by vestige' (*per vestigum*), whereas the imagination contemplates God in vestige (*in vestigum*). This distinction between *per* and *in* is not explicated in the text itself, but Turner points out that Bonaventure makes the distinction elsewhere in his *Commentary on the Sentences* of Peter Lombard, where the distinction refers to two degrees of encountering God: the mere revealing of God in contrast to making God present;[23] a mere pointing to in contrast to the displaying of a presence. This distinction in degrees of intensity is again reflected in the next stages of reason (*ratio*) and intellect (*intellectus*) whose focus is respectively God 'by image' (*per imaginem*) and 'in image' (*in imagine*) which are apprehended in the interiority of the mind rather than in the exterior world through the senses. Moving deeper we have the level of intelligence (*intelligentia*) that can comprehend God through and in light (*per/in lumen*) culminating in the apex of mind (*apex mentis*) where God is perceived ecstatically (*exstasis*). This echoes earlier schemes, particularly Boethius' levels of sensation, imagination, reason, and understanding.[24] In this ecstatic state God, who was an object of mind, becomes one with the mind/soul. In Aristotelian fashion, as the mind takes on the form of its objects, so the mind takes on the form of the supreme object, God. Taking the form of God entails an ecstatic experience of union.

The term that Bonaventure uses for the soul is *mens*. The primary designation of this term is 'mind', but it can be rendered as 'soul' for it refers to the essential part of the person that makes the journey to God and which contains the faculties of memory, intelligence, and will. The soul/mind makes its journey to God within interiority, a journey from exteriority to interiority, and transcendence. Although this journey belongs to the soul, it yet occurs within the body because the soul is not a substance apart from the body. For Bonaventure, in line with orthodox Christian thinking, the human person is a body and soul together. Elsewhere he discusses the relation of soul to body at some length. At his time there were two main contenders for understanding

[21] For a clear account and useful diagram of these various correspondences, see McGinn, *The Flowering of Mysticism*, pp. 106–7.

[22] Bonaventure, *Itinerarium* 5.2.

[23] Turner, *The Darkness of God*, p. 109.

[24] Boethius, *The Consolation of Philosophy*, trans. V. E. Watts (London: Penguin, 1969), pp. 157–8. See McMahon, *Understanding the Medieval Meditative Ascent*, pp. 214–26.

this relationship: the theory of traducionism, that held that the soul is created with the body and 'led out' (*traducere*) from the body; and the theory of creation, that the soul is created and then infused into the body. Bonaventure seems to be more of a traducionist in that he argues that God creates the soul with the body.[25] The soul and body are one substance and they are united because of the principle of *unibilitas*, the ability of them both to be formed as a single substance.[26] Indeed, it is this quality of 'unibility' that distinguishes humans from angels who are both intellectual substances. Unlike souls, angels do not need to have bodies, as they exist on a purely non-material level of the cosmos in the empyrean heaven.[27] Like Aquinas, Bonaventure does not regard the soul alone to be the complete person; there must be a body as the soul is the form of the body and the person is created as an embodied entity. The soul then inhabits the body not as a distinct entity somewhere within it, but pervading the body as its separable life force. It is both the perfection and mover of the body (*perfectio et motor*); it 'perfects through its essence what it moves through its power'.[28] The soul then imparts life to the body and also sensitivity and intelligence. Through the soul the person's body is sensitive to the world; the body functions as an organ of perception that is open to a world.

In discussing the human person, Bonaventure agrees with the classical understanding of Boethius that the person is a rational, individual substance (*individua substantia rationalis naturae*). By 'individual', Bonaventure means something that is singular, incommunicable, and having supereminent dignity,[29] of particular importance being incommunicability, by which he means that something is not part of something else; thus, a foot is communicable because it is a part of a person, but the person itself is incommunicable because it is not part of something else. On this view, the disembodied soul is therefore not a person because it is communicable,[30] and when separated it cannot be complete as it has desire to be embodied. Bonaventure's journey to God, where it realizes the highest vision through grace, is therefore necessarily

[25] Bonaventure, *Commentarius* in II *librum Sententiarum* d.18, a.2, q.3, in Christopher M. Cullen, *Bonaventure* (New York: Oxford University Press, 2006), p.132.

[26] Thomas M. Osborne Jr. 'Unibilitas: The Key to Bonaventure's Understanding of Human Nature', *Journal of the History of Philosophy*, 37/2 (1999), pp. 227–50.

[27] For a study of medieval angelology, see Tiziana Suarez-Nani, *Les anges et la philosophie: Subjectivité et fonction cosmologique des substances séparées au XIIIe siècle* (Paris: Vrin, 2002); *Connaissance et langage des anges selon Thomas d'Aquin et Gilles de Rome* (Paris: Vrin, 2003). Also the substantial paper on angels in Olivi: Tiziana Suarez-Nani, 'Pierre de Jean Olivi et la subjectivité angélique', *Archives d'histoire doctrinale et littéraire du Moyen Âge*, 2003/1 (Tome 70), pp. 233–316.

[28] Osborne, 'Unibilitas', p. 234.

[29] Osborne, 'Unibilitas', p. 246.

[30] Osborne, 'Unibilitas', p. 234. Osborne quotes Bonaventure's commentary on the sentences: 'I call the distinction of incommunicability, that something is not part of something or coming to the composition of a third thing.' *Disctintionem incommunicabilitatis dico, quod aliguid non sit alicuius pars sive veniens in compositonem tertii . . .'*

within the body. It is not as though the soul leaves the body but rather realizes this vision within the embodied person—within interiority that is also transcendence. There is perhaps an attempt to avoid a paradox here that the soul transcends the body and yet is embodied, a paradox that is important to the Christian mystical vision generally: the human person is indeed embodied, and yet the experience of transcendence that occurs in the body is also a reality. The soul of necessity is embodied, for without the body the soul, according to Bonaventure, would have no dignity. Indeed, the fullness or completeness of the living person as soul plus body is expressed in our ability to laugh, for only embodied souls can laugh (hence angels cannot laugh); risibility is a proof of the soul's animation of the body.[31] The incommunicable embodied person, enlivened by the soul which gives the body particularity, individuality, and risibility, is close to God and reflects God as its image. Although the person can never be God, there is yet union with God in the height of ecstatic contemplation that the person reaches through the graded hierarchy of being, through climbing the ladder of interiority.

Hierarchy, as in all scholastic theology, is central to Bonaventure's understanding. We have a hierarchy of society for human persons desire the company of others, possessing social affection (*affectus socialis*) that expresses itself in the hierarchies of matrimony (where the husband is superior to the wife), parenthood (where the parent is superior to the child), and the civil realm (where the superior stands over the subordinate).[32] We have the hierarchy of the Trinity, the hierarchy of the Church, and the angelic hierarchy. The natural order of society reflects the cosmical hierarchy, and although human reality has its place in the hierarchy and the peaceful running of the system entails each being functioning within the totality of the system, the human person can experience God directly through the mystical ascent of the hierarchy to the divine realm.

Reading 7

After our mind has beheld God outside itself through his vestiges and in his vestiges, within itself, through his image and in his image, and above itself through the similitude of the divine light shining above us and in the light itself, insofar as this is possible in our state as wayfarers and through the exercise of our mind, when finally in the sixth state our mind reaches that point where it contemplates (*speculetur*) in the first and supreme principle and in the mediator of god and man, Jesus Christ, those things whose likenesses can in no way be found in creatures and which surpass all penetration by the human intellect; it now remains for our mind by contemplating (*speculando*) these things to transcend and pass over (*transeat*) not only this sense world but even itself. In this passing over, Christ is the way and the door and Christ is the ladder and the

[31] Osborne, 'Unibilitas', p. 249. [32] Cullen, *Bonaventure*, p. 108–9.

> vehicle, like the place of atonement (*propitiatorium*) placed above the ark of god and the sacrament hidden from the world (*saeculum*).[33]

Here Bonaventure gives us a good summary of the soul's mystical journey to the divine light within and above us. In the sixth stage of contemplation there is the vision of Christ who himself is now described as the ladder that transcends the intellect which cannot understand or apprehend the first principle and so to do this must leap over itself through grace to be drawn into God.

This perceiving the first principle in the highest state is an ecstasy which is both a 'standing outside' (*ex-stasis*) oneself on the highest peak of contemplation, and also the very deepest sense of God within the self. At the end of the soul's journey into God, Bonaventure quotes the Pseudo-Denys:

> **Reading 8**
> But you my friend concerning mystical visions with your journey more firmly determined leave behind your senses and intellectual activities, sensible and invisible things, and nonbeing and being; and in this state of unknowing be restored insofar as is possible to unity with him who is above all essence and knowledge. For transcending yourself and all things by immeasurable and absolute ecstasy of a pure mind, leaving behind all things, and freed from all things, you will ascend to the superessential ray of the divine darkness.[34]

All practitioners on the inner path are aiming at such a superessential ecstasy. The term exstasis, or contemplative ecstasy, is used by Bonaventure to describe the vision of his teacher Francis as a term for the ultimate experiential good of human life. It is a fairly common term to designate the person's experience of God that is understood as a kind of personal annihilation, although Bonaventure is following in the Victorine tradition of its usage (see 'Richard of St Victor on the Inner Life', p. 89). Newman observes how the Latin translations of the Pseudo-Denys use the term *exstasis*, which reflects God's nature as a loving ecstasy (*eros ekstatikos*) and he also uses the term *excessus mentis*, an excess of mind, which is found eight times in

[33] Bonaventure, *Itinerarium* 7.1: . . . *postquam mens nostra contuita est Deum extra se per vestigia et in vestigiis, intra se per imaginem et in imagine, supra se per divinae lucis similitudinem supra nos relucentem et in ipsa luce, secundum quod possibile est secundum statum viae et exercitium mentis nostrae; cum tandem in sexto gradu ad hoc pervenerit, ut speculetur in principio primo et summo et meditiore Dei et hominum, Iesu Christo, ea quorum similia in creaturis nullatenus reperiri possunt, et quae omnem perspicacitatem humani intellectus excedunt: restat, ut haec speculando transcendat et transeat non solum mundum istum sensibilem, verum etiam semetipsam; in quo transitu Christus est via et ostium, Christus est scala et vehiculum tanquam propitiatorium super arcam Dei collocatum et sacramentum a saeculis absconditum.* Cousins' translation modified.

[34] Bonaventure, *Itinerarium* 7.5, quoting *De mystica theol* c.1, 1 (PG3 997B; PL 122, 1173A): *Tu autem, o amice, circa mysticas visiones, corroborato itinere, et sensus desere et intellectuales operationes et sensibilia et invisibilia et omne non ens et ens, et ad unitatem, ut possibile est, inscius restituere ipsius, qui est super omnem essentiam et scientiam. Etenim te ipso et omnibus immensurabili et absoluto purae mentis excessu, ad superessentialem divinarum tenebrarum radium, omnia deserens et ab omnibus absolutus, ascendes.*

the Vulgate.[35] Bernard of Clairvaux uses this phrase to refer to an inner state of mind that goes beyond reason: 'in that state the inner self transcends the bounds of reason and is rapt above itself'.[36] This trance-like state of ecstasy in which the soul is in rapture (*raptus*) with Paul in the third heaven is also the condition for fully understanding scripture.[37] The indexical or everyday 'I' is overwhelmed and swept away by the vision of the seraphs that leads to the transcendence of God. Here we have the hallmarks of classical mystical theology: the state of unknowing, unity with God, freedom, ecstasy, and paradoxical language ('ray of divine darkness'). In this state the individual will, the 'I will' (*volo*) is replaced by the divine will, and the ordinary self is forgotten.

There are paradoxes here. On the one hand Bonaventure understands the complete person to be the embodied soul, while on the other we have the idea that a person's completion is in the ecstatic vision of God such that the limited self is forgotten and the usual sense of identity abandoned. In one sense, in everyday transaction the self as the subject of first person predicates predominates. 'I will' or 'I want' are the paradigmatic statements of intentional consciousness in the world, and in this ordinary state transcendence is lost to the absent God, the *deus abscondis*. Conversely, in deep interiority the sense of the indexical 'I', the 'I will' or 'I want' is abandoned[38] and the self is filled with the presence of God: the self goes beyond the mind to absorption in a pure transcendence. Indeed, within the logic of the mystical ascent the 'I' must become absent; it must erase itself, or become erased through grace, such that only God lives within the self. This 'ecstasy' (*extasis*) or 'excess of mind' (*exessus mentis*) or 'rapture' (*raptus*) is the love of God that makes us like him. In Aquinas' terms, becoming like God is indeed the goal of life, and 'God loves us to the extent that we become like him' (*deus intantum diligit nos*

[35] Longère 'Introduction', in Jean Châtillon and Monique Duchet-Suchaux (ed. and French trans.), *Richard de Saint-Victor: Les Douzes Patriarches ou Beniamin Minor* (Paris: Cerf, 1997), p. 55, n. 2. The term *excessus* in the Vulgate has the implication of leaving the world. It is used in the context of the death of Christ and Jesus, Moses, and Elijah in the Transfiguration. Also see Barbara Newman, 'What did it Mean to Say "I Saw?" The Clash between Theory and Practice in Medieval Visionary Culture', p. 9, *Speculum*, 80/1 (2005), pp. 1–43.

[36] *Sed aliquando homo interior rationem excedit et supra se rapitur, et dicitur excessus mentis.* Bernard Sermons 115, Opera 6/1, p. 392, quoted and translated by Newman, 'What did it Mean to Say "I saw"?', p. 9.

[37] Newman, 'What did it Mean to Say "I saw"?', p. 10.

[38] In a slightly different, later context de Certeau makes an interesting observation that pure volition creates a void in language as it 'passes through'. That is, language as a system seems to be opposed to the 'I' as agent. The 'I' '. . . is what language always "forgets" and what makes the speaker forget language'. I think de Certeau means that the subject of first person predicates in the statement 'I will' is inevitably erased through the total language system which is greater than the subject. Michel de Certeau, *The Mystic Fable*, vol. 1: *The Sixteenth and Seventeenth Centuries*, trans. M. B. Smith (Chicago, IL: Chicago University Press, 1992), p. 174.

inquantum ei assimilamur).[39] Bonaventure speaks above that the mind 'transcends and passes over not only the sense world as such but truly even itself' (*transcendat et transeat non solum mundum istum sensibilem, verum etiam semetipsam*). There is a self-forgetting that is simultaneously a remembering of God, and in the remembering of God the self is annihilated: this is a mystical union or knowledge which, in Pseudo-Denys' terms, is a kind of unknowing. This understanding is not a monism but a realization that God is the ground of one's being, although the disappearance of the indexical-I is close to an absorption, and Harmless notes that the use of the *in Deum* for 'into God' of the *Itinerarium's* title is 'more bold' than the possible *ad Deum*.[40]

This elimination of the indexical-I, the paradoxical eradication of the will through an act of will,[41] which is described as ecstatic, is also wisdom. Indeed Bonaventure identifies ecstasy with Christian wisdom (*sapientia christiana*), which is his highest realization. It is the cognition of God by experience (*cognitionem Dei experimentalem*),[42] an ascent of the soul/mind in which all curiosity (*curiositas*) is silenced and the limited sense of self is forgotten. God and wisdom are in fact synonyms for Bonaventure,[43] and to realize wisdom is to realize God and achieve union with God.

This ecstatic union is a key to the symbolic universe. Through penetrating God's wisdom the person can understand the ways in which the image and the vestige reflect God, and how the written word of God—the divine revelation—reflects the organization of the cosmos. Both the written word and nature are symbols of the divine in that they have an inner connection to each other. Part of the work of theology is to reveal these connections and to allow the devotee to understand the deep relationship between the symbolic world of the text, the divine revelation of the Bible, and the symbolism of the world, between the *allegoria in verbis* and the *allegoria in facta*, to use de Certeau's phrase, between rhetoric and the ontic.[44] Both text and world are signs of the divine will and theology is the task of correctly understanding the system of signs. Christian wisdom allows us to understand things as they are and things as they are pointed to by the symbolic order. Indeed, the text might be said to speak the facts and the facts speak the text. In Bonaventure's phrase: 'God does not only speak by words (*non tanquam loquitur per verba*), but also by facts (*verum eitam per facta*). Because for him, to say is to do and to do is to say

[39] Persson, *Sacra Doctrina*, p. 111.

[40] W. Harmless, *Mystics* (OUP, 2005), p. 86.

[41] On this see my *The Ascetic Self: Subjectivity, Memory and Tradition* (Cambridge: Cambridge University Press, 2004), pp. 196–200.

[42] Bonaventure, *Commenatrius* in III *librum Sententiarum* d. 35. U. 1, quoted in Cullen, *Bonaventure*, p. 24.

[43] Cullen, *Bonaventure*, p. 23.

[44] De Certeau, *The Mystic Fable*, p. 91.

(*qui ipsium dicere facere est, et ipsius facere dicere*).'[45] Thus Holy Scripture describes the entire universe (*sic dexcribit totum universum*),[46] and the task of theology is to decipher its meaning. Indeed the soul's mystical, inner ascent to God and ecstatic wisdom is a kind of interpretation of the cosmos—a kind of reading. This theme of reading the book of nature was to be taken up by later mystics. Boehme, for example, was to see God as the 'signature of all things', and romantic nature mysticism sees the divine in nature, but here we have lost the textual revelation as allegory. For Bonaventure and his contemporaries, to understand the nature of the self is to understand where the human person is in the cosmic scheme and to existentially understand the inner journey in ecstatic union. This is to still the mind, allow the 'indexical I' to become a vehicle for the divine will, and achieve a totalizing vision with no new vistas to be opened. Standing on the peak of the self within interiority is the highest wisdom that is the eradication of curiosity, since *curiositas* is a fault that distracts the mind and keeps it from the fixed point of God.

VISION AND MYSTICAL ASCENT

The *Itinerarium* presents us with a compact symbolic world that leads from the outer world into interiority and ultimately silence. It is a text that assumes not only that world as a symbolic system, but a text that assumes a praxis and sees itself as part of a system of practice involving the ascetic life of contemplation and sacred reading. Focusing the mind in contemplation became the central concern of monastic institutions and the contemplative life. While some texts such as *The Cloud of Unknowing* emphasize the soul dwelling in darkness, in 'nothing' which is 'everything',[47] there is another tradition of visualization as a method through which to be receptive to the grace of God. Eventually all vision is left behind, but it is an integral element of the inner journey. We have seen in the last chapter the proliferation of vision texts bearing witness to more spontaneous visions; in addition to such literature there are theological accounts of cultivated visions or visualization techniques associated with the soul's journey to God. There is a thin line between vision and visualization—or the active cultivation in imagination of divine images.

[45] *Breviloquium* 4.4 (V. 206a), quoted in French translation in Emmanuel Falque, *Saint Bonaventure et l'entrée de dieu en théologie* (Paris: Vrin, 2000), p. 49. Falque makes the point that this precedes Austin's idea of language as performativity.

[46] Falque, *Saint Bonavanture*, p. 38.

[47] *The Cloud of Unknowing*, chapter 69, ed. Phyllis Hodgson, *The Cloud of Unknowing and the Book of Privy Counselling* (Oxford: Oxford University Press, 1944).

Indeed we might say that the ideal was for visualization, a cultivated practice, to lead to vision, a spontaneous divine gift.[48] Long hours of prayer cultivated absorbed states of mind, and theological texts such as the *Itinerarium* map out various stages of the development of the mind or soul that is envisaged as a journey towards God through levels of ascending purification. These stages came to be conceptualized as a movement through three stages of purgation, illumination, and union, particularly in the later mystical tradition.

According to Newman, a key source that most medieval thinkers would have been aware of, particularly Bonaventure, is Augustine's threefold classification of a hierarchy of perception from the visual, to the visionary, to pure intuitive insight that he describes in a later text, *De Genesi ad Litteram*, the 'Literal Commentary on Genesis'.[49] Indeed Augustine is a key figure in the development of inwardness in the Christian West, adapting Plato's idea of inwardness in the service of a Christian vision. For Augustine truth, or God, lies within and the inner world—or inner space contains the truth of God perceived in deep introspection. 'God is behind the eyes' for Augustine, 'as well as the One whose ideas the eye strives to discern clearly before it'.[50] As outlined in the *Confessions*, the soul needs to turn towards itself and ascend through the stages of the visual or ordinary perception, through the visionary or imaginative vision, to intuitive, imageless, insight or intellectual vision (*visio intellectus*). To know God is to know the self. The inwardness that begins by being oneself is finally revealed as God. The trinity of memory, sight, and will that are present within us recapitulates the divine trinity.[51] As we move inwards towards God, the mind is purified of lust for the sensible world and can see the ideas of the divine mind.

This inner turn is both an ascent within the body and away from the body, a journey through memory (*memoria*) to God. Indeed the inner memory becomes like a vast inner landscape, and Augustine compares it to a great chamber containing not only memories of the past, but the forms of knowledge; a place where all images are stored and, above all, the place where God is found[52]—the ultimate meaning of human life. *Memoria* for Augustine has an

[48] Newman in a very interesting and useful article notes that this was the case at the end of the fourteenth to early fifteenth centuries. She notes that popular manuals, such as *Meditations of the Life of Christ*, diffused techniques of prayer to a wide, even illiterate, audience. Newman, 'What did it Mean to Say "I Saw"?', pp. 1–43.

[49] Newman, 'What did it mean to say "I saw"?', p. 6–7.

[50] Charles Taylor, *Sources of the Self* (Cambridge and New York: Cambridge University Press, 1989), p. 136.

[51] Augustine, *De Trinitate* XIV. 3. 5, in Gareth B. Matthews (ed.), *Augustine on the Trinity*, Books 8–15 (Cambridge: Cambridge University Press, 2002), pp. 140–3. *Patrologia Latina*, vol. 42, col. 1038–9.

[52] Augustine, *Confessions* 10.8.14: 'So I must go beyond this natural faculty of mine as I rise by stages towards the God who made me. The next stage is memory which is like a great field or a spacious palace, a storehouse of countless images of all kinds which are conveyed to it by the

ambiguous quality. On the one hand it prevents the soul's journey towards God through raising obstacles such as desire and curiosity, but on the other it facilitates the journey as a power that enables the recollection of God. Neoplatonic language would have the soul rising towards the One within interiority, but Augustine's treatise is far less clinical and he dwells on the idea of inwardness identified with the vastness of *memoria*, but which is also intimate and particular to oneself. Indeed, he relates the verb 'I think' (*cogito*) to 'I gather' (*cogo*) as life gathers memories through time.[53] Although influenced by Platonic and Manichean dualism, Augustine is no dualist in his mature thinking. Rather for him—as for the later Bonaventure—the person (*persona*) is a conjunction (*coniunctum*) of soul and body, a rational being with these two aspects even though the soul, the inner aspect, is 'but the better part of man, and that the body is not the whole man, but the inferior part of man, and it is when both are joined together that they receive the name of man' (*sed pars melior homnis anima est; nec totus homo corpus, sed inferior hominis pars est; sed cum est utrumque coniunctum simul, habet hominis nomen*).[54] He finely balances the Platonic view of the soul as distinct from, and indeed imprisoned in, the body, with the Christian insistence on the sanctity of the body and creation. It is not the body itself that is evil and keeps us from the vision of God, but sin that pervades the body and stops us realizing our true destiny, which is the beatific vision.

Augustine's view is very influential and is the backdrop for discussions about the nature of vision and the spiritual path. With theological texts we have an account of the journey, as we have seen with Bonaventure, and also an account of how the journey is to be made; an account of the spiritual habitus to be developed. Bonaventure himself was influenced by a mystical tradition in a monastic centre near Paris, the Augustinian abbey of St Victor, whose monks became known as the Victorines. Of particular importance for Bonaventure was Hugh of St Victor (d.1142) whose writings he refers to; but it is to another influential thinker of that school that I wish to turn to for an account of interiority—Hugh's younger contemporary, Richard.

senses.' Trans. R. S. Pine-Coffin, *Saint Augustine Confessions* (London: Penguin, 1961), p. 214. *Patrologia Latina*, vol. 32, col. 784: *Transibo ergo et istam vim naturae meae, gradibus ascendens ad eum qui fecit me; et venio in campos et lata praetoria memoriae, ubi sunt thesauri innumerabilium imaginum de cujuscemodi rebus sensis invectarum.* On memory in Augustine, see Philip Cary, *Augustine's Invention of the Inner Self* (New York: Oxford University Press, 2003), pp. 125–9. Paul Ricoeur, *Memory, History, Forgetting*, trans. Kathleen Blamey and David Pellauer (Chicago, IL: Chicago University Press, 2004), pp. 96–102.

[53] Augustine, *Confessions* 10.11.

[54] Augustine, *City of God* 13.24.2, in R. W. Dyson (ed. and trans.), *Augustine: The City of God Against the Pagans* (Cambridge: Cambridge University Press, 1998), p. 575. B. Dombart (ed.), *Santi Aurelii Augustini Episcopi De Civitate Dei*, vol. 1 (Bibliotheca Scriptorum Graegorum et Romanorum Teunmeriana, 1877), p. 593.

RICHARD OF ST VICTOR ON THE INNER LIFE

Richard of St Victor (d.1173) was Scottish by birth and joined the community of St Victor about ten years after Hugh's death in 1141, and before the death of the abbot Gilduin in 1155. Richard composed various treatises, particularly on mystical theology, including commentaries on scripture, theological and philosophical treatises, and works on spirituality, as well as letters and sermons.[55] He is perhaps best known for his work on the Trinity.[56] Richard privileges knowledge over faith, is deeply concerned with interiority, and is part of what Chenu has called the extraordinary efflorescence of doctrine and experiences of love between the years 1120 and 1160.[57] The direct apprehension of God in interiority through analogical reading and prayer is a journey into the self. This path is pursued through one's own efforts initially, through the dual process of exegetical reading and contemplation, but in the end the 'inner man' (*interior homo*) is achieved by God's grace. Humankind is corrupted due to the Fall, but redemption through Christ, and following the inner path to God, is possible. In his book about sin, *On the Status of the Inner Man After the Fall* (*De statu interioris hominis post lapsum*), Richard writes that 'our inner man' (*interior homo noster*) has incorruption entangled in corruption in the post-lapsarian world,[58] but purification is possible and we can apprehend the vision of God within which is granted through divine grace. In his exposition of the dream of Nebuchadnezzar and Daniel, he writes: 'Just as the body has no power without life itself, it is without soul, so our inner man has no good power without divine grace.'[59] The unfolding of the inner self is the unfolding of the vital principle of life, which is also a discovery of God within.

Richard composed a text, *The Mystical Ark* (*De Arca Mystica*, also known as the *Benjamin Major*) that had influenced Bonaventure, and a smaller work on contemplation, the *Twelve Patriarchs*, or *Benjamin Minor*. This is a work about contemplation through an allegorical reading of the Moses' arc for the

[55] For a list of his works, see the introduction by Jean Longère in Châtillon and Duchet-Suchaux, *Richard de Saint-Victor*, pp. 14–17. I have used this edition of the Benjamin Major. On his life, see Grover Zinn, 'Introduction', *The Twelve Patriarchs; The Mystical Ark; Book Three of the Trinity* (New York: Paulist Press, 1979), pp. 1–49. For a general introduction to his contemplative thought, see Spijker, *Fictions of the Inner Life*, pp. 129–84.

[56] Nico den Bok, *Communicating the Most High: A Systematic Study of Person and Trinity in the Theology of Richard of St Victor (+1173)* (Paris and Turnhoult: Brepols, 1996), p. 8.

[57] M. D. Chenu, *L'eveil de la conscience* (Montreal: Institut d'Études Médiévale; Paris: Libraire Philosophique, Vrin, 1969), p. 33.

[58] *De statu interioris hominis post lapsum*, ch. 19, col. 1130B, *Patrologia Latina*, vol. 196. The only translation to my knowledge is J. Ribaillier, 'De statu interioris hominis de Richard de Saint Viktor', *Archives d'histoire doctrinale et littéraire du Moyen Âge*, tome 42, 1967, pp. 7–128.

[59] *De Eruditione Hominis Interioris Libri Tres*. Paul Migne (ed.), *Patrologia Latina*, vol. 196, ch. III, col. 1236A: *Sicut enim corpus nihil potest sine vita sua, id est sine anima, sic interior homo noster nihil boni potest sine gratia divina.* (My translation.)

former text, and the story in *Genesis* (29: 18–20 and 30–3), of Jacob and his two wives, for the latter. In the Genesis story, Jacob marries Leah and her sister Rachel and has children with them, as well as with their two handmaids. Together they have twelve sons—the twelve patriarchs—and a daughter. In the famous story, after seven years working for Laban, his uncle, Jacob would be given the hand of Rachel in marriage. However, Jacob is deceived into marrying her elder sister Leah. Jacob loves Rachel, who is beautiful, but not Leah, who is not. On condition that he work for a further seven years, he is also given Rachel to marry. Leah bears six sons and a daughter, Rachel bears two sons, and their handmaids bear Jacob two sons each. There is a long tradition of commentary on this text, which is read allegorically by the medieval commentators. Generally, Rachel represents contemplation and love of God, and Leah the active life and affection or will, directly parallel to Mary and Martha in the New Testament. In this spiritual reading, Richard sees the text as necessitating an interior inquiry; thus the history of Israel becomes the history of each person, and the characters come to represent different human qualities. The narrative of the nation is recapitulated in the narrative of the inner quest for God.

Reason (*ratio*) and affection (*affectio*), represented by Rachel and Leah, constitute a double force (*gemina uis*) of human beings—the ability to judge and the ability to love: reason for truth and affection for virtue.[60] *Ratio*, the power of judgement, is concerned with the external senses and their objects, corporeal realities (*corporalia*) that are necessary for any further knowledge of the self. Furthermore, imagination is within the purview of reason, although subordinate to it. But although subordinate to reason, imagination is an important faculty for Richard, as it is the power of the soul by which it ponders or meditates.[61] Bilhah, Rachel's servant, represents imagination, while her two sons, Dan and Naphtali, represent the spheres where imagination operates, and the images of pain and joy in the next world.[62] The first four sons of Leah, or affection—Reuben, Simeon, Levi, and Judah—represent fear (*timor*), sorrow (*dolor*), hope (*spes*), and love (*amor*), virtues which are sufficient for salvation, but not for perfection.[63] Confronting and controlling these emotions in the sensual world (*sensualitas*) through patience (*patienta*) and abstinence (*abstinenta*), the soul can rise up and ascend towards God: it can know the invisible realities of itself (*invisibilia sua*) and of God (*invisibilia*

[60] *Benjamin Minor* 2: 'Two powers have been given to each reasonable spirit by the Father of Lights which is the perfect gift for all and perfect grace.' *Omni spiritui rationali gemina quadam uis data est ab illo Patre luminum, a quo est omne datum optimum, et omne donum perfectum.* English translation S. V. Yankowski, *Benjamin Minor* (Ansbach: E. Koomeier and E. G. Kostetzky, 1960).

[61] *Benjamin Minor*, ch. 17, col. 12B: *Imaginatio ergo, quando instrumentum significat, est vis illa animae*... 'Therefore imagination, as a significant instrument, is the power of the soul...'

[62] *Benjamin Minor*, pp. 18, 22.

[63] *Benjamin Minor*, p. 7.

divina).[64] Leah then gives birth to Issachar, Zebulun, and the daughter Dinah, who represent joyous inner sweetness (*gaudium*), hatred of sin (*odium*), and sense of shame or modesty (*pudor*). Only after this does Rachel give birth to Joseph—the power of discretion (*discretio*) or discerning truth—that in turn leads to contemplation, represented by Benjamin, after whose birth Rachel dies. Discretion is the occupation or habit of reason and also of the spirit.[65] The sons of Zilpah, Leah's handmaid, are Gad and Asher, representing abstinence and patience. The scheme that Richard operates is as follows:[66]

Jacob = God
Sons of Leah:
1. Reuben = fear of God
2. Simeon = sorrow of sin
3. Levi = hope of forgiveness
4. Judah = love of God
5. Issachar = joy of inward sweetness
6. Zebulun = hatred of sin
7. Dinah = shame of sin

Sons of Rachel:
8. Joseph = discretion
9. Benjamin = contemplation

Sons of Bilhah (Rachel's handmaid):
10. Dan = vision of pains to come
11. Naphtali = vision of joys to come

Sons of Zilpah (Leah's handmaid):
12. Gad = abstinence
13. Asher = patience

Having thus transcended its lower or sensual nature, the soul can know contemplation symbolized by Benjamin. In the *Benjamin Major*, Richard defines contemplation as 'the free, high perception of the mind in wisdom, suspended with wonder'.[67] He classifies this into six types according to their objects or spheres, two in each of the three realms of senses (*sensibilia*), the

[64] *Benjamin Minor*, p. 72.

[65] On Richard's distinction between *ratio*, *discretio*, and *intelligenita*, see Joseph Ebner, *Die Erkenntnislehre Richards von Sr Viktor*, Beitäge zur Geschichte der Philosophie des Mittelalters, vol. 19, pt 4 (Münster: Ashendorffschen Buchhandlung, 1917), pp. 32–3.

[66] Based on the diagram in the Middle English translation of the *Benjamin Minor* by the author of *The Cloud of Unknowing*. Barnes, *Richard of St Victor's Treatise of the Study of Wisdom*, p. 31.

[67] *Benjamin Maior*, I. 4. Paul Migne (ed.), *Patrologia Latina*, vol. 196, col. 67D: *Contemplatio est libera mentis perpciacia in sapientiae spectacula cum admiratione suspense.*

intelligible realm (*intelligibilia*), and the intellectual realm (*intellectibilia*), which correspond to the faculties of imagination, reason, and intelligence that apprehend those worlds.[68] The two seraphim flying above the arc of the covenant are symbols of contemplation for Richard, representing six types by their six wings: the contemplation of the sensible world through imagination, of the ideas behind the sensible world in imagination and reason, the nature of invisible things by reason, of spirits by reason, of God, and of the Trinity.[69] Thus the first kind of contemplation is in the realm of imagination without reason, the second in imagination according to reason, and so on.[70] The *Benjamin Minor* only takes up the last two kinds of contemplation, numbers five and six, which are both above reason, the fifth not being beyond it but the sixth being both above and beyond it. Some truths cannot be understood by reason, such as the unity of the Trinity or the body of Christ, but only taken on incontestable authority (the authority of scripture and the Church).[71] The former is represented by the death of Rachel, that is, the death of *ratio*; the other is represented by the ecstasy or mental excess of Benjamin (*Beniamin excessum*). This latter term, *excessus*, is used by Richard in a second classification of inner states found in the *Benjamin Major*, but not in the *Minor*, except here. This classification is in terms of 'modes', the subjective state of contemplation rather than its objective correlates or objects (as in the above list of types). Richard lists three modes: the dilation of the spirit (*dilatatio mentis*), the elevation of the spirit (*sublevatio* or *elevatio mentis*), and the alienation or excess of the spirit (*alienatio* or *excessus mentis*). These are successive grades (*gradus*) of attainment, although facilitated not by industry but by grace.[72] What precisely is meant by these terms, or why they are chosen, is open to speculation. *Dilatatio mentis* refers to the natural state of the soul and is a synonym for *sinus mentis*,[73] where *sinus*, whose literal meaning is 'fold', seems to refer to the innermost recess of the mind.

[68] Longère, 'Introduction', in Châtillon and Duchet-Suchaux, *Richard de Saint-Victor*, pp. 51–2. For a study of contemplation in Richard see Ebner, *Die Erkenntnislehre Richards von St Viktor*, p. 105. On the role of imagination in meditation, pp. 24–7; on the objects of the six types of contemplation pp. 111–19.

[69] *Benjamin Maior*, books 1–4.

[70] The scheme in the *Benjamin Major*, chapter 6 is as follows: First contemplation in imagination only; second is in imagination and according to reason; third in reason and according to imagination; fourth in reason and according to reason; fifth above, but not beyond, reason; and sixth above and beyond reason.

[71] *Benjamin Minor* 86.

[72] *Benjamin Maior*, V. 2. See Longère, 'Introduction', in Châtillon and Duchet-Suchaux, *Richard de Saint-Victor*, pp. 53–4.

[73] Jean Châtillon, 'Les trios modes de la contemplation selon Richard de Saint-Victor', p. 4, n. 5, *Bulletin de Littérature Ecclésiastique*, 41/1 (1940), pp. 3–26.

Finally, Richard makes a contrast between contemplation and meditation, the one succeeding the other, as Benjamin and Joseph kiss when they meet. He concludes the *Benjamin Minor*:

Reading 9

Strictly speaking, Benjamin designates pure intelligence and Joseph pure wisdom (*prudentia*). By Benjamin (is meant) the type of contemplation that is of invisible things (and) by Joseph the type of meditation that is of moral behaviour (*mors*). Indeed, the comprehension of invisible realities pertains to pure intelligence; careful consideration (*circumspectio*) of moral behaviour pertains to true wisdom. We say pure intelligence is that which is free from any mixture with imagination. On the other hand, true wisdom is said to be different from wisdom of the flesh. True wisdom is that which obtains, increases, and conserves true goods, but wisdom of the flesh is about transitory goods, as 'the sons of this world are declared wiser than the sons of light (L:16.8)'. Therefore Joseph falls to the neck of Benjamin as often as meditation comes to contemplation. Then Benjamin receives his brother who falls into his arms, as the soul rises up as result of the effort of meditation to contemplation. Then as Benjamin and Joseph exchange kisses, so divine revelation and human reasoning assent to a shared attestation of truth.

Do you see how divine Scripture changes the mode to signify one and the same thing, and for all that does not allow the sense to be concealed completely but adds to (the meaning)? In the death of Rachel contemplation ascends above reason; in the entry of Benjamin into Egypt, contemplation descends all the way to imagination; in the affectionate kissing of Benjamin and Joseph, human reason applauds divine revelation.[74]

Here the allegory of Benjamin and Joseph is made explicit. In line with the general Victorine theology, all that is external is but allegory for what is internal. Benjamin, who is contemplation, is also intelligence (*intellegentia*), and Joseph is wisdom (*prudentia*) and meditation. I have rendered *prudentia* as 'wisdom' here as it is associated with practical life or moral behaviour (*mors*) that stems from the character or *habitus* we develop. The combination

[74] *Benjamin Minor* 87: *Proprie tamen et expressius per Beniamin designatur intelligentia pura, per Ioseph uero prudentia uera. Per Beniamin, scilicet illud genus contemplationis, quod est de inuisibilibus; per Ioseph, illud genus meditationis quod est in moribus. Comprehensio siquidem rerum inuisibilium pertinet ad intelligentiam puram; circumspectio uero morum pertinet ad prudentiam ueram. Intelligentiam puram dicimus, quae est sine admixtione imaginationis; prudentiam autem ueram, ad differentiam eius quae dicitur prudentia carnis. Prudentia uera est de acquirendis, multiplicandis, conseruandis ueris bonis; prudentia autem carnis est, de bonis transitoriis, secundum quam filii huius saeculi dicuntur prudentiores filiis lucis (Luc. XVI). Totiens ergo Ioseph super collum Beniamin ruit, quotiens meditatie in contemplationem desinit. Tunc Beniamin fratrem suum super se ruentem excipit, quando ex studio meditationis animus in contemplationem surgit. Tunc Beniamin et Ioseph oscula iungunt, quando diuina reuelatio et humana ratiocinatio in una ueritatis attestatione consentiunt. Videsne quomodo diuina Scriptura circa unam eamdemque rem significationis modum alternat, ubique tamen aliquid adiungit unde sensum suum ex toto latere non sinat? In morte Rachel contemplatio supra rationem ascendit; in introitu Beniamin in Aegyptum, contemplatio usque ad imaginationem descendit; in deosculatione Beniamin et Ioseph, divinae revelationi humana ratio applaudit.* (My translation.)

of intelligence and wisdom is the combination of contemplation and meditation in Richard's scheme. The object of intelligence and contemplation is the invisible world, whereas the object of wisdom and meditation is this world and the appropriate modification of behaviour. Here, intelligence seems to mean a higher mental faculty, or even concentration, that penetrates beyond the world in contemplation. These uses of *intelligentia* and *prudentia* to mean, on the one hand, a mode of concentration to develop 'ecstasy' or 'mental excess', and *prudentia* to mean practical wisdom, are attested elsewhere. In the *Benjamin Major*, Richard uses *prudentia* as a synonym for *sapientia*, a usage that reflects other sources.[75]

Contemplation and meditation are interrelated in this passage and mutually implicated. In the earlier passage defining contemplation from the *Benjamin Major*, Richard goes on to define meditation as 'wise gaze of the soul engaged in the vehement inquiry into truth'. Both contemplation and meditation contrast with ordinary thinking (*cogitatio*), which is 'heedless looking about of the soul inclined to wandering'.[76] The two practices of contemplation and meditation are higher faculties of the mind for Richard that can counteract wandering thoughts and lead us to higher levels of the cosmos where, in time, we will be granted the vision of God. In Richard's scheme, contemplation is a function of the intellect in apprehending invisible worlds above the imagination, while meditation is linked to moral development and appropriate behaviour; cultivating the correct *habitus* in order that contemplation can develop. Richard is using 'meditation' in a way consonant with the Victorine tradition. *Meditatio* was understood by his predecessor, Hugh of St Victor, as a mental activity that followed from *lectio*, study of texts, as the memorization of texts and thinking about their truth such that the truth of what is read becomes part of one's life and is integrated into one's behaviour (into one's

[75] *Benjamin Major* 9: 'in what manner wisdom scatters itself on the earth, and wisdom is established in heaven, to what extent wisdom takes away hell . . .' . . . *quomodo sapientia sua fundavit terram, et stabilivit coelos prudentia, quomodo sapientia illius eruperunt abyssi* . . . This is a standard trope as almost the exact phrase is found in other sources where it occurs in a liturgical context, e.g. Thomas Cisterciensis commentary on the *Cantica Canticorum* Book 1, ch. 1, 65B, Paul Migne (ed.), *Patrologia Latina*, vol. 206: 'The Lord spreads wisdom over the earth, establishes wisdom in heaven. Wisdoms attack the abyss . . .' *Dominus sapientia fundavit terram, stabilivit coelos prudentia. Sapientia illius irruperunt abyssi* . . . *In Nomine Patris* . . . Paul Migne (ed.), *Patrologia Latina*, vol. 86, col. 671D: *Dominus sapientia fundavit terram, stabilivit coelos prudentia. Sapientia illius eruperunt abyssi. Prudentia* in other places is a close synonym occurring in lists, thus Lactantius, *Liber tertius et Falsa Sapientia Philosophorum*, chapter 20, Paul Migne (ed.), *Patrologia Latina*, vol. 6, col. 347C–446B, expanded notes 415D: 'Here "in the heart" (means) instead of the soul, prudence, wisdom . . .', *Hic cordis ponitur pro animo, prudentia, sapientia*. Also Marius Victorinus (fourth century), *Adversus Arium* 1111A: *dictus est enim prudentia, sapientia, omniumque rerum scientia, ita enim de eo subjungit*, Paul Migne (ed.), *Patrologia Latina*, vol. 8, 1039B–1138B.

[76] *Benjamin Major*, ch. IV, col. 67D: *meditatio est providus animi obtutus in veritatis inquisitione vehementer occupatus; cogitatio autem est improvidus animi respectus ad evagationem pronus.*

habitus). *Lectio*, says Hugh, trains the mind in 'order and method' (*ordo et modus*) using grammar, but *meditatio* allows the mind free range (hence Richard's definition cited above). Meditation for Hugh is the internalization of what has been read through three stages of understanding—namely correct, useful, and habitual (*rectus, utilis, necessarius*). In correct meditation, the mind memorizes scripture and reflects on the virtues of the saints; in the second stage, what has been understood in reflection is applied to life where the virtues read about in others are made 'my own' (*meas faciam*); and the third stage is where virtue and knowledge are completely combined in oneself.[77] Meditation then is not only reflection on what has been read and memorized in *lectio divina*, but the internalization of that reading and its implementation in life. Thus in the *De Meditatione*, Hugh distinguishes created things, scripture, and conduct as objects of meditation.[78] It is the building of what might be called character, which, as Carruthers observes, in the Greek *charaktér* refers to the mark on a seal or stamp;[79] the person is stamped with moral fibre through the internalization of his or her reading in meditation. Not simply concentration, meditation is the cultivation of virtue within the self and its expression in action.

For Richard, *contemplatio* is a higher functioning of the mind in which the intellect rises above imagination; as Ebner remarks, it is the highest mode of inner activity[80] characterized by degrees of intensity. But the English term 'intellect' does not cover the semantic range of *intelligentia*, which refers to a higher faculty of thinking; a faculty that creates insight into the nature of things. Indeed, Richard tells us that *contemplatio* is above reason and above the thoughts of the earth. According to this particular scheme there are three stages in the knowledge of God, three degrees of *excessus*: the first stage below reason, the second with reason, and the third above it, which are also related to three degrees of knowing God and levels of heaven.[81] These three levels can also be related to the three realms of knowledge that Richard inherits from Boethius, the *sensibilia* known through imagination, the *intelligibilia* known by reason, and *intellectibilia* known by intelligence or higher understanding. Finally, contemplation is the direct or the immediate apprehension of God,

[77] Hugh of St Victor, *De arca Noe morali* II.6, Paul Migne (ed.), *Patrologia Latina*, vol. 176, 693D–640C). Quoted and explained by Mary Carruthers, *The Book of Memory: A Study of Memory in Medieval Culture* (Cambridge and New York: Cambridge University Press, 1990), pp. 162–3. On Hugh's understanding of meditation, see Spijker, *Fictions of the Inner Life*, pp. 75–6. On Hugh's use of language to express interiority, see Cédric Giraud, 'Du silence à la parole: Le Latin spirituel d'Hughes de Saint-Victor dans le vanitate mundi', *Archives d'histoire doctrinale et littéraire du Moyen Âge*, 77/1 (2010), pp. 7–27.

[78] Spijker, *Fictions of the Inner Life*, pp. 75–6.

[79] Carruthers, *The Book of Memory*, p. 180.

[80] Ebner, *Die Erkenntnislehre*, p. 98: Die contemplatio ist der hochste modus der inneren Betatigung.

[81] *Benjamin Minor* 74. See Châtillon, 'Les trois modes', p. 8.

also referred to by Richard as 'the super-eminence of spiritual theory' (*de supereminentia spiritualium theoriarum*).[82] The term *theoria* had been used in the monastic tradition since Augustine to denote direct knowledge of God, the goal of the spiritual life.

For Richard, the term *excessus* is used synonymously with *exstasis*. Chenu points out the ambiguity of mentis excessus, referring both to a part of oneself, and as an 'extravagent conformity' to the other.[83] He also uses the term *somnium* ('a dream') as a synonym in relation to the dream of Nebuchadnezzar and Daniel. In the following passage we see *somnium mentis* associated with *alienatio* and mystical ascent.

Reading 10

Because through bodily dream-rapture bodily sense is put to sleep, alienation is correctly apprehended through mental dream-rapture by which all external memory is completely interrupted. But to perceive dream-rapture there is in divine contemplation a secret passing over from the mind. And so he sleeps and perceives the dream-rapture who by departure from the mind ascends to sublime contemplation.[84]

This passage presents us with a general understanding of what contemplation is. I have rendered *somnium* by 'dream-rapture' because clearly Richard does not simply mean 'dream' here. The general idea is that there is a rapture of body in which the senses are suppressed, followed by a rapture of mind in which memory or the usual fluctuation of the mind is suppressed. Alienation is the separation of the soul from the lower functioning of the mind and body. Thus, divine contemplation is rising into a rapture beyond the mind; it is something hidden that passes over or transcends the mind. In this state, the one who prays appears to be asleep and is unconscious of the lower functioning of the senses and normal mental activity. With the departure from the level of the mind he ascends to sublime contemplation. This sublime contemplation is an *exstatis*, a rapture and a dwelling with or in God. The parallels here with Indian yogic texts are so striking as to evoke comment, but we will defer a discussion of comparative issues until Chapter 6.

In our exposition of this and the previous reading, we need to say something about Richard's understanding of perception. There were two competing models of perception: extramission, from Plato, that the eye exudes a beam of light that touches objects of perception; and intromission, from Aristotle,

[82] *Beniamin Minor* 75.

[83] Chenu, *L'eveil de la conscience*, p. 35.

[84] *De Eruditione Hominis Interioris* Book II, ch. 2, col. 1300A: *Quia per somnium corporis, sensus corporeus sopitur, recte per somnium mentis alienatio intelligitur, per quam exteriorum omnium memoria funditus intercipitur. Somnium autem videre, est in divinae contemplationis arcanum mente transire. Dormit itque et somnium videt qui per mentis excessum in sublimium contemplationem ascendit.* (My translation.)

that the eye passively receives light from external objects.[85] In particular, extramission is important in affecting popular piety in so far as viewing sacred objects such as relics, icons, or the host itself, was believed to be touching them, which was thought to have salvific effects,[86] a view not dissimilar to India of the same period. Indeed, perception was not morally neutral as the mind distracted by sensory delights is a mind drawn towards sin;[87] and conversely, the mind focused on sacred images is drawn towards purity. The spiritual journey envisaged by both Bonaventure and Richard is one in which perception is withdrawn from the visible world and focused internally in intellectual vision or the focusing on methods of concentration to a form of inner perception stripped of images, beyond imagination, which is a perception of God. In the model of extramission the eye touches the objects of perception, and once the external world is left behind the model still operates of the inner eye of the mind 'touching' objects of imagination (images, prayers) and finally moving to the transcendence of *theoria* which touches God.

Lastly, we need to note that mystical ascent within the self is also an ascent in the love of God for Richard. To love God is to become like an angel and 'to hammer out for ourselves (*excudere*) in some manner the form of the angelic likeness'.[88] Becoming like an angel is a development of self-knowledge and a higher refinement of it in love.[89] Richard writes a book on four degrees of love in which the love of God enters the soul and the soul returns to itself; then the soul ascends above itself in love, and passes into God entirely. The fourth stage is descending from God out of compassion.[90] The ascent to God is the ascent through the erotic experience of love in which the lover burns with longing

[85] Suzanne Conkin Akbari, *Seeing through the Veil: Optical Theory and Medieval Allegory* (Toronto: University of Toronto Press, 2004), pp. 23–7. Conkin puts the distinction well, p. 24: 'Intromission takes place when the visible form is literally "sent into" the one who sees. The appearance of the object comes forth to meet the subject, creating a fundamentally passive viewer who receives the image of the object before him. Extramission, conversely, implies an active viewer, who radiates some sort of actualizing power that facilitates the transmission of the image of the object back to the subject. The extramitted visual beam "sent outward" from the viewer, reaches out (as it were) and apprehends the object of vision.'; Fernando Salmón, 'Medieval Theories of Vision in the Medical Classroom', *Endeavour*, 22/3 (1998), pp. 125–8. Also see C. Lindberg, *Theories of Vision from Al-Kindi to Kepler* (Chicago, IL: Chicago University Press, 1976). The origin of extramission seems to be Plato's *Timaeus* 45b–46a.

[86] Christopher Joby, 'The Extent to which the Rise in the Worship of Images in the Late Middle Ages was Influenced by Contemporary Theories of Vision', *Scottish Journal of Theology*, 60/1 (2007), pp. 1–36.

[87] The moral nature of perception seems to have been first developed by Peter of Limoges in his Moral Treatise on the Eye (*c.* 1275–89). See Richard G. Newhauser, 'Peter of Limoges, Optics, and the Science of the Senses', *Senses and Society*, 5/1 (2010), pp. 28–44.

[88] *Patrologia Latina*, vol. 196, 136D. Quoted in Peter Dronke, *Medieval Latin and the Rise of the European Love Lyric*, vol. 1: *Problems and Interpretations* (Oxford: Clarendon Press, 1968), p. 63.

[89] Spijker, *Fictions of the Inner Life*, p. 149.

[90] *Tractatus de Gradibus Charitatis, Patrologia Latina*, vol. 196, col. 1195A–1208B.

inflamed by passion, breathlessly sighing and so on. Although the language of the *Benjamin Major* and *Minor* is not that of love, the love mysticism of Richard's text is not incompatible with his treatise on mystical ascent and other allegorical writing. The resources to know and love God are within the human person, and to know God is to love God: love is a form of divine knowledge.

Focusing on Bonaventure and Richard of St Victor has enabled us to understand something of how the person was theorized in relation to God and cosmology in the Christian Middle Ages. Of course there are large philosophical differences and disputes that lasted through many generations. One of the issues that is to come to sharper focus in later centuries is the distinction between voluntarism and intellectualism, where the voluntarist mystical theology focuses on the affective union with God, in contrast to the intellectualist that is less concerned with 'experience' as an affective state, but more as an intellectual process. This distinction partly maps onto another important distinction in medieval mysticism, highlighted by Oliver Davies, between 'nuptial mysticism' (*Brautmystik*), where God is perceived as bridegroom to the bride soul, and 'the mysticism of being' (*Wesenmystik*), the union of the self with the being of God.[91] The mysticism of being finds its expression from Dionysius the Pseudo-Areopagite to *The Cloud of Unknowing* and Meister Eckhart which, while it might be suspicious of vision, nevertheless propagates a particular kind of inwardness as shared being and as detachment or non-attachment to self and world. As Turner points out, Bonaventure inherits the apophatic tradition of Dionysius, that we might call an intellectualist tradition, while also presenting a strong voluntarist account in emphasizing the transcendence of intellect in a union with God, which is a union of love.[92] While the mysticism of Bonaventure and Richard lack the emphasis on emotional devotion and the focus on *eros* that we find in Bernard of Clairvaux and the later Carmelite mystics in the *Brautmystik* tradition, particularly Theresa of Avilla, there is nevertheless a strong dimension of love in their work as characterizing the nature of mystical union. Indeed, as we have seen, Richard even writes a treatise on love.

Bonaventure and Richard shared a world view in which the human person can only be understood as being within a created cosmos. The theologians developed philosophical arguments about the human person within the constraints of revelation and the authority of the Church. The person is in the image of God and has an interiority within which God appears. Such appearance or vision, called the beatific vision beyond faith and reason, becomes a goal for many people, particularly in monastic communities—seeing God in

[91] On this distinction, see Oliver Davies, *God Within: The Mystical Tradition of Northern Europe* (London: Darton, Longman and Todd, 1988), pp. 2–4.

[92] Turner, *The Darkness of God*, p. 131.

this life—before death or final Judgement. This realization comes through developing moral character, through prayer and meditation on the scriptures, which leads into more intense degrees of interiority until the vision of the Lord is attained, initially through industry and then through grace. Humans have their place in the Christian narrative as beings characterized by interiority, but an inwardness that is both potentially shared by all and unique to each. The human person is part of a total order, a cosmos, that the theologians articulated: the true nature of human being as sacred.

THE SENSE OF AN ENDING

The cosmological psychology that we have seen in Richard of St Victor and Bonaventure's inner journey as located within mainstream theology begins to come to an end with the Renaissance and the Reformation. Although a cosmological inwardness does carry on into the sixteenth and even to the eighteenth centuries, particularly in the Hermeticist and Neo-Kabbalist tradition from Ficino through Mirandola to Bruno, Campanella, and Fludd,[93] it is under threat from new rationalist conceptions of the person developing due to the rise of science that challenged a religious understanding of the world based on revelation.[94] The end of cosmological inwardness occurs in conjunction with the rise of rationalism and empiricism. By the time of the Renaissance, the old world was being questioned by scientific developments. As science advanced so religion retreated from claims about the nature of the empirical universe. Copernicus abolished the geocentric universe, and Galileo was condemned for his discoveries supporting the heliocentric view.[95] Yet in spite of trying to hold on to a world that was rapidly changing, the Church was forced to relinquish its prerogative on explanation.

Subjectivity becomes stripped of cosmology and retreats from mainstream religion, although it does survive in esoteric pockets through to modernity. The decline of a cosmological inwardness and the shift to a modern world

[93] Frances Yates, *Giordano Bruno and the Hermetic Tradition* (London: Routledge, 2002 (first published 1964)).

[94] For example, the new rationalism will have nothing to do with Renaissance magic: Descarte's friend 'le bon père' Marin Mersenne rejects Campanella and later launches a diatribe against Fludd—see Yates, *Giordano Bruno*, pp. 431, 472–9, 484–7. See also the controversy between Kepler and Fludd, pp. 479–83. On the shift from the old world view to the new scientific one, see Edward Grant, *Planets, Stars and Orbs: The Medieval Cosmos* (Cambridge: Cambridge University Press, 1996), pp. 667–73; Alexander Koyré, *The Astronomical Revolution*, trans. R. E. W. Maddison (London and New York: Routdedge, 2009 (first published 1973)). On Copernicus' heliocentric model that replaces the more complex geocentric model, see pp. 43–54.

[95] On this, and for further reference, see my *The Importance of Religion: Meaning and Action in Our Strange World* (Oxford: Wiley-Blackwell, 2012), pp. 155–6.

view was a complex process, and we can identify a number of historical trajectories marked or demarcated by events and persons as signs of important changes in the conception of the person; markers of an ending and signs of a beginning. While it is not possible to develop a detailed account, it is important to trace three overlapping historical trajectories. Firstly, we have the death of cosmological psychology of the kind we have seen; secondly, we can trace the continuance of a cosmological inwardness through into the sixteenth and seventeenth centuries, where it becomes a more sidelined discourse; and thirdly, developing from this we have a romantic inwardness that leads into modernity.

The End of Cosmological Inwardness

Standing at the end of the medieval world in the middle of the fifteenth century, Denys the Carthusian, the Ecstatic Doctor, surveys the history of Christian mysticism in his book *On Contemplation* (*De Contemplatione*). He traces the history of mystical theology or contemplation (both are synonymous for him) from the Pseudo-Areopagite through Origen, Augustine, Bernard of Clairvaux, Hugh and Richard of St Victor, Bonaventure, to Jan von Ruusbroec.[96] Turner notes that the list of who is and who is not included itself indicates some of his contemporary concerns about theology and mysticism and their relationship. Thus he included Gallus, who is significant for his mysticism rather than his theology, and excludes Scotus, famous for his theology rather than his mysticism.[97] That is, mysticism has become more clearly demarcated from theology by his time, and even anti-intellectual in its emphasis on experience. We might even read the ecstatic doctor's work as nostalgia for the earlier age where mysticism and theology were integrated into a single enterprise.[98] Denys bears witness to the beginnings of a separation of theology as an intellectual exercise from inwardness. We see the beginnings of new understanding of theology, with Duns Scotus and his rejection of the Thomistic Aristotileanism in favour of a nominalism that emphasized the particularity of the world, haecicity, and an invitation to build theories about

[96] Turner, *The Darkness of God*, p. 214. I have largely relied on Turner's account as, to my knowledge, there is no translation of *De Contemplatione*.

[97] Turner, *The Darkness of God*, p. 215.

[98] Turner, *The Darkness of God*, p. 219: 'The significance of Denys the Carthusian therefore seems to lie in his predicament: temperamentally as a synthesiser, he is confronted with fragmentation. Pulled spiritually by the attractions of a pietistic affectivism, his loyalty to his Dionysian apophatic tradition resists a voluntarist anti-intellectualism. In principle yearning for the comprehensiveness of the thirteenth century synthesis of a Bonaventure or Thomas, he is faced with the academicism of a speculative theology which could little serve the purpose of the Victorine style of mysticism he so favoured.'

the world on a rational basis of paying attention, in phenomenological terms, to what shows itself. Rational theology further develops with Ockham and Bacon who underline the importance of a scientific understanding of the world that, in the end, was to be the destruction of theology as a total explanatory system.

Protestantism responded more favourably to the new mechanistic sciences than Catholicism and presented a new view of interiority that was much more privatized and individualistic. Although we can see continuities with the medieval world, Protestantism emphasized conscience and the direct, unmediated connection between self and God. No longer embedded and embodied within a magical world, the Protestant self became more amenable to the separation of the secular from the religious, of governance from privacy, claiming for itself a stripped down inwardness which had tried to rid itself of cosmology and ritual mediation in favour of a direct connection between the inner self and God, an encounter especially seen in morality and in human conscience. With Protestantism we begin the 'disenchantment of the world' to use Weber's phrase developed by Gauchet, where the divide between myth and reason becomes entrenched.[99]

With the bifurcation between theology and inwardness we have the development of an affective mysticism that reached its highpoint in the sixteenth century, particularly with the Carmelites, stretching into the seventeenth century with the Christian Platonists such as Ralph Cudworth.[100] Retaining elements of cosmological psychology, this form of mysticism becomes increasingly marginalized from mainstream theological, and by now philosophical, thinking. Descartes' philosophical model of dualist interactionism is built upon the technological mechanistic models available to him, and subjectivity, the essential self, has retreated within, away from world and body, to the Cartesian monad causally interacting with material reality. The cosmological person has given way to the private *cogito*. This private *cogito* of Descartes is a long way from the Victorines' cosmological psychology or Bonaventure's integral understanding of soul, body, and world. The inwardness of Descartes is propositional and an isolated consciousness—the 'I think' (*cogito*). This is further developed by Locke who develops, or even 'invents', the modern concept of consciousness in which any traditional sense of inwardness is written out of the account of human reality, culminating in the Enlightenment view of the self as having autonomy and being void of any innate ideas: we are

[99] Marcel Gauchet, *The Disenchantment of the World: A Political History of Religion*, trans. Oscar Burge (Princeton, NJ and Chichester: Princeton University Press, 1997). Gauchet presents an interesting thesis, that we cannot assess here, that disenchantment begins with transcendence where God withdraws from the world in the major theistic religions. This reduction of otherness is the promotion of interiority, which erodes the religious or sacred: 'immanence presupposes severance from the foundation', p. 51.

[100] Taylor, *Sources of the Self*, p. 165.

born as a blank slate—a *tabula rasa*. With Locke, as Ricoeur observes, any echo of Platonism or Neoplatonism is no longer perceptible.[101] There is a shift in the seventeenth century from a philosophy of Being in the medieval period, to a new philosophy of consciousness in which the person has become a being with a subjectivity stripped of the ancient cosmology, to be replaced with a theory of rights and obligations and without an inherent teleology.[102]

New Forms of Inwardness

Apart from the mainstream Christian mystical tradition, a second trajectory of cosmological inwardness can be traced arising in the Renaissance and inspired by Platonism. Of particular note is Marsilio Ficino (1433–99), a student of Plotinus and Proculus, who wished to combine Platonism with Christianity in his magnum opus, the *Platonic Theology* (*Theologia Platonica*) whose subtitle says that he wishes to state only what is approved by the Church (*tantus assertum esse volo quantum ab ecclesia compobatur*). In this work we find ideas familiar from earlier centuries that there are five levels of being in ascending order, and three levels of rational souls. These teachings, Ficino tells us, are found in the ancient Egyptian works of Hermes Trismegistus.[103] This hermetic tradition, interested in magic, alchemy, and the inner cosmos, attracted much interest through the sixteenth century, some of its adherents having political influence, such as John Dee and Robert Fludd in Elizabethan England, and one important thinker, Giordanno Bruno, being tried and burned for heresy at Rome in 1600.[104] Indeed, Bruno is possibly the last to lose his life for propagating a certain kind of Platonic interiority.

In spite of religion's retreat from cosmology, the sixteenth century and early seventeenth century witnessed what some consider to be the apogee of mysticism. Jean Joseph Surin (1660–5) for example, analysed by de Certeau, says that we can know God through faith and through experience, and that every age produces those mystics who know God directly.[105] Surin is a controversial

[101] Ricoeur, *Memory, History, Forgetting*, p. 102.

[102] For an excellent account of interiority in the history of philosophy, see Seán Hand, 'Working Out Interiority: Locations and Locutions of Ipseity', *Literature and Theology*, 17/4 (2003), pp. 422–34.

[103] Marisilio Ficino, *Platonic Theology*, trans. Michael J. B. Allen, Latin text ed. James Hankins (Cambridge, MA, London: Harvard University Press, 2001), vol. 1, book 4.

[104] See note 92. On the current of Western esotericism, see the (still) engaging book by Désirée Hirst, *Hidden Riches: Traditional Symbolism from the Renaissance to Blake* (London: Eyre and Spottiswoode, 1964). For a more recent treatment, see A. Faivre and W. Hanegraaf (eds.), *Western Esotericism and the Science of Religion* (Leeven: Peters, 1998); N. Goodrick-Clarke, *The Western Esoteric Traditions: A Historical Introduction* (New York: Oxford University Press, 2008).

[105] De Certeau, *The Mystic Fable*, pp. 179–80, 223–35.

figure: the main participant in the exorcisms of Loudun, he became possessed as a result of inviting the Devil to come into him rather than possessing the nun, Jeanne des Anges, who he was exorcizing.[106] Other figures, such as Madame Guyon (1648–1717) advocated inner prayer in order to experience the grace of God, although she was imprisoned in France for her beliefs and publications. Cosmological inwardness remains within mystical Protestantism in the work of Jacob Boehme (1575–1642), a shoemaker from Gorlitz (now in Poland), who had an inner experience of God while gazing at a pewter dish, a catalyst for work that he produced twelve years later. Again, his work was subject to censure, although he was not imprisoned. Boehme privileged the will over the intellect and emphasized the resurrection of the body—the regeneration of the flesh as foundational to human hope;[107] but we are a long way here from orthodox theology and from the main intellectual concerns of the age. In the wake of Boehme we have his disciple Gichtel, made famous by his engravings showing the cosmic spheres circulating around and within the body, who also influenced Blake and what we might call romantic inwardness, which can be traced particularly in poetry through the work of Yeats, Rilke, Wallace Stevens, and even Hart Crane. Indeed, Novalis' young hero, Heinrich von Ofterdingen, longing for his blue flower, is the beginning of this romantic inwardness. We also have the strong inwardness of religious existentialists, particularly Kierkegaard, and the secular existentialists who emphasize an inwardness that is, in essence, nothing. But this new kind of interiority is individualistic and largely divorced from broader collectivities—in spite of Kierkegaard's longing for Christendom—such as the Church or monastic institution. Modern interiority becomes focused on expression or expressivism rather than religious transformation. But we will defer a discussion of this contrast between the collective subjectivity or cosmological psychology of the medieval world and the romantic subjectivity that develops from the eighteenth century and goes through to modernity, to a later chapter.

CONCLUSION

We have come a long way in our account from a world peopled with invisible beings and in which the totality of the external cosmos was contained within interiority. Taylor's 'porous self' of the premodern world—which is also a self where God is located within the depth of the soul, as is the totality of the

[106] Michel de Certeau, *The Possession at Loudun*, trans. M. B. Smith (Chicago, IL: University of Chicago Press, 2000).

[107] Norman O. Brown, *Life Against Death* (London: Routledge and Kegan Paul, 1959), pp. 33–4.

cosmos—comes to be replaced by the self of modernity in which subjectivity is stripped of cosmology in favour of a secularized individualism. It is almost as though the medieval world view of inwardness or collective subjectivity became fragmented into a number of discourses and expressed in a number of genres. The mysticism of the High Middle Ages and the doctrines of inner ascent come to be displaced with the rise of science and the retreat of religion from a cosmological world view. Rather than a mystical theology being central to accounts of self and world, we have a separation of mysticism from theology and the development of mystical writings in vernacular languages. Following ideas of inwardness into modernity we have the rise of the idea that we are beings 'with inner depths', a movement that has been so thoroughly described by Taylor, and a romanticism that highlights inwardness as longing for the infinite. This romanticism unfolds into an existential modernism on the one hand, and the negation of inwardness in postmodern discourse on the other. But before we turn to a discussion of these developments it is time to introduce a comparison of the material we have presented and to begin to develop a thesis about the truth within as a collective subjectivity and cosmological psychology.

4

Inwardness and Visual Contemplation in Hinduism

The truth within has been a constant theme in the history of Hindu traditions from an early period, a truth conflated with the idea of the self (*ātmā*), and the quest to realize or find the self became the highest value in Brahmanical tradition. A concern with the self was a philosophical preoccupation and ascetic traditions developed that focused on the self in the belief that realizing the self would free the ascetic from the bonds of suffering and reincarnation. The self lay hidden within the person, conceptualized in terms of the truth lying within the heart. This truth is concealed and hidden, a secret that can only be discovered by the most discerning practitioner through long hours of contemplative practice. This self is the true reality, realizing which one wakes up to the truth that frees us from the bonds of matter and reincarnation. The hidden, inner self, the *antarātman*, is an eternal truth, more real than the everyday reality that entraps us, but hidden in the depths of our being. To realize this hidden, secret self is the highest goal of life, and this knowledge, which is not simply a knowing that—a kind of knowledge that knows that the sky is blue or that three is a prime number—but an existential cognition involving a turnaround of one's whole being. This is liberation and life's highest and complete fulfilment. The history of Hinduism could be read as the unfolding of this central idea, but of course things are more complicated and that history is tied up with the history of society, politics, and other competing truth claims, particularly that it is not the self that is found within the heart, but God.

But one of the roots of the Hindu traditions is the self and the fundamental idea that through introspection this hidden truth can be found. The truth within us is the truth of the self that never dies and was never born. In contrast to the unmoving, unchanging self are action (*karma*) and the vicissitudes of everyday temporal life. The realization of the self is the transcendence of action and its realm. This idea can be located very early in the history of Hinduism in texts called Upaniṣads and dates from at least 800 BC. Later, the idea of a distinct theistic reality is introduced by around the second century BC, but the fundamental idea of the self, hidden in the heart, is never lost.[1]

This simple idea that within us, metaphorically conceptualized as hidden in the cave of the heart, we have a hidden, deeper self that is our true identity comes to be articulated through different genres of text with different degrees of emphasis and different philosophical conceptions as to what this self is. The philosophy of the Vedānta was concerned with the nature of the self and expressed a number of positions from the view that the self is, in the end, the only true reality and is the same in all of us, to the view that there are innumerable distinct selves embodied in a real world. Other philosophies developed that our true self is distinct from matter and the goal of life is to free our self from its bonds. This Sāṃkhya philosophy is one of the most ancient in India with connections to Buddhism as well. Along with the philosophy of the hidden self, a social institution developed devoted, at least theoretically, to this realization, namely the institution of renunciation. We have strong debates about the nature of this self and how this inner truth can be reconciled, if at all, with life in the world and obligation to family, clan group, and kingdom. And while philosophy comes to be centrally concerned with the nature of the self, there are popular genres of literature that also contain the theme of the self hidden within and the quest for its realization. Indeed, the great epic about internecine war, the Mahābhārata, ends with the hero Yudhiṣṭhīra gaining final liberation after all his long toil.

The history of the truth within, the history of the self in Hinduism, is a vast topic, so in order to present a focused discussion compatible with the Christian material we have presented, we will restrict our inquiry to the medieval period, which I take to refer to the post-Gupta era (after CE *c.*600) when strong traditions of textual reception and practice had developed which were mutually aware of each other and sometimes mutually antagonistic at a theological or philosophical level. Our procedure here, as with the Christian material, will be to offer an overall account of the truth within and develop the theme of inwardness, firstly at a pre-philosophical level of culture that, while articulated and sophisticated, is not theologically reflective, and which is shared by different philosophies and theologies. At this pre-philosophical layer we have pan-South Asian texts in Sanskrit that are concerned with spiritual practices in order to gain both power in this world and liberation from it, along with texts of devotion.

[1] This idea of the self has been expounded clearly by Jonardon Ganeri in *The Concealed Art of the Soul: Theories of Self and Practices of Truth in Indian Ethics and Epistemology* (Oxford and New York: Oxford University Press, 2007), pp. 13–38. On views of the self in Mīmāṃsā, Nyāya, and Vedānta see C. Ram-Prasad, *Knowledge and Liberation in Classical Indian Thought* (London: Palgrave, 2001), pp. 19–26, 60–77, 209–14.

Of particular interest for our present project, that parallel the Christian material of roughly the same period, are what I have called 'vision texts'. This textual material is usually part of a larger corpus of work concerned with daily and occasional ritual within the tantric genre, although not all of these texts are technically 'Tantras'. As we will see, there are striking parallels in similar texts of different traditions—Buddhist, Śaiva, and Vaiṣṇava—that are concerned with finding the truth within through the creation of an inner reality, formed in the visual imagination that the practitioner learns to inhabit. This inner visionary world forms part of the practitioner's daily ritual procedure and, although the deities and metaphysical systems differ, the fundamental structure of internalization and the intensification of inwardness to realize the inner truth is common. All the different theologies draw on and assume a shared cultural inheritance and structures of practice are consistent across different traditions. Explicitly following Sanderson's lead, in order to understand Indian conceptions of personhood we need to go beneath the surface of philosophical abstraction to discourses from which concepts of the person were drawn. Of particular importance, as Sanderson has shown, were the traditions of Kashmir from the ninth to thirteenth centuries where 'materials at all levels have achieved great sophistication and mutual consciousness'.[2] One explanation of this common cultural platform might be that different systems shared a common source of practice, although such a claim is impossible to substantiate at the present time due to the problem of establishing the chronology and date of texts.

But before we develop an account of this pre-philosophical cultural layer we need to begin at a very broad and general level in order to sketch the historical trajectory of ideas that were to become more sharply defined in the medieval period. To help us understand the idea of an inner truth that is our true self, we need to begin our account with some general remarks about the category of the person in the history of Indian religions, before going on to focus on the medieval tantric and devotional traditions as they developed not only in Kashmir, but in Nepal and South India too.

THE PERSON IN INDIAN RELIGIONS

Mauss regarded the individual, as we have seen, to be a unique product of the West in its fullest expression. Although India did have a concept of the individual it never developed, according to Mauss, due to the dampening

[2] Alexis Sanderson, 'Purity and Power Among the Brahmans of Kashmir', p. 191, in M. Carrithers, S. Collins, and S. Lukes (eds.), *The Category of the Person: Anthropology, Philosophy, History* (Cambridge: Cambridge University Press, 1985), pp. 190–216.

effect of the world-renouncing traditions of Buddhism, the Vedānta and Sāṃkhya.[3] Mauss' student Louis Dumont developed the idea of the individual in the West after writing a definitive work on society, specifically the caste system, in India. We shall here briefly return to Dumont, who we need to discuss in the context of three general features of the notion of the person that stand out in the history of South Asia: firstly social group or caste, secondly possession, and thirdly reincarnation. While, as I am arguing, there are parallels between understandings of inwardness in Christian Europe and Hindu India, the broad parameters within which the idea of the person develops are nevertheless quite specific to India. We need to say something about each of these.

Dumont presented a strong argument for the development of individuality in Europe that is politically linked to the notion of the citizen and to the idea of equality in contrast to the hierarchy of India, although he did argue for the existence of the individual in India as the world-renouncer in contrast to the householder who is not an individual because embedded within a social, transactional world. In a particularly influential essay, 'World Renunciation in Indian Religions' ('Le renoncement dans les religions de l'Inde'),[4] Dumont argues that the ancient Brahmanical understanding of a human being fell under a categorization that differentiated between a 'man in the world' ('l'homme dans le monde') and 'the renouncer' ('le renonçant'), the former resting on the institution of caste, the latter on the renunciation of caste. The orthodox Brahman male adhered to the duties of caste and saw his highest obligation to perform virtue or duty (*dharmaḥ*) within the boundaries of his social position, in contrast to the renouncer who gave up worldly obligations or human purposes of virtue (*dharmaḥ*), prosperity (*arthaḥ*), and pleasure (*kāmaḥ*) in order to seek the higher goal of salvation or liberation (*mokṣaḥ*). In giving up worldly obligations and desires the renouncer thereby became an individual through focusing on his own salvation and rejecting the social codes and roles that define the householder as a purely social being. The householder is not an individual, therefore, whereas the renouncer is an individual but an individual-outside-the-world ('l'individu-hors-du-monde') in contrast to the Western individual-in-the-world. The man-in-the-world is the householder who is not an individual but defined by social relationships, defined by caste. While admittedly the Brahmanical householder did develop ideas and traditions, it is the renouncer who is the source of all innovation in Indian religions, the individual outside of the social structure who has the creativity of the individual.

[3] Sanderson offers a strong critique of this view in 'Purity and Power', pp. 190–1. Indeed, this whole article can be read as evidence against Mauss' view.

[4] Louis Dumont, 'Le renoncement dans les religions de l'Inde', in *Homo Hierarchicus: Le system des castes et ses implications* (Paris: Gallimard, 1966), pp. 324–50; trans. Mark Sainsbury, Louis Dumont, and Basia Gulati as *Homo Hierarchicus: The Caste System and its Implications* (Chicago, IL: Chicago University Press, 1970), pp. 267–86.

For Dumont, traditional societies are holistic, the emphasis being on society as a whole, in contrast to modern, Western society, which is individualistic. Dumont argued that the fundamental organizing principle of Indian society is the distinction between purity and pollution, along the scale of which different social groups are organized with the Brahmans at the top as the most pure and the untouchables at the bottom as the most impure. Furthermore there is a fundamental distinction between ritual status and secular power,[5] which are competing sources of authority, the Brahmans being the possessors of sacred purity and the kings holding secular authority.[6] More broadly, the ruling, land-owning caste in a region employed Brahmans for ritual services in return for payment and also employed lower castes for other social functions such as labour. There was a reciprocal relationship between the land-owning castes and other groups,[7] but the crucial point being the distinction between purity and power. Dumont has been criticized for presenting too simple a picture of a complex social phenomenon,[8] and for reading back into the past a contemporary social structure. Other scholars have emphasized the distinction between auspiciousness and inauspiciousness to be more important as an organizing principle of social reality,[9] particularly the removal of the inauspicious through

[5] Dumont, *Homo Hierarchicus*, pp. 212–13.

[6] Dumont, *Homo Hierarchicus*, pp. 231–3.

[7] Dumont develops this idea, particularly in 'The Conception of Kingship in Ancient India', published as Appendix C in *Homo Hierarchicus*, pp. 287–313.

[8] E.g. N. Dirks, *The Hollow Crown: Ethnohistory of an Indian Kingdom* (Cambridge: Cambridge University Press, 1987), pp. 3–7, 256–61; D. Quigley, *The Interpretation of Caste* (Oxford: Clarendon Press, 1993), pp. 21–53. Milner has understood caste in a much broader, macro-sociological context as an extreme exemplification of the idea of the status group, developed by Max Weber, found in other civilizations. Both the ideology of caste and its actual social features are rooted in a more fundamental logic of status. Murray Milner Jr., *Status and Sacredness: A General Theory of Status Relations and an Analysis of Indian Culture* (New York: Oxford University Press, 1994), p. 139. Chris Bayly has supported Dumont to some extent, arguing that, although there are other important sociopolitical factors, caste hierarchy based on purity and pollution was long established at ancient centres of Hindu learning. C. Bayly, *Indian Society and the Making of the British Empire* (Cambridge: Cambridge University Press, 2002), p. 156. Also see Susan Bayly, *Caste, Society, and Politics in India from the Eighteenth Century to the Modern Age* (New Delhi: Replika Press, 1991), pp. 195–6; Dipankar Gupta, *Interrogating Caste: Understanding Hierarchy and Difference in Indian Society* (New Delhi: Penguin, 2000); M. Searle-Chatterji and Urshula Sharma (eds.), *Contextualising Caste: Post-Dumontian Approaches* (New Delhi: Rawat, 2003). On Dumont's reception see Robert Parkin, *Louis Dumont and Hierarchical Opposition* (New York and Oxford: Berghahn Books, 2002), pp. 102–29. For critique and a robust defence of his book see the symposium edited by T. N. Madan et al. (eds.), 'On the Nature of Caste in India: A Review Symposium on Louis Dumont's *Homo Hierarchicus*', *Contributions to Indian Sociology*, 5/1 (1971)—especially see Madan's 'Introduction', pp. 1–13; for a strong critique, among others, see Gerald D. Berreman, 'The Brahmanical View of Caste', pp. 17–23 and Louis Dumont's defence, 'On Putative Hierarchy and Some Allergies to it', pp. 58–81. For a summary of the issues see Rowena Robinson, *Sociology of Religion in India* (New Delhi: Sage, 2004).

[9] John Carman and Frédérique Apffel Marglin (eds.), *Purity and Auspiciousness in Indian Society* (Leiden: Brill, 1985); F. A. Marglin, *Wives of the God-King: The Rituals of the Devadasis of Puri* (Delhi: Oxford University Press, 1985), pp. 283–303. Gloria Raheja, in *The Poison in the Gift* (Chicago, IL: Chicago University Press, 1988), argued for the centrality of inauspiciousness and

ritual[10]—some scholars even maintaining that caste is virtually the invention of colonialism that serves a colonial, political purpose.[11] Clearly the colonial constructionist view of caste is an extreme exaggeration as we know that the hierarchical model of class (*varṇaḥ*) is as old as the *Ṛg-veda* 10.90—the *Laws of Manu* or *Manusmṛti*, composed between the second century BC and the third century AD, testifies to a distinction between the twice-born Brahman and the untouchable 'dog cooker' and is extremely prescriptive about marriage within and between castes.[12] Even the fifth-century Chinese Buddhist pilgrim Fa-hsien mentions groups of people who had to bang pieces of wood together to warn of their coming so that the Brahmans could avoid ritual pollution.[13] The historicity of a hierarchical or structured social system is surely not at issue, although its precise character at different periods is problematic.

While the assessment of these arguments and counterarguments is not directly relevant to our project, arguably Dumont's distinction between status and power is supported by both modern ethnography[14] and history. Epigraphic evidence shows us that caste disputes were mediated through reference to law books,[15] which indicates the complex nature of caste throughout history. One suspects that the system of four classes—Brahmans, Nobles or Warriors, Commoners, and Serfs—was an organizing system rather than a concrete social reality. The social reality was caste (*jātiḥ*) marked by endogamy: one had to marry within one's caste although outside of one's family or clan group (*kulam*), and commensality: one could eat only with others of the same caste affiliation.

As Quigely has observed, regardless of what the underlying constraints are, what is important and what all scholars agree about is that caste is linked to kinship. Indeed, kinship is arguably one of the most enduring patterns of human life and to understand the idea of the person in the history of South Asia we need to understand the kind of society she would have been born into. There is then compelling evidence from our texts and epigraphy that caste was

rituals to remove it among the Pahansu community in northern India. She also argued that a centre–periphery model of society with landowning castes at the centre is a more accurate description than a hierarchical one.

[10] Raheja, *The Poision in the Gift*, pp. 36, 251.

[11] R. Inden, *Imagining India* (Oxford: Blackwell, 1990).

[12] *Manusmṛti* 5.85, trans. Patrick Olivelle as *The Law Code of Manu* (New York: Oxford University Press, 2004).

[13] Wade Giles, *Travels of Fa-hsien (399–414 AD) or Record of the Buddhist Kingdoms* (Cambridge: Cambridge University Press, 1923), p. 21.

[14] E.g. Jonathan Parry, *Caste and Kinship in Kangra* (London: Routledge and Kegan Paul, 1979), cited in Quigley, *The Interpretation of Caste*, p. 62.

[15] E.g. the wheelwrights (*rathakāraḥ*) disputed their place in the social hierarchy and a stele records the decision that there were two types of wheelwright, one of high status and one of low, supported by reference to the law books. M. Derrett, 'Appendix by the Translator', in R. Lingat, *The Classical Law of India*, trans. J Duncan and M. Derrett (Berkeley and Los Angeles, CA: University of California Press, 1973), p. 273.

an important feature of South Asian society in the medieval period and evidence for Dumont's distinction between status and power. Kings in medieval Hindu civilization, within what Pollock calls 'the Sanskrit cosmopolis',[16] employed Brahmans and Brahmans vied for patronage.[17] The family you were born into defined who you were and caste itself was understood as a property of the body, generally inalienable,[18] although some tantric traditions believed that this property could be eradicated through initiation and so was not an impediment to liberation. Ideas about inwardness were formed within this social world in which Brahmans were regarded as pure and regarded themselves as pure and so subject to pollution that had to be avoided (and also possession) through a strict ritual regime.

A second feature in the medieval Hindu notion of the person is that there is an interpenetration of what we would call the natural and the supernatural. What Taylor has described as the 'porous self', the self whose boundaries are open to external forces, is apposite in the South Asian context.[19] The person, as in medieval Europe, was subject to invasive supernatural influences and lived in a magical or enchanted world. Illness was understood in terms of possession (*āveśaḥ*), particularly madness (*unmadaḥ*) and epilepsy, and possession was a feature of everyday life that needed to be dealt with through ritual means. The Brahman tried to avoid it through strict ritual control ensuring, for example, that he had carried out all of his requisite ritual performances so as to avoid demons entering through the 'hole' (*chidram*) of his shadow. Although after the nineteenth century such beliefs were put under the sign of superstition, these were not simply popular folk beliefs but permeated all strata of society.[20] Indeed, even high-caste, erudite philosophers

[16] S. Pollock, *The Language of the Gods in the World of Men: Sanskrit, Culture and Power in Premodern India* (Chicago, IL: Chicago University Press, 2006), pp. 16–18.

[17] We know that even kings of South East Asia employed Brahmans from India for royal consecrations and purposes of ritual purification. A. Sanderson, 'The Śaiva Religion among the Khmers of Kashmir, Part 1', *Bulletin de l'Ecole française d'Extrême-Orient*, 90–1 (2003–4), pp. 349–463.

[18] Sanderson, 'Purity and Power', p. 204, citing the *Mataṅgaparameśvaravṛtti*, pp. 150–1.

[19] Other scholars have made this distinction. Martin Hollis spoke of 'plastic man' to refer to a passive understanding of a person subject to external forces versus 'autonomous man' with independence and control. *Models of Man: Philosophical Thoughts on Social Action* (Cambridge, New York, Melbourne: Cambridge University Press, 1977), pp. 65–6. Godfrey Leinhardt spoke of the Dinka as having a conception of the self governed by external forces. Even memories were conceptualized in this way. *Divinity and Experience: The Religion of the Dinka* (Oxford: Clarendon Press, 1987 (first published 1961)), p. 149. See also Paul Heelas and Andrew Lock (eds.), *Indigenous Psychologies: The Anthropology of the Self* (London: Academic Press, 1981), 'Introduction', pp. 3–18; Gavin Flood, *The Importance of Religion: Meaning and Action in Our Strange World* (Oxford: Wiley-Blackwell, 2012), p. 57.

[20] On contemporary ritualized possession with particular reference to Kerala see Rich Freeman, 'Purity and Violence: Sacred Power in the Teyyam Worship of Malabar', PhD dissertation, University of Philadelphia, 1993. For a historical survey of possession in South Asia see Frederick M. Smith, *The Self Possessed: Deity and Spirit Possession in South Asian*

would be thinking within this world view (just as in the West Gregory of Nyssa, a highly refined Christian theologian, believed that cabbages should be thoroughly washed because demons lurked in the folds of the leaves). Some ritual manuals devoted sections to the diagnosis and prognosis of possession. The *Īśānaśivagurudeva-paddhati* (eleventh century), a Śaiva Siddhānta text from Kerala, devotes several chapters to it and describes possession in terms of social stratification and gender. Thus people of a low caste behaving as though they were Brahmans is a sign of possession and people on the social margins or behaving outside of Brahmanical social norms were subject to possession. For example, women behaving in particular ways that Brahman males might disapprove of, when laughing, when naked, when 'standing at a cross roads' were subject to these forces.[21] Even snake bites were understood in these terms as snakes were within the range or control of supernatural snake-beings called Nāgas.[22] We can discern here, as Fred Hardy observed more generally throughout South Asia, three styles of ritual existing at village level (*grāmya-*), tantric (*tāntrika-*), and orthodox (*vaidika-*).[23]

Thirdly, reincarnation seems to have been a widely held belief, although just how widely held is impossible to say as we only have textual evidence to go on. At a popular level it is unclear to what extent belief in reincarnation was dominant as it is not necessarily universal even today, particularly among lower caste groups where life after death is conceptualized as simply going to another world, to the world of the ancestors, or in a pluralist fashion with different parts of a person going to different locations.[24] This reflects in a contemporary context the very ancient idea attested in the *Ṛg-veda* that different parts of a person go to different locations, thus the eyes go to the sun, the breath goes to the wind, and the essence of the self goes to the ancestors.[25] The idea of reincarnation in 'Hindu' sources is first attested in the Upaniṣads where it appears as a secret doctrine. King Ārtabhāga asks the sage Yājñavalkya about the fate of a person after death who reveals to him the

Literature and Civilization (New York and Chichester: Columbia University Press, 2006). On specifically tantric possession and its textual representation see Gavin Flood, *The Tantric Body* (London: Tauris Press, 2006), pp. 87–96.

21 *Īśānaśivagurudevapaddhati* Mantrapāda 2.43.1–8.

22 The *Tantrasāra-saṃgraha* by Nārāyaṇa, critically ed. M. Duraiswami Aiyangar (Madras: Government Oriental Manuscripts Library, 1950). See Andrew Rawlinson, 'Nāgas and the Magical Cosmology of Buddhism', *Religion*, 16/2 (1986), pp. 135–52.

23 Fred Hardy, *The Religious Culture of India: Power, Love, Wisdom* (Cambridge, New York, Melbourne: Cambridge University Press, 1994), p. 94.

24 E.g. Freeman's interview with an elderly person who thought that part of a person went to another world at death, part went into the earth, and part became a crow. Freeman, 'Purity and Violence', pp. 114–15. This belief would seem to be linked to the practice of making food offerings (*piṇḍa*) to the dead, which are eaten by crows. On different beliefs in practice see Jonathan Parry, *Death in Banaras* (Cambridge, New York, Victoria: Cambridge University Press, 1994).

25 *Ṛg-veda* 10.16.

secret that good action leads to merit (*puṇyaḥ*) and evil action leads to further evil (*pāpam*).[26] By the time of the late Upaniṣads the doctrine is firmly established and the *Śvetāśvatara-upanisad* (perhaps 400–200 BC) says that the soul wanders through its own action (*saṃcaret svakarmabhiḥ*).[27] This cycle to which all beings are subject is conceptualized as one of suffering from which the highest goal of life is to escape. The soul is trapped in the body and the highest purpose of life, the highest good, is to escape from the cycle of suffering. This doctrine held true for Jainism and Buddhism too, although it becomes a more complex idea in Buddhism due to the doctrine of no-self.[28] Rather than an unchanging entity going from body to body there is a process of change, a causal link but no unchanging essence that links the chain of lives.

The implications of the reincarnation doctrine on the understanding of inwardness are perhaps less significant than might at first be supposed. But what is important about the doctrine is that it is another facet that shows how the person is deeply linked to the broader cosmos and to all other beings. The human person is but another kind of being in a vast cosmos of an infinity of beings, both natural and supernatural. There is a hierarchy of beings in the cosmos that reflects the hierarchy of social being and the forces in the cosmos can enter into the person as the consciousness within a person can leave the body and enter other bodies. The *Mālinivijayottara-tantra*, for example, lists a hierarchy of births (*jātiḥ*) in the community of beings (*bhūtagrāmaḥ*) from the vegetable kingdom, to insects, to birds, to wild and domestic animals, to the human world. These categories are simply within the material world and there are other classes of beings beyond this realm.[29]

Dumont's work has had a huge impact upon our understanding of the history of South Asian social institutions and conceptions of the person. Dumont claims that the renouncer is the only individual in the history of Indian religions, but an individual outside of society. His evidence to back the claim is derived from indigenous classifications such as the three goals of life (*trivargaḥ*) being relevant to the householder in contrast to the final goal, *mokṣaḥ*, being relevant to the renouncer. Although Dumont has a point that

[26] *Bṛhadāranyaka-upaniṣad* 3.2.13. See Olivelle, *The Early Upaniṣads.*

[27] *Śvetāśvatara-upaniṣad* 5.7. See Olivelle, *The Early Upaniṣads.*

[28] See the volume of papers edited by Wendy Doniger. W. Doniger O'Flaherty (ed.), *Karma and Rebirth in Classical Indian Traditions* (Berkerley and Los Angeles, CA: University of California Press, 1980).

[29] *Mālinīvijayottara-tantra* 5.7–9ab: *caturdaśavidho yatra bhūtagrāmaḥ pravartate / sthāvaraḥ sarpajātiśca pakṣijātistathāparā //7// mṛgasaṃjñaśca paśvākhyaḥ pañcamo 'nyaśca mānuṣaḥ / paiśāco rākṣaso yākṣo gāndharvaścaindra eva ca //8// saumyaśca prājāpatyaśca brāhmaścātra caturdaśa* / 'There are fourteen kinds in the community of beings: the five (groups of) plants, insects, above them birds, and those known as wild animals and domestic animals and then humans and demons, fiends, spirits, along with heavenly musicians and also (those belonging to) Indra, beings pertaining to the Moon, Lords of Creatures, and Brahmas. Here (these comprise) the fourteen.'

innovation seems to come from renouncers—one thinks of Śaṅkara and Rāmānuja—to claim that they are individuals is problematic. Indeed, the renouncer in some sense gives up his individuality. At renunciation he, and it is usually although not exclusively a he, takes on a new name, burns his sacred thread in the ersatz funeral pyre, and stripped bare of his old way of life takes on the mantle of renunciation and dedication to a life of homeless wandering, seeking his liberation. At least this is a romanticized ideal. In truth many renouncers join monastic communities (*maṭhaḥ*), some of which are, in effect, old people's homes and rather than sites of individual contemplation they 'are places of group life'.[30] But is individuality enhanced through renunciation? Arguably rather than an emphasis on individualism the renouncer is participating in a broader tradition that highlights communality and identity with others in the same order. As we saw with Christian monasticism, the renouncer internalizes the tradition and its expectations through long years of practice, through ritual, prayer, and asceticism. Rather than individuality the renouncer emphasizes a subjectivity that is formed by and within tradition.

CLASSICAL HINDUISM

Within these general parameters of conceptions of the person, classical Hinduism[31] developed a range of philosophical accounts of the self, from the materialists who asserted the materiality and reality of the person as body, to Vedānta idealists who understood materiality to be unreal.[32] The Vedānta or 'end of the Veda' refers to the Upaniṣads and the tradition that stems from them. The Upaniṣads themselves are the first texts that espouse the idea of a hidden, inner truth that is identified with the self. The *Bṛhadāranyaka* is the earliest text (*c.*800 BCE) that presents the idea that the deepest reality hidden in

[30] Sondra Hausner, *Wandering with Sadhus: Ascetics in the Hindu Himalayas* (Bloomington, IN: Indiana University Press, 2007), p. 116.

[31] The terms 'classical' and 'medieval' are, of course, derived from the study of Western history and imposed upon the subcontinent. The general idea of Western scholarship has been that the reign of the Guptas in India (CE 320–600) followed by a political fragmentation and the invasion of the Hūṇas parallels the reign of Rome followed by the fragmentation of the empire and the invasion of the Germans. Later both Europe and India were threatened by the rise of Islam. In this context the term 'medieval' has brought with it a value judgement connoting a fall from a more pristine era. In this study no judgement is intended; the term 'medieval' is used purely through convention and refers to the post-Gupta civilization when devotional and tantric traditions developed along with the sharper delineation of philosophy. On the problem of the 'medieval' see Ronald Inden, Jonathan Walters, and Daud Ali, *Querying the Medieval: Texts and the History of Practices in South Asia* (New York: Oxford University Press, 2000), pp. 16–19.

[32] For a survey see Richard King, *Indian Philosophy* (Edinburgh: Edinburgh University Press, 1999).

the heart is the self and furthermore this self is identical with the absolute self of the universe, the Brahman. Although there is a rhetoric of searching for the self within, this self—as Ganeri points out[33]—is not the object of consciousness but the deepest subject. The perceiver cannot perceive itself and cannot be known in a conventional sense, about it one can only say 'no, no' (*neti neti*).[34] This idea is developed in the *Chāndogya* where we find the famous story of how Āruṇi educates his son Śvetaketu in the truth of the self, how one should seek the essence of all things and how the essence of the self constitutes the whole world: 'that is what you are' (*tat tvam asi*).[35] As time develops this idea becomes modified in the *Śvetāśvatara-upaniṣad* where we have the idea of a God who is the focus of worship and yogic concentration, who is the source of the universe, a magician (*mayī*) who weaves the web of the world (*māyā*) and who is the substrate and support of self and world. He reigns over all the worlds and yet resides hidden in all beings (*sarvabhūtaguhāśayaḥ*).[36]

Towards the end of the first millennium BC there was a massive expansion of Sanskrit learning and texts, as Pollock has documented in great detail, from the edicts of Aśoka in the Maurya dynasty (320–150 BC).[37] At a popular cultural level, by the end of the first millennium AD Sanskrit literary culture began to develop, with the gradual composition of the great epics the *Rāmāyaṇa* and *Mahābhārata*. Texts debated the four purposes of life, virtue (*dharmaḥ*), prosperity or wealth (*arthaḥ*), pleasure (*kāmaḥ*), and liberation (*mokṣaḥ*), and which was of higher value. The *Kāma-sūtra* (third or fourth century AD), for example, discussed (mostly erotic) pleasure as expressing the fundamental nature of the person, which had legitimate expression within the broader social context. This text was composed mostly for the high-caste urbanite, the *nāyaka*, and points to a lack of inhibition that modern sensibilities (even in the West) are averse to. Teachings about pleasure, the Kāma Śāstra literature, articulated with a literary culture concerned with love, passion, beautiful women, and handsome princes, the literary forms which later found expression in religious, devotional literature, particularly the poetry focused on Kṛṣṇa and his girlfriends.[38] Indeed, a history of inwardness could be written from the perspective of literary culture and the development and refinement of human emotions (*bhāvaḥ*) expressed as aesthetic emotions (*rasaḥ*).

[33] Ganeri, *The Concealed Art of the Soul*, pp. 27–30.

[34] *Bṛhadāraṇyaka* 4.5.15, in Patrick Olivelle (ed. and trans.), *The Early Upaniṣads* (New York and Oxford: Oxford University Press, 1998).

[35] *Chāndogya* 6.1.3-6, in Olivelle, *The Early Upaniṣads*.

[36] *Śvetāsvatara* 3.1 and 11. See Olivelle, *The Early Upaniṣads*.

[37] See Pollock, *The Language of the Gods*, pp. 59–74 for a shortened overview.

[38] E. Dimock and D. Levertov, *In Praise of Krishna: Songs from the Bengali* (New York: Anchor Books, 1967).

Alongside refined literary culture and the aestheticization of human experience for the ruling elites in the urban environment, we have the development of literatures concerned with liberation and the raising of spiritual sensibilities that sought transcendence of the world. This kind of literature has liberation (*mokṣaḥ*), the search for the inner self, as its concern and the transcendence of worldly life. Thus it is within the realm of renunciation, although increasingly the values of renunciation come to find a place in the values of the householder. The *Bhagavad-gītā*, for example, espouses the value of virtue (*dharmaḥ*) and the virtue of love (*bhaktiḥ*) for God as the highest value beyond pleasure. The ideal human on his way to perfection should be without desire, detached from the fruits of action, and offering those fruits to God. The yogi who cultivates discipline and is controlled (*yuktaḥ*) or steadfast, who has faith or confidence in the Lord, enters into the Lord.[39]

Texts on more intense forms of spirituality are also being composed at this time, such as Patañjali's *Yoga-sūtra*, a synthesis of teachings about concentration practice that eradicates the traces of past actions and prepares the self for final liberation, conceptualized as inner solitude (*kaivalya*). Each monadic self is contained within itself in liberation, quite detached from the comings and goings of the world. This text develops an intense sense of inwardness through concentration on a single point that transforms consciousness. Consciousness takes on the forms of its objects, so focusing on a pure, transcendent object such as the Lord (*īśvaraḥ*) transforms the person to a level that transcends all limiting conditions and worldly constraints. This idea of the realization of the inner self that transcends the outer self associated with the body is a theme that we find throughout the soteriological literature of the classical and medieval periods. A rich tradition of yoga texts develops that cuts across sectarian divisions. Thus, for example, the Jain philosopher Hemacandra can write a text on yoga, the *Yogaśāstra*, that echoes other traditions. The text makes a distinction between the inner self (*antarātmā*) and the outer self (*bahirātmā*). The person who perceives himself to be the body is said to be external whereas the person who perceives the inner self as ruling over the body is full of bliss and has consciousness as its nature.[40]

[39] *Bhagavad-gītā* 6.47: *yoginām api sarveṣāṃ mad-gatenāntarātmanā / śraddhāvān bhajate yo māṃ sa me yuktatamo mataḥ*. 'Also, of all yogis, the one whose inner self has come to me, who worships me, rich in his faith, is thought to be the most steadfast.' Gavin Flood and Charles Martin (trans.), *The Bhagavad Gita: A New Translation* (New York and London: Norton, 2012). For a good account of the human person and theistic reality in the text, see Julius Lipner, *Hindus, their Religious Beliefs and Practices* (2nd edn, London: Routledge, 2012), pp. 160–5.

[40] Hemacandra, *Yogaśāstra* 12.7–8, in Olle Quarnström (trans.), *The Yogaśāstra of Hemacandra: A Twelfth Century Handbook on Śvetambara Jainism* (Cambridge, MA and London: Harvard University Press, 2002), p. 188.

The yogin and the nāyaka both develop a kind of inwardness, the one expressing an ascetic value, the other an aesthetic value. Both the ascetic and the aesthetic were possibilities for the Brahman, although the value of renunciation and transcendence arguably came to be the dominant paradigm.

MEDIEVAL HINDUISM

Alongside the systematic or even scientific exposition of pleasure in the *Kāmasūtra*, playwrights and poets composed works in Sanskrit for an educated, urban elite developing in towns with increasing economic prosperity.[41] Poets such as Kālidāsa (fourth century AD) wrote of longing and tragic love and even a science of literature developed, the inquiry into literature (*Kāvyamīmāṃsā*) by the poet Rājaśekhara.[42] Tensions between the worldly, urban community and religious renouncers expressing a different value system came to be expressed, for example in Bhaṭṭanārāyaṇa's play *Āgamadaṃbara*.[43] But by the medieval period the ideals of renunciation, namely other worldly power and liberation, had become pervasive and penetrated the householder ideal. With the tantric traditions from around the seventh century AD, the ideal of renunciation came to be an inner attitude that the married householder could maintain—as we find with the highly orthodox Vedānta and *Bhagavad-gītā*, which advocates virtuous action in the world but with a spirit of detachment from the fruits of action. Not only could the householder—Dumont's man-in-the-world—achieve worldly success and enjoy the fruits of the householder life, but he could also aim at liberation in this very life through participating in householder versions of renunciate traditions.

In the medieval period four forms of religion developed that are particularly important: the religion of Śiva or Śaiva tradition, the religion of Viṣṇu or Vaiṣṇava tradition, the religion of the Goddess or Śākta tradition, and we might add the purely Brahmanical religion of the Brahmans. The Brahmans followed the secondary revelation or *smṛti* (that which is remembered) called the Smārtas in contrast to the followers of the primary revelation, *śruti*, who in earlier centuries had been the dominant performers of the solemn (*śrauta-*) vedic ritual. The Purāṇas are texts expounding narratives of the gods and lineages of kings, and were the purview of orthodox Brahmans within all four

[41] On increasing economic prosperity see R. Gombrich, *Theravada Buddhism* (London: Routledge, 1988), pp. 57–8. Pollock, *The Language of the Gods*, pp. 75–114.

[42] Pollock, *The Language of the Gods*, pp. 200–1. For a good introduction and translation of plays from this period see Lyne Bansat-Boudon, *Théâtre de l'Inde ancienne* (Paris: Gallimard, 2006).

[43] *Agamadaṃbara*, trans. Csaba Dezso as *Much Ado About Religion* (New York: New York University Press, 2005).

traditions. These were the textual foundation of devotion (*bhaktiḥ*) that focused on a personal deity as Lord (*bhagavān*) or Goddess (*bhagavatī*). For bhakti traditions the truth within is the Lord in the heart who, for Vaiṣṇava tradition, is the inner controller yet who is also transcendent. With the arising of an alternative revelation, the Tantras, tantric forms of Hinduism came to dominate the medieval world and some Purāṇas overlap with some Tantras in matters of ritual and visualization. Although some Tantras were antinomian in character, in the belief that orthodox Brahmanical restriction or inhibition restricted the achievement of liberation, most Tantras were supportive of general devotional life of the high-caste Hindu and tantric initiation was supererogatory to vedic initiation.[44]

This is not the place to describe the historical development of medieval Hinduism but we do need to present a brief sketch of the sociopolitical condition in which we can locate the practices and philosophies I shall discuss. In the medieval period, as Sanderson has shown, kingdoms developed in which kings adhered to the religion of the Brahmans, who practised strict adherence to caste and discipline or life-stage (*varṇāśramadharmaḥ*), and were also initiated into one of the newer religions focused on the gods Viṣṇu, Śiva, the Goddess (Bhagavatī), or the Sun (Sūrya/Ādiya). While Buddhism and Jainism also thrived during this period, arguably the most important religion in regional kingdoms was Śaivism, and Sanderson has justifiably called the period from the fifth to thirteenth centuries the 'Śaiva Age'.[45] Śaivism became the paradigm religion for others to imitate to attract patronage.[46] The Śaiva religion itself was subdivided into various branches that Sanderson has mapped. On the one hand we have Purānic Śaivism, the religion of Śiva expressed in the Purāṇas and maintained by devotees called Maheśvaras or Śiva bhaktas. On the other hand we have non-Purānic worship of Śiva that the later tradition divided into two broad categories, the Higher or Outer Path (*atimargaḥ*) and the Path of Mantras (*mantramārgaḥ*). The Atimārga represents the earlier form of Śaivism from around the second century AD, of ascetic groups (particularly the Pāśupatas, who became an important monastic order) who had gone beyond (*ati-*) the social order[47] out from which the Mantramārga emerged. The Mantramārga is what we refer

[44] For a general introduction see Alexis Sanderson, 'The Śaiva and Tantric Traditions', in F. Hardy et al. (eds.), *The World's Religions* (London: Routledge, 1988), pp. 190–216. See also André Padoux, *Comprendre le tantrisme: Les soures Hindous* (Paris: Albin Michel, 2010); Flood, *The Tantric Body*.

[45] A. Sanderson, 'The Śaiva Age: The Rise and Dominance of Śaivism during the Early Medieval Period', in Shingo Einoo (ed.), *Genesis and Development of Tantrism* (Tokyo: Institute of Oriental Culture, 2009), pp. 41–350.

[46] Sanderson, 'The Śaiva Age', pp. 43–5.

[47] Alexis Sanderson, 'Śaivism and Brahmanism in the Early Medieval Period', Gonda Lecture 2006 <http://www.alexissanderson.com/uploads/6/2/7/6/6276908/gondalecture2.pdf> (accessed 28 May 2013).

to as tantric Śaivism and was concerned with the propitiation of Mantra gods and gaining power (*siddhiḥ*) and liberation (*mokṣaḥ*) through mastering them, as Sanderson has documented in great detail. Evidence of the Mantramārga occurs from about the fifth century, and by the seventh it had royal patronage. What differentiated the Mantramārga from earlier kinds of religion was the emphasis on initiation (*dīkṣā*); liberation is guaranteed through the requisite initiation by a Śaiva master or guru. It was made up principally of the Śaiva Siddhānta, which is the main tradition, normative Śaivism still extant in South India. The Śaiva Siddhānta worshipped Śiva in the form of the liṅga and as the five-headed Sadāśiva. Along with the development of this religion, other traditions developed focused on a ferocious god Bhairava, thought to be a higher manifestation of Śiva and/or the goddess who is his power (*śaktiḥ*). These non-Saiddhāntika groups assumed the ritual and cosmological structure of the Śaiva Siddhānta but interpreted it in a generally non-dualistic way.[48]

These groups of ascetics were generally antinomian and flouted vedic ritual purity rules in the belief that liberation through the path they offered transcended that of the Brahmanical followers of the Veda. The textual revelation that they revered is itself divided into texts focused on Bhairava, called the mantra-corpus (*mantrapīṭham*), and texts focused on the goddess Kālī or Kālasaṃkārṣinī or her forms, called the wisdom-corpus (*vidyāpīṭham*). These antinomian groups taught that in order to achieve liberation, vedic inhibition (*śaṅkhā*) has to be transcended through going against Brahmanical purity rules by consuming forbidden substances—namely alcohol, blood, and sexual fluids obtained through ritual sex that broke caste restrictions.[49] Some traditions, such as the Krama or Gradation school, performed extreme non-dualistic practice (*advaitācāraḥ*) that entailed transcending disgust in the consumption of faeces, urine, and vomit, as well as an orgiastic dimension to the ritual between high-caste male practitioners and low-caste women (lower than Śudras) in the 'gathering of the heroes' (*vīramelāpaḥ*).[50] The *Vijñānabhairava-tantra* even says that ritual purity (*śuddhiḥ*) prescribed by vedic authority is impurity in the Śaiva system (*śambhudarśanam*).[51] Many of these cults were propagated by ascetics in cremation grounds, such as the skull-carrying Kāpālikas, who had dropped out of conventional society and were seeking power in this and other worlds. Of particular importance was the Trika, the threefold tradition that worshipped a triad of goddesses called Parā,

[48] For a simplified account of these traditions see my *An Introduction to Hinduism* (Cambridge: Cambridge University Press, 1996), pp. 151–73.

[49] See David White, *The Kiss of the Yoginī: Tantric Sex in its South Asian Contexts* (Chicago, IL: Chicago University Press, 2003), pp. 67–93.

[50] Alexis Sanderson, 'The Śaiva Exegesis of Kashmir', pp. 282–8, in Dominic Goodall and André Padoux (eds.), *Mélanges tantriques à mémoire d'Hélène Brunner* (Pondichéry: Institut Français de Pondichéry, 2007), pp. 231–442.

[51] *Vijñānabhairava tantra* verse 123.

Parāparā, and Aparā on a trident diagram or *maṇḍala* within the body and also on an external diagram as Sanderson has so lucidly explained.[52] In time, ritualized sex for producing impure substances to offer to deities became aestheticized and the focus shifted from the production of substances for offering to deities, to sexual experience as the reflection of the bliss of liberation and the bliss of the union of Śiva and the goddess. Probably always a minority practice, this erotic worship could be performed purely mentally in the imagination. Thus there is a graded hierarchy of external ritual with impure substances, to erotic worship in the imagination, to direct realization of the inner truth of non-dual awareness.[53] Indeed, esoteric worship came to be modelled on exoteric, vedic rites and this esoteric worship and system of deities in turn interpreted in purely idealistic ways by non-dualist commentators.[54]

The Trika came to have a sophisticated philosophical articulation in the philosophy of the Recognition school or Pratyabhijñā, of which the most important and influential exponent was Abhinavagupta (*fl. c.*975–1025 AD). He took the practices and doctrines of these sects and made them palatable and adaptable to the Śaiva householder. Thus there was no longer a need for the external accoutrements of the cult, such as wearing human bones, covering oneself in cremation ground ash, and carrying a skull-topped staff. The new, householder Śaiva was esoteric: internally a follower of Śākta-Śaivism (the goddess-orientated cults of the Mantramārga) but externally a follower of conventional Śaivism and vedic practice.[55] This is no overt subversion but functions within the restrictions of convention while flouting those conventions as an inner practice. Freedom from restriction is an inner state of consciousness.

In parallel to the development of Śaivism we have the religion of Viṣṇu, which similarly can be divided into orthodox Purāṇic worship and tantric Pāñcarātra, a tradition that revered a textual revelation in a corpus of texts called Saṃhitās. The Pāñcarātra became, and remains, the common ritual structure for the main Vaiṣṇava tradition in South India, the Śrīvaiṣṇava. A parallel, although in some ways rival, sect is the Vaikhānasa, which regards itself as non-tantric although both traditions share rituals and deities.[56] Although outside of the vedic fold, Buddhism followed a similar pattern of

[52] Alexis Sanderson, 'Maṇḍala and Āgamic Identity in the Trika of Kashmir', in André Padoux (ed.), *Mantras et Diagrammes Rituelles dans l'Hindouisme*, Équipe no. 249: L'Hindouisme: Textes, doctrines, pratiques (Paris: Éditions du Centre National de la Recherche Scientifique, 1986), pp. 169–214.

[53] Alexis Sanderson, 'Meaning in Tantric Ritual', pp. 87–90, in Ann-Marie Blondeau and Kristopher Schipper (eds.), *Essais sur le rituel III* (Louvain, Paris: Peeters, 1995), pp. 15–95.

[54] Sanderson, 'Meaning in Tantric Ritual', pp. 70–5.

[55] Jayaratha's commentary on the *Tantrāloka* 4.251ab, cited by Sanderson, 'The Śaiva Exegesis of Kashmir', p. 232.

[56] G. Colas, *Viṣṇu: ses images et ses feux: Les metamorphoses du dieu chez les Vaikhānasa* (Paris: EFEO, 1996), pp. 168–71.

the Vajrayāna becoming a distinct tradition from the Mahāyāna but conceptually reliant on it, and even tantric Jainism developed.

VISUAL CONTEMPLATION

It is within this rich cultural and religious context that what we might call an intensification of inwardness occurs in order to realize the liberating truth within the self. Some renouncers and householders seeking a more intense religiosity adopted mystical or spiritual practices that involved the visualization of the deity or group of deities, with a view to identification with the imagined image. This visualization and identification with the image was practised in order to gain, for some, magical power in this world—such as power to gain supernatural power, defeat enemies, and attract women—but also ultimate liberation from the cycle of reincarnation through the liberating gnosis of the inner self. The practice of visual contemplation is probably ancient and seems to have precursors in Buddhist meditation practices involving the visualization and realization in the mind's eye of a photic image called the *nimitta*. This image would take the practitioners into the various states of absorption (*dhyānam*/Pāli: *jhānam*), namely the four absorptions of form (*rūpajhānam*) and the four formless absorptions (*arūpajhānam*) (see 'Early Meditation Practice', pp. 172–4).[57] These states are linked with kinds of practice that focus on a concrete or external image such as a circle of light on the wall, or a colour, or a diagram (*maṇḍalam*) called *kasiṇa*. Thus, very early on the term *dhyānam* seems to have been associated with a visual image, and by the time of the medieval texts has come to refer to visualization. Thus texts might describe visualizations that they refer to as *dhyāna* not only in Buddhist but Hindu traditions as well.

These visualizations usually occurred within the context of the tantric practitioner's daily ritual. For example, an orthodox Brahman belonging to the mainstream religion of Śiva, the Śaiva Siddhānta, would practise at the three junctures of the day: dawn, noon, and dusk. This ritual procedure, which is a standard pattern in all tantric traditions, involves bathing, the purification of the body (*bhūtaśuddhiḥ*), the divinization of the body through placing mantras upon it (*nyāsaḥ*), inner or mental worship of the deity (*antar-/mānasa-yāgaḥ*), and external worship (*bahya-yāgaḥ*), making offerings to a deity externalized in an icon or the aniconic *liṅga*.[58] We need to remember

[57] Sarah Shaw, *Buddhist Meditation* (London: Routledge, 2010), pp. 88, 146–7. L. Cousins, 'Vittaka/Vitarka and Vicāra: Stages of Samādhi in Buddhism and Yoga', *Indo-Iranian Journal*, 35 (1992), pp. 137–57.

[58] I have described these elsewhere. Flood, *The Tantric Body*, pp. 106–7.

firstly that the deity visualized is also or primarily a mantra, a sound formula which is the deity's body, and secondly that to worship a god one must become a god—'having formed one's own body with mantras of Śiva in due order, the well purified self who has become Śiva should undertake the worship of Śiva'.[59] This need to become Śiva ritually is true even of metaphysically non-dual traditions such as the Śaiva Siddhānta. During the ritual process the practitioner burns up the physical body in his imagination and recreates his body as a body comprising mantras of the god, thereby replacing his own body with the body parts of the deity. The god within is identified with the totality of the practitioner's body.

Visualization is part of this daily process, but particularly during the inner or mental worship, during which the practitioner imagines the throne of the deity in his heart, onto which he brings the deity in his imagination through the central channel of his body from the crown of the head to seat him or her on the throne. The god is then worshipped in the heart before the performance of external worship. Dominic Goodall coined the term 'tantric prayer' to designate this kind of visual prayer that developed in Hindu traditions from about the eighth century in both north and south of the subcontinent, but arguably 'visual contemplation' is perhaps a better rendering of *dhyāna*, as the mode of address entailed by prayer in a tantric context is lost in the sense that the visualization is a 'prayer' to oneself. This visual contemplation involves visualizing a deity on a throne or seated on a lotus in the heart along with a retinue of minor deities. Although the deities differ depending upon tradition and texts, the process of internalization is shared among Śaivas, Śāktas, and Vaiṣṇavas, along with Buddhist and Jain traditions.

During the mental or inner sacrifice the practitioner constructs a visualized throne in his heart with legs in the form of lions or theriomorphic beings as supports. A lotus emerges out from the throne upon which the central deity is installed. While there are some variations in the details, what is striking about the throne image is that it remains consistent across different tantric traditions, regardless of theology. It is as if there is a ritual level of engagement operating with only weak reference to a tradition's metaphysics although the vertical visual structure of the throne is identified with different levels of the Śaiva or Pāñcarātra cosmos. There is a shared cosmological ritual that seems to function independently of a tradition's ontological or metaphysical commitments about identity and the nature of transcendence. We are here dealing with a pre-philosophical, shared level of spiritual practice that is differently instantiated according to text and tradition. Let us present four examples from the Śaiva Siddhānta, non-Saiddhānta Śaivism, and the Pāñcarātra. Our

[59] *Sarvajñānottara* 5.2: *alaṅkṛtya svakaṃ dehaṃ śivamantrair yathākramam / śivībhūtaḥ supūtātmā śivasyārcanam ārabhet*

examples move from mainstream, orthodox Śaivism to more esoteric interpretations of the tradition, to non-Śaiva religions.

The first example is the visualization of Śiva in the dualistic Śaiva Siddhānta tradition that originated in Kashmir and flourished in the South with an added dimension of Tamil devotionalism. The central deity of the Śaiva Siddhānta is the five-headed Sadāśiva, although in practical terms he is usually worshipped in the form of the *liṅga*, at first internally as part of the devotee's daily practice and then externally in the image.[60] The sources of these descriptions are from devotional or liturgical hymns (*stotram*), ritual manuals (*paddhatiḥ*), and from descriptions in tantric revealed texts, the Āgamas or Tantras.

TEXTUAL EXAMPLES

Let us take examples from the ritual manuals: the prestigious and most famous manual of Somaśambhu (eleventh century), the abbot of the Śaiva monastery at Golakīmaṭha near Tripurī in Central India, called the *Somaśambhupaddhati*, and the later *Īśānaśivagurudevapaddhati*. Both of these texts are based on the Saiddhāntika revelation that we find in texts such as the *Kāmikāgama*. In the *Somaśambhupaddhati* we find the following description of the throne visualized in the heart:

Reading 11

The injunction concerning the worship of Śiva's throne.

47. Then seated on the stone (in the form of) a tortoise, he should worship the power whose nature is support, the form of the sprout in the seed, whose body is white as the ocean of milk. *Oṃ hāṃ*, homage to the power that supports. 48. Having the appearance of a bud of a lotus rising from the stem, white like the moon and jasmine, mounted on the tortoise stone, he should worship the throne of Śiva, which is Ananta. *Oṃ hāṃ*, homage to the seat of Ananta. *Oṃ hāṃ*, homage to Ananta. 49. (One should worship) the feet of the throne of Śiva having the appearance of wonderful lions, showing their backs to each other, (representing) the ages, Krta, Treta, and so on. 50. One should worship them in due order, (they being) Virtue (*dharmaḥ*), Knowledge (*jñānam*), Detachment (*vairāgyam*), and Majesty (*aiśvaryam*), (and they are) white, red, golden, and black. *Oṃ hāṃ*, homage to Virtue etc. 51. Having worshipped the same lotus Ananta, which is white with eight petals in bloom, he should show the lotus gestures above the faces of the lions. 52. *Oṃ hāṃ*, homage to the lotus. Then one should worship the pericarp containing fifty seeds, the colour of molten gold, (along with) the

[60] For a thorough account of the daily and occasional rituals of the Śaiva Siddhānta see the four volumes by H. Brunner of the *Somaśambhupaddhati*. A good English account is R. Davis, *Ritual in an Oscillating Universe: Worshipping Śiva in Medieval India* (Princeton, NJ: Princeton University Press, 1991).

sixty-four fibres (of the lotus stem). *Oṃ hāṃ*, homage to the pericarp. 53. (Then one should visualize the eight energies as) the colour of the dawn, with three eyes, four arms, a chignon (*jaḍām*) adorned with a crescent moon at the top (? *akuṭakhaṇḍendumaṇḍitā*), and holding a whisk, 54–5, whose hands make the boon giving and fearless gestures, whose (fourth) hand rests upon Śiva. From the eastern direction to the end (the N-E), in due order, at the tips of the stamens where the petals are, he should worship the eight energies and demonstrate the gesture of salutation. (He should worship) the energy Manonmanī, white as cow's milk, in the pericarp. *Oṃ hāṃ*, homage to Vāmā and so on (Jyeṣṭhā, Raudrī, Kālī, Kalavikaraṇī, Balavikaraṇī, Balapramathaṇī, Sarvabhūtadamanī). 56. Having visualized the throne of the god of gods, pervaded by the levels beginning from the earth to Śuddha Vidyā, one should worship it. 57. There on the lion throne (one should install) the god who is without taint like a pure crystal. (He has) five faces, three eyes on each face, (and) ten arms . . .[61]

Here we see the lion throne of the deity with a lotus growing out of it, visualized in the heart, upon which the deity to be worshipped is installed surrounded by a retinue of his energies established on the petals of the lotus. The cosmical hierarchy that comprises various stages and categories, particularly the thirty-six categories or *tattva*s that comprise the cosmos, is mentally identified with this vision. There are many features of this visualization particular to the Śaiva Siddhānta, such as the goddess Manomanī who is visualized below Sadāśiva and the deities of the directions located on the petals of the lotus.

This ritual pattern is echoed in many other texts and the structure of the throne is virtually the same, with cosmological principles identified with the legs of the throne and so on. In worshipping Śiva in the form of the sun,

[61] *Somaśambhupaddhati* vol. 1 III. 47–57: *śivāsanapūjāvidhiḥ: tataḥ kūrmaśilāsīnāṃ kṣīrodasitavigrahām / yayed bījāṅkurākārāṃ śaktimādhārarūpaṇīm //47//oṃ hāṃ ādhāraśaktaye namaḥ / kundendudhavaloddaṇḍapayojamukulākṛtim /yajet kūrmaśilārūḍhaṃ śivasyānantam āsanam // 48//oṃ hāṃ anantāsanāya namaḥ /oṃ hāṃ anantāya namaḥ /vicitrakesariprakhyān anyonyaṃ pṛṣṭhadarśinaḥ /kṛtatretādirūpeṇa śivasyāsanapādukān //49//dharmaṃ jñānaṃ ca vairāgyamaiśvaryaṃ ca yathākramam /karpūrakuṇkumasvarṇakajjalābhāni pūjayet // 50// oṃ hāṃ dharmāya nama ityāgneyyām /oṃ hāṃ jñāāya nama iti nairṛtyām /oṃ hāṃ vairāgya nama iti vāyavyām /oṃ hāṃ aiśvaryāya nama ityaiśānyām /utphullāṣṭadalaṃ śvetaṃ tadevānantapaṅkajam/ saṃpūjya siṃhavaktrordhvaṃ padmamudrāṃ pradarśayet // 51//oṃ hāṃ padmāya namaḥ / taptacāmīkaracchāyāṃ paṇcaśadbījagarbhitām / kesarāṇāṃ catuḥṣaṣṭyā karṇikāṃ pūjaet tataḥ //52// oṃ hāṃ karṇikāyai namaḥ / udyaddinakarābhāsās trinetrāśca caturbhujāḥ / jaḍāmakuṭakhaṇḍitā dhṛtacāsarāḥ //53//varadābhayahastāśca śivāsaktakarāmbujāḥ / pūrvādīśāntapatrasthakesarāgreṣv anukramāt //54//śaktīḥ saṃpūjayedaṣṭau namomudrāṃ radarśayet / gokṣīradhavalāṃ śaktiṃ karṇikāyāṃ manonmanīm //55// oṃ hāṃ vāmāyai namaḥ / oṃ hāṃ jyeṣṭāyai namaḥ / oṃ hāṃ raudryai namaḥ /oṃ hāṃ kālyai namaḥ /oṃ hāṃ kalavikraṇyai namaḥ / oṃ hāṃ balavikraṇyai namaḥ /oṃ hāṃ balapramathanyai namaḥ /oṃ hāṃ sarvabhūtadamanyai namaḥ / oṃ hāṃ namonmanyai namaḥ // kṣityādiśuddhavidyāntatattvavyāpakam āsanam /saṃcintya devadevasya pūjayettadanantaram //56//oṃ hāṃ śivāsanāya namaḥ / vidyādehadhyānam: tatra siṃhāsane devaṃ śuddhasphaṭikanirmalam /pañcāsyaṃ daśadordaṇḍaṃ prativaktraṃ trilocanam //57//*

the *Īśānaśivagurudevapaddhati*, as in Somaśambhu's text, identifies Ananta with the throne and the legs of the throne (*pīṭhapādāḥ*) with the mental dispositions or bhāvas in the higher mind or *buddhi*, namely *dharma*, *jñāna*, *vairāgya*, and *aiśvarya* and their opposites.[62] Again these are represented in animal form. A white lotus rises out of the throne, forming the seat for the deity.[63]

In Aghoraśiva's liturgical hymn the *Pañcāvaraṇa-stava*, the hymn to the five circles of deities edited by Goodall and his colleagues, is a collection of hymns that are visualizations to be practised during the daily ritual (*nityapūjā*) of the initiate. The text ignores external ritual and focuses only on visualizations to be performed as part of the Saiddhāntika's daily routine—in Goodall's phrase, 'instructions for mental worship . . . formulated as expressions of praise'.[64] Each day the practitioner would visualize these deities and recite the text itself as part of the daily rites; the text is a practical liturgical manual of a kind not dissimilar to those of other traditions. The daily practice begins with the visualization of Śiva as the sun, then the guardians of the doorways of the mental place of worship, the visualization of the throne of worship, and then Sadāśiva seated on the throne surrounded by his retinue (*yāgaḥ*) of male deities. Aghoraśiva's text gives all five circuits of deities although later Tantras give fewer.[65] The description of the throne is virtually identical to that of Somaśambhu.

Reading 12

17. I praise the Support Energy (earth goddess), who is like the ocean of milk, a coiled form of a sprout in the seed, the support of all, steadfast in the middle, established on the tortoise stone. 18. I bow down to the white Ananta, the lotus throne of illusion, the Lord of the mantra, established on the stone that is Brahma, (who has) pervaded manifestation. 19. (I bow down to) the feet (which form) the corners (of the throne) beginning with fire, on the throne of the Lord, whose nature is identical to Ananta, and with the form of lions. (They are identified with) Virtue and Knowledge which are white and red, with Detachment and Majesty which are yellow and very black.[66]

[62] These *bhāvas* are cosmological and psychological impulses that we find in the Saṃkhya system existing within the level of *buddhi*. See the *Sāṃkhya-kārikās* 43–6. See G. Larson, *Classical Samkhya: An Interpretation of its History and Meaning* (Delhi: MLBD, 1969), pp. 191–4, 271.

[63] *Īśānaśivagurudevapaddhati* 3.12.24–26. Also 4.56.38.

[64] Dominic Goodall, N. Rout, R. Sathyanarayanan, S.A.S. Sarma, T. Ganesan, and S. Sambandhasivacarya (eds.), *Pañcāvaraṇastava of Aghoraśivācārya: A Twelfth-Century South Indian Prescription for the Visualisation of Sadāśiva and his Retinue* (Pondichéry: Institut Français de Pondichéry, 2005), p. 17.

[65] Goodall, *Pañcāvaraṇastava*, p. 25.

[66] *Pañcāvaraṇastava* 17–18: *ādhāraśaktiṃ kṣīrodavarṇāṃ bījāṅkurākṛtim /sarvādhārāṃ bhaje madhye sthirāṃ kūrmaśilāsthitām //17//prapañcavyāptito brahmaśilāsthaṃ mantranāyakam /māyāpadmāsanaṃ śvetam anantaṃ praṇamāmy aham //18//dharmajñāne śvetarakte*

Two final examples from the Śaiva material, the non-Saiddhāntika text from Kashmir, the *Svacchandabhairava-tantra* and the *Netra* or *Amṛteśvara-tantra*, which describe a similar throne to be visualized during the internal worship.

In the *Svacchanda-tantra* we read:

Reading 13

54. He should worship the god of gods with various foods, flowers, incense and perfumes, prepared only by the mind. 55–6. Having visualized himself as Bhairava, then he should practise the coming into the heart (of the deity). Having fixed the bulb (below) the navel, he should imagine the stalk twelve fingers (from there) to the heart, where he should visualize a very brilliant lotus with eight petals, filaments, and the pericarp. 57. (He should meditate) there on the bulb, which is made of power, in the filament those very worlds of the Rudras which are the ornaments (of the Lord), O best of women. 58. The knot whose nature is illusion is established in the impure path. The very brilliant lotus of knowledge is embellished with seeds in the pericarp. 59–60. And there, O Goddess, the Lords of Knowledge (Vidyeśvaras) are known as the lotuses (= the seeds). Having visualized the pure, great lotus, comprising all the gods in this way, one should first perform the imposition of power, then afterwards on the bulb. One should imagine Ananta as established in the stalk (and) bulb. 61. He is splendid, very pure, and shining as a trembling light. He should (then) fix Virtue, Knowledge, Detachment, and Majesty in due order. (They are) white, red, yellow, and black, established in the directions beginning with the south-east. (These are) the feet whose form is a lion; they have three eyes and a ferocious manner.[67]

The lion feet are also identified with the four Vedas and four Yugas (65ab). This introduces further cosmological elaboration. Here the central deity is Bhairava, a ferocious form of Śiva who is held to be superior in this tradition to Sadāśiva of the Śaiva Siddhānta, identified by the non-dualistic commentators on these texts as the fullness of pure consciousness.

supītaṃ vairāgyaṃ caiśvaryamīḍe 'tikṛṣṇam /siṃhākārānantasāmarthyarūpān śambhoḥ pīṭhe 'gnyādikoṇasthapādān.

[67] *Svacchanda-tantra 2. 54–62. gandhair dhūpais tathā puṣpair vividhair bhakṣyabhojanaiḥ / pūjayed devadeveśaṃ manasaiva prakalpitaiḥ // 2.54 // ātmānaṃ bhairavaṃ dhyātvā tato hṛdyāgamācaret / nābhau kandaṃ samāropya nālaṃ tu dvādaśāṅgulam // 2.55 // hṛdantaṃ kalpayed yāvat tatra padmaṃ vicintayet / aṣṭapatraṃ mahādīptaṃ kesarālaṃ sakaṇīkam // 2.56 // kandaṃ śaktimayaṃ tatra nāle vai kaṇṭakāstu ye / bhuvanāni ca tāny eva rudrāṇāṃ varavarṇini // 2.57 // māyātmako bhaved granthir aśuddhādhvavyavasthitaḥ / vidyāpadmaṃ mahādīptaṃ kaṇīkābījarājitam // 2.58 // puṣkarāṇi ca deveśi tatra vidyeśvarāḥ smṛtāḥ evaṃ dhyātvā mahāpadmaṃ sarvadevamayaṃ śubham // 2.59 //śaktinyāso bhavet pūrvaṃ kandaṃ tu tadanantaram / aṅkuraṃ nālavinyāsamanantaṃ parikalpayet // 2.60 // tejomayaṃ mahāśubhraṃ sphuratkiraṇabhāsvaram / dharmaṃ jñānaṃ ca vairāgyamaiśvaryaṃ ca kramānnyaset // 2.61 // sitaraktapītakṛṣṇā āgneyyādīśadiggatāḥ / pādakāḥ siṃharūpāste trinetrā bhīmavikramāḥ // 2.62 //* Also see 2.161–3.

The *Netra-tantra* contains a number of visualizations of different forms of Śiva and these, in a similar way, involve the deity seated on a lotus in the heart and on the lion throne. Here we have the visualization of Bhairava:

Reading 14

10.1–6. So now I will speak about the division of the Bhairava revelation (the southern path). (Bhairava) has five faces, having the appearance of a mass of black collyrium, whose nature is the destructive fire at the end of an era, mounted on a corpse [i.e. Sadāśiva], with ten arms, fearful, appearing with a retinue with black faces, roaring a terrifying noise, whose mouth is gaping with fangs, frowning with crooked eyes, mounted on the lion throne, decorated with a snake garland, adorned with a garland of skulls, holding a sword and shield, the god holding the noose and goad, whose hands make the boon giving and fear not gestures, who holds a thunderbolt/lightning symbol, the great hero, who holds an axe weapon. Having worshipped Bhairava one should visualize (the goddess) sitting on his hip.[68]

In general terms the structure of the throne or the throne as a lotus is shared in these different traditions. We should also note that in the internal visualization of the Trika, the goddesses of that tradition are visualized on the prongs of a trident that pervades the body upon which the different levels of the Śaiva cosmos are mapped. Sanderson has shown how the different levels of identity of the practitioner are related to this hierarchical visualization, from adherence to Brahmanical social norms to adherence to orthodox Śaiva Siddhānta practice, to transcendence of that identity in the worship of the goddesses mounted upon the blazing corpse of the Śaiva Siddhānta deity, Sadāśiva. Sanderson has given a full account of this vision and its meaning in the Trika system.[69]

My last and best example of the lion throne from a non-Śaiva source—the *Jayākhya-saṃhitā* of the Pāñcarātra or tantric Vaiṣṇava tradition—among other things, deals with the identification of the practitioner with the universe and clearly outlines the four ritual stages I mentioned earlier. Here the macrocosm is contained in the microcosm in this classic text. After the purification of the body and the divinization of the body we have the mental worship in which a throne is constructed in the imagination in the heart and the god Nārāyaṇa, a form of Viṣṇu, brought down into it from the crown of the head and worshipped there. The visual prayer reads as follows:

[68] *Netra-tantra* 10.1-6: *athedānīṃ pravakṣyāmi bhairavāgamabheditam / bhināñjanacaya-prakhyaṃ kalpāntadahanātmakam //1// pañcavaktraṃ śavārūḍhaṃ daśabāhuṃ bhayānakam / kṣapāmukhagaṇaprakhyaṃ garjantaṃ bhīṣaṇasvanam //2// daṃṣṭrākarālavadanaṃ bhru-kuṭīkuṭilekṣaṇam / siṃhāsanapadārūḍhaṃ vyālahārai virbhūṣitam //3// kapālamālābharaṇaṃ dāritāsyaṃ mahātanum / gajatvakprāvṛtapaṭaṃ śaśāṅkakṛtaśekharam //4// kapālakhaṭvāṅga-dharaṃ khaḍgakheṭakadhāriṇam / pāśāṅku śadharaṃ devaṃ varadābhayapāṇikam //5// vajra-hastaṃ mahāvīraṃ paraśvāyudhapāṇikam / bhairavaṃ pūjayitvā tu tasyotsaṅgagatāṃ smaret //6//*

[69] Alexis Sanderson, 'Maṇḍala and Āgamic Identity in the Trika of Kashmir', pp. 178–81.

Reading 15

1. So having formerly become Viṣṇu, the practitioner should then worship Viṣṇu with the mental sacrifice. 2–3b. Imagining (the area) between the genitals and the navel filled with four parts, he should visualize the energy whose form is the earth (*ādhārarūpinīm*), above that the fire of time (*kālāgniḥ*), above that Ananta, and then the Earth Goddess (*vasudhā devī*). 3c–5b. From the bulb [of the lotus] to the navel is divided into four parts. Visualizing the ocean of milk in the navel and then a lotus arising (out of it), extending as far as a thousand petals and whirling with a thousand beams, having the appearance of a thousand rays, he should fix the throne on its back. 5c–7. The fourfold (disposition) Virtue, Knowledge, Detachment, and Majesty descend by means of their own mantras to the four (directions) of fire (the south-east) and so on, fixing those four up to the abode (*gocaram*) of the Lord Īśāna (the north-east). As for the four feet of the throne, they are white with lion faces, but the forms of men in their bodies endowed with exceeding strength. 8–9b. The parts from the eastern direction up to the northern abode are fixed with the opposites of Virtue, Knowledge, Detachment, and Majesty. These have human form, blazing like the red midday flower (*bandhukah, Pentapetes Phoenicea*). 9c–10. The four (scriptures), the *Ṛg-veda* and so on have the form of a horse-man, are yellow and (situated) in between the east and the direction of the Lord (north-east), between the east and the direction of Fire (south-east), between the south-west and Varuṇa (west), and between the wind (north-west) and Varuṇa (west). 11–12b. The group of world-ages, namely Kṛta and so on, have the form of a bull-man, are black, and located in the directions between the Lord (north-east) and Soma (north), between Antaka (Yama = south) and the Demon (Yakṣana = south-west), and the Moon (north) and the Wind (north-west). 12c–13b. They each have four arms: with two they support the throne and with two they make obeisance to the Lord of the Universe. 13c–15b. Above them he should firstly fix a white lotus (and then) the threefold (form, namely sun, moon, and fire), way above with those mantras, arising from himself and previously articulated, O Nārada. On the back of that he should establish both the King of Birds and the Boar. Having imagined (the area) from the navel to the heart (divided) by five equal sections he should worship the presence of mantra-throne.[70]

[70] *Jayākhya-saṃhitā* 12.1–15. *evaṃ viṣṇumayo bhūtvā svātmanā sādhakaḥ purā mānasena tu yāgena tato viṣṇuṃ samarcayet // 12.1// nābhimeḍhrāntare dhyāyec chaktiṃ cādhārarūpiṇīm kālāgniṃ ca tadūrdhve tu anantaṃ tasya copari // 12.2 // tadūrdhve vasudhāṃ devīṃ caturbhiḥ pūritāṃ smaran kandān nābhyavasānāc ca caturdhā bhājitaiḥ padaiḥ // 12.3 // nābhau kṣīrārṇavaṃ dhyātvā tataḥ padmaṃ samutthitaṃ sahasradalaparyantaṃ sahasrakiraṇāvṛtam // 12.4 // sahasraraśmisaṅkāśaṃ tatpṛṣṭhe cāsanaṃ nyaset dharmaṃ jñānaṃ ca vairāgyam aiśvaryaṃ ca caturthakam // 12.5 // avatārya svamantreṇa āgneyādicatuṣṭaye catuṣkam etad vinyasya yāvadīśānagocaram // 12.6 // pīṭhapādacatuṣke tu sitās simhānanā amīśarīrāt puruṣākārāḥ parotsāhasamanvitāḥ // 12.7 // tatpūrvadigvibhāgādi yāvaduttaragocaram nyasyādharmaṃ tathā 'jñānam avairāgyam anaiśvaram // 12.8 // puruṣākṛtayas tv ete bandhūkakusumojvalāḥ prāgīśānadigante tu prāgāgneyadigantare // 12.9 //yātuvāruṇamadhye tu vāyavyavaruṇāntare ṛgvedādyaṃ catuṣkaṃ tu pītaṃ hayanarākṛtim // 12.10 // īśānasomadigmadhye antakāgnidigantare yāmyarākṣasamadhye tu saumyasāmīraṇāntare // 12.11 // kṛtādyaṃ yugasaṅghaṃ ca*

I shall not dwell on the details here but simply point out that this is a visually complex description in which the practitioner imagines a hierarchy of deities in his body, with a lotus growing up from the navel to the heart and a throne being established upon it whose feet are made up of theriomorphic aspects of the cosmic emanation, namely the constituents of the cosmic intellect (*buddhiḥ*), the scriptures, and the world ages. The text goes on to describe the bringing down of Nārāyaṇa through the central channel from above the crown of the head (the *dvādaśāntaḥ*) and establishing him on the throne where he can be worshipped purely in the imagination. Yet although the Lord is brought into the heart in imagination, in reality the Lord dwells in the inner self of all beings (*sa vasty antarātmasu*).[71]

After this internal worship the deities are worshipped externally in the world in an image and what was done internally, the praise and offering of flowers and incense, done externally.

INWARDNESS WITHOUT RITUAL

These examples are sufficient to establish that we are in a shared world of visual contemplation practice in which the truth within is realized through the imagination. Different metaphysical systems are overlaid on top of this shared ritual and cosmological structure. Furthermore, this elaborate visual field is constructed internally within the practitioner in a heightened intensification of imagination. Inwardness is understood in explicitly visual terms and we have a stress on subjectivity, but a subjectivity that conforms to the norms of text and tradition. The subjectivity of these tantric practitioners is meant to restrict individuality in favour of a shared subjectivity. The narrative of the tradition, namely the cosmological world view of cosmic emanation, that lower levels emanate from and are coagulations of higher, is recapitulated within the person: the macrocosmic world is internalized in the microcosm of the self.

Alexis Sanderson has shown how these textual traditions borrowed from each other, although mostly the non-Śaiva texts imitated the Śaiva,[72] and although the question of historical influence remains important, my examples

kṛṣṇaṃ vṛṣanarākṛtim sarve caturbhujās tv ete dvābhyāṃ sandhārayanti ca // 12.12 // pīṭham añjalinā dvābhyāṃ praṇamanti jagatprabhum eṣām upari vinyasya sitapadmāditas trayam // 12.13 // prāguktais svoditair mantrair upary upari nārada tatpṛṣṭhe pakṣirājaṃ ca varāhaṃ tūbhayaṃ nyaset // 12.14 // ānābhi hṛdayāntaṃ ca pañcadhā susamaiḥ padaiḥ vikalpya bhāvayed vyāptim asya mantrāsanasya ca // 12.15 //

[71] *Jayākhya-saṃhitā* 12.117.

[72] Alexis Sanderson, 'History Through Textual Criticism in the Study of Śaivism, the Pañcarātra and the Buddhist Yoginītantras', in François Grimal (ed.), *Les Sources et le temps. Sources and Time: A Colloquium, Pondicherry, 11–13 January 1997*, Publications du département

raise interesting questions about the relation between practice and theology. For here we have practice that is already highly elaborated and theorized in the mapping of the cosmos onto the throne structure and onto the body, and which undergoes a further theorization by the philosophers or theologians of the tradition. Indeed one of the central concerns of the Kashmiri exegetes was establishing a non-dualist interpretation of sacred revelation against the dualist exegetes of the Śaiva Siddhānta, which entailed incorporating all other systems within the system of the non-dualist traditions. Thus Kṣemarāja writes commentaries on both the *Svacchanda-* and *Netra-* Tantras, claiming them for his monistic idealist vision.

Alongside predominantly ritual texts we have seen, albeit with a stress on interior ritual, we have purely meditational or contemplative and devotional texts that developed during this period for the purpose of personal, devotional practice. One of these that Kṣemarāja writes a commentary on is the *Vijñānabhairava-tantra*. This is a text of the Trika tradition that contains various meditational practices that go beyond the usual ritual structures of focusing on mantra, deity, and sacred diagram. The focus of the text is pure interiority understood as absolute consciousness (*pūrṇāhantā*) located within the self.[73] The truth within is the truth of this pure, absolute consciousness. True ritual (*pūjā*) is not making offerings of flowers and so on but dissolution of the self in the 'great sky' (*mahāvyoman*) of consciousness beyond thought-construction (*nirvikalpaḥ*)[74] and this is the truth within the self. This realization is the cognition that the subject and object of knowledge are in essence the same.[75] The focus is on the body and its esoteric interiority, which is understood to have a subtle structure through which the subtle energy (*prāṇaḥ*) of the divine flows. The habitual pattern of the mind is to move out into the world through the senses, through the 'nine doors' or apertures of the body. By controlling this outwardly directed attention and bringing concentration within the self, the practitioner is able to rise up through the levels of the cosmos, mapped onto the body, to achieve liberation conceptualized as union with Bhairava. This is realization that the true nature of the self is one with absolute consciousness personified in its fullness as Bhairava: the essence of one's own self (*svātmā*), the inner truth, is simply autonomy, bliss, and consciousness (*svatantrānandacinmātrasāraḥ*).[76] In the end there is no need of external

d'Indologie 91. (Pondichéry: Institut Français de Pondichéry/École Française d'Extrême-Orient, 2001), pp. 1–47.

[73] As Lilian Silburn says, 'Le Vijñānabhairava est entièrement axé sur l'expérience de l'intériorité, une intériorité absolue de la conscience (*pūrṇāhantā*)' in *Le Vijñānabhairava: Texte traduit et commenté* (Paris: de Boccard, 1961), p. 10.

[74] *Vijñānabhairava* 147.

[75] *Vijñānabhairava* 137cd: *ekam ekasvabhāvatvāt jñānaṃ jñeyaṃ vibhāvyate*. 'Knowledge and object of knowledge appear as one due to their one essence.'

[76] *Vijñānabhairava* 152.

ritual, for all that is needed is the recognition of one's innate essence as absolute consciousness realized in the interiority of meditation. And even this inner practice needs finally to go beyond all visualization: 'meditation is the mind which is unswerving, without image or support. Meditation is not a mental image of (god with) body, eyes, mouth, and hands etc.'[77] The fruits of this practice are liberation and complete detachment in which one's attitude to friend and foe is the same (*samaḥ*)[78] and where there is no distinction between the pure and the impure. Indeed, if there is only consciousness then wherever the mind goes there is the ultimate condition of Śiva.[79]

There are ethical considerations here implied by these practices that we will need to discuss. (If there is only one reality, what are the grounds for morality? See Chapter 6.) But for now let us take a passage to see the kind of inwardness entailed by this (external) ritual transcending tradition.

Reading 16

34. Having placed the mind within the skull, with eyes closed, gradually fixing the mind, he may perceive the highest object of perception. 35. The middle channel is situated in the middle (of the body), whose form is like the stem of a lotus. One should visualize it as the Goddess, which is (also) inner space, (then) God is revealed. 36. By means of the weapon through which perception is blocked, by the hands, the drop (*binduḥ*) is perceived due to this stopping of the doors (of the senses) and the piercing of the (knot between) the eyebrows. (The drop) gradually disappears (and) in the middle of that (sky of consciousness, the practitioner) is established in the supreme. 37. (The practitioner sees) a form like a red mark (*tilakam*) as a subtle fire, arisen trembling within the place (of the inner eye). Meditating on this drop in the heart and at the crown of the head in its dissolution, (he himself goes to) dissolution. 38. One who is immersed in the absolute sound, the unstruck, uninterrupted sound in the receptacle of the (inner) ear running (like) a river, goes to the supreme absolute.[80]

At first reading this passage is somewhat obscure. Here we have an inner practice in which the practitioner concentrates within his own cranium, with eyes shut, on the 'highest object of perception' (*lakṣyam uttamam*). This is the absolute, whose sign within the practitioner is a point of light (*binduḥ*), which

[77] *Vijñānabhairava* 146cd: *dhyānaṃ hi niścalā buddhir nirākārā nirāśrayā / na tu dhyānaṃ śarīrākṣimukhahastādikalpanā //*

[78] *Vijñānabhairava* 125–6.

[79] *Vijñānabhairava* 115: *yatra yatra mano yāti bāhye vābhyantare 'pi vā / tatra tatra śivāvasthā vyāpakatvāt kva yāsyati*. 'Wherever the mind goes, inside or outside, there is the condition of Śiva. Due to its all-pervasiveness where can (the mind) go?'

[80] *Vijñānabhairava* 34–8: *kapālāntarmano nyasya tiṣṭhan mīlitalocanaḥ / krameṇa manaso dārḍhyāt lakṣayet lakṣyam uttamam //34// madhyanāḍī madhyasaṃsthā bisasūtrābharūpayā / dhyātāntarvyomayā devyā tayā devaḥ prakāśate //35// kararuddhadṛgastreṇa bhrūbhedād dvārarodhanāt / dṛṣṭe bindau kramāt līne tanmadhye paramā sthitiḥ //36// dhāmāntaḥ kṣobhasambhūtasūkṣmāgnitilakākṛtim / binduṃ śikānte layānte dhyāyato layaḥ // 37 // anāhate pātrakarṇe' bhagnaśabde sariddrute / śabdabrahmaṇi niṣṇātaḥ param brahmādhigacchati //38//*

Kṣemarāja glosses as a meditative support (*ālambanam*), that is one's own luminous light.[81] This inner light perceived in the mind's eye is like a red mark or ornament on the forehead (*tilakam*). The inner light is accompanied by the inner sound of the absolute (*śabdabrahma*) that resounds as if uncaused or unstruck (*anāhataḥ*) and flows like a river to the supreme. This is not perceived, Kṣemarāja reminds us, by the receptacle of the ear as such, but is an inner attainment or hearing (*antarupalabhye*), where one perceives the inner sound flowing swiftly. This inner perception is achieved by physically blocking off the senses of hearing and seeing, the eyes and the ears, with the hands. Kṣemarāja tells us that the instruments (the 'weapon') here are the thumb and forefinger which serve to temporarily shut off outer perception for the duration of the practice.[82] The idea of inner sound is well attested throughout the medieval texts. Abhinavagupta refers to the doctrine as a subtle resonance within all living beings,[83] whose extensional analogue is the drop (*binduḥ*) or point of light perceived in inner meditation.

The passage above can be read in terms of a progression in inner practice. The practitioner meditates, focusing attention inside the cranium. This is assisted by the practice of blocking the outer senses—eyes and ears—with the hands in order to eradicate external sound and to perceive the inner light and sound. The meditator experiences a central channel in the body through which the energy of the Lord moves. He sees the inner light or drop, which is understood as piercing or breaking the 'knot' (*granthiḥ*) between the eyebrows.[84] He then perceives and comes to be absorbed in the sky of consciousness (*saṃvidgaganam*), which is to be established in the supreme, and which is also for Bhairava to become manifested.[85] Kṣemarāja glosses 'the middle channel' as the *susumnā*, a term used in yoga for an esoteric channel that they believed ran through the centre of the body and was used for visualization

[81] *Vijñānabhairava-vivṛti*, p. 29: . . . *svaprakāśe prabhāvare jyotiṣi ālambane* . . .

[82] This practice of listening to an inner sound that is the sound of the absolute is common in the Indian yogic traditions, developed in later yogic Upaniṣads such as the *Nādabindu-upaniṣad*, and in haṭha yoga texts such as *Haṭhayogapradipika*. The practice comes down to the present in traditions such as the *Radhasoami*. See Huzur Maharaj and Sawan Singh, *Philosophy of the Masters* series 1, English trans. (Punjab, India: Radha Soami Satsang Beas, 1963), pp. 94–9.

[83] *Tantrāloka* 3.113cd: *yo'sau nādātmakaḥ śabdaḥ sarvaprāṇiṣvavasthitaḥ*. 'This sound, whose nature is resonance, is established in all living beings.'

[84] *Vijñanbhairava-vivṛti*, p. 31: *bhrumadhyagranthividāraṇāt*.

[85] *Vijñanbhairava-vivṛti*, p. 31: *aṅguṣṭhatarjanyādikrameṇa karābhyāṃ ruddhāni dṛgupalakṣitāni mukharandhrāṇi yena tādṛśasya yogino'steṇa bhrūmadhyasthagranthividāraṇāt hetorbindau dṛṣte kramādekāgratāprakarṣāt līne saṃvidgagane eva madhye'sya yoginaḥ pramā sthitiḥ bhairavābhivyaktiḥ syatityarthaḥ*. 'The meaning (of the verse) is that the supreme abode of the yogin is the manifestation of Bhairava in the 'middle' (channel) which is being dissolved in that very sky of consciousness. (This is) seen due to the gradual pull of one-pointed concentration. The two drops (?) are the causes of the breaking of the knot between the eyebrows. With the weapon of the yogi, the perception (through) the apertures in the face are blocked by the two hands with the thumbs and forefinger in due order.'

purposes. This channel is a conduit through which the divine energies move, the most important of which is the goddess Kuṇḍalinī who, once awakened by meditation practice, moves up through the body to unite with Śiva at or above the crown of the head in the 'twelve finger point' (*dvādaśāntaḥ*), i.e. the point twelve fingers' length above the eye centre or twelve fingers' length above the crown of the head.[86] This symbolic journey is reflected here in our verse, the implication being that the perception of the inner light is the result of the awakening of power within the body. On this verse Kṣemarāja comments:

Reading 17

The 'middle channel' is called *suṣumnā*, 'situated in the middle' means it is situated in the middle of the heart. Due to its subtlety its form is like the thread of a lotus shoot, 'meditated' (means) visualized (*cintitam*) and 'inner sky' (means) whose nature is the space of consciousness. (The experience of the central channel) is to be attained. Thus 'by the goddess' (means) by the method (of her arising within the body) and 'god' (means) the light becomes manifest. It is empty in the middle channel, whose nature is the space of consciousness (and) the energy of breath, whose nature is consciousness, pours out as reflexive consciousness from that . . .[87]

Kṣemarāja interprets the passage in the light of his metaphysics, using the terminology of non-dual Śaivism that the god is really the light of consciousness (*prakāśaḥ*) and the goddess in the breath is reflexive consciousness (*vimarśaḥ*). Through visualizing this power arising within the body, the practitioner then focuses on the inner light, which itself is dissolved into the pure sky of consciousness and his identity as the absolute reality is realized within his meditation.

RITUAL THINKING AND THE PERSON

Having established the shared ritual substrate of tantric visual contemplation in our texts, I wish to move to a higher level of abstraction and away from this textual description in order to re-approach it from a different angle. I wish to

[86] Kuṇḍalinī is a particularly important practice in later haṭha yoga associated with practices such as inserting the tongue into the nasal cavity to prevent the flow of the nectar of immortality escaping. See James Mallinson, *The Khecarīvidyā of Ādinātha: A Critical Edition and Annotated Translation of an Early Text of Haṭhayoga* (London: Routledge, 2007), pp. 132–4. On the rising of breath in haṭha yoga see Jason Birch, 'The Meaning of Haṭha in Early Haṭhayoga', *Journal of the American Oriental Society*, 131/4 (2011), pp. 527–54.

[87] *Vijñānabhairava-vivṛti* p. 30: *madhyanāḍī susumnākhyā, madhyasaṃsthā hṛdayamadhyasthā bhavatīty anvayaḥ sūkṣmatvāt mṛñālasūtratulyarūpayā dhyātaṃ cintitamantarvyoacidākāśātmajaṃ yasyāṃ sā, tathāvidhayā devyā devaḥ prajāśaḥ prakāśate, madhyanāḍyāmantaścidākāśtmakaṃ śūnyamevāsti, tasnāt prāṇaśaktirniḥsarati iti vimarśena prakāśaprādurbhāvaḥ . . .*

make three observations about visual contemplation and inwardness. Firstly I wish to suggest a thesis that imagination is a guide to understanding these texts, secondly that these texts present us with ritual thinking and point to a layer of culture that is below a clearly articulated philosophical discourse and yet structurally higher or more complex than daily transaction—a cultural level which entails the eradication of individuality and a shared or collective subjectivity—and thirdly that they point more broadly to what might be called an ontology of process, a process of subjectivization and textualization.

Imagination as a Guide

A number of verbs used in the texts might be translated by 'meditate', 'visualize', or 'contemplate', verbs that in English perhaps imply a more somatic engagement with a mental process than merely verbs such as 'reflect' or 'consider' or 'think'. The texts use gerund forms, *dhyātvā*, *cintayitvā*, *śrutvā*, and the third person optative, *dhyāyet*, *cintayet*, and *smaret*. We even have *vikalpya*, 'having imagined', and *vikalpayet*, 'one should imagine'. These terms are used synonymously. But what is the force of 'imagine' here? Clearly these terms do not indicate something considered as unreal. These texts are committed to a realist position with regard to practice in the sense that practice is a serious matter that leads to liberation from suffering. Kṣemarāja, in his commentary on the *Netra* and *Svacchanda* Tantras, is clearly intellectually committed to the serious nature of these practices, and that the texts have been preserved through repeated copying over many generations bears witness to their high regard. Imagination here does not mean a mental process that takes us away from reality but rather the opposite, a mental process that intensifies the real and a practice—the practice of the imaginal—that opens up a world for the practitioner that is, indeed, more real than the world of daily transaction. We have then the subject of these practices, the subject of the verbs, and the object, namely the visualized throne and the deities installed upon it transposed upon the body, so in a sense the subject of practice is also the object of practice.

The use of liturgical hymns, as in our example above, and visualization more generally is not restricted to the tantric traditions but is also found in bhakti, and Frank Clooney has described such visualization in the practice of 'exteriorising the form' of God (*uluveḷippāṭa*) found in the *Tiruvāymoli* and its commentaries.[88] So we are probably looking at fairly widespread spiritual exercises that are not simply restricted to the tantric genre.

[88] F. Clooney, *Seeing Through Texts: Doing Theology Among the Śrīvaiṣṇavas of South India* (Albany, NY: SUNY Press, 1996), pp. 138–41.

The visualization of the throne is still, in one sense, an outer practice compared to the deeper interiority of the *Vijñānabhairava* where the text speaks of meditation on the 'drop' (*binduḥ*), which dissolves into the light that is emptiness. Questions then arise concerning the relation not only of the subject to the object of contemplation, but of the object of contemplation, the visualized image, to the presence of which it is a sign.

To clarify these issues we might turn to hermeneutical phenomenology, which is useful in helping us understand these texts through giving us an account of imagination. In phenomenology from Husserl we have the fundamental distinction between the process of knowing, the *noesis*, and the object of knowledge, the *noema*. The question of the being of the *noema* is suspended through bracketing, through the *epoché* (see 'Description', pp. 258–9). Now in our texts the visualized object, the *noema*, points to different referents in the different traditions we have looked at. Thus for the Śaiva Siddhānta, Sadāśiva who is established on the throne is the transcendent Lord as goal of practice, ontologically distinct from devotees, while for the *Netra* and *Svacchanda* Tantras it is Bhairava on the throne, above the corpse of Sadāśiva, and there is an ambivalence about the self–deity relationship that is exploited, if you will, by Kṣemarāja in his non-dualistic commentaries on those texts. To frame the question in a Paul Ricoeurian way, to what extent is the image as the product of imagination a trace of *presence* or an indicator of *absence*?

Of course, there is no answer to that question, but it is nevertheless important to ask it, as the question does bring into relief the processes or procedures at work here and sets these practices within a broader context of religious intention and the nature of religious interiority or subjectivity. Paul Ricoeur is helpful in clarifying the issues for us. He observes that imagination, as Kant highlighted, is 'a rule-governed form of invention . . . or a norm-governed productivity', and secondly it is 'the power of giving form to human experience' or 'the power of redescribing reality'.[89] Certainly our verbs *dhyāyet*, *cintayet* and so on represent the power of redescribing reality, but a redescription at a higher level, reconstituted within subjectivity. But this subjectivity is not individualism or the romantic understanding of the subject, but is rather constituted by tradition as a shared or collective subjectivity. We see here image, the icon of the deity, turned into a kind of metaphor.

This process of visualization followed by the outer ritual, the *bahyayāga*, is suggestive of the way these traditions understand the world and its relation to a spiritual practice. Through practice the world comes to be seen in its true light, as the place the practitioner wants to escape to, but also the place that allows transformation to occur.

[89] Paul Ricoeur, 'The Bible and the Imagination', in *Figuring the Sacred: Religion, Narrative and Imagination* (Mineapolis, MN: Fortress Press, 1995), p. 144.

Shared Subjectivity

While these texts are deeply concerned with inwardness, with inner practices, they cannot be described as being concerned with the individual. Indeed, individualism, which in modernity we associate with inwardness and subjectivity, is eradicated in these traditions. These texts bear witness not to the development of individualism—as Dumont thought of renunciation—but rather point to a shared or collective subjectivity.[90] This is the heart of tradition. We have the intensification of inwardness at a deep cultural level that entails the development of subjective experience which is not individual, and which furthermore gives access to the world through a complex process of imagination. While a political reading of this material—that these traditions were vying for patronage and that is one of the main reasons why they would mimic each other—is clearly apposite, there is also a non-political reading that points to a process concerned with the practitioners undergoing change and accessing what the traditions regard as a higher good, beyond mere worldly success. The practitioner identifies with the deities of the tradition and his own sense of self is overwhelmed by the other, by the implied self of tradition. While these traditions claim to be transformative—their stated goal is liberation and power—they are also conservative in their expectation that practitioners conform. The structure through which this occurs is the internalization of the symbolic system, or what we might call the entextualization of the body.[91] The subjectivity that is experienced is collective, a shared imagination constrained by the texts and practices.

Put simply, these texts demonstrate an intensification of subjectivity that, although practised by a particular person, is not individual. The practitioner's identity is subsumed within the narrative of the tradition and the body is inscribed by the text and subjective experience aligned with the expectations of tradition. The tantric practitioner lives within the canopy of the tradition, within the *maṇḍala* of his practice.

This move from constructing a reality within the human mind to constructing an external reality in the external ritual parallels the formation of the world itself in the cosmologies of these religions: as an emanation of Śiva's consciousness for the non-dualists, of Nārāyaṇa for the Pāñcarātra, an emanation of matter itself from an unmanifest state for the dualists, or the appearance of emptiness for the Buddhists. There is a move from consciousness to world,

[90] This would seem to be borne out ethnographically too. See Hausner, *Wandering with Sadhus*, p. 47, on sadhus as set apart yet connected with each other. Hausner writes: 'To understand contemporary renouncers' lives, I argue, we need to see them as members of a community (which Dumont significantly underplayed) and at the same time, we need to understand how that community is premised upon a collective split from householder social life (which Dumont cogently argued)', p. 52.

[91] See Flood, *The Tantric Body*, pp. 3–30.

with the important proviso that the world is not something other than the reality formed in meditation. The forms of the world give themselves to the practitioner in communion with the mind; the external rite reflects the internal rite at a lower level. So these practices are not only in the mind but form part of the structure of the world, and through their practice the adept participates in the higher reality to which he aspires. Indeed, theologically we might see visual contemplation as the self giving of the deity in worldly form and a manifestation of a kind of divine self-opening, something that clearly has parallels in Christianity.

The Social Imaginary

These examples from what are, from one perspective, obscure texts tell us something important about religion and about human subjects, namely that these are cultural forms that mediate the human encounter with mystery, which is to give access to a human reality. Far from being escapist fantasies, we might see these practices as intensifying imagination and, through that, opening out a world that is regarded as real even though imaginal. That is, as poetry or metaphor allow humans to inhabit a social imaginary, a real, although imagined, world, so these visualization texts and practices allow their communities to inhabit real, although imagined, worlds. These texts have existential import as well as being indicators of the political positions of social actors in medieval Kashmir or Nepal. The texts provide formal indications of processes at the heart of being religiously human, and of particular importance is the fact that they are pre-philosophical and exemplify what we might call ritual thinking—a mode of thinking articulated in text that reflects practices in the world and in turn prescribes practices and experience.

Clooney has used the phrase 'thinking ritually' to indicate the centrality of thinking, along with somatic practices and reflection on those practices, as one of the central concerns of what we might call theological reflection. This is a layer of culture that is specific and yet shared across a very broad spectrum of social agents. If, following Rappaport, we take ritual to be 'the performance of more or less invariant sequences of formal acts and utterances not entirely encoded by the performers',[92] the sequence of formal acts in our texts entails imaginative or mental acts with a high degree of complexity developed within the mind, within a person's interiority and yet which are not individualistic in the sense that the practitioner through this mental prayer takes on the attributes of tradition. This pre-reflexive, pre-philosophical layer of tradition, structurally higher than the worldly habitus, is a level of process that is shared

[92] Roy A. Rappaport, *Ecology, Meaning and Religion* (Berkeley, CA: North Atlantic Books, 1979), p. 207.

across traditions, and we might even speak of an ontology of process that is fundamental to the human temporal condition and can be identified within religious cultures through a comparative process.

These visualization practices are deeply conservative in reinforcing the religious structures of tradition. They offer no social critique. Even the secret practices of some tantric traditions that break Brahmanical prohibition rules depend on the existence of Brahmanical norms for their effect. Indeed, after the ritual procedure, after the annual erotic ritual, the Brahman householder goes back to his daily routine of conformity to the wider vedic values of his community.

Yet to see these practices purely in terms of hegemony or internalized ideology is to miss something of fundamental importance about tantric prayer. Such prayer clearly serves to reinforce cultural bonds and social structures, yet also offers a model of community that is shared for those who stand within it, who have the necessary qualification or *adhikāra*. Visual contemplation is not democratic or even particularly egalitarian, yet it does make claims about the world and aspires to the perfection of the human condition. There is no social utopia here but there is a vision of a perfected world through its divinization, a social imaginary in which devotees share a subjectivity that participates in divinity.

CONCLUSION

During the medieval period (post-Gupta) tantric traditions developed throughout the subcontinent. Tantric practices of visual contemplation are shared by different traditions and are expressed in genres of literature—the Tantras, or primary revelation itself, and secondary texts such as ritual manuals based on that textual revelation. This pre-philosophical literature articulates an idea of inwardness in which the cosmos as a hierarchy of levels is mapped onto the vertical structure of the human body. There are varying models and terminologies in the different traditions but the paradigm is the same. The truth within is located through these visualization and ritual practices and we can see this across a range of texts.

Lastly, then, these texts make methodological claims on us in that they entail a kind of phenomenology of the religious life. If we characterize phenomenology along Heideggerian lines as letting be seen that which shows itself, as showing what was hidden, then this is a first level of encounter. This encounter entails a formal indication of the life of the practitioner represented by the text that we can recognize because of our shared bodily being. As we are dealing with history and text in the first instance, this material must be dealt with through the methods of historical and textual analysis. That is, we need philology in the establishing of texts and their intertextuality and historical inquiry to set them in their social and political setting. But these texts are not simply of historical interest, but of philosophical, or more strongly, existential importance. The first-level mapping of what shows itself through philology and historical analysis, our first-level phenomenology, gives way to a deeper engagement, a second-level phenomenology that confronts us with questions of human truth and the power of imagination. This material points to the importance of religion as giving access to the world, or what we might even call the real, and to a realm of material causation that is implicitly understood by these traditions.

Through seeking the truth within by developing this social imaginary, the community of practitioners infuses life with meaning at an almost pre-discursive, cultural level. I say almost because already we have a strong overcoding of a basic imaginal structure with heavily interpreted cosmological categories. Below the intellectualized, discursive level of the commentaries, we have a layer of human practice that functions within the imaginal, which offers an intensification of experience that transcends the boundaries of inner and outer, and in which subjectivity is overwhelmed by a collective subjectivity, a shared world that is cosmic and ultimately real for those practitioners who stand within it. On top of this pre-philosophical cultural layer we have philosophy and theology, the interpretations of the philosopher-theologians of the different schools who claimed these practices as their own. Kṣemarāja writes a commentary on the *Svacchanda-* and *Netra-* Tantras, filling them with his non-dual interpretation and thereby rescuing the text from a dualistic, Saiddhāntika reading, and it is to examples of this philosophical articulation of shared subjectivity to which we must now turn.

5

A Hindu Philosophy of Inwardness

Within the broader Indic civilization, and built upon the textual revelations of the kind we have seen, various philosophical or theological arguments about the nature of the person developed within the Brahmanical class. These philosophical traditions were expressed in Sanskrit and written in texts, often as commentaries on revelation. There has been much discussion about whether these intellectual traditions can be regarded as philosophy or theology, and whether there can be a 'Hindu theology'.[1] One of the problems is that the history of thought in India has not formally divided itself between philosophy and theology in contrast to the West where, in the early modern period, philosophy comes to be a critique of theology and inherently atheistic.[2] In India, intellectual discourse through the medium of Sanskrit took the form of commentaries upon texts, although not all philosophy was commentarial and there were styles of thinking that were less exegetical and more analytical, particularly as regards logic. One could restrict 'theology' to discourse about a 'theos'—about 'God'—but this would be to rather arbitrarily exclude early Mīmāṃsakas or even Śaiva monists from the discussion. So for current purposes I shall use the term 'philosophy' as a rendition of the terms *darśana* and *dṛṣṭi*, whose literal meaning is 'vision' or 'view', and of *mata*—systematic doctrine. All the thinkers who could be designated as philosophers, from the Buddhist Dharmakīrti to the theist Rāmānuja, were engaged in an intellectual project that was largely, but not exclusively, exegetical, and which claimed to have the highest good as its object. This highest good is liberation from the

[1] In an interesting essay, Francis Clooney first raised the issue of whether there is or what could be 'Hindu theology'. 'Restoring "Hindu Theology" as a Category in Indian Intellectual Discourse', in G. Flood (ed.), *The Blackwell Companion to Hinduism* (Oxford: Blackwell, 2003), pp. 447–77. One of the problems is the tradition-specific history of the term and the separation of theology from philosophy in the early modern period. I am inclined to agree with Bronkhorst in seeing early Indian philosophy as akin to Greek philosophy along Pierre Hadot's line as 'a way of life'. Johannes Bronkhorst, *Aux origines de la philosophie Indienne* (Paris: Infolio, 2008), pp. 11–16.

[2] Simon Critchely, *Very Little . . . Almost Nothing: Death, Philosophy, Literature* (London and New York: Routledge, 1997), p. 3.

cycle of suffering (*mokṣaḥ*) for many, and virtue or correct action (*dharmaḥ*) for the Mīmāṃsā.

In the course of time there arose the idea that there were six orthodox systems of philosophy (*darśanam*): the so-called *astika* schools that regarded the Veda as authoritative, in contrast to the *nāstika* schools such as the Buddhists, Ajīvikas, and Jains, who disclaimed this revelation. The classification of these specific six is, however, fairly late (post-twelfth century and perhaps much later[3]) and is problematic in that it excludes the Śaiva systems and loses the sense in which intellectual traditions, both 'Hindu' and 'non-Hindu', interacted in dynamic exchange and shared a common style of discourse. Among these the Vedānta that flows from the Upaniṣads is clearly a very important tradition that thematizes the idea of the truth within. The Vedānta developed into a number of philosophical schools, generally affiliated to the religions of Viṣṇu, notably Advaita Vedānta, the non-dual tradition of Śaṅkara (AD *c.*788–820), the Viśiṣṭādvaita Vedānta or qualified non-dualism of Rāmānuja (*fl. c.*1017–1137), and the Dvaita Vedānta or dualism of Madhva, all of who wrote of the self within, but who conceptualized the relationship between self and absolute reality in monotheistic or theistic terms.[4]

By the tenth century, especially in Kashmir, there was a Śaiva intellectual tradition that reacted against the earlier Buddhism in the valley. The theologians of the Śaiva Siddhānta, such as Bhaṭṭa Rāmakaṇṭha (*fl. c.*950–1000), Bhojadeva (eleventh century), and Aghoraśiva (twelfth century), wrote commentaries on key scriptures—the Tantras—expounding a dualistic understanding of self and world, that the soul hidden within the body is eternally distinct from the world and from the transcendent Lord. This is not so much dualist as pluralist in that this view accepts the reality of three substances: the Lord (*patiḥ*), the soul (literally 'beast', *paśuḥ*) and the cosmos or bond (*pāśaḥ*) that binds the soul as a noose binds a cow. A rival interpretation of scripture came from the non-dualistic, Śaiva idealists who successfully argued against the Siddhānta that there is a single reality of consciousness only. This philosophical idealism was known as the recognition school (Pratyabhijñā) because of the doctrine that liberation is recognition of one's true nature as absolute

[3] See G. Gerschheimer, 'Les "Six doctrines de speculation" (*ṣaṭtarkī*): Sur le catégorization variable des système philosophiques dans l'Inde classique', in K. Preisendanz (ed.), *Expanding and Merging Horizons: Contributions to South Asian and Cross-Cultural Studies in Commemoration of Wilhelm Halbfass* (Wien: Verlas der Österreichischen Akademie der Wissenschaften, 2007), pp. 239–58. A Jain author Haribhadra Suri (eighth century) seems to have been one of the earliest to use six systems, although different to the later six. K. Satchidananda Murty, *Ṣaḍdarśana samuccaya: A Compendium of Six Philosophies* (2nd edn, Delhi: Eastern Book Linkers, 1986), pp. 98–100. Thanks to Rembert Lutjeharms for this reference.

[4] On Advaita, see C. Ram-Prasad, *Advaita Epistemology and Metaphysics: An Outline of Indian Non-Realism* (London: Routledge-Curzon, 2002), pp. 25–92. On theories of consciousness, see Ram-Prasad, *Indian Philosophy and the Consequences of Knowledge* (Aldershot: Ashgate, 2007), pp. 51–99.

consciousness. This tradition was founded by Śomānanda (*fl.* AD *c.*900–50) in his *Vision of Śiva* (*Śivadṛṣṭi*) and developed by his student Utpaladeva (*fl.* AD *c.*925–75) who wrote *Stanzas on the Recognition of the Lord* (*Īśvara-pratyabhijñā-kārikā*).[5] His student's student, Abhinavagupta (*fl. c.*975–1025), was the most famous thinker in this tradition who wrote a commentary on Utpaladeva's text, along with other works, and his student Kṣemarāja (*fl. c.*1000–1050) wrote commentaries on scripture and an independent work, the *Pratyabhijñāhṛdaya*, propagating the monistic vision of his master. Kṣemarāja's student Yogarāja (*fl. c.*1025–75) wrote a commentary on Abhinavagupta's *Paramārthasāra*. Whether these thinkers were practicing theology or philosophy is a matter of perspective. In one sense they were not theologians because they refuted the idea of a deity distinct from consciousness; yet in another sense they were because they revered the scriptural authority of the Tantras. As Ratié points out, a characteristic of theology is reference to scriptural authority, which the Śaiva non-dualists make; yet they also argue without reference to scriptural authority, and in this sense their work is philosophy.[6] On balance, perhaps the term 'philosophy' is more inclusive than 'theology', particularly if we take it along the lines of Hadot's understanding of Greek philosophy as a way of life, rather than simply a dry intellectual pursuit.

ABHINAVAGUPTA

Abhinavagupta, one of the greatest thinkers of the Śaiva Age, is a philosopher of interiority who systematically presents a doctrine of the truth within. He wrote on aesthetic appreciation and the links between such appreciation and mystical experience in his commentary on a classic text of poetics by Ānandavardhana, the *Dhvanyāloka*.[7] On the other hand, he wrote on Śaiva ritual, and meditation in order to achieve liberation, in an erudite ritual manual *The Illumination of the Tantras* (*Tantrāloka*) which he summarized in *The Short Exposition of the Tantras* (*Tantrasāra*),[8] along with commentaries on

[5] For an intellectual history of the Pratyabhijñā, especially the place of Somānanda, see John Nemec, *The Ubiquitous Śiva: Somānanda's Śivadṛṣti and his Tantric Interlocutors* (New York: Oxford University Press, 2012), pp. 25–78.

[6] Isabelle Ratié, *Le soi et l'autre: Identité, difference et altérité dans la philosophie de la Pratyabhijñā* (Leiden: Brill, 2011), pp. 13–14. Ratié presents a good discussion of this issue pp. 11–14.

[7] D. H. H. Ingalls, J. M. Masson, and M. V. Patwardhan (trans.), *The Dhvanyāloka of Ānandavardhana, with the Locana of Abhinavagupta* (Cambridge, MA: Harvard University Press, 1990).

[8] Sanderson's title: 'A Commentary on the Opening Verses of the Tantrasāra of Abhinavagupta', pp. 103–5, in Ernst Fürlinger (ed.), *Sāmarasya: Studies in Indian Arts, Philosophy, and Interreligious Dialogue* (New Delhi: D. K. Printworld, 2005), pp. 89–147.

scriptures (the commentary on the first chapter of the *Mālinīvijayottara-tantra* and the *Supreme Trident* (*Parātriṃśika-vivaraṇa*), and another independent work, *The Essence of Supreme Meaning* (*Paramārthasāra*)). Lastly, he composed a work that reflects his mature thinking, learned commentaries on Utpaladeva's text that is particularly important as a critique of the Buddhist impersonalists (the *Īśvarapratyabhijñāsūtravimarśiṇī* and the *Īśvarapratyabhijñāvivṛttivimarśiṇī*). We do not know much about his life other than hints he leaves in colophons, such as that his parents were not native to Kashmir but came from the south, and that he was conceived in a tantric sexual ritual.[9] Whether this was or was not the case, Abhinavagupta's self-description tells us that he sees himself as located centrally within what we might call the tantric Śaiva tradition.[10]

The broader culture around Abhinavagupta was pluralistic with various traditions vying for patronage of the royal court. There had been a successful and thriving Buddhist monasticism in Kashmir articulated in the philosophy of the Sarvastivādins. By the time of Abhinavagupta, Vaiṣṇava and Buddhist religion had been thriving in Kashmir and Śaivism attracted royal patronage.[11] Indeed, Śaivism remained the most important religion for the kings of the subcontinent for many years.[12] Abhinavagupta was a Brahman who wished to propagate a non-dualistic idealism and impose this view on the Śaiva scriptural corpus that he regarded as his revealed textual authority. One of the main opposing systems for Abhinavagupta's formulating his philosophy of the person was philosophical Buddhism, and we shall pay some attention to his refutation of it in due course. But he was also concerned to establish the supremacy of Śaiva non-dualism within the broad parameters of Brahmanical Śaivism. To do this his general strategy was to incorporate the complexity of different Śaiva systems into his own. While this strategy produced some very artificial correspondences, it was nevertheless successful in showing that popular apotropaic and other magical practices could be accommodated by his high Śaivism. Through this method of incorporation of texts and practices into a much broader, overarching system, lower, popular cultural levels could be incorporated into a higher intellectualism. Indeed, even socially marginal

[9] Alexis Sanderson, 'Abhinavagupta', in Mircea Eliade (ed.), *The Encyclopedia of Religion* (New York: Macmillan, 1987), vol. 1, pp. 8–9. See also K. C. Pandey, *Abhinavagupta: An Historical and Philosophical Study* (Varanasi: Chowkhamba Sanskrit Series, 1963 (first published 1936)), pp. 1–21.

[10] See Alexis Sanderson, 'Abhinavagupta'. On Abhinavagupta's works, see Sanderson, 'The Śaiva Exegesis of Kashmir', pp. 352–63, 370–83, in Dominic Goodall and André Padoux (eds.), *Mélanges tantriques à mémoire d'Hélène Brunner* (Pondichéry: Institut Français de Pondichéry, 2007), pp. 231–442. Also see Pandey, *Abhinavagupta*, pp. 6, 9–12.

[11] See Mark Dyczkowski, *The Doctrine of Vibration* (Albany, NY: SUNY Press, 1988), pp. 1–3.

[12] Alexis Sanderson, 'The Śaiva Age: The Rise and Dominance of Śaivism during the Early Medieval Period', in Shingo Einoo (ed.), *Genesis and Development of Tantrism* (Tokyo: Institute of Oriental Culture, 2009), pp. 41–350.

practices of the Krama and Kaula traditions that involved caste-free sex or polluting substances could find intellectual justification through the doctrine of non-dualism.

ABHINAVAGUPTA'S THEORY OF THE PERSON

That Abhinavagupta draws on religious traditions that were often antinomian reflects a particular understanding of the person that is both descriptive and aspirational. He intends to present an analysis of the human situation, especially in response to other competing philosophical systems, and he intends to promote a particular vision of human liberation and the highest good. Monistic systems tend to have difficulty in consistently presenting a non-dual view of the world as the very use of language implies a distinction between subject and object. Abhinavagupta is aware of the problem and circumvents it in terms of levels of existence. From one perspective Abhinavagupta accepts the general Indian world view that we are caught in a web of suffering with all creatures, being born and dying repeatedly until liberated from the cycle. Yet from the highest perspective of pure consciousness there is only the appearance of repeated birth and death, for in reality a person is identical with the one truth of pure consciousness—the absolute subject or 'I-ness' (*ahaṃtā*) that is found within themselves. The human person is an appearance of pure consciousness, which becomes differentiated into subjects and objects in a process of development in which unity becomes fragmented. But even this language of emanation in some ways compromises the pure non-dualism Abhinavagupta wishes to promote. Be that as it may, from the human perspective the cosmos is the result of a series of unfolding stages that progressively become more solidified and differentiated, in which entities become, or appear to become, clearly distinct. There are different systems of cosmical hierarchy in the scriptural revelation that Abhinavagupta calls upon, perhaps the most important for him being the hierarchy of levels called *tattva*. These are used in ritual, as we have seen, but also are presented as purely philosophical notions in Abhinavagupta's explanation of the world. Indeed, as Sanderson has observed, Abhinavagupta attempts to transform ritual into pure thought.[13]

In his exposition of the cosmos, Abhinavagupta accepts the terminology and cosmological structure of the Śaiva Siddhānta, but gives this a non-dualist

[13] In one of his commentaries Sanderson writes: 'His [Abhinavagupta's] exegesis of the Parātriṃśikā is an exercise in translating ritual into pure thought, and ultimately into a metaphorical description of an absolute reality which cannot descend without distortion even into the sequence of ratiocination.' Alexis Sanderson, 'The Visualisation of the Deities of the Trika', p. 82, in A. Padoux (ed.), *L'Image divine: Culte et méditation dans l'Hindouisme* (Paris: Éditions du Centre National de la Recherche Scientifique, 1990), pp. 31–88.

reading. A human being is the result of a process of cosmological unfolding, a chain of beings that Śiva emanates from himself. Our true nature is therefore light (*prakāśaḥ*) and reflexive consciousness (*vimarśaḥ*), the perception of which is restricted by cosmological forces that constrain us into our particularity. There are different terminologies that express these cosmological forces. One terminology is impurity (*malam*) which itself is divided into the power of individuality (*āṇava-*), the illusory differentiation into subjects and objects (*māyīya-*), and action (*kārma-*). These come into play at a certain stage of cosmic unfolding below the pure level of the cosmos, or pure course (*śuddhādhvā*).[14] Another terminology used within the hierarchy of the thirty-six levels, or *tattvas*, is that of coverings over the soul (*kañcukaḥ*) which are five—namely, particular agency (*kalā*), limited knowledge (*vidyā*), attachment to sense objects (*rāgaḥ*), time (*kālaḥ*), and causal restriction (*niyatiḥ*). In the Śaiva cosmos that Abhinavagupta inherits, the bound soul (*paśuḥ*) needs the constraints of time, attachment to sense objects, causal force and so on, in order to experience the world and experience the fruits of action. That these very forces are simply the expansion of consciousness is a liberating cognition that is the goal of the practitioner in Abhinavagupta's tradition. This realization of pure consciousness is liberation while living (*jīvanmuktiḥ*) and the recognition of pure consciousness within interiority. Indeed, in another way of speaking, this realization is that the entire manifestation of the cosmos—both the visible worlds of mundane experience and the invisible worlds that only yogins can enter—is understood as exteriority (*bāhyatva*), in contrast to the pure interiority of consciousness. This exteriority is, however, only apparent as the universe does not exist outside or independently of consciousness.[15]

Given that the totality of the cosmos, on this view, is only consciousness, we can nevertheless analyse the way in which persons function and how limited personal experience based on ignorance can be transformed to the unlimited cosmic experience of Śiva as the only true subject. True identity, for Abhinavagupta and others in his school, is the unchanging self as one with the light of consciousness. What changes is the empirical self, the self of whom there is a story, the narrative self embroiled with time, attached to the spheres of the senses, but who nevertheless reflects the cosmic self of Śiva in his acts of willing, thinking, and acting. Abhinavagupta, in particular, defended this view against the Buddhist impersonalists in his magnum opus, the commentary on Utpaladeva's Recognition of the Lord (*Īśvarapratyabhijñā-vimarśiṇī*).

This work represents the mature thinking of Abhinavagupta and promotes a view that the self is identical with absolute consciousness, from which perspective variegated consciousness is unreal. At the same time the work

[14] See André Padoux, *Vāc*, trans. J. Gontier (Albany, NY: SUNY Press, 1990), p. 104, n. 54; Gavin Flood, *Body and Cosmology in Kashmir Śaivism* (San Francisco: Mellen, 1993), pp. 55–83.

[15] For a good account of exteriority, see Ratié, *Le soi et l'autre*, pp. 17–18.

is an analysis of mundane experience and the functioning of limited consciousness—that is, how human beings think and experience the world. From an account of the human person in relation to the world, Abhinavagutpa develops a kind of theistic view that all experience depends upon a transcendent God which he rereads in the light of his monism as a claim that self-experience is in fact the experience of pure, reflexive consciousness: consciousness becoming aware of itself. This pure non-dualist position is inevitably at the expense of theistic language, which becomes metaphor or a way of speaking about non-dual awareness drawn from a lower level revelation.

Central to this work is an analysis of how cognitions arise and how memory constitutes a central factor in personal identity. In order to experience a world, Abhinavagupta tells us, particularized consciousness—consciousness embodied in particular persons—requires the powers of knowledge or cognition (*jñānam*), memory (*smṛtiḥ*), and differentiation or exclusion (*aphohanaḥ*). The power of knowledge gives us understanding of an apparently objective world, memory gives us understanding of who we believe ourselves to be in providing a continuity of thought and identity, and the power of exclusion allows us to differentiate between entities and between self and world. All this rests upon absolute consciousness, which can be spoken of in theistic terms as the Great Lord. Utpaladeva's final verses of the second chapter of his book read as follows:

Reading 18

> Thus the functioning of the human world—which stems precisely from the unification of cognitions, in themselves separate from one another and incapable of knowing one another—would be destroyed if there were no Maheśvara who contains within himself all the infinite forms, who is one, whose essence is consciousness, possessing the powers of knowledge, memory and exclusion.[16]

Abhinavagupta notes that the human world of experience assumes a certain unity, that cognitions are related to the same objects in our memory, and that in order to account for this continuity we need to posit the notion of a permanent subject of experience. The powers of knowledge, memory, and differentiation enable the subject to experience a world, and Abhinavagupta offers an exposition of these powers in his commentary on the text in Reading 18.

In order to account for how objects of consciousness appear, we must accept that they are constituted within consciousness itself. But if, as the Buddhists maintain, this consciousness is constantly changing, then there could be no continuity of objects because memory would not be stable. Consciousness

[16] Utpaladeva, *Īśvarapratyabijñākārikā* 1.3.6–7. I quote Torella's translation of the verses themselves. The translations of Abhinavagupta's commentary are my own, although I have been guided by Pandey's English translation and Ratié's rendering of some passages.

therefore must be one, and must include 'objective' reality within it as it differentiates objects through the power of knowledge. This reality of objects—all the infinite forms of the universe—is, of course, only constituted within interiority (*antaḥkṛta-*) by consciousness itself. Yet how does it do this? Abhinavagupta's commentary on the verse reads:

Reading 19

Nobody denies that consciousness is manifested. But if consciousness is resting only within itself, how does it manifest its object? For if the object has an objective property (*dharmaḥ*) and the manifestation of the object is contained (*paryavasitaḥ*) (within itself), the distinction between perceiver and perceived is lost.[17]

Objects of consciousness, although they appear distinct, cannot have their own self-illuminating nature, for if they did, then there could be no relation between subject and object because two self-illuminating entities could not 'shine' or illuminate the other. Rather, the objects of consciousness are constituted purely within consciousness and the internal (*antarmukhaḥ*) self-luminosity of consciousness remains constant in spite of the differentiation of the objects of cognition. On this model, consciousness manifests its objects and that which is manifested, and while appearing to be separate from consciousness, in fact is not; it is 'mere appearance'. In the relationship between 'I' and 'this', the object ('this') only appears to be distinct from the subject; the object becomes external (*bahirmukhaḥ*) and oriented towards the outside although, as Ratié observes, this extraversion (*bahirmukhatva*) is simply the way in which consciousness appears to itself. When I imagine an apple it appears to be external, but in reality it is constituted only within consciousness.[18] Consciousness remains aware of its having become apparently externalized through the powers of memory, knowledge, and differentiation. The object of consciousness is internal to it (*tadrūpāntaragataḥ*), and although the Buddhists accept this, Abhinavagupta points out that if the subject of experience, who illuminates objects, were changing at each moment, as the Buddhists maintain, then memory would not be possible.[19] That is, the presence of memory requires there to be a continuity of a conscious subject. Memory is the residual trace due to previous experience (*purvānubhava-saṃskārāt*):[20] the direct object (*viṣayaḥ*) of a previous experience becomes the object of memory, and this experience must be of a subject. In his commentary on Utpaladeva's verse, Abhinavagupta raises the Buddhist objection that if this is so, then there is no need to posit a permanent self; all experience can be accounted for in terms of residual traces of previous

[17] *Īśvarapratyabijñāvimarśinī* 1.3.7, p. 141: *saṃvit tāvat prakāśate iti tāvat na kecit apahnuvate / sā tu saṃvit yadi svātmamātraviśrāntā arthasya sā katham prakāśaḥ/ sa hi arthadharma eva tathā syāt, tataśca arthaprakāśaḥ tāvatyeva paryavasita iti galito grāhygrāhakabhāvaḥ /*

[18] Ratié, *Le soi et l'autre*, p. 176.

[19] *Īśvarapratyabijñāvimarśinī* 1.3.7, p. 141.

[20] *Īśvarapratyabijñākārikā* 1.2.5.

experience. Abhinavagupta retorts that memory is a quality (*guṇaḥ*), and as a quality cannot stand alone; it needs a substratum (*āśrayaḥ*) to be embedded within. That substratum is the permanent self (*ātmā*).[21] If there were no conscious subject, there could be no chain of memories. But this is no individual self, as is held by other Hindu schools such as the Vaiśeṣikas and Sāṃkhya, but is self-luminous consciousness itself, outpouring its intentional objects and consuming them through its power of freedom. Which intentional objects appear to consciousness from an infinite possibility of appearances is due to the power of knowledge, which brings to light particular objects, and memory, which links appearances to a subject.

But these are not enough to account for human perception. We need something more that controls events into their particularity, and that is the power of exclusion. On this power, Abhinavagupta writes:

Reading 20

It also has to be admitted as following (from our analysis) that whatever is manifested is separate from consciousness, one consciousness from another consciousness, and an object of consciousness from another object of consciousness. But in reality this separation is not possible (so) it is called merely an appearance of separation. But this is not, for all that, deprived of ultimate reality; (appearance) is that very ultimate reality of all that is created. It is called differentiation because it differentiates all parts. That appearance is the meaning of the power of exclusion. All worldly transactions (are formed) by that triad of powers.[22]

The power of separation is the power that differentiates states of consciousness from each other along with the objects of consciousness. The text uses the strong term *paricchedaḥ* that has the implication of 'cutting' from the verbal root *chid*, 'to cut'. I have rendered it 'differentiation' as the power that controls each appearance into its particularity. Furthermore, the diversity of appearances is not deprived of ultimate reality; appearance *is* that very reality. That is, the world or totality of appearances is not an illusion, as in Advaita Vedānta, but is nevertheless identical with absolute consciousness in this philosophy: the world simply is consciousness. As Ratié observes, Abhinavagupta is

[21] *Īśvarapratyabijñāvimarśinī* 1.2.5, p. 99.

[22] *Īśvarapratyabijñāvimarśinī* 1.3.7, pp. 142–3: *idam api pravāhapatitam ūrikāryam—yat kila tad* [conjecture: Sanderson in Ratié, p. 182] *ābhāsyate tat saṃvido vicchidyate, saṃvic ca saṃvidantarāt, saṃvedyaṃ ca saṃvedyāntarāt. na ca vicchedanaṃ vastutaḥ saṃbhavatīti vicchedanasyāvabhāsamātram ucyate / na ca tad iyatāpāramārthikam, nirmīyamāṇasya sarvasyāyam eva paramārthaḥ / yataḥ eṣa eva paritaśchedanāt pariccheda ucyate, tadavabhāsanasāmarthyam apohanaśaktiḥ / anena śaktitrayeṇa viśve vyavahārāḥ.* I have been guided by Ratié here in reading *iyatāpāramārthika* rather than *iyatā pāramārthika* as the editor of the KSTS edition has done, and even the commentator Bhāskara. Ratié notes that Pandey does not translate this passage and comments on the reasons for choosing this reading. Ratié, *Le soi et l'autre*, p. 182, n. 28.

claiming that the being of consciousness is precisely the appearance.[23] It is not so much that the world is an unreal illusion but rather that the real world is identical to consciousness. Consciousness appears as the objective world through the powers of knowledge, memory, and exclusion that underpin all worldly transaction.

Let us sum up what Abhinavagupta is saying. In his view, consciousness contains within itself the entire universe of objects, but although the mass of objects (*artharāśiḥ*) is contained within consciousness, it only causes some to appear (*ābhāsayati*) as distinct from it. This is brought about by the power of knowledge. Having manifested some objects from the mass of potentiality, consciousness becomes aware of its having become apparently external to itself in what appear to be new cognitions (*navaṃ jñānam*). These always new cognitions arise and disappear, they come and go, but the self-luminosity of consciousness in itself remains intact and does not change. This externality (*bahirmukham*) is grasped by consciousness that nevertheless remains within its interiority (*antarmukham*). But the power of knowledge, or the capacity of consciousness to manifest existents outside of itself, must be supplemented by another power in order to explain the relative permanence of the objects of consciousness.[24] We need to explain the continuity of objects once they have been manifested. Understanding that these apparently external, changing objects, even when they appear to be new cognitions, are identical with consciousness, occurs through the power of memory. That is, even apparently new cognitions are to be recognized as being identical with universal self-luminosity in relation to particular objects. Objects of cognition appear to consciousness in the present—they are directly perceived—but objects that were present to consciousness but that have gone into the past are understood through memory. Finally, the power of exclusion or differentiation is responsible for manifesting one thing as distinct from another. It is this power that particularizes or controls an entity into its particularity, making it distinct from others. At the end of the day, of course, all is mere appearance (*avabhāsamātram*); this does not mean illusion, but rather that appearance is only consciousness. The entire mass of objects that comprise our experience is constructed internally (*kroḍīkṛtaḥ*) within absolute consciousness and their apparent differentiation is due to the three powers. These three powers control all worldly transaction, yet rather than the individual person, it is the Lord who knows or cognizes, remembers, and differentiates. Indeed, Abhinavagupta concludes, the many ways in which these powers are manifested is due to the Lord's power of freedom (*svatantram*).[25]

[23] See Ratié, *Le soi et l'autre*, pp. 183–4. This is a good example of how a monistic idealism, that the world is identical with consciousness, is not the same as an emanationism, although the language of emanation and the language of identity tend to be found together. It might be argued that Bhāskara's commentary on the text tends towards emanationism rather than a pure idealism.

[24] See Ratié, *Le soi et l'autre*, p. 180.

[25] *Īśvarapratyabijñāvimarśinī* 1.3.7, pp. 141–3.

THE FLOW OF EXPERIENCE

The intentional objects of consciousness, the appearances (*ābhāsāḥ*), appear in a continuous flow. They are controlled into their particularity by the power of exclusion and are successive. From another perspective, this succession is the flow of time which, Utpaladeva says, is nothing other than the succession (*krama eva sa tattvataḥ*) of appearances.[26] This power of time (*kālaśaktiḥ*) is itself nothing other than a power of the Lord who manifests the variety of appearances. From the perspective of ultimate reality, of course, which is pure subjective consciousness, there is no time. In the eternal subject of knowledge (*pramātā*) whose nature is consciousness (*saṃvidrūpaḥ*) there is no temporal succession, not even of the apparent objects of consciousness because they exist only within consciousness. The experience of time, then, is one of the major differences between the limited subject of consciousness, the empirical self, and absolute subjectivity.[27]

The same is true, says Abhinavagupta, of space and spatial relations between the subject and object of experience. He writes:

Reading 21

So, even spatial succession appears in the limited self whose nature is circumscribed, as one's own self, body (and the experience of) emptiness and so on (as in the statement) 'I am standing here.' And it appears in existents also in relation to oneself as in 'what is in close proximity to me is near and what is otherwise is far'. To the unlimited reality of consciousness whose nature is free from constraint, objects appear as one's own self, the existence of 'I', so as such are perfect. Their nature is such that it is unconstrained. Such is the reality that is his own self.[28]

The experience of oneself as a body and other objects of consciousness, from the mundane awareness that 'I am standing here' to more subtle experiences such as emptiness, are all in reality within consciousness. Although our experiences of body and self, along with the objects of experience or existents (*bhāvāḥ*), appear to be distinct from us, such that we can distinguish between near and far, for example, in truth they are coextensive with us as perfected consciousness. In reality, consciousness is free from constraint and only circumscribed by the self-limiting action of the powers described above. Human experience appears to be constrained by limitation: the limitation of time and space and the limitation of causation; but this limitation is only

[26] *Īśvarapratyabijñāvimarśinī* 2.1.3.

[27] See Ratié, *Le soi and l'autre*, pp. 208–11.

[28] *Īśvarapratyabijñāvimarśinī* 2.1.7, p. 22: *evaṃ deśakramo 'pi mitātmanaḥ paricchinnasvarūpasya śūnyādeḥ dehāntasya svātmani bhāti iha tiṣṭhāmi iti, svāpekṣayā ca bhāveṣvapi 'yat mama saṃyogapārimityena vartate tadantikam itarat dūram' iti / amitasya svarūpeyattāśūnyasya tu saṃvittattvasya bhāvāḥ svātmanā ahaṃbhāvena yato bhānti tataḥ pūrṇāḥ - aparicchinnasvarūpeyattākāḥ, yataḥ svātmā tasya tathābhūta eva . . .*

apparent as all of reality is identical with consciousness and arises due to its spontaneous freedom.

Spatial and temporal awareness are cognitions of types of relation (*saṃbandhaḥ*). Our experience of the world, constrained by the powers of knowledge, memory, and exclusion, is also characterized by the relationship of self to world, of consciousness to its objects, and of subject to predicate in a sentence. The idea of relation was important to Abhinavagupta because he wished to establish an unchanging, self-identical consciousness in contrast to the Buddhist philosophers who maintained that the self is empty of essence and who criticized the notion of relation. According to the Buddhists there can be no relation between a self that does not exist and the objects of its experience, nor between subject and predicate.[29] But for Abhinavagupta the idea of relation is crucial for establishing a connection between consciousness and its intentional objects. Relation, he says, is 'the practicable life of this entire world' (*sakalalokayātrānuprāṇitakalpa-*).[30] The principal relation is between cause and effect which can be directly perceived as a necessary relationship because the objects of consciousness inhere within it, which is to say, are within the Lord's awareness. But the causal relationship is not simple in the sense that the intentional object is partly determined or constrained by interest. Our perception of apparently external objects is partly conditioned by our interiority. In his commentary on a verse by Utpaladeva that describes how different phenomena such as 'being', 'pot', and 'substance' are the references of a word, Abhinavagupta describes how the same phenomenon can give rise to different responses. In this way we can account for different intentional objects. Thus Abhinavagupta rather touchingly writes, a man who is broken hearted (*hṛdbhaṅgaḥ*) 'finding that there is nothing', when he sees a pot simply perceives bare existence (*sattvābhāsam eva*)—simply, 'it is'. A man who is thirsty perceives the appearance 'pot', a man who simply sees the pot as something to be taken to different places perceives 'a thing', while a man who is keen on price sees 'gold' in the pot, and so on.[31] That is, our motivation and orientation, the type of person we are, colours our perception of the world.

Although he differs from other schools, Abhinavagupta's general model of human experience is largely congruent with the broader Hindu understanding that a person is essentially a soul incarnated into a human body due to its past

[29] C. Lal Tripathi, *The Problem of Knowledge in Yogācāra Buddhism* (Varanasi: Bharat-Bharati, 1972). Tripathi presents an account of the Yogācāra view in relation to its critique. The general point is the rejection of relation in Buddhism (pp. 222–7), the real being essentially non-dual (pp. 331–2); David Lawrence, *Rediscovering God with Transcendental Argument* (Albany, NY: SUNY Press, 1999), pp. 81–2. Ratié, *Le soi et l'autre*, pp. 92, 100, 298. On the Buddhist critique of universals, see R. R. Dravid, *Problem of Universals in Indian Philosophy* (Delhi: Motilal, 2001), pp. 61–7.

[30] *Īśvarapratyabijñāvimarśinī* 2.2.6, p. 54.

[31] *Īśvarapratyabijñāvimarśinī* 2.3.4, p. 99.

actions, its desires, and motivations. We experience a world in an appropriate body that is conditioned by our past, and we are attached to our experiences, which keeps us bound in the cycle of rebirth. The sense of who we are in our everyday lives, the sense of 'I', is not who we *really* are, but is constrained by body and world. The kind of body we have determines the kind of world we experience. Limited I-consciousness is affected by the residual traces (*samskāraḥ, vāsanā*) of past experience. This limited I-consciousness is not the true self, says Abhinavagupta, because it is a determinate cognition (*vikalpaḥ*). Personal identity is the worldly or everyday sense, which for Abhinavagupta is regarded as 'impure' (*aśuddhaḥ*). This impure sense of the 'I' as the subject of first person predicates takes two forms: one of direct experience—as in the experience of 'I am fat'—and the other of a unified sense of a life, that past experiences happened to me, as in 'I who was fat am now thin', or 'I who was a child am now young or old.'[32] The ignorant state of being a subject, who most people think they are most of the time, is a constriction of the highest freedom of the Lord. When I make a statement that contains the first person pronoun, I am particularizing myself in a certain time and place, thereby excluding all other possible appearances. This limited sense of self, Abhinavagupta contrasts with the true self, the true sense of 'I' as universal subject. Following Utpaladeva he writes:

Reading 22

I-consciousness is two kinds: pure and that which is within material power (*māyā*). In this, (the I-consciousness) which is pure is nothing but (absolute) consciousness, non-distinct from the universe, or (it is that) which is in the pellucid self, blended with the reflections of the universe. But the impure (I-consciousness comprises) objects of knowledge such as body and so on. As regards pure I-consciousness, there is nothing contrary (to it) that can be excluded, because even a pot and so on should not be negated on account of its opposition (to pure consciousness because all objects) have as their essence the light of consciousness. How can it be regarded as a determinate cognition? The impure which has as its nature the object of knowledge such as body and so on, which is distinct from another body, pots and so on, is certainly a determinate cognition.[33]

From the highest perspective, universal I-consciousness is the true reality designated as 'pure' by Abhinavagupta, in contrast to limited I-consciousness which is within material power (*māyā*). The term *māyā*, that in some contexts

[32] *Īśvarapratyabijñāvimarśinī* 1.6.5, pp. 314–15: *yo 'haṃ sthūlaḥ . . . ahaṃ sthūlaḥ . . .*

[33] *Īśvarapratyabijñāvimarśinī* 1.6.5 pp. 313–14: *aham ity avamarśo dvidhā—śuddho māyīyaśca, tatra śuddho yaḥ saṃvinmātre viśvābhinne viśvacchāyācchuritasvacchātmani vā, aśuddhas tu vedyarūpe śarirādau / tatra śuddhe'hampratyavamarśe pratiyogī na kaścid apohitavyaḥ saṃbhavati ghaṭāder api prakāśasāratvenāpratiyogitvenānapohyatvāt ityapohhyābhāve kathaṃ tatra vikalparūpatā / aśuddhas tu vedyarūpe śarīrādāv anyasmād dehāder ghaṭādeś ca vyavacchedena bhavan vikalpa eva /*

can be rendered as 'illusion' in the Pratyabhijñā context, is better rendered as 'material power' in the sense that it is a limitation on consciousness that occurs at a particular level of cosmological unfolding, below the 'pure creation'. With *māyā*, the various coverings or constraints come into play that limit consciousness into the particularity of individual subjects or knowers and objects of knowledge.

On this view, both subject and intentional object of consciousness are formed through cosmological, limiting constraints; so from this perspective, even the limited sense of 'I' is a determinate cognition (*vikalpaḥ*) akin to body and other intentional objects. But from the perspective of the highest I-consciousness, even these intentional objects—such as the body, pots, and other realms of experience—do not negate the highest sense of 'I' because they are nothing other than that supreme consciousness. All limitation is only apparent. In short, my true nature is absolute subjectivity, 'I-am-ness' (*ahantā*), which has become limited I-consciousness through a process of cosmic unfolding. And as worlds of experience open up, so a sense of this absolute subjectivity closes down; and conversely, the opening up or realization of absolute subjectivity is the closing down of the experience of multiple realities. The Lord manifests himself as the cosmos through various levels, including seven types of experient.[34] Human experience is the result of a cosmological process of limitation, and the material world in which we find ourselves is but one world among many thousands that we cannot perceive with the senses of our limited bodies. But those who have practiced a spiritual discipline can perceive these other, more subtle worlds, and Abhinavagupta

[34] For example, Kṣemarāja's commentary on the *Spanda Kārikās* the *Spandanirṇaya* 1.1, p. 4. Here Ksemarāja lists the seven kinds of experient in the cosmos that the Lord becomes, namely Śiva, the highest experient at the top of the cosmos, Mantramaheśvaras, Maheśvaras, Mantras in the pure cosmos, and Vijñānakalas, Pralayakalas, and Sakalas in the impure cosmos. He writes: *śrīmaheśvaro hi svātantryāśaktyā śivamantramaheśvaramantreśvaramantravijñānākala-pralayakalasakalāntām pramātṛbhūmikāṃ tadvedyabhūmikāṃ ca gṛhṇānaḥ pūrvapūrvarūpatāṃ bhittibhūtatayā sthitām apy antaḥ svarūpāvacchādanakriydayā nimeṣayannevonmeṣayati uttarottararūpatām avarohakrameṇa, ārohakrameṇa tūttarottararūpatāṃ nimeṣayanneva jñānayoginām unmeṣāyati pūrapūrvarūpatāmata evottaram uttaraṃ pūrvatra pūrvatra saṃkocātmatāṃ jahad-vikasitatvenāsāvābhāsayati, pūrvaṃ pūrvaṃ tu rūpam yathottaraṃ vikasitatāṃ nimajjayan saṅkucitatvena sarśayati.*

'The supreme Lord by his own power of freedom assumes the levels of subjective experient Śiva, Mantramaheśvaras, Maheśvaras, Mantras, Vijñānakalas, Pralayakalas, and Sakalas along with their objective correlates. Closing in the previous condition by the play of covering his true nature, which is by splitting (himself), gradually descending, he opens out further and further (levels). But by gradual ascent, closing in those very subsequent forms, he opens out previous forms for cognition yogis. Abandoning previous contraction he makes manifest higher (levels) by opening them up. He shows himself by contraction, closing in previous form, opening out subsequent (forms).'

The idea here is that the Lord manifests lower forms, which entails a concealing of higher forms, while conversely the opening out of higher levels, as in the case of yogis, entails a contraction or closing in of lower levels. This systole and diastole movement refers both to the cosmos and of the yogi's journey.

mentions that yogis reverse the process of cosmic unfolding and limitation through ascending back to the source of all, namely absolute subjectivity, the pure sense of 'I'. For yogis on the path to enlightenment, the 'ascent higher and higher' (*uttarottaram ārohataḥ*)[35] is a journey back through the cosmos and so back through the stages of limitation, to the absolute subjectivity.

A number of types of language or discourse can be discerned in Abhinavagupta's account. Firstly, from the highest perspective of absolute subjectivity all is consciousness. Abhinavagupta can speak of this also in theistic terms—that the self who is light of consciousness is that very Supreme Lord (*prakāśātmā parameśvara eva*).[36] From the highest perspective there is no impurity or limitation. Secondly, there is also a cosmological language in Abhinavagupta, and he speaks of the unfolding of the hierarchical universe through a series of levels which, he says, have various terms in different scriptures. He mentions, for example, the standard Upaniṣadic idea of the states of waking, dreaming, and sleeping as corresponding to levels of the cosmos which are integrated into the cosmological system of the *Mālinīvijayottara-tantra* that he refers to.[37] Lastly, there is the language of philosophy concerning the relation of the subject of consciousness to intentional object, causation, and means of knowing that are standard topics in Indian philosophical discourse. Although the language or discourse of Abhinavagupta's commentary on Utpaladeva, his last work, is predominantly philosophical, these other discourses of cosmology and spiritual practice also make their appearance and are seamlessly integrated into his account.

One of the reasons for this is that Abhinavagupta has a vision of the human person that sees it as an outpouring of unlimited absolute freedom. The Lord chooses self limitation in the human person and other phenomena because the Lord's nature is spontaneous freedom. Nevertheless, from the unenlightened human perspective, realizing the true nature of reality as pure subjectivity is a long way off; but the potential for realizing this is within us all, according to Abhinavagupta. The limited human person reflects the divine person of Śiva, and the limited human powers of willing, knowing, and acting reflect Śiva's powers of willing, knowing, and acting.[38] While the human faculties are partly to blame for human bondage in the world of the senses, it is also human faculties that can be used to transcend the human condition. Indeed, Abhinavagupta bases his soteriological system on the transforming effects of the faculties of willing, knowing, and doing. Through their being put to the service

[35] *Īśvarapratyabijñāvimarśinī* 1.6.5, p. 322.

[36] *Īśvarapratyabijñāvimarśinī* 1.6.8, p. 334.

[37] *Īśvarapratyabijñāvimarśinī* 1.6.5, p. 322. The *Mālinīvijayottara-tantra* presents a cosmological structure at 2.36–8, 41–6, 49–58. See Flood, *Body and Cosmology*, pp. 122–35; Somdeva Vasudeva, *The Yoga of the Mālinīvijayottara-tantra* (Pondichery: EFEO, 2004), pp. 215–33.

[38] Abhinavagupta, *Parātriṃśikālaghuvṛtti*, p. 17, ed. and French trans. André Padoux as *La Parātriṃśikālaghuvṛtti: Texte traduit et annoté* (Paris: de Boccard, 1975).

of a spiritual discipline, the human person is transformed, realizes his true nature as pure subjectivity, and is released from bondage. Partly on the basis of this classification Abhinavagupta develops the idea of different paths to liberation, to which we must now turn.

THE WAYS TO LIBERATION

Of particular importance for Abhinavagupta was one of the main scriptures of the Trika, the *Supreme Victory of the Goddess Mālinī* (*Mālinīvijayottara-tantra*), itself a dualist text, according to Sanderson, that was appropriated by Abhinavagupta.[39] This is a text that offers a cosmology, ritual, and meditation practice including visual contemplations of the kind we have already seen. From this text, Abhinavagupta takes a classification of three types of religious experience that forms the basis for his monumental *Tantrāloka*, which is a manual or *paddhati* for this text. These three practices are referred to as 'immersions' (*samāveśāḥ*) that the text refers to as divine (*śambhuḥ*), powerful (*śāktaḥ*), and individual (*āṇavaḥ*).[40] Abhinavagupta takes this as the basis of his exposition relating each of the three ways with the faculties of will (*icchā*), cognition (*jñānam*), and action (*kriyā*). Indeed, this classification becomes the basis of his exposition in the *Tantrāloka* and its summary the *Tantrasāra*, and his student Kṣemarāja uses it as a heuristic device through which to read one of the founding texts of this form of Śaivism, Vasugupta's *Śiva-sūtras*.[41]

Abhinavagupta's central organizing principle in these works is the path to liberation, which he understands as the realization or recognition of a person's innate divinity: that individual consciousness is coterminous with absolute consciousness that he justified philosophically in the work we have just considered. Abhinavagupta divides the way to realization into two categories: the method or means (*upāyaḥ*) that he takes to be the immersions of the *Mālinīvijayottara*, and the method that is no method, the non-means (*an-upāyaḥ*), which is to take the goal, immersion in the absolute consciousness of Śiva, as the means. The *anupāya* is Abhinavagupta's innovation that recognizes the problem of a monistic metaphysics that any notion of a distinction between a means and an end, a path and a goal, meditator and object of

[39] Alexis Sanderson, 'The Doctrine of the *Mālinīvijayottaratantra*', in T. Goudriaan (ed.), *Ritual and Speculation in Early Tantrism: Studies in Honour of André Padoux* (Albany, NY: SUNY Press, 1992), pp. 281–312.

[40] *Mālinīvijayottara-tantra*, 2. 20–3.

[41] Alexis Sanderson, 'Review of Lilian Silburn's *Śivasūtra et Vimarśinī de K.semarāja. (Études sur le Śivaïsme du Cachemire, École Spanda.) Traduction et introduction*, Publications de l'Institut de Civilisation Indienne 47, Paris, 1980.', *Bulletin of the School of Oriental and African Studies*, 46/1 (1983), pp. 160–1.

meditation, undermines that very non-dualism. If there is only one reality, then all language that distinguishes between means and end is, in last analysis, illusory. All methods, even those regarded as interior, are the light of consciousness, which is the innate essence of Śiva.[42] From the absolute perspective, there can be no ignorance if there is only knowledge; there cannot be the cessation of the 'coverings' over consciousness (*āvaraṇam*) if, in reality, there are no coverings.[43] In the light of the non-means there is no need for the restriction of mantra repetition, external worship, meditation, and correct conduct (*mantrapūjādhyānacaryādiniyantraṇam*).[44] The truth is that Śiva is the only true subject in the universe, and this reality is constituted by light (*prakāśaḥ*) and reflexive awareness (*vimarśaḥ*) which can be theistically understood as Śiva and the Goddess or Power (*śaktiḥ*)—although in the ultimate sense this is simply a way of speaking about reflexive consciousness. Waking up to this awareness could be conceptualized in theistic terms as Śiva's grace or the descent of his power (*śaktipātaḥ*),[45] although even this language somewhat compromises the pure non-dualism Abhinavagupta wishes to promote.

From a lower perspective, if a person was not receptive to the descent of power (*śaktipātaḥ*), a range of methods were available, themselves arranged in a hierarchy from *śambhu*, to *śākta*, to *āṇava*, which used the human faculties of will (*icchā*), cognition (*jñānam*), and action (*kriyā*) respectively. To understand Abhinavagupta's philosophy of the person we need to understand how a person can be transformed and divinized through these means.

The Divine Means

The third chapter of the *Tantrasāra*, summarizing the third chapter of the *Tantrāloka*, explains the first method, the *śāmbavopāya*, which we might literally render as 'the method relating to the one who exists for happiness': Śambhu is a name for Śiva, which means 'existing (*bhu*) for happiness (*śam*)'.

[42] Abhinavagupta, *Tantrāloka* 2.15: *kiṃ ca yāvadidaṃ bāhyamāntaropāyasaṃmatam / tatprakāśātmatāmātraṃ śivasyaiva nijaṃ vapuḥ*. 'Even though this externality is regarded as an internal method, it is only the light of consciousness; the innate essence of Śiva.' That is, what the ignorant might regard as an internal method is still external compared to the light of consciousness. The semantic range of the term *vapus* includes 'body'. This points to the extended notion of body in this tradition and can refer to the cosmic body of Śiva. On this term, see A. Padoux (trans.), *La Lumière sur les tantras* (Paris: CNES, 1998), p. 162, n. 36. Also see my *Body and Cosmology*, pp. 107, 134.

[43] Abhinavagupta, *Tantrasāra*, pp. 8–9.

[44] *Tantrasāra*, p. 9.

[45] On śaktipāta, see Christopher Wallis, 'The Descent of Power: Possession, Mysticism, and Initiation in the Śaiva Theology of Abhinavagupta', *Journal of Indian Philosophy*, 36/2 (2008), pp. 247–95.

Although its origins are in the tradition of the *Mālinīvijayottara*, not far removed from cremation ground possession cults in its doctrine of immersion (*samāveśaḥ*), Abhinavagupta relates *śāmbhava* to the will, and calls this the method of will (*icchopāyaḥ*), although by *icchā* he means a force that is wider than the semantic range captured in the term 'will' to refer to preconceptual force within the person and, moreover, within the absolute as the impulse to creation or manifestation. He opens the chapter:

Reading 23

If (the practitioner) cannot enter there into the whole circle (in the way described in the preceding chapter), which is the reality of Śiva whose nature is light as already stated, then perceiving nothing but its power of autonomy as predominant, he experiences the immersion into Bhairava, which is devoid of thought-construction. This is its teaching. All this mass of existents is merely a reflected image in the sky of consciousness, due to its having the characteristic of a reflection. For the characteristic of a reflection is that a reflection appears only as infused with something else. It is without power, (only) appearing as difference, like the form of a face in the mirror, like saliva to taste, like smell to the nose, like sexual intercourse to the organ of pleasure, like a sharp stomach pain to the faculty of inner sensation, or like an echo in space.[46]

Here, Abhinavagupta presents the heart of his doctrine. The apparent theistic reality of Śiva is nothing other than consciousness with which the practitioner is identical. Bhairava is the fullest expansion of consciousness, immanent in the world, and the enlightened person realizes his immersion into this fullness. Once a person is in this condition of enlightenment there is no longer any thought-construction, which takes the practitioner away from realization of highest reality, but simply spontaneous expression of one's true nature as reflexive awareness. Abhinavagupta glosses *icchā* as the power of spontaneous freedom (*svātanryaśaktiḥ*), without the perception of which the practitioner cannot otherwise realize himself as divine and cannot, in Abhinavagupta's words, 'enter into the whole circle'. This 'whole circle' is the absolute reality of consciousness, a totality without boundary that spontaneously expresses its totally free nature. The term *icchā* here does not mean individual drive and intention but refers to Śiva's power of creation, the drive within Śiva to manifest the cosmos that is reflected imperfectly in individual intention.

[46] *Tantrasāra*, pp. 10–11: *Yad etat prakāśarūpaṃ śivatattvam uktam, tatra akhaṇḍamaṇḍale yadā praveṣṭuṃ na śaknoti, tadā svātantryaśaktim eva adhikāṃ paśyan nirvikalpam eva bhairavasamāveśam anubhavati, ayaṃ ca asya upadeśaḥ—sarvam idaṃ bhāvajātaṃ bodhagagane pratibimbamātraṃ pratibimbalakṣaṇopetatvāt, idaṃ hi pratibimbasya lakṣaṇaṃ—yat bhedena bhāsitam aśaktam anyavyāmiśratvenaiva bhāti tat pratibimbam, mukharūpam iva darpaṇe, rasa iva dantodake, gandha iva ghrāṇe, mithunasparśa iva ānandendriye, śūlakuntādisparśo vā antaḥsparśanendriye, pratiśrutkeva vyomni.* See also *Tantrāloka* 3.24–34. My understanding of the *Tantrasāra* was greatly enhanced by reading some sections of the text in a class with Alexis Sanderson.

Indeed, the term 'intention' or 'intentionality' does convey something of the meaning of *icchā* in so far as Śiva's consciousness is always intentional, it always has an object, and if there is no outer object then its object must be itself.

This pure reflexivity of awareness is one of the key doctrines of the non-dual Śaivas. Indeed, they agree with Husserlian phenomenology in maintaining that all consciousness is intentional; consciousness is always 'consciousness of'. While the objects of restricted or contracted consciousness, which is the nature of the limited person, appear as external to the subject, in reality consciousness is simply aware of itself and becomes aware of its own projections as the path towards final enlightenment unfolds. The objects of consciousness, which appear to be external, outside the self, are in fact simply reflections (*pratibimbham*) and as such cannot be separated from what they are reflections of. The mass of existing things is merely a reflected image. Just as a face in a mirror, so smell in the nose, sexual union in the organ of pleasure, or a sharp stomach pain, are only reflections. Just as these examples appear as reflected, so this world appears in the light of Supreme Śiva. Playing the protagonist, Abhinavagupta asks: but 'reflections of what? What is the original (*bimbam*)?' And he replies that there is none (*mābhūt kiṃcid*); there is no original object. But there being no original object does not mean that the appearance of the multiplicity of objects is without a cause; rather, the cause is the energy of the Supreme Śiva, which is autonomy (*svatantryam*). The nature of this universe is that it is like a reflection, it has 'reflection bearing-ness' (*pratibimbadhāritvā*) as its nature, which is the inverse of supreme consciousness; indeed, the universe as a reflection is inert or unconscious (*jaḍam*).[47]

Having presented an account of the nature of reality as a reflection that, in truth, is pure reflexive consciousness, Abhinavagupta goes on to present an account of emanation in terms of the Sanskrit language understood as a

[47] *Tantrasāra*, pp. 11–12: *eṣaṃ yathā etat pratibimbitaṃ bhāti tathaiva viśvaṃ parameśvar-aprakāśe / nanu atra bimbaṃ kiṃ syāt? mābhūt kiṃcit / nanu kim akāraṇakaṃ tat? hanta tarhi hetupraśnaḥ—tat kiṃ bimbavācoyuktyā, hetuśca parameśvaraśaktireva svātantryāparaparyāyā bhaviṣyati, viśvapratibimbadhāritvāc ca viśvātmakatvaṃ bhagavataḥ, saṃvinmayaṃ hi viśvaṃ caitanyasya vyaktisthānam iti, tadeva hi viśvam atra pratīpam iti pratibimbadhāritvam asya, tacca tāvat viśvātmakatvaṃ parameśvarasya svarūpaṃ na anāmṛṣṭaṃ bhavati, citsvabhāvasya svarūpānāmarśanānupapatteḥ / svarūpānāmarśane hi vastuto jaḍataiva syāt, āmarśaśca ayaṃ na sāṃketikaḥ.* 'Although this world appears as reflected, it is (truly) in the light of the Supreme Śiva. But surely, what is the original? There is none. Is that then without a cause? So then, your question is about cause. Why this talk of the image? The cause will be nothing but the energy of Paramaśiva, which has autonomy as a synonym. And because the Lord supports the reflection of the universe, he is immanent. For this universe is made of consciousness, consisting of consciousness. For the universe here is the inverse (of pure consciousness) in being a reflection. Moreover, of course, this fact of being all embodying is not not perceived because of the impossibility (*anupapatti*) of that which has consciousness as its very nature, not being aware of its nature. The absence of cognition of its own nature in reality is nothing other than unconscious. This awareness is not one that depends on convention.'

representation of the emanation and reabsorption of the cosmos from and back into pure consciousness. At the highest level, when the universe is potential, the pure representations (*śuddhāḥ parāmārśāḥ*) of consciousness move out through the power of freedom and take on (*bhajante*) the forms of deities, the Vidyeśvaras, in the pure realm from where they proceed to grosser forms of manifestation.[48] Here the entire universe which comprises the powers (*śaktiḥ*) of Śiva is conceptualized as an expansion of the first three letters of the Sanskrit alphabet, *a*, *i*, and *u*, which emerge into manifestation.[49] This is also understood as the emanation of sound on three levels: namely, 'the seeing one' (*paśyantī*) in which there is no differentiation, the middle layer (*madhyamaḥ*) of mental representation, and the transactional (*vaikharī*) layer of actualized speech in which subjects and objects are distinguished.[50] This is a more philosophical account of the cosmological concept of the universe as pervaded by divine sound that the yogin perceives in inner meditation that we saw in the last chapter.

Why does Abhinavagupta present this material here? Firstly, the methods are themselves a reflection of cosmic emanation and so it is important for him to present an account of sonic emanation in the *śāmbhāvopāya*. Any account of the human and of how salvation is achieved necessarily needs to present an account of the cosmos because understanding how the person is located within the hierarchy of levels is to gain an existential knowledge or cognition that is believed to liberate. Secondly, his exposition needs to accommodate and incorporate different systems within it in order to establish the Pratyabhijñā interpretation of reality. Abhinavagupta's metaphysics, then, is that in the highest reality the cosmos is identical with reflexive consciousness, reflected within normal acts of cognition. Normal acts of cognition are intentional, which means consciousness has an object. Mental representation (*parāmārśaḥ*) is an act of cognition in which the subject of knowledge (*pramātā*) perceives an object of knowledge (*prameya*), which is represented in consciousness. The flow of these representations is, however, not merely related to the individual, but is a power that expresses wider, cosmic forces. Drawing on the Kālī cult of the Krama and Kula traditions, Abhinavagupta refers to these powers of consciousness as Kālikā. There is a process of consciousness projecting out and then those projections being contracted. This occurs within the individual and reflects the cosmic projection and contraction entailed in Śiva's five cosmic actions (emanation, maintenance, destruction, revealing himself, and concealing himself).[51] On this fairly simply idea of mental representations

[48] *Tantrasāra*, p. 18. [49] For an excellent account, see Padoux, *Vāc*, pp. 233–43.

[50] See Padoux, *Vāc*, pp. 166–222.

[51] On the cosmic acts, see Kṣemarāja, *Pratyabhiñāhṛdāya* 10, in *Pratyabhiñāhṛdāya by Kṣemarāja*, ed. J. C. Chatterji (Srinagar: Kashmir Series of Texts and Studies, 1911). Also D. Goodall (ed. and trans.), *The Parākhya Tantra: A Scripture of the Śaiva Siddhānta* (Pondichéry: Institut Français de Pondichéry, 2004), 3. 122–9.

reflecting cosmic processes, Abhinavagupra superimposes a variety of categories from the different systems he is familiar with in order to bring them within the ordering system of his own religion.

The Powerful Means

The second means to achieve liberation that Abhinavagupta deals with is the 'powerful' (*śākta-*) method, which uses the faculty of cognition. By contemplating a pure thought-construction (*śuddhavikalpaḥ*) such as 'I am Śiva', the practitioner can realize the truth of this statement in due course through the mind's gradual purification. The idea behind this is that once one thought (*vikalpaḥ*) is purified then it engenders another similar, pure thought forming a causal chain of thoughts that become increasingly, step by step, more purified until enlightenment, the immaculate essence without thought-construction,[52] is reached. Discursive cognition, conditioned by memory and past traces, can nevertheless become a liberating force when directed in the correct way. Such directing of thought is, in fact, a form of meditation (*bhāvanā*), which is a kind of theoretical reflection or speculative reasoning called *tarka* founded on truth revealed in true scriptures and in the teachings of a true master.[53] Because of the power of dichotomizing cognition, Abhinavagupta claims, people falsely believe themselves to be bound in the cycle of reincarnation; but this is a false belief (*abhimānaḥ*). In order to counter this false belief we need to cultivate a true belief, that is, a discursive thought that is also true, such as that 'I transcend all and am embodied as all'.[54]

Discursive cognition that leads either to entanglement in the world of the senses or to enlightenment and freedom from entanglement is conceived by Abhinavagupta as a power (*śaktiḥ*). The processes of cognition are in fact powers of supreme consciousness that expand and contract, which Abhinavagupta conceptualizes in terms of twelve goddesses called Kālī who become manifested as sense perception and which withdraw back into their source, pure consciousness, conceptualized as the Supreme Goddess Kālasaṃkārṣinī. These twelve Kālīs are the goddesses of the Krama pantheon that Abhinavagupta integrates into his philosophical account of the purification of discursive thought.[55] Consciousness projects (*kalayati*) itself in the form of these

[52] *Tantrāloka* 4.6cd: *saṃvidabhyeti vimalāmavikalpasvarūpatām*. Consciousness becomes pure, an essence without thought-construction.

[53] *Tantrasāra*, p. 21.

[54] *Tantrasāra*, p. 21: *ato viśvottīrṇo viśvātmā ca aham iti.*

[55] Alexis Sanderson, 'Meaning in Tantric Ritual', pp. 73–5, in Ann-Marie Blondeau and Kristopher Schipper (eds.), *Essais sur le rituel III* (Louvain, Paris: Peeters, 1995), pp. 15–95. The twelve are Sṛṣṭi-, Rakta-, Sthitināśa-, Yama-, Saṃhāra-, Mṛtyu-, Rudra-, Mārtanda-, Paramāraka-, Kālāgnirudra-, Mahākāla-, and Mahābhairavacandograghora-. These are also described in the *Tantrāloka* 4. 148–81. See Sanderson, 'Meaning in Tantric Ritual' for a description.

goddesses, firstly into sphere of intentional objects (*prameya*), then reabsorbs itself into the sphere of processes of cognition or means of knowing (*pramāṇaḥ*), and finally into itself as the subject of knowing (*pramātā*). This process of extension and return occurs in all moments of consciousness and is analysed here into its specific stages as an account of the way experience arises and is destroyed. The supreme reality is self-revealing because it is omniform in everything, and the enlightened practitioner who has realized this is said to be spontaneously initiated by the Goddess.[56] No formal or external initiation is needed in someone who has realized the inner power of the Goddess in thought.

On the one hand, Abhinavagupta describes the processes of cognition in what we might call the mythological language of the Krama tradition; yet on the other, he describes the processes of cognition in terms of traces from the past colouring the sequence of discursive cognition. Both of these are ways of speaking about the same process. This purification of thought is initiated by the master whose function (*vyāparaḥ*) lies in the explanation of scripture, which in turn creates proper discursive thought (*samucitavikalpaḥ*), that in turn is the cause (*nibandhanaḥ*) of generating a sequence of pure thoughts. The correctly directed sequence of thoughts, which is in fact a manifestation of powers and is also true reasoning, leads to enlightenment and the removal of duality. Indeed, Abhinavagupta identifies true reasoning with meditation (*bhāvanā*) as the method that develops dichotomizing cognition and leads from a state of being unclear to a state of lucidity. True reasoning therefore is not simply a kind of philosophical thought process, but is a meditation, and so is classified as one of the auxiliaries of a six-fold yoga (*ṣaḍaṅgayogaḥ*),[57] with the other parts playing a supporting role. We might render the term *tarka* as 'contemplative reasoning' or even 'insight' as it refers to the power of judgement that allows the practitioner to discern between a pure cognition and an impure one. Indeed in many ways *tarka* is akin to insight meditation (*vipaśyanam*) in Buddhism which cultivates deep understanding of the nature of reality as having no self, being impermanent and being a condition of suffering, and which can be contrasted with absorbed meditation (*dhyānam*). For Abhinavagupta, the traditional yoga of absorption—wherein the yogi concentrates upon an object and becomes absorbed in it—is a restriction of consciousness and should be avoided.[58] Focused meditation on an object is the

[56] *Tantrasāra*, p. 23.

[57] The six auxiliaries are breath control (*prāṇāyamaḥ*), retraction of senses (*pratyāhāraḥ*), meditation (*dhyānam*), concentration (*dhāraṇaḥ*), reasoning (*tarkaḥ*), and absorption (*samādhiḥ*). The earliest formulation of this list occurs in the *Maitryupaniṣad* 6.18. See the interesting discussion of these in Somadeva Vasudeva, *The Yoga of the Mālinīviyayottaratantra*, pp. 367–82. I have followed Vasudeva, who follows Sanderson in translating *aṅga* as 'auxiliary' or 'subsidiary' rather than 'limb' (p. 367, n. 1).

[58] Thanks to Alexis Sanderson for drawing my attention to this point.

opposite of *bhāvanā*, which is about the expansion of consciousness to realize its full extent. Abhinavagupta writes:

> **Reading 24**
> Thus as it has been said, the removal of duality is made by discursive thought. This ultimate truth—whose true nature is shining forth, having gradually expelled the condition of its real nature not being apprehended, a state that it has itself spontaneously assumed—begins to expand, then expands, then is fully expanded. In this way it shines forth.[59]

The purification of discursive cognition leads to the removal of duality that is the non-apprehension of the true nature of reality. This very duality is itself due to the spontaneous self-limiting of consciousness, simply because it is the very nature of ultimate truth to spontaneously manifest (i.e. limit) itself. This ultimate consciousness expands through stages until it is fully expanded, personified in the bulging eyes of the image of Bhairava. For the practitioner to realize ultimate truth through contemplative reasoning is to expand consciousness through various stages to its full expansion. This realization of the full expansion of consciousness is a higher gnosis.

All external accoutrements of tradition are, for Abhinavagupta, merely supports for the realization of non-dual awareness. Thus contemplative reasoning is supported by external ritual such as making offerings into the sacred fire, the standard Brahmanical practice, and repetition of mantras. The offerings of fragrant flowers, liquids, and powders that are aesthetically pleasing to Paramaśiva is nothing other than offering these things to consciousness, which devours them.[60] Thus Abhinavagupta's scheme moves from external ritual to internal practice in which fire offerings are understood as simply supports for inner practice of mental purification; ultimately all the contents of consciousness are consumed, even the very light of consciousness itself, which he interprets purely as support for the inner processes of purification.

The Individual Means

Finally, the last method outlined by Abhinavagupta uses the faculty of action. The 'individual means' includes all outer ritual practices as well as meditational practice and mantra repetition. *Āṇava* is an adjective derived from *aṇu*, atom, which is used to denote the individual soul. The *āṇāvopāya* is for the Śaiva who is not proficient enough to follow the *śāmbhava* or *śākta* methods and is the

[59] *Tantrasāra* pp. 24–5: *ato dvaitāpāsanaṃ vikalpena kriyata ity ukteḥ [/] ayaṃ paramārthaḥ—svaruṇpaṃ prakāśamānam akhyātirūpatvaṃ svayaṃ svātantryāt krameṇa projhya vikāsonmukham, atha vikasat, atha vikasitam ityanena krameṇa prakāśate.* Removal of *daṇḍa* emendation by Alexis Sanderson.

[60] *Tantrasāra*, p. 25.

lowest in Abhinavagupta's hierarchy of means. Rather than developing pure discursive cognition, the follower of the individual method is only able to develop a discursive cognition with the support of external phenomena such as mantra, meditation on the body, and external objects. The *Mālinīvijayottara* speaks of *āṇava* as comprising the arising mantra (*uccāraḥ*), the performance of yogic posture (*āsanam*), meditation (*dhyānam*), concentration on syllables (*varnaḥ*), and focusing on loci of meditation (*sthānaprakalpanam*).[61] Although the text itself does not deal systematically with these, particularly mantra practice,[62] Abhinavagupta goes into some detail in the *Tantrāloka* (Chapter 3), summarized in the *Tantrasāra* (Chapter 5). Within this classification, Abhinavagupta regards only the meditation locations as 'external injunction' (*bāhyavidhiḥ*), the others being internal (*antara*-).

The details of these various practices are complex, but all share the general idea of energy within the body moving or being directed upwards to the crown of the head where, or above which, Śiva is symbolically seated. We need at this point to say something about Abhinavagupta's conception of the body. Although this is more developed in later yogic traditions, the body at one level is a physical entity that experiences the sensory world; but there are also more subtle levels to it. This subtle body (*sūkṣmaśarīraḥ*) is pervaded by many channels (*nāḍīḥ*), of which three are the most important. One, called the *suṣumnā*, runs up the central axis of the body from the anal region to the crown of the head and even 'twelve fingers' (*dvādaśāntaḥ*) length beyond that, with two channels circumvoluting it from the nostrils to the base. Along this central axis are located centres of power called 'circles' (*cakrāni*), 'supports' (*ādhārāḥ*), and 'knots' (*granthayaḥ*) which are thought to correspond to levels of the cosmos. Through yogic practice such as control of the breath and the repetition of mantras, the Goddess is awakened and moves up this central channel to the place of awakening at or above the crown of the head.[63] There is an elision between breath or energy (*prāṇam*) and the coiled or serpent Goddess Kuṇḍalinī who is coiled within the body. This journey of energy up through the body is simultaneously the journey of the yogi through the hierarchical cosmos to liberation and the opening out of the fullness of consciousness. This is not the place to elaborate the details of this practice, but it is notable that Abhinavagupta describes in some detail the developing of the breath and mantra, locating the phoneme (*varṇaḥ*) within the arising of the mantra (*uccāraḥ*) which occur within the subtle breath (*suḳṣmaprāṇam*).[64] The last method, the meditation on 'place' (*sthānaprakalpanaḥ*), refers to

[61] *Mālinīvijaottara-tantra* 2.21ab.

[62] Vasudeva notes that other Śaiva scriptures fill in the details of the practice of *uccāra*. Vasudeva, *The Yoga of the Mālinīvijayottara-tantra*, pp. 283–4.

[63] See L. Silburn, *Kuṇḍalinī: The Energy from the Depths*, trans. Jacques Gontier (Albany, NY: SUNY Press, 1990).

[64] *Tantrasāra*, p. 42.

meditation on three locations: the breath, body, and external object.[65] Abhinavagupta lists external objects as themselves comprising eleven types, such as the ritual arena and the rosary.[66] These external rites involved visualizing deities, performing ritual worship to images, and following the pattern of Śaiva worship. Such worship involved the ritual identification of the body with the cosmos in 'six paths' (*ṣaḍadhvā*) that we find in standard Śaiva Siddhānta liturgy.[67] But with all of these practices, the externality is only apparent because all appearances are identical with supreme consciousness and are vibrations of it for Abhinavagupta, and he clearly says that the external injunction nevertheless 'still shines within the Supreme Lord'.[68]

The question of the nature of the self and the nature of consciousness is not simply a cognitive question for Abhinavagupta. He sees it as fundamental to the truth of the human person and to the relief of suffering in this world. His great intellectual project is to draw religious systems—different revelations from a divine source along with their yogic and ritual systems—into the gravitational pull of his monistic metaphysics. In this he has varying degrees of success. The simple model of three methods that he identifies with three human and divine faculties of willing, thinking, and acting, serves to control a vast and complex array of systems. There is almost a compulsive desire to map different systems onto each other, with the twelve Kālīs of the Krama being identified with the three Goddess of the Trika, for example, and the yogic system of different cosmic levels in the *Mālinīvijayottara* being identified with the four states of waking, dreaming, sleeping and the transcendent fourth that we find in the Vedānta tradition, and so on. These complex mappings that take up many pages of commentary illustrate that, by this period, a diverse number of traditions had developed. What is important for us is that Abhinavagupta's philosophical articulation of the nature of a person articulates pre-philosophical practices based on a variety of different revelations. The true identity of the person is non-gendered and not determined by caste, but has an innate, spontaneous freedom as absolute consciousness without duality. Our ignorant sense of who we are is based on false pride that identifies with attachment, but the very forces within us that keep us bound in the cycle of

[65] *Tantrasāra*, p. 45.

[66] *Tantrāloka* 6.1–4. The eleven places are the diagram (*maṇḍalam*), earth platform (*sthaṇḍilam*), chalice (*pātram*), rosary (*akṣapsūtram*), text (*pustakam*), the symbol of Śiva (*liṅgam*), an inscribed skull (*tūraḥ*), painting on cloth (*paṭaḥ*), clay image (*pustaḥ*), metal image (*pratimā*), and other image (*mūrtiḥ*). See Alexis Sanderson, 'Meaning in Tantric Ritual', pp. 27–8. The *Netra-tantra* 7.26 lists eleven *sthāna*-s situated within the body. A. Padoux, *La Lumière sur les Tantras*, p. 111, n. 67.

[67] See H. Brunner (ed. and French trans.), *Somaśambhupaddhati* (Pondichéry: Institut Français de Pondichéry, 1977), vol. 3, pp. xiii–xxii; R. Davis, *Ritual in an Oscillating Universe: Worshipping Śiva in Medieval India* (Princeton, NJ: Princeton University Press, 1991), on the purification of the *kalās*, pp. 95–100. On the six paths, see Padoux, *Vāc*, pp. 330–71.

[68] *Tantrasāra*, p. 45: *sa ca parameśvara eva antarbhāti.*

suffering can be harnessed and used in support of liberation. His account of the nature of a human person, and how perception operates, is linked to the structure of his soteriology: that the paths out of suffering, the paths to enlightenment, are founded upon the structures of human existence. In a sense, human nature itself provides the basis upon which to build systems of salvation.

CODA: THE INTELLECTUAL HISTORY OF THE SELF

Emerging from this, at times necessarily dense, textual discussion, we lastly need to present the themes that Abhinavagupta is dealing with in a broader intellectual framework. As to the question of whether there is an intellectual history in India, the material presented here supports the idea that there is, and that this intellectual tradition, spread over a vast continent, was concerned with fundamental issues of human importance: the nature of the human person, the nature of the world, and how we should act. By the time of Abhinavagupta, the religions of South Asia had developed a sophisticated philosophical vocabulary and different intellectual positions were well established and resourced. As we have seen, one of the key themes emerging in Abhinavagupta's world was the idea and nature of the self; that the self within is the truth of the world, and that realizing this self is a liberating cognition. The nature of the self had been a focus of concern from the very foundations of Indian philosophy in the Upaniṣads, where we first have the idea of the truth within as universal, cosmic and proto-Sāmkhya speculation and are presented with an atomic notion of the self. Indeed, we have two trajectories in this early period that are to resonate through the history of Indian philosophy: on the one hand, the monism exemplified in the *Bṛhadāranyaka-* and *Chāndogya-*Upaniṣads, in which the self (*ātmā*) is identical with absolute reality (*brahma*); and on the other, a monadic view of the self exemplified by Sāmkhya, in which the self is particular but eternally cut off from matter and other selves—a pure spirit apparently trapped in the material world. Both of these views maintain that this self is hidden within the body and realizing this is the highest goal and value of life. These two opposing doctrines work their way through to the modern period. In addition to this we have Buddhist and materialist doctrines that deny the reality of the self as a self-identical reality through time. The Buddhist impersonalists came to be an important intellectual force, with large monastic universities such as Nālandā, working out the implications of this doctrine and arguing with other, opposing positions. Abhinavagupta responds to this challenge in presenting his arguments, particularly in the *Īsvarapratyabhijñāvimarśinī*, in a considered way that takes seriously the Buddhist doctrine of momentariness, but critiques the fundamental Buddhist position of impersonalism (*anātmā*). While the tradition continues to some extent after Abhinavagupta with his students, there is no continued dialogue with the Buddhists, and serious debate in this particular trajectory remains silent.

But the debate about the self does not, of course, end here, and we have not touched upon the vitally important tradition of Vedānta, which promoted an orthodox, Brahmanical view of the self in varying degrees of identity with the absolute, nor the Vaiśeṣika and Nyāya particularist views of the self. This tradition was to see a second flowering in the early modern period in Bengal and Varanasi, with innovative doctrines in dialogue with Islam developing.[69] Indeed, interaction with Islam—or, more precisely, the engaging of Islam with the new thinking—was an important development in the history of ideas, particularly with Dārā Shukoh's translation of the Upanisads, which is thought to be the world of God, into Persian. This 'new reason' flourished throughout the seventeenth century, developing a fresh style 'which digs up the deep or hidden meaning (*gūḍhārtha*) in the ancient text',[70] and parallels the philosophical developments of Descartes and Bacon in Europe and their responses to scholasticism. Ancient questions as to whether the self is unitary and the self's relation to God are re-examined, and new thought developed on the metaphysics of mathematics, for example. As in seventeenth-century Europe there was a rejection of medieval and Renaissance ideas about the universe in favour of a mechanized vision, so in South Asia during the sixteenth and seventeenth centuries we have a rejection of earlier philosophical concerns about truth and the self in favour of concerns about language, meaning, and knowledge. This was especially the case with the New Reason Thinkers of the Nyāya school, which underwent a revival in Benares and Navadvīpa, as Ganeri has shown. This school, beginning with Raghunātha Śiromaṇi (1460–1540) developed new thinking about the world and expressed itself in independent, short treatises or pamphlets,[71] although commentaries do continue to be written. Although it might not be accurate to speak of a total disenchantment with the old way of thinking, the cosmological world view of earlier centuries, there was nevertheless a sense of a new philosophical vision and confidence in the power or reason that is more focused on the clarification of philosophical and epistemological issues and less on the idea of cognition as somehow salvific. With colonialism and the imposing of a new system of education in the nineteenth century, traditional learning comes to be subordinated to the official model up to the present time. The quest for the truth within becomes relegated to religious institutions, with philosophical concerns becoming identical to those of British and European universities.

[69] See R. Ganeri, *The Lost Age of Reason: Philosophy in Early Modern India 1450–1700* (Oxford and New York: Oxford University Press, 2011), pp. 22–30, 36–8, 40–1.

[70] Ganeri, *The Lost Age of Reason*, p. 6.

[71] Ganeri, *The Lost Age of Reason*, pp. 96–8.

CONCLUSION

What I have called the pre-philosophical literature of the medieval religions comes to have philosophical articulation in schools of debate. Non-dualistic Śaivism finds its philosophical expression in the Recognition School or Prayabhijñā, of which Abhinavagupta was the finest spokesman. We can see his exposition of the inner truth that is the self identical with the absolute consciousness of Śiva, in his *Tantrasāra*, the essence of the Tantras, and in his commentary on Utpaladeva's *Īśvarapratyabhijñā-kārikās*. In this text we have seen how he defends the view that inwardness as constituted by an absolute subjectivity is metaphysical truth.

Although Abhinavagupta's legacy in Kashmir only continues in a truncated way, he is a key figure in the broader intellectual history of the subcontinent, giving voice to popular religions of salvation and a deep concern about the human person that is to continue in other streams and eddies into the colonial period. It is with the rise of modernism that the view of the self Abhinavagupta advocates comes to be challenged in a way that parallels the challenge to the traditional self with modernity. Indeed, as will already be emerging, and as we will examine in more detail in Part III, there are resonances with his medieval counterparts in Europe, not only in the style of scholasticism but in the participatory view of the self. Although the content of philosophical perspective is quite different, it is this deeper sense of the human person as connected to a broader cosmos and community that is threatened by the passage of modernity. But before we embark upon a more explicit comparison, we will turn to another parallel tradition—that of Buddhism.

6

Inwardness Without Self

Buddhism presents us with a dilemma. On the one hand it begins with the idea of truth within, the inner enlightenment experience of the Buddha that spawns a civilization, yet on the other it denies the notion of the self. What precisely the Buddha meant by 'no-self' is contentious and later Mahāyāna Buddhism even reintroduces the notion of a self (in the *Laṅkāvatāra-sūtra* for example). If my claim is that inwardness is central to the idea of religious personhood, then how does Buddhism substantiate such a thesis? Clearly Buddhism does not agree philosophically with the Hindu traditions we have encountered—there were lively debates on the notion of the self and the notion of God—and Buddhism is philosophically diverse even within itself. Yet, that being said, the notion of inwardness does have leverage in the tradition and does tell us something about the mode of being a person and the mode of spiritual development that the tradition proclaims. The famous story of Siddhārtha Gautama testifies to the importance of inwardness that lies at the root of the tradition. Siddhārtha gives up his luxurious life as a prince to seek an end of suffering, he practises austerities, and finally realizes enlightenment, the end of suffering, within himself. He woke up to the truth of nirvāṇa that had always been there, at least according to the later religion. The strong tradition of meditation in Buddhism is where we see inwardness in the sense described here, where a focus on watching the mind and its contents and developing concentration leads the practitioner to the understanding or realization of Buddhist truth.

The pre-philosophical layer of Buddhist meditation and ritual culture does have significant overlap with the Hindu material we have examined, some of which can be accounted for through historical influence, even though later philosophers distanced themselves from the mythological dimensions of the tradition.[1] Thus the early Buddhist doctrine of the meditation absorptions or *dhyāna/ jhāna* influenced Patañjali's *Yoga-sūtras* and, conversely, Śaiva

[1] On Buddhism as philosophy in contrast to religion, see Bernard Faure, *Double Exposure: Cutting Across Buddhist and Western Discourses*, trans. Janet Lloyd (Stanford, CA: Stanford University Press, 2000), pp. 64–7.

cosmology and practice influenced later Buddhism.[2] Elements of Buddhist practice go back before the time of the Buddha and the Buddha himself is said to have been taught forms of meditation and asceticism that he was eventually to reject in favour of the middle way between extremes of asceticism and indulgence. Early ascetics called Śramaṇa, that included groups such as the Buddhists, Jains, and Ājīvikās, were contrasted with Brahmans, who revered the sacred Hindu scriptures and kept to purity rules and ritual injunctions. The two groups were antagonistic towards each other and the grammarian Patañjali compared their relationship to that between a mongoose and a snake.[3] Within the narrative structure of the life of the Buddha, he was taught meditation methods, in particular the technique of developing calm (*śamathaḥ* (Sanskrit)/*samatha* (Pāli)) and refined states of consciousness called *dhyāna/jhāna*. What the Buddha brings to the Indian religious field is insight meditation (*vipaśyanam/vipassanam*), which enabled enlightenment to arise (although meditation cannot be said to have produced enlightenment since it is uncaused).[4] This insight is into the nature of life as being suffering, impermanent, and not-self (*anātmā/anatta*). The Buddha taught for forty years or so, and after his death the community began to diversify until eventually there were two broad traditions: the Mahāyāna, which in turn proliferated into many traditions and spread throughout Asia, and what was pejoratively termed the 'lesser vehicle' or Hīnayāna but which can be descriptively called Nikāya Buddhism,[5] which comprises various schools of which the Theravāda is the only surviving living tradition that has come down to us. The Buddha's insight was that liberating truth dwelled within the person and that through deep introspection we could have knowledge of it. This knowledge was not simply knowing that, but an existential liberation from the bonds of birth, death, and rebirth. Through developing the eightfold path that can be seen as a moral basis to living (*śīlaḥ*), absorbed meditation (*samādhiḥ*), and insight (*vipaśyanam*), the practitioner cultivates wisdom that leads to enlightenment or *nirvāṇa*.

[2] E.g. *vitārka, vicāra, ānanda, asmitā, egāgratā* are clearly derived from the *jhāna* factors *vittaka, vicāra, pītī, sukkha, ekāgattā*. See Lance Cousins, 'Vittaka/Vitarka and Vicāra: Stages of Samādhi in Buddhism and Yoga', *Indo-Iranian Journal*, 35 (1992), pp. 137–57; Johannes Bronkhorst, *The Two Traditions of Meditation in Ancient India* (Delhi: MLBD, 1993), pp. 71–4. On the Śaiva influence on Buddhism see Alexis Sanderson, 'Vajrayāna, Origin and Function', in *Buddhism into the Year 2000: International Conference Proceedings* (Bangkok and Los Angeles, CA: Dhammakāya Foundation, 1995), pp. 89–102.

[3] Romila Thapar, *Interpreting Early India* (Delhi: Oxford University Press, 1993), p. 63.

[4] R. Gombrich, *What the Buddha Thought* (London: Equinox, 2009), pp. 147, 171. On *dhyāna* in relation to other Indian meditation practices see Bronkhorst, *The Two Traditions of Meditation*, pp. 78–111.

[5] I adopt Nikāya Buddhism to refer to non-Mahāyāna schools defined by allegiance to a particular transmission of monastic rules from Alf Hiltebeitel, *Dharma: Its History in Law, Religion and Narrative* (New York: Oxford University Press, 2011), pp. 103–4.

The justification of examining this process as a type of inwardness is that it conforms to the pattern that the practitioner gains wisdom through introversion, and furthermore that through the inward gaze the practitioner sees himself as integrated into the cosmos and that the cosmos is recapitulated within the self. For the early Buddhist this process culminated in the realization that there is no substantial self. This is, of course, paradoxical, for who is the subject of the insight into non-self? But although we have this problematic about the nature of the narrative coherence that we call the self, that meditation is a kind of interiority is in the tradition from its roots.

BARE INWARDNESS

An early text of meditation found in the Pāli Canon, the discourse on the four foundations or bases of mindfulness (*Satipaṭṭhāna-sutta*), presents an account of introversion in which the monk becomes aware of the body, feeling, mind, and mental categories (*dhamma*). In the text the Buddha exhorts his monks to pay attention to the body and to observe it with detachment; similarly he should observe feeling (*vedanā*), which in Buddhism means aversion, attraction or indifference, followed by observance of the mind (*cittam*) and the categories. With the mindfulness of body, for example, the monk should be aware of bodily posture, breathing, and all the contents and functions of the body. The text reads:

Reading 25

And how, monks, does a monk practise contemplating the body in the body? Here, monks, a monk goes to a forest, or the roots of a tree or an empty place and sits, folding his legs in a cross-legged position, making his body straight and sets up mindfulness in front of him. Mindful, he breathes in; mindful, he breathes out. As he breathes in a long breath, he knows, 'I am breathing in a long breath', or as he breathes out a long breath he knows, 'I am breathing out a long breath'. As he breathes in a short breath, he knows, 'I am breathing in a short breath', or as he breathes out a short breath, he knows, 'I am breathing out a short breath'. He trains thus: 'experiencing the whole body, I will breathe in'; he trains thus: 'experiencing the whole body I will breath out'.[6]

[6] *Majjhima Nikāya* 10, *Satipaṭṭhāna-sutta* in Sarah Shaw, *Buddhist Meditation* (London: Routledge, 2010), p. 81. Shaw's translation: *athañcabhikkhave bhikkhu kāye kāyānupassī viharati? 1. Idha bhikkhave bhikkhu araññagato vā rukkhamūlagato vā suññāgāragato vā nisīdati pallaṅkam ābhijitvā ujum kāyaṃ panidhāya parimukhaṃ satim upatthapetvā. So satova assasati, sato passasati. Dīgham vā assasanto dīgham assasāmīti pajānāti. Dīghaṃ vā passasanto dīghaṃ passasāmīti pajānāti. Rassam vā assasanto rassam assasāmīti pajānāti. Rassam vā passanto rassam passasāmiti pajānāti. Sabbhakāyapatisamveī assasissāmīti sikkhati.*

This is a very early text composed during the first centuries BC, after the Buddha's death around 400 BC. Although it is well before the time frame of this study, it is important in that it captures the spirit of Buddhist meditation that carries on through the centuries to the present time in South East Asia and now in the West. In this text we are presented with the cultivation of a heightened state of awareness. It is not explicitly about inwardness in the sense of visionary or absorbed states of mind in which awareness of the external world is attenuated. Yet I would be reluctant to say that this text is not about inwardness. It seems to me that we have here a uniquely Buddhist understanding that sees the person in terms of process (bodily processes, breathing, locomotion, and so on) and attention reflexively turned to that. As reflexivity this text clearly concerns inwardness, yet an inwardness that is highly focused on the present moment and the arising and passing of bodily and mental functions that only exist in the present. This is a stripped down or bare inwardness with the minimal content of simply watching the body, feeling, mind and existents.

The term translated as 'mindfulness' is *sati*, or in Sanskrit *smṛti*, whose primary designation is 'memory'. But rather than the recollection of the past, it is the bringing to awareness of the present. It designates a kind of ambient awareness. Warder translates the term as 'self-possession'[7] and Guenther as 'inspection'.[8] The primary meaning of the verbal root *smṛ* is to remember or recall, but it is also used in a more general sense of awareness, and is used in later Hindu tradition to designate 'meditate' or 'visualize', particularly in the third person optative, 'one should meditate' (*smaret*). In early Buddhism the primary designation of *sati* is mindfulness. Shaw cites an early sutta illustrating that to be mindful is to be alert and awake: *sati* is like a gatekeeper of a citadel who allows in only those he knows but not those he does not.[9] Thus mindfulness alerts us to the cultivation of wholesome (*kusalam*) states of mind and the rejection of unwholesome states (*akusalam*).

The text therefore exemplifies a kind of inwardness generated through reflexive awareness that is also reportable and brings awareness into language through a kind of narrative sequence. Thus, while awareness itself escapes description, the text is keen to advocate a verbal understanding of what is happening. The subject of first person predicates becomes the focus of awareness through the acts that it is performing. In self-awareness the 'I' comes into view through its activity. Here, through focusing on the breath the monk becomes aware of the subject of breathing: that 'I am breathing in' or 'I am breathing out'. The monk is aware and this awareness is reportable with a

[7] A. K. Warder, *Indian Buddhism* (Delhi: MLBD, 1970), p. 83.

[8] Herbert V. Guenther, *Philosophy and Psychology in the Abhidharma* (Berkeley, CA: Shambala, 1976), p. 111.

[9] Shaw, *Buddhist Meditation*, p. 76.

minimal narrative produced. Ideally the monk will be engaged in a continuous self-narrative in which the four foundations are the objects of attention that can be continually narrated. Such reflexive awareness is the key to eventually awakening in that it pays attention to the here and now, and in so deepening consciousness of the present moment eventually leads to the enlightenment experience in the here and now.

In the Christian and Hindu material we have seen how inwardness is closely associated with participation in tradition and cosmos. But in what sense then is mindful awareness participation? It would seem that this text exemplifies not a recapitulation of tradition but an implicit *rejection* of tradition in saying that the only relevant thing, the only available truth, is awareness of the present moment. This is clearly the emphasis of the text, yet even here the inwardness it presents is in conformity with the Buddha's vision. While the internalization of tradition is not so explicit as in Hindu and later Buddhist practice, where the deities of the tradition are so culturally specific, there is still an internalization of the teachings. That is, the Buddha teaches awareness and how it is to be achieved, a teaching recorded in the texts that become tradition, and so when the monk is practising awareness or mindfulness of breathing he is recapitulating the practice of the Master. In narrating his own life in terms of an inner running commentary on what he is doing, the monk is reproducing in himself the Master's life and teachings. There is still a tradition here but a tradition that is stripped of much content other than bare awareness of the 'I am', or rather 'there is this awareness'. Mindfulness is cultivated through habit, the habit of regular meditation, yet undermines mere habit through cultivating awareness. Habitual practice counts for nothing if there is no awareness.

There is a deeper level of inwardness implied here. Through this reflexive awareness the monk is led to the understanding that in fact the subject of this experiencing is no subject. The 'I' is non-substantial and merely a conventional way of speaking. Thus the sutta at one point focuses on mindfulness of death, contemplating dead bodies in different states of decay and applying that insight to the meditator's own body. Through contemplating death in such a concrete way the practitioner is given awareness of his own mortality and the insight that within the body there is nothing permanent, even the self. The last base of mindfulness is contemplating *dhamma*. *Dhamma* (Sanskrit *dharma*) is a semantically broad term that embraces the Buddha's teaching, but is also a term for an existent that is an object of consciousness. Thus the four truths of the Noble One are *dhamma* in both senses, as the teaching of the Buddha and as object of consciousness.[10] Mindfulness of *dhamma* here means to be aware

[10] See Hiltebeitel, *Dharma*, pp. 103–79. The Abhidharma defines teaching (*dhamma*) as name, phrase, and syllable as well as the Buddha's speech. Collett Cox, *Disputed Dharmas: Early Buddhist Theories on Existence* (Tokyo: International Institute for Buddhist Studies, 1995), p. 161.

of suffering, the cause of suffering, the end of suffering, and the path leading to that end. Similarly the five hindrances to meditative development (sense desire, ill will, sloth and torpor, restlessness and worry, and doubt) and the seven factors of enlightenment are *dhammas* or objects of consciousness. Thus from bare reflexive awareness the text moves to awareness of doctrine and the way in which the teachings are internalized and made specific to the person. This is a subtle doctrine, integrating fairly abstract ideas into the life of the practising monk.

EARLY MEDITATION PRACTICE

While mindfulness is an integral part of Buddhist meditation, there are other forms of meditation that cultivate inwardness in a much more elaborated way. Through sitting still and focusing the mind on an object of concentration the meditator goes into an absorbed state called *dhyāna* (Sanskrit) or *jhāna* (Pāli). These states were classified in early Buddhism into four absorptions of form (*rūpajhānaḥ*) and four formless absorptions (*arūpajhānaḥ*), which leads in turn to the six higher knowledges (*abhiññā*) which include magical powers (*iddhiḥ*). Of these higher knowledges, three are mundane (*lokiya-*) and three are transcendent (*lokuttara-*). The transcendent knowledges are the divine eye (*dibbacakku*), which gives insight into the current action traces of all beings that propel them into future rebirths, the ability to see one's own rebirths, and knowledge of the destruction of the 'outflows' (*āsavaḥ*), the roots of attachment that keep a being bound to the cycle of rebirth. These higher knowledges therefore give insight into the Buddha's doctrine of suffering, impermanence, and no-self.

From its foundations, then, Buddhism has been concerned with cultivating inwardness through meditation practice. Of particular importance is the development of *dhyāna/jhāna*. Through cultivating the five *dhyāna* factors and repressing the hindrances, the practitioner creates the conditions for an inner sign or eidetic image to arise (*nimittam*), that takes the mind into a state of concentration or absorption. *Vitàrka* has the meaning of 'reasoning', but within the context of meditation it refers to the faculty of the mind that directs or throws attention onto an object. Keeping the mind in this state of attention, stopping the mind from wandering, is 'deliberation' or *vicāra*. These two processes of *vitarka* and *vicāra* are present in all cognition but harnessed and developed in meditation. Through the cultivation of these faculties the mind develops joy (*prīti*), followed by contentment (*sukham*), which leads in turn to one-pointedness (*ekāgratā*). Each of these counteracts one of the hindrances—thus *vitarka* counteracts indolence, *vicāra* doubt, *sukha* counteracts frivolity, *prīti* ill-will, and *ekāgratā* sense desire. When all five factors are present in a sufficiently intense degree, then the first *dhyāna* arises. In the second *dhyāna*, *vitarka* and *vicāra* fall away and the meditator is left with joy, contentment, and one-pointedness. The further *dhyānas* are refinements until in the fourth *dhyāna* only one-pointedness remains. There is some dispute over *prīti* and *sukha*,[11] but on the whole this structure of meditation is common to the Nikāya Buddhism and the Mahāyāna in the tradition of reflection upon the mind, the Abhidharma. But other schools of the Mahāyāna overlay this scheme with their own ornate elaborations, particularly the tantric traditions. Nevertheless, the *dhyāna* scheme continues through the tradition, and even the *Guhyasamāja-tantra* describes five kinds of *nimitta*: the form of a mirage (*marīcikā*), smoke, fireflies, light, and constant light like a cloudless sky.[12]

We have in the early tradition a technical vocabulary for the development of inwardness found in the Pāli Canon and still used in the living Theravāda meditation tradition. There is a developed vocabulary of the processes of cognition and a sense of interiority in that the meditator goes on a journey within. The Buddha himself spoke of *nibbāna* as the 'further shore' and used the metaphor of the journey or path (*margaḥ/magga*) within. The texts also use the metaphor of a mountain. As the meditator develops in practice the mind becomes more and more refined and purified in a way akin to climbing a mountain 'to the transparent air of the mountain peak',[13] or attaining *jhāna* is like a cool pool in which joy and happiness pervade the body.[14] This meditative inwardness can be cultivated through a number of techniques such as focusing on a circle of light shining on a wall in the *kasina* exercises, and although it is insight that is the facilitator of enlightenment, the practice of the *dhyānas* has a central place in the history of Buddhism. There would seem to be a link between concentration and the arising of the sign and the later practice of visualization and, indeed, the term *dhyāna* becomes synonymous with visualization in the Buddhist and non-Buddhist tantric traditions of the medieval period.

The kind of meditation practice in Buddhism is akin to the inwardness developed in the medieval Hindu traditions. From its inception, the Buddhist meditator tries to achieve stillness: stillness of body, stillness of breath, and stillness of mind, in order to unleash or realize a higher state of mind that is purely internal. As with the Hindu material, this inwardness is not individualistic although it happens to a particular person, but is collective in so far as the practitioner conforms to a predetermined pattern. Indeed, the practitioner is copying the Buddha, who paved the way, in developing concentration, as the

[11] Guenther, *Philosophy and Psychology in the Abhidharma*, p. 121. Guenther provides a good account of the *dhyāna* factors, pp. 120–6.

[12] *Guhyasamāja-tantra*, ch. 18, p. 164. Cf. *Śvetāśvara-upaniṣad* 2.11 (see Olivelle, *The Early Upaniṣads*).

[13] Guenther, *Philosophy and Psychology in the Abhidharma*, p. 122.

[14] Shaw, *Buddhist Meditation*, p. 64.

Buddha did, that will hopefully lead to final enlightenment in this life. The Buddhist practitioner meditates alone and yet is part of a collective body or community (*saṅgham*) with a shared goal, shared metaphysical structures, and shared institutions to inhabit. As we have seen with previous examples, the same is true here. The Buddhist monk practises to erase his attachment that forms a superficial personality. What might be associated with individual personality characteristics or personality types is eradicated in meditation practice. The only way in which individuality, defined as a distinct personality, is relevant is in the effectiveness of practice. Early Buddhist texts of the Pāli Canon refer to different kinds of personality as being driven by greed (*lobhaḥ*), hate (*doṣam*), or delusion (*mohaḥ*), and different practices can counteract these tendencies. Thus someone driven by lust, associated with greed in meditational psychology, should practise the meditation on death,[15] or someone driven by hate should practise loving kindness (*maitrī/mettā*), the first of the pre-Buddhist practices of 'divine abidings' (*brahma-vihāraḥ*).

In these early practices we see the same correspondence between inner state of mind and cosmos. The three realms of the Buddhist cosmos, the realm of desire (*kāma-lokaḥ*), the realm of form (*rūpalokaḥ*), and the formless realm (*arūpalokaḥ*), are experienced in interiority as the meditator leaves the realm of desire and enters the first *jhāna*. Each of the subsequent *jhānas* is associated with particular worlds in the Buddhist system. Thus the various heavens where beings can be reborn are located in the realm of the *jhānas*. Exactly as we saw in the Hindu systems, as we rise up through the cosmic system, the distance between consciousness (*cittaḥ*) and the world of experience (*lokaḥ/bhuvanaḥ*) becomes less. Thus in the formless realm the name of the worlds is not differentiated from the name of the four states of mind—namely the realm of infinite space, infinite consciousness, nothingness, and neither perception nor non-perception. These refined states of consciousness, however, are not regarded as necessarily leading to enlightenment, and rather like the Śaiva condition of the experients whose object is the dissolution of the cosmos (*pralayakevalī*), the practitioner of the *arūpa-jhānas* cannot be liberated from that state. In the early Buddhist scheme it is only from the fourth *jhāna* (not from the *arūpa-jhānas*) that the higher knowledges can be cultivated and liberation achieved. Indeed, the Buddha is said to have achieved enlightenment in the fourth *jhāna* and to pass into the final enlightenment or *parinibbāna* from the fourth *jhāna*.[16]

[15] A contemporary practice of Thai monks is to contemplate pictures of pin-up girls juxtaposed to decomposing corpses: a modern innovation on the Buddhist meditation on death.

[16] *Mahāparinibbāna-sutta* 6.9. Trevor Ling (ed.), *The Buddha's Philosophy of Man* (London: J. M. Dent, 1981), pp. 139–213. There was some debate about whether one could be enlightened without going through the *jhānas*, and a category developed in the commentarial literature of the 'dry visioned' enlightened being or *sukhavippāsaka* who is enlightened by insight only and not by

LATER BUDDHISM

Later Mahāyāna Buddhism understood its own development in terms of 'three turnings of the wheel of the teachings' (*dharmaḥ*), namely the lesser vehicle (Hinayāna), the greater vehicle (Mahāyāna), and the tantric tradition or diamond vehicle (Vajrayāna).[17] The main shift in the self-perception of the Mahāyāna is that it claims that it unites compassion (*karuṇaḥ*) and wisdom (*prajñā*) and the highest goal is the state of the enlightenment-being or bodhisattva, who has put off his own final enlightenment until all beings are enlightened. This is, of course, a paradoxical teaching in that out of compassion the bodhisattva vows to save all beings and yet in his wisdom he knows that they are empty of essence and so there are no beings to save.[18]

The origins of the Mahāyāna are obscure, whether it developed from a monastic community or a lay community for example. Its proliferation is probably linked to the development of writing, but alongside this some scholars think that the Mahāyāna originates in meditation experiences. Practitioners meditating in remote areas for many hours over long periods have visions of the Buddha and transmit the teachings they perceive themselves to have received. As Paul Harrison says, one of the purposes of concentrated meditation is 'to provide practitioners with the means to translate themselves into the presence of this or that particular manifestation of the Buddha principle for the purpose of hearing the *dharma* which they remember and propagate'.[19] The transmission of the Mahāyāna sūtras flows from their being received in meditation—hearing the *dharma* from a realized master and communicating what has been heard. This legitimates new teachings and also legitimates the idea that these teachings are indeed the word of the

meditation in the *jhānas*. Such a person has enlightenment by wisdom, *paññavimutti*, in contrast to someone who is enlightened from developing the mind (i.e. the *jhānas*), *cetovimutti*, or enlightened 'both ways' (*ubhatobhāgavimutti*). The Buddha himself was *cetovimutta*. The dry visioned (*sukkhavipāssaka*) arhat does not possess magical powers, even though enlightened, because he has not developed the *jhānas*, Majjhima Nikāya 1.437. Ref from K.N. Jayatilleke, *Early Buddhist Theory of Knowledge* (London: Allen and Unwin, 1963), p. 467. This debate seems to have been lost sight of in the later tradition.

[17] The *Saṃdhinirmocana-sūtra* seems to have been the first text to espouse this doctrine. See Paul Williams, *Mahāyāna Buddhism: The Doctrinal Foundations* (2nd edn, London: Routledge, 2009), pp. 85–6.

[18] Thus the *Vajracchedikā Prajñāparamitāsūtra* 3. says: 'As many beings as there are in the universe of beings . . . all these I must lead to Nirvana, into that Realm of Nirvana which leaves nothing behind. And yet, although innumerable beings have thus been led to Nirvana, no being at all has been led to Nirvana.' Conze's translation, Buddhist Wisdom Books (London: George Allen and Unwin, 1958), p. 25.

[19] Paul Harrison (trans.), *The Samādhi or Direct Encounter with the Buddhas of the Present: An Annotated English Translation of the Tibetan Version of the Pratyuttpana-Buddha- Saṃmukhāvasthita-Samādhi-Sūtra* (Tokyo: The International Institute for Buddhist Studies, 1990), p. xx.

Buddha. Rawlinson argues that sound and meaning are fused in this meditative experience of the inner truth (*adhyātmikadharmaḥ*).[20]

Greatly simplifying a complex historical development, we might say that the early Buddhism that emphasized *jhāna* meditation transformed into a Buddhism that stressed consciousness and developed into the doctrine of the consciousness-only school, the Cittamātra or Yogācāra, in contrast to the Buddhism that emphasized insight or wisdom and developed into the emptiness doctrine of the Madhyamaka. While the Yogācāra cultivates inwardness and articulates a philosophy of consciousness only, the Madhyamaka cultivates insight into no-self and the emptiness of the world (or specifically emptiness of the constituents or *dharmas* that make up the world). In one sense there is no inwarndness with the Madhyamaka because both inner and outer are identically empty. The reality of the world is sameness (*samatā*), which is empty (*śunyam*) of any essence or own-being (*svabhāvaḥ*). To speak of 'inside' and 'outside' is therefore delusional.

On the cusp of the development of these two major schools we have the proliferation of a number of pre-philosophical texts, the sūtras that claim to be the word of the Buddha (*buddhavacanam*). The first turning of the wheel of the *dharma* was by the historical Buddha Śakyamuni, but the Mahāyāna also claims to be the direct teaching of the Buddha from a higher form given in a vision. These texts claim to be a revelation from the Buddha who is dwelling at a higher, non-material level in a non-material body (the *samboga-kāyaḥ*). In contrast to the earlier teachings and the Pāli Canon, which claimed that the Buddha had no closed fist[21] (i.e. no esoteric teachings), the Mahāyāna sources claim that the Buddha has esoteric teachings for those with the ability to understand. The Hinayāna was for those of lower understanding concerned with the selfish desire for their own enlightenment (the Śrāvakas or 'Hearers' and the solitary Buddha or Pratyekabuddha tradition). A number of Mahāyāna sūtras arose declaring a proliferation of named meditative states. For example, an early Mahāyāna text, the *Śūraṃgamasamādhi-sūtra*, presents a long list of *samādhis*, lauding itself as the supreme.[22] The early Pure Land scriptures, the larger and smaller *Sukhavativyūha*, can be seen as early visionary texts and their descriptions of the Buddha Amitābha's realm are similar to descriptions of more explicitly vision texts such as the *Gandhavyūha* that particularly developed in China.[23]

[20] Andrew Rawlinson, 'Visions and Symbols in the Mahāyāna', in P. Connolly (ed.), *Perspectives on Indian Religion: Papers in Honour of Karel Werner* (Delhi: Sri Satguru, 1986), pp. 191–214.

[21] *Mahāparinibbāna-sutta* 2.25.

[22] E. Lamotte, *Śuraṃgamasamādhisūtra: Concentration of Heroic Progress: Early Mahāyāna Buddhist Scripture*, trans. Sarah Boin-Webb (London: Curzon Press, 1998), pp. 18–19.

[23] See D. T. Suzuki, *Essays in Zen Buddhism*, vol. 3 (London: Rider, 1953), pp. 75–102.

These texts elaborate the idea of inwardness and meditative states or *samādhi* in which the practitioner experiences different realms, the innumerable Buddha fields (*buddhakṣetram*) that comprise the universe. The idea of the neat categorization of the *jhānas* becomes overlaid with other vision-systems in an infinite universe. An example of this is an early meditation text, the *Pratyutpanna-sūtra*, translated into Chinese by Lokakṣema in CE 179.[24] Here the meditator recollects the Buddha Amitābha, visualizing him in his pure land, and after practising for seven days he sees the Buddha in a dream or vision. Indeed, the full name of the text can be translated as 'the meditation in which one is brought face to face with the Buddhas of the present' and reflects the older practice of the recollection of the Buddha (*buddhānusmṛtiḥ*).[25] Paul Harrison and Paul Williams have both emphasized the importance of protracted meditation for the formation of Buddhist literature, and while Sanskrit equivalents of 'inwardness' such as *pratyātmavedya* are not that common, the whole context of the formation of the Mahāyāna sūtras is meditation. Meditation, along with the transmission of texts that were received, is an important feature in the development of the tradition.[26] In the *Pratyutpanna-sūtra* the Buddha declares the merits of the practice and what it achieves and although this text foreshadows the Pure Land tradition, it also foreshadows the Yogācāra. At one point the Buddha says that bodhisattvas can hear the Buddha of the present through recollection, a recollection that should not be on the Buddha as a thing nor purely as a construction, but as empty. The text reads:

Reading 26

'For example, Bhadrapāla, there are certain women or men with a natural bent for washing their hair and putting on jewellery, who might decide to look at themselves in a vessel of clear oil, or a vessel of clear water, or a well-polished round mirror, or a patch of ground smeared with azurite [?]. If they see therein their own forms, Bhadrapāla, what do you think? Does that appearance of the forms of the men or women in the vessel of clear oil, or vessel of clear water, or well-polished round mirror, or patch of ground smeared with azurite mean that there are men or women who have gone inside those things or entered them?'

Bhadrapāla said:

'No Reverend Lord, it does not. Rather, Reverend Lord, because the oil and water are clear and undisturbed, or the round mirror is highly polished, or the patch of earth smeared with azurite is clean, the reflections stand forth; the bodies of the men or women have not arisen from the water, or mirror, or patch of earth; they have not come from anywhere nor gone anywhere; they have not been produced from anywhere, nor have they disappeared anywhere.'

24 Paul Harrison, 'Translator's Introduction', p. 1, in *The English Tripiṭaka: The Pratyuttpana Samādhi Sūtra, The Śūraṅgama Samādhi Sūtra* (Berkeley, CA: Numata Center, 1998). Translated from the Chinese.

25 Harrison, 'Translator's Introduction', p. 2.

26 Williams, *Mahāyāna Buddhism*, pp. 40–1; Harrison, *The Samādhi or Direct Encounter With the Buddhas of the Present*, p. xx.

The Lord said:

'Well done, well done, Bhadrapāla! You have done well, Bhadrapāla. So it is, Bhadrapāla. As you have said, because the forms are good and clear the reflections appear. In the same manner, when those bodhisattvas have cultivated this *samādhi* properly, those Tathāgatas are seen by the bodhisattvas with little difficulty. Having seen them they ask questions, and are delighted by the answering of those questions. In thinking: "Did these Tathāgatas come from anywhere? Did I go anywhere?", they understand that the Tathāgatas did not come from anywhere. Having understood that their own bodies did not go anywhere either, they think: "Whatever belongs to this triple world is nothing but thought. Why is that? It is because however I imagine things, that is how they appear.

"That thought is not apprehended as being inside, nor as being outside, nor as neither of the two. On the contrary, it is produced on the basis of objectification. That which is [in this way] produced conditionally has no substantial existence. That which has no substantial existence is unborn. That which is unborn is not apprehensible as an object. That which is not apprehensible as an object is empty of essence (*svabhāva-śūnya*). That which is empty of essence is indefinable. That which is indefinable is unable to be seen, discerned, fixated upon, demonstrated, destroyed, or established.

"Thought creates the Buddha, thought itself sees him. Thought is the Buddha, thought the Tathāgata. Thought is my body, thought sees the Buddha. Thought cannot itself know thought, thought cannot itself see thought. Thought with [false] apperceptions is stupidity; thought without [false] apperceptions is nirvāṇa. These *dharmas* lack anything enjoyable. They are all produced by thinking. Since thinking is empty, then whatever is thought is thus ultimately non-existent. Bhadrapāla, such is the vision of the bodhisattvas established in the Samadhi."'

Then at that time the Lord uttered these verses:

By thought is the Buddha produced;
And by thought alone is he seen.
The Buddha is only thought for me,
Thought alone is the Tathāgata.

Thought alone is my body.
And the Buddha is seen by thought.
Thought alone is my awakening;
Thought itself is without essence (*svabhāva*).

Thought does not know thought,
Thought does not see thought,
The appearance of thought is ignorance,
The non-apperception of thought is nirvāṇa.

These dharmas are insubstantial,
They arise from (mis)conception.
Whatever is conceived with regard to emptiness,
That conception is here empty.[27]

[27] Harrison, *The English Tripiṭaka*, ch. 3 K–O, pp. 41–4. I do not present the Chinese text.

This is a rich passage. The young man or woman looking into the mirror is akin to the practitioner looking into himself in meditation. As the reflection becomes clear so the mind becomes clear through its purification. Indeed, the image of cleaning a mirror for the cleansing of the mind is an old one. As a reflection, the image does not come from the outside yet nor does it arise from within, but the clarity of a clean reflection is an image for the clarity of mind that sees things in their true nature. Furthermore, this truth is akin to the Buddha, for if one wishes to see him he is there and can be questioned in this vision. Because of the Buddhist teaching about the emptiness of reality the practitioner should perceive such visions to be empty—the Buddha comes from nowhere and the practitioner goes to nowhere. This is very close to classical Perfection of Wisdom teachings about emptiness. The Buddha is empty of essence, as indeed is the self and whole of reality.

Yet at this point another idea is introduced into the text: that the entire Buddhist cosmology comprising the triple world, the three realms that we encounter from early Buddhism, is simply made of thought, exists only in consciousness. The text even goes so far as to say that the mind creates the Buddha and so in a sense creates itself because the mind is the Buddha. Yet, linking this idea to the earlier vision, even the mind and its *dharmas*, the objects of consciousness, themselves are empty. The mind cannot perceive itself but the mind free from imaginative conceptions (*vikalpaḥ*) realizes its true nature as empty and as the very Buddha who has been a putative object of meditation.

Concepts that were to flower in the Mahāyāna are present in the text. We have the vision of the Buddhas, and in particular Amitābha, who is to become the main focus of the Pure Land school (and the *Pratyuttpana* is revered by the tradition as an early Pure Land text), the mind-only doctrine that all reality is within consciousness only, and the philosophy of emptiness. As is common with this material, a number of ideas are overlaid on top of each other: thus the Buddha is identified with a purified consciousness, which is identified with emptiness and with nirvāṇa. Of particular note for our concern is the idea that the Buddha is within the practitioner. There was the historical Buddha certainly, but the truth of the Buddha, the very nature of the Buddha, is located within the living person. This doctrine came to be formulated in the idea that all beings have the seed of enlightenment or thought of enlightenment (*bodhicittam*) within them. This came to be identified with the womb or embryo of the Buddha, the *tathāgatagarbha* that is within all beings.[28] Although this did not develop into a distinct school of Buddhism akin to the

[28] Williams, *Mahāyāna Buddhism*, pp. 103–28; D. S. Ruegg, *La Théorie du Tathāgatagarbha et du Gotra* (Paris: École Française d'Extrême Orient, 1969); S. K. Hookam, *The Buddha Within: Tathāgatagarbha Doctrine According to the Shentong Interpretation of the Ratnagotravibhāga* (Albany, NY: SUNY Press, 1991).

Madhyamaka and Yogācāra, it nevertheless represented a strong idea expressed in a number of texts that the truth is within. As in the passage from the *Pratyuttpana-sūtra* cited above, the Buddha is identical to the mind, and although initially identified as 'my mind' is seen to be universal in the course of practice.

INWARDNESS IN THE MAHĀYĀNA

The Buddha within or the seed of enlightenment within becomes fused with the doctrine of consciousness only propounded by the Yogācāra school. One of the foundational texts of the school, the *Laṅkāvatāra-sūtra*, while promoting the view that all is consciousness, propounds the doctrine that the *tathāgatagarbha* is equated with the consciousness that underlies all of reality, the storehouse consciousness (*ālayavijñānam*).[29] This truth is realized within the person in introspection. In the opening chapter of the text, the demigod Rāvaṇa, the anti-hero of the Hindu epic, addresses the Buddha:

Reading 27

1. Show me here, O Lord, the principle of truth, that points to inwardness, that is indeed free from impurity, gone beyond views [and] without self, the injunction to truth which is the principle of the essence of consciousness.
2. Now is the time. May he go to Lanka, O sage, the Buddha whose body has stored up auspicious virtues, which is manifested as transformed and transforming, who is intent upon the truth of the abode of inwardness.[30]

In these verses Rāvaṇa questions the Buddha directly. He asks the Buddha to show him the 'principle of truth' that translates the Sanskrit compound *dharmanaya*, where *naya* can mean 'system' or even 'conduct'. 'Principle' here would seem to be a good rendering, as the phrase seems to indicate more than simply the teaching, but a foundational reality that is the *dharma*. This would seem to be in accord with other uses of *dharmanaya* in the Buddhist tantric canon. Thus the *Mañjuśrīmūlakalpa* speaks of 'the entry into the principle of truth of the Mahāyāna which is the purpose of the Bodhisattva'.[31]

[29] *Laṅkāvatāra-sūtra*, trans. D. T. Suzuki as *The Laṅkāvatāra Sūtra* (London: Routledge and Kegan Paul, 1932), ch. 6, p. 191. Sanskrit text pp. 220–1.

[30] *Laṅkāvatāra-sūtra* ch. 1, verse 1–2. Sanskrit text p. 3: *cittasvabhāvanayadharmavidhiṃ nairātmyaṃ dṛṣṭivigataṃ hy amalaṃ / pratyātmavedyagatisūcanakaṃ deśehi nāyaka iha dharmanayaṃ /1.1/ śubhadharmasaṃcitatanuṃ sugataṃ nirmāṇa-nirmita-pradarśanakaṃ / pratyātmavedyagatidharmarataṃ laṅkām hi gantu samayo'dya mune /1.2/.* My translation guided by Suzuki—Suzuki's translation is rather free. I have taken the accusatives *sugatam* etc. as objects of the verb in each verse.

[31] *Mañjuśrīmūlakalpa* ch. 1, p. 23: *bodhisattvasambhāramahāyānadharmanayasaṃpraveśanataḥ.* Although the term *naya* could also imply 'practice' as in 'pursuing the entry into the practice of

But what is particularly interesting is that the principle of truth points to the abode (*gati-*) of 'inwardness'. The term I have translated as 'inwardness' here is *pratyātmavedya-*, which can be literally rendered as 'that which is to be known in oneself'. The compound *pratyātmavedya-* thus connotes inwardness in the sense of reflexive awareness and introspection. It would seem to be an almost uniquely Buddhist expression, occurring only once in Abhinavagupta's work.[32] We can take this to mean that the truth, the principle of *dharma* that is also the truth of the Buddha, is within oneself. The compound *pratyātmavedya-* is found elsewhere in the ninth or tenth century—*Lamp that Integrates the Practices* (*Caryamelapakapradipa*), attributed to third-century Aryadeva, for example, where 'the supreme truth has inwardness as a characteristic' (*paramārthikam evedaṃ pratyātmakavedyalakṣaṇam*).[33] The phrase also occurs in the foundational text of the *tathāgatagarbha* tradition, the *Ratnagotravibhāga* ('The Germ of the Jewels'):

Reading 28
I bow before the sun of the doctrine,
Which is neither non-being nor being,
Nor both being and non-being together,
And neither different from being nor from non-being;
Which cannot be speculated upon and is beyond explanation,
But revealed [only] by introspection and is quiescent.[34]

Takasaki translates *pratyātmavedya* as 'introspection' and the passage makes clear that the truth of the Buddha within, the germ of the Buddha, is ineffable and has to be directly experienced through introspection. This truth is outside of the usual categories of being and non-being and all the possible combinations of those terms. The utter transcendence of this reality beyond words is yet not outside of experiential understanding, and is brought within the realm of articulation in the Buddhist tradition.

The idea of the *tathāgatagarbha* expressed in the *Ratnagotravibhāga* is, in effect, the truth within the person. *Ratnagotra* is translated by Takasaki as the 'germ of the three jewels' (i.e. the jewels of the Buddha, the Dharma and the

ritual, the purpose of conduct, and various mantras' *vicitramantracaryārthakriy ādharmanayapraveśānuvartinī* (p. 24). The same ambiguity between 'practice' and 'principle' is found in the *Guhyasamāja-tantra* 13 (45). 1: 'Ah the tranquil practice/principle of virtue, and the firm practice/principle of mantra', *aho dharmanayaṃ śāntaṃ aho mantranayaṃ dṛḍham.*

32 Abhinavagupta, *Īśvarapratyabijñāvimarśinī* 28. 19, p. 247.

33 *Caryamelapakapridipa*, p. 29. Christian K. Wedemeyer (ed. and trans.), *Aryadeva's Lamp that Integrates the Practices (Caryamelapakapridipa): The Gradual Path of Vajrayana Buddhism According to the Esoteric Community Noble Tradition* (New York: Columbia University Press, 2007).

34 *Ratnagotravibhāga* 2.9. Jikido Takasaki, *A Study on the Ratnagotravibhāga (Uttaratantra), Being a Treatise on the Tathāgatagarbha Theory of Mahāyāna Buddhism* (Rome: Istituto Italiano per il Medio ed Estremo Oriente, 1966), p. 163.

Saṅgha or community), where *gotra* is identified with 'seed', or 'element', or 'cause'. It is also a common word meaning 'family' or 'clan' and perhaps we have the implication that the jewel that is within all beings unites them into a family. But the main point is that within the person lies the truth of the Buddha, an absolute reality, and that this truth is to be realized by oneself (*pratyātmavedanīya-*) as the Buddha realized this truth for himself.[35] It is in this text, too, that we come across the term *vajra*—'thunderbolt' or 'lightning'—to denote the absolute truth of enlightenment. This truth, says the text, is not capable of being explained but must be realized—that phrase again—by oneself (*pratyātmavedanīya-*).[36] This compound or variants of it are used several times in the text. The truth is an awakening through introspection (*pratyātmādhigama-dharmaḥ*). Thus Buddhahood is 'having been realized' (*adhigamya*) by oneself, which is the understanding or realization (*avabodhaḥ*) of the saints that they achieved through wisdom of their own (*pratyātmā*). This wisdom is achieved by the bodhisattvas through introspection, which purifies their perception. The purity of perception through the cultivation of inwardness is also moral purity. A person with the highest compassion towards others, who renders service to others, is the bodhisattva whose perception is pure and who realizes the truth within,[37] the highest nirvāṇa through self-introspection (*pratyātmaveditam*).[38]

The *tathāgatagarbha* tradition is a fine example of the Buddhist idea of the truth within and provides strong evidence for inwardness in Buddhism in spite of the doctrine of not-self. Indeed, the *tathāgatagarbha* doctrine that becomes linked to the Yogācāra idea that the mind is brightly shining (*prabhāsvaracittam*) is very close to the Hindu notion of the self (*ātmā*): it is rather the emptiness tradition that is more clearly demarcated, and indeed it is a moot point whether one can speak of inner truth in relation to emptiness. The Madhyama Nāgārjuna is no philosopher of inwardness but of radical, uncompromising emptiness of self and other. If all is empty, even emptiness itself is empty, then all talk of inner truth in contrast to externality is illusory, or at best purely a relative way of speaking.

TANTRIC BUDDHISM

By the tenth century Buddhism in India was dying out and what remained of the religion vied for patronage with others.[39] It adopted forms of tantric

[35] Takasaki, *Ratnagotravibhāga*, p. 26. [36] Takasaki, *Ratnagotravibhāga*, p. 142.
[37] Takasaki, *Ratnagotravibhāga*, p. 179. [38] Takasaki, *Ratnagotravibhāga*, p. 326.
[39] Ronald M. Davidson, *Indian Esoteric Buddhism: A Social History of the Tantric Movement* (New York: Columbia University Press, 2002), pp. 99–102.

Śaivism and the higher yoga teachings of tantric Buddhism can be traced to Śaiva prototypes.[40] Perhaps the earliest tantric Buddhist text is the *Arya-mañjuśrīmūlakalpa*, composed some time between the sixth and fifteenth centuries, although the core of the text probably towards the earlier period.[41] It is a long scripture that was translated into Tibetan and Chinese and belongs to a class of Tantras called kriyā, Tantras concerned with ritual practice. This is a precursor of the later *Guhyasamāja-tantra*, assigned by its editor to the third century AD but probably later,[42] that contains some of the same deities but represents a more developed and systematic phase of the doctrine and practices. Finally, the last Buddhist Tantra to be composed in India was the *Kālacakra-tantra*, still widely used today in Tibetan Buddhism. Here we have an elaborate system of cosmology and ritual, much of it derived from Hindu systems such as the six-limbed yoga.[43] This text is concerned with the cosmos, the macrocosm, or the external (*bāhya-*) and how it is recapitulated in the individual, the microcosm, or internal (*adhyātma-*). Here the individual is part of a social body, the *vajra* family or group of practitioners, and is moreover identified with the *vajra* group itself.[44] The winds of action (*karmavātaḥ*) that control the external cosmos are recapitulated within the person as winds of energy or breath (*prānaḥ*) that form the person. The same forces that shape the outer cosmos, namely the elements, also form the body,[45] and the inner experience of meditation shows this: that the body and cosmos are coterminous and this is part of the higher gnosis of enlightenment.

An important doctrine that we find in the Buddhist Tantras is that of the families of Buddhas, the five Jinas or Dhyāni Buddhas that constitute a ritual

[40] See Sanderson, 'Vajrayāna, Origin and Function'.

[41] A version of the text based on a single manuscript was published by Ganapati Sastri although this was not a critical edition. A further manuscript has emerged in Nepal, the *Manjuśrīyamūla-kalpa* (probably the original title). A diplomatic edition of this text is planned by the Early Tantra Project. See <http://www.tantric-studies.uni-hamburg.de/projects/manjusrimulakalpa/>: 'The importance of the *Mañjuśriyamūlakalpa*, aka. *Mañjuśrīmūlakalpa*—traditionally regarded as belonging to the *kriyā* class of Tantras—within the history of Buddhist esotericism has long been known (through the studies of Przyluski, Lalou, Macdonald and others). However the Sanskrit text that has been available so far is merely a transcription in book-form of a single manuscript, and the editor has made no attempt to solve the many problems regarding the difficult language of the text and the corruptions of the manuscript. The importance of an ancient Nepalese palm-leaf manuscript has been pointed out by Mitsutoshi Moriguchi, but the manuscript itself has yet to be published. It is planned to produce a volume in which the text of the Nepalese manuscript will be made available in a diplomatic transcription, together with an introductory study of the significance of this recension as compared with the published version of the Sanskrit, and also with the Tibetan and Chinese translations. The volume will additionally offer a comparison of the system of this Tantra with early Śaiva and Vaiṣṇava tantric traditions.' (Accessed 13 June 2012.)

[42] Benoytosh Bhattacharya, 'Introduction', p. xxxvii, in Bhattacharya (ed.), *Guhyasamāja Tantra or Tathāgataguhyaka* (Baroda: Oriental Institute, 1967).

[43] Vesna Wallace, *The Inner Kalacakratantra: A Buddhist Tantric View of the Individual* (New York: Oxford University Press, 2001), p. 189.

[44] Wallace, *The Inner Kalacakratantra*, pp. 109–33.

[45] Wallace, *Kalacakratantra* 5.165–8.

diagram or *maṇḍala* used in outer rites and in visualization.[46] In tantric Buddhist theology, supreme enlightenment has become 'great happiness' (*mahāsukham*) and associated with the 'adamantine being' or Vajrasattva. The term *vajra* means both 'diamond' and 'thunderbolt', thereby emphasizing the dynamic, firm nature of enlightenment. The maṇḍala of the Dhyāni Buddhas represents the totality of the cosmos and the path to liberation. Although the particular Buddhas who are located in it have their origin in earlier texts, the maṇḍala as a whole only comes into being in the *Guhyasamāja-tantra*. Here the Lord manifests the maṇḍala, transforming himself as the different Buddhas by assuming different meditations or visualizations. These five Buddhas are Akṣobhya in the east, Vairocana or Vajradhāra in the centre, Ratnasambhava in the south, Amitābha in the West, and Amoghasiddhi in the north. Each of these has a set of symbolic associations, linked up with other classifications of sets of five, such as the five 'heaps' (*skandhaḥ*), five postures, five elements, five locations in the body, and five families (*kulam*) of faults. Thus Vairocana is associated with the form *skandha*, the colour white, the Bodhisattva Samantabhadra, the *kula* of delusion (*mohaḥ*), the head, and so on.[47] Most significantly, each of these Buddhas—which are in effect tantric deities—is in sexual union with a consort or 'wisdom' (*prajñā*), thereby representing the union (*yugalam*) of compassion and emptiness and skilful means and wisdom.[48]

A practitioner or sādhaka would become affiliated with a particular family of Buddhas through initiation and would visualize the deities within that lineage in a way almost identical to Śaivism. The inwardness of the practitioner developed in meditation is thus directly associated with the cosmological scheme of the Dhyāni Buddhas. From focused concentration that leads into the levels of meditative absorption (*dhyānam*) in the early tradition we have come to the visualization of meditation Buddhas within a particular lineage (*gotram*). The person's true nature is realized in the imaginative construction of the Buddha in the maṇḍala, which is a visual representation of the Buddha in a Buddha field, a realm of the universe governed by a particular Buddha. Through identifying with the Buddha in this way in the depth of sustained meditative practice, the practitioner becomes one with the Buddha and gains access to the source of this entire manifestation, namely the adamantine being or Vajrasattva. This is to achieve an end of suffering and attain great happiness (*mahāsukham*).

The inner truth in the late Vajryāna text, the *Kālacakra-tantra*, is an elaboration of the early tradition fused onto a non-Buddhist tantric system.

[46] For an account of the five Dhyāni Buddhas see the still excellent S. N. Dasgupta, *Introduction to Tantric Buddhism* (Berkeley, CA and London: Shambala, 1974), pp. 84–8.

[47] Dasgupta, *Introduction to Tantric Buddhism*, p. 87.

[48] See Bhattacharya, 'Introduction', *Guhyasamāja Tantra*, pp. xxv–xxvi.

The cosmos is found within the body and both comprise the five elements. The person in one sense becomes individual in being the focus of meditative attention as the possessor of the cosmos, yet this is also the eradication of any sense of separate identity. The inwardness the text develops is in order to erase any sense of distinction and to establish the identity of the person, with the social body or *vajra* group to which the practitioner belongs, with the wider cosmos. Indeed, as the universe will be destroyed by the fire of time personified as the deity Kālāgni (again from tantric Hinduism), so the body will be destroyed by the power of terrible Goddess Caṇḍalī, located in the navel. This incineration of the body is in fact the awakening of knowledge (*jñānam*). The structure here parallels the Hindu systems where the Goddess Kuṇḍalinī lies dormant in the root centre of the body to be awakened through breath control to rise to the crown of the head, symbolically destroying the body and facilitating a higher gnosis in the Sādhaka (see 'Visual Contemplation', pp. 119–20). Here, however, the equivalent Goddess Caṇḍālī is located at the navel, the lowest centre in the Buddhist system, which has four centres at the navel, heart, throat, and head corresponding to the four bodies of the Buddha in the Vajrayāna system. The gross or physical body of the Buddha (*nirmānakāyah*) is at the navel, the truth body of the Buddha is in the heart (the *dharmakāyā-cakram*), the subtle, enjoyment body of the Buddha (*sambhogakāyah*) is at the throat, and the 'own-being body' (*svabhāvikakāyah*) is in the head. This in itself is interesting, for the hierarchy of the bodies is slightly rearranged so that the truth body can be located in the heart. In a strict hierarchy it would be above the sambhogakāya, but here two models are being conflated: a hierarchical model with a model in which the centre of the cosmos and the centre of the person, the body of truth, must be located in the centre of the person, the heart.

These symbolic associations seem somewhat random to the outside observer but they are regarded as having great significance due to the interpenetration of all aspects of reality. Thus the subjectivity of the practitioner is linked to the objectivity of the cosmos and both, at the end of the day, are simply manifestations of emptiness.

INWARDNESS AND MORAL REVERSAL

The conceptual generosity of the Buddhist tantric systems allowed the embrace of different traditions within it. The Higher Yoga Tantras (Anuttara Yoga Tantras) absorb and adapt Śaiva texts directly with almost no change other than the deity's name. But what is most striking about the Buddhist tantric systems is the degree to which they absorb and develop the antinomian dimensions of tantric practice. Tantrism is infamous for these aspects, particularly ritualized sex, even though these texts represent a small minority of the total tantric oeuvre and were probably practised by a minority. Nevertheless these traditions are important for what they tell us about tantric Buddhist conceptions of the person and about the malleability of traditional mores.

In the old view of the Theravāda and the Mahāyāna, inwardness as meditative quest was developed to attain the goal of nirvāṇa and, with the Mahāyāna, Buddhahood. It was important to develop a strong moral base on which to build meditation and wisdom, and with the Mahāyāna this becomes the six and then ten stages of the bodhisattva's path to enlightenment, again based on a strong ethical teaching of compassion for all creatures and developing virtues such as not taking that which is not given, not drinking alcohol, not lying, celibacy for monks and nuns, and constrained sexual behaviour for the laity. There is strong continuity of moral base between the Theravāda and Mahāyāna teachings, alongside which there is the development of other aspects of doctrine. We see a general shift from the traditional teachings of the Buddha—the four truths of the Noble One, the twelve links of dependent origination, the three characteristics of existence—to an emphasis in the Mahāyāna on the emptiness of all things (an extension of the not-self doctrine) along with the infinite variety of all things (an extension of the doctrine of the constituents of reality or dharmas). There are as many Buddha fields or universes as there are grains of sand in the Ganges, yet all of these universes are empty and all the universes are, in the 'consciousness' strand of the Mahāyāna, manifestations of emptiness.

Within this grand metaphysics and symbolic universe, sexual imagery becomes important as representing the supreme happiness (*mahāsukham*) of enlightenment and the union of opposites. The union of Vajradhāra with his consort Vajreśvarī represents the union of skilful means with wisdom and of compassion with emptiness, the active and the passive poles of a symbolic world. There is a 'secret' symbolic codification of terms such that metaphysical principles—compassion and emptiness—and ritual objects—the *vajra* and bell—also mean male and female sexual organs (*bodhicitta* means semen and so on). Conversely sexual terms refer to metaphysical principles. This is known as 'twilight' language (*sandhabhāṣaḥ*).[49]

This symbolism is reflected in practice and it is here that controversy lies and the shock value of the Vajrayāna comes into play. The practitioner, through initiation, seeks to gain release from the cycle of rebirth within a single lifetime, and for the adept this entails ritualized sex or sexual yoga. Part

[49] See Agehananda Bharati, *The Tantric Tradition* (London: Rider, 1965), pp. 164–84 and the discussion by David Snellgrove, *Indo-Tibetan Buddhism: Indian Buddhists and Their Tibetan Successors* (London: Serindia Publications, 1987), pp. 132–3. For a list of terms see David Snellgrove, *The Hevajra Tantra*, vol. 1 (London: Oxford University Press, 1959), pp. 99–100.

of the South Asian world view was that semen is retained in the head and its preservation leads to long life. Conversely the emission of semen leads, inevitably, downward to death. Sexual ritual must be seen in this context: the male sādhaka should not emit semen, and through not doing so experience bliss in union with his partner, although there seems to be some ambiguity about this and some texts advocate the emission of semen (this is certainly the case in extreme Hindu Tantras where sexual substances are offerings to ferocious deities).[50] The use of sex in a ritual setting or simply in the imagination is an integral part of the esoteric dimensions of tantric Buddhism and is regarded as the quick route to enlightenment.[51] The gaining of power (*siddhiḥ*) and release (*nirvāṇam*) through the quick path is to overturn the traditional moral values of Buddhism. But it is not merely that some of the texts enjoined sexual practice in order to reflect the union of Vajradhāra with Vajreśvarī—in one sense, at least for the laity, that is not so shocking—but that they also advocated the overcoming of disgust and horror. It is certainly true that in some texts the bliss of human sexual union reflects the great bliss of enlightenment symbolized by the copulating deities, but other texts also emphasize the horrific nature of the deities visualized and the need to overcome disgust and fear. Part of this follows from the internal logic of the tradition. If all is empty of essence and all is 'sameness' (*samatā*) and, as the philosopher Nāgārjuna teaches, the limit of samsāra is the limit of nirvāṇa, then the practitioner should perceive equality in the world and overcome distinctions between right and wrong, good and bad, pleasure and displeasure. Thus the *Caṇḍamahārośana-tantra* describes a variety of sexual positions alongside the consumption of bodily excretions that should be undertaken with equanimity.[52] Indeed 'tantric feasts' (*melaḥ*) entail the consumption of taboo substances, namely human flesh from a corpse, cow, elephant, horse, and dog meat.[53] The *Guhyasamāja-tantra* is clear that the old morality is being overturned by this new ordinance in order to hasten enlightenment. Traditional, 'right thinking' bodhisattvas fainted with fear at the new teaching, the text says, and the *Hevajra-tantra* tells us that 'you should slay living beings . . . speak lying words . . . take what is not given . . . (and) frequent others' wives . . .'[54] The *Guhyasamāja* teaches that all social laws should be

[50] On the Hindu equivalents see Sanderson, 'Meaning in Tantric Ritual', pp. 80–3, in A.-M. Blondeau and K. Schipper (eds.), *Essais sur le rituel III* (Louvain, Paris: Peeters, 1995), pp. 15–95.

[51] Vesna Wallace, *Kālacakra Tantra, The Chapter on Sādhanā, Together with the Vimalaprabhā Commentary: A Study and Annotated Translation* (New York: American Institute of Buddhist Studies, 2010), pp. 137–8.

[52] C. S. George (trans.), *The Caṇḍamahārośana-tantra*, Chapters II–VIII (New Haven: Oriental Society, 1974), pp. 131–2.

[53] Snellgrove, *Indo-Tibetan Buddhism*, pp. 160–70.

[54] Snellgrove, *Indo-Tibetan Buddhism*, pp. 170–3.

disregarded by the yogi who has realized the truth of emptiness, because for him the world appears as an insubstantial drama.[55] This is a complete reversal of traditional Buddhist precepts.

On reading this material one does wonder about the degree to which the texts represent practice or the imagination of the authors, but that such material is included in a sacred text regarded as revealed raises interesting questions about its function and how and why there is this challenge to normative Buddhist practice. Furthermore, what does this tell us about inwardness?

We have seen that there is a concern with inwardness in traditional Buddhism in the emphasis on meditation. We have seen this with the development of meditative absorptions and the idea of looking within, of introspection or inwardness encapsulated in the compound *pratyātmavedya* and also in the idea of mindfulness. With the Mahāyāna we see the development of this inner concern through the cultivation of intense visualization practices that create an inner reality as an analogue for the world. This meditational trajectory leads into the development of the Yogācāra school of philosophy and is developed as a significant feature of tantric Buddhism. The maṇḍala is constructed in imagination that the practitioner lives within. But we also have, overlaid on this interiority, magical practices concerned with the acquisition of magical power and the sexual and 'disgusting' practices developed in the name of traditional values of wisdom and compassion. This is surely partly about overcoming death through confronting the horrors of life, and as such reflects the traditional Buddhist meditation on death (see 'Bare Inwardness', p. 171), but I think that we need to understand this complex material as the person being integrated within a cosmology and transcending the boundaries of limitation in order to understand the deeper connection between self and world. As we have seen with the Hindu and Christian material we have discussed, inwardness in those traditions is deeply implicated in the structure of the universe and the spiritual path is a journey through the cosmos to God within. In a parallel way, with Buddhism we have a spiritual path that is a journey through the Buddhist cosmos to the truth of enlightenment within. With the Theravāda we see this in the structure of the *dhyāna* meditation levels that correspond to worlds of experience: as is awareness (*cittam*) so is world (*lokaḥ*), the level of *dhyāna* corresponds to the level of the cosmos. This idea is carried over into the Mahāyāna and the Vajrayāna, where we have a proliferation of meditative absorptions (*samādhiḥ*) and a proliferation of worlds or Buddha fields.

With tantric Buddhism the logic continues in understanding ordinary human practices in cosmological terms. The sexual act is not simply that, but reflects a cosmological truth of the union of opposites. Furthermore, the mundane prohibitions and inhibitions of everyday, transactional life prevent

[55] Bhattacharya, *Guhyasamāja Tantra*, p. xiii.

us from realizing the higher truth of emptiness and sameness. If in reality all is empty and equal, then there should be no discrimination between pleasure and disgust, good and bad. Such distinctions are only conventional and do not hold from an absolute perspective. Thus extreme tantric practice can be seen in this light, that conventional morality and cultural norms are just that, conventions that must be overturned for a higher realization to occur. Thus for the novice the Buddhist moral precepts must be strictly adhered to, but for the adept yogi they are mere conventions whose flouting can facilitate a higher awareness. What would be harmful for a beginner is transformative for someone advanced along the path of enlightenment. I think this is the kind of reasoning at work here.

We can generalize from this to say that there is a link between cosmology and morality. Indeed, with the tantric traditions we see morality placed in the service of cosmology in that awakening to the higher truth of the universe—that all is interpenetrated and all is empty and the same—entails a denigration of conventional morality. We might even say that in strongly monistic systems or emanationist cosmologies, as tantric Buddhism, there is a weakening of the moral order. Conversely we might say that a strong moral order often occurs in systems that are not monistic or in which cosmology is not so much emphasized. For all his disapproval, Zaehner was perhaps insightful in understanding monistic systems as being inherently susceptible to moral erosion. With the sense of the transcendence of time and death, the disappearance of the everyday 'I' or ego, and the sense of oneness, there is inevitably a sense in which morality is mere convention, including killing and being killed.[56] Certainly, in traditions with an emphasis on conscience and morality there is less emphasis on cosmic participation, and in strongly cosmological traditions participation in the structure of the cosmos is more important than morality per se. That morality is adhered to in such systems might be because it is part of the structure of reality and so gives us access to that reality. Seeing morality to be part of the structure of the universe is to see morality linked to perception: to act morally is to perceive the universe in a trans-egoistical way. This sense of morality is quite different from a non-cosmological morality (such as a contemporary Protestant or humanist sense of morals).

[56] Zaehner, in a highly entertaining if somewhat exaggerated book, cites a notorious mass murderer in the 1960s, Charles Manson, as an example of action that follows from a monistic world view. After quoting a Hindu tantric text about a tantric 'meeting', he writes: 'There is much nobility and probably much truth in the theory of the union of opposites proclaimed by Heraclitus and the Upanishads alike, and Aldous Huxley is not far wrong in calling it the "perennial philosophy" since it crops up everywhere, in every form, and at all times. But it needs to be rigorously checked by the rational mind which it would destroy. If not, then "all things are lawful". And is it a coincidence that this particular sect [in the tantric text cited] called itself the "Family" as Charlie Manson called his own devoted band? Or is there a mysterious but real solidarity in what Manson called the "total experience", which for this Tantric family was "Bliss" and "participation in the Divine"?' R. C. Zaehner, *Our Savage God* (London: Collins, 1974), pp. 102–3.

CONCLUSION

Buddhism presents a challenge in the inquiry into inwardness. It has distinct views about ontological foundations and differs from Hindu systems as regards the metaphysics of the self. On the one hand Buddhism poses the doctrine of not-self, while on the other throughout the long tradition there is an emphasis on meditation, inner experience, and the quest for enlightenment regarded as the truth within. Indeed, the whole tradition stems from the inner experience of the Buddha as depicted in so many representations of the Buddha with eyes half closed, seated in meditation, and the Mahāyāna itself arguably grows out of meditative practices. There is clearly an idea of the truth within that is sought through dedicated and sustained practice over many years.

This fundamental structure of introspection is overlaid with different kinds of metaphysical terms and ideas, but there is a core understanding of reflection—as we saw in the idea of mindfulness—that is minimally cosmological but nevertheless focused on bodily processes and processes of awareness. Even in the early tradition, the emphasis on meditational absorptions links inwardness to cosmological structure, an emphasis that we find in the later Mahāyāna and tantric traditions. The inner truth of the Buddha, which in some ways is the simple insight that life is suffering, impermanent, and that persons contain no unchanging essence, is articulated in complex ways through the generations as Buddhism transforms in different cultural and political contexts. With the growth of the *tathāgatagarbha* doctrine, which easily relates to the consciousness-only doctrine of the Yogācāra, inwardness is emphasized as the mode in which the inner truth, the inner Buddha, is realized. For the earlier Mahāyāna this inner perception is a moral purification, but by the time we come to the Vajryāna there is a flouting of traditional morality in favour of the intensification of meditational and ecstatic experience—the spontaneous realization of the truth of enlightenment.

In teachings that emphasize the emptiness of all things, as in the philosophy of Nāgārjuna, there is a denial of the inner/outer distinction: the practitioner simply needs to wake up to the truth of emptiness. In more gradualist teachings, such as the Theravāda and Yogācāra, there is an emphasis on the gradual purification of the mind through introspective awareness. By meditation and focusing on an inner point, the truth of the Buddha is realized within awareness. There are parallels here with the Hindu material we have seen, although the doctrinal dimensions are so diverse and the Buddhists rigorously argued against their Hindu counterparts. But it has been important to bring Buddhism into the scheme in order to show how, in spite of doctrinal distinction, Buddhism too lays stress on the development of the inner life and the realization of the truth within. We now need to examine these proximities in a more structured way.

Part II

Theory

Having surveyed the truth within through the readings of inwardness from the history of Indian religions and Christianity we are in a position to draw together some of the uniting themes and to further develop the theory of inwardness entailed by our descriptions. The theory of religious inwardness that I wish to develop from the thick textual accounts I have presented, as a comparative enterprise, necessarily needs to engage with phenomenology, sociology, philosophy, and history. In particular, we need to ask how our phenomenology of inwardness speaks to a sociological and macro-historical account. Furthermore, we need to articulate how this can be done in a comparative context.

Approaches to inwardness in the history of philosophy have been complex. On the one hand, we have a tradition of subjectivism or philosophy of consciousness focused on the individual mind that develops in the rationalist tradition from Descartes, of whom, for all their differences, Locke, Kant, and Husserl are fine exemplars. On the other, we have the rejection of this kind of subjectivism and a critique of inwardness that emphasizes broader historical and social forces at work in the formation of the person. This critique has followed three broad historical trajectories what we might call (a) Marxist, (b) semiotic, and (c) sociological. (a) The Marxist critique can be traced from Hegel through Marx to Lukács, to the later dialectical thinkers of the Frankfurt School, and through to contemporary dialectical thinkers such as Jameson. Here, inwardness is seen as the product of historical forces that must take precedence in any account of human formation: inwardness is a kind of luxury or epiphenomenon of historical and economic processes. Thus Lukács can say that interiority is the product of bourgeois alienation. (b) The semiotic critiques the philosophy of consciousness, partly developing from Marx, finds its articulation in the philosophy of the sign of Voloshinov/Bakhtin, through to Kristeva, to other twentieth-century semioticians, and through to post-structuralism and postmodernism. Here the emphasis is on language and the formation of subjectivity in and through language. We might even include the deconstruction of subjectivity in psychoanalysis from Freud to Lacan within this trajectory, where inwardness is understood as being formed in and through the unconscious. (c) Finally, the sociological critique of inwardness itself can be divided into a functionalist tradition stemming from Durkheim to his students Hertz, Mauss, through to Dumont, and a *verstehen* tradition from Weber with a focus on social values. Both the Durkheimian and Weberian traditions of sociology stress the importance of macro-social forces in the formation of the person, although there is no total disparagement of inwardness in that individual agency can have effects on the social body. The fault lines in the debate are not, of course, always as neat as this; we have the contemporary Marxist Badiou, for example, defending subjectivity against a purely semiotic critique, and anthropologists such as Csordas emphasizing the importance of subjectivity understood phenomenologically.

In the second part of the book I aim to develop a theory of religious inwardness from the material presented in Part I that addresses some of the problems presented by critiques of inwardness. The three chapters enact a comparative religion that draws on the readings presented in Part I, arguing that a premodern inwardness must be understood in terms of a shared subjectivity and collective imagination. Yet the disjunction between the cosmological premodern and modern subjectivity should not be exaggerated, and there are continuities that enable us to identify as inwardness the kinds of religious subjectivity we have seen. There is variable indexicality of the first person pronoun. Indeed, a phenomenology of inwardness shows that we can characterize it as self-reflection, being reportable, and disclosed through a system of signs. This leads finally in our last chapter to a consideration of the relation between such subjectivity and broader historical processes that we need to consider in any comparative analysis of the truth within. What might be called act theory argues for the impact of inwardness on history through the act itself that results in the event. Events in turn constrain further subjective judgements. Thus, distinctions between subjectivity and language, self and narrative, person and history, consciousness and sign, must be understood in terms of inwardness articulated as act.

7

A Theory of Religious Inwardness

With the completion of the historical and textual account we are in a position to develop in this and the next chapter a thesis about the truth within based on the comparative material. This will need us to engage with a range of literature—primarily with phenomenology, but also with semiotics and sociology. We will need to raise questions about what these discourses tell us about inwardness, and how the micro-subjective understanding of inwardness revealed through phenomenology relates to the broader, macro-historical perspective. This necessitates an oscillation between different kinds or levels of exposition, from the narrowly focused study of textual particularities, to an account of the broad sweep of history.

In one sense the thesis is simple and can be sketched in the following terms. Hinduism, Buddhism, and Christianity contain the idea that there is a truth within the human person that can be understood or realized through the cultivation of spiritual practices. This notion of inner truth entails an account of the human person as characterized by subjectivity or inwardness and that the cultivation or realization of such inwardness has salvific value; it is a transcendence of restriction. The truth within entails a notion of inwardness in which there is participation in a cosmos greater than the individual. In the traditions we have examined, this participatory model of inwardness can be distinguished from individualism as a characteristic feature of modern understandings of the person. This is not to argue, of course, that medieval religions did not have a concept of a person; but we need to distinguish individualism as a feature of modernity from individuality as a shared property of persons.

THE DEIXIC FIRST PERSON

In more technical terminology we might say that the floating signifier of the 'I', the deixic reference or marker that carries cultural and social values, has variable boundaries such that the signifier identifies different kinds of subjectivity. The floating signifier 'I', while referring to the individual person, does not entail individualism and, as we have seen, can refer to a kind of inwardness that is an index of a broader tradition or corporate imagination. In the religions we have examined, such an imagination is characterized as a cosmology related to a psychology in which the deixic marker 'I' carries with it a cosmological implication generally absent from late modern uses of the pronoun. The variable boundaries of the 'I' mean that statements such as 'I will', 'I can', and 'I do', and their Latin, Sanskrit (and other vernacular) equivalents, have different implications in premodern religions. We can distinguish inwardness as a shared subjectivity from individualism where individualism is a kind of social value that emphasizes the particular carrier of the 'I' as self-assertion against the social group. Individualism has developed in modernity with the loss of holistic societies (to use Dumont's term) and the loss of cosmological religions that emphasized inwardness in a collective sense. This is accompanied by the development of technology, communication, and globalization, and negatively, disenchantment and social fragmentation. By contrast, the meaning of the 'I' and its transformational possibilities in the premodern religions we have looked at depends upon the cosmological structure of those traditions. Thus, participation of the 'I' in the practices of tradition is participation in the broader cosmos, which gives meaning to life and which is believed to have soteriological consequences. This participation is what is meant by shared subjectivity.

The literature we have examined from the histories of Christianity and Indian religions articulate a partially theorized, pre-philosophical expression of this shared subjectivity that is formed through spiritual practices. Arguably developing out of such pre-philosophical partially theorized cosmological assumptions, we have the philosophical expression or theorized culture in which the implicit understandings of the truth within the human person become explicit. Let us develop some of these themes: firstly, the participatory model of inner truth that can be contrasted with individualism; secondly, individuality as a feature of common humanity; and thirdly, the pre-philosophical formation of inwardness.

THE PARTICIPATORY MODEL OF INWARDNESS

I have argued that the texts we have seen present us with a view of the truth within. These texts themselves are an index of broader cultural attitudes about the human person. I have taken as exemplars texts from different genres or cultural levels: a sophisticated philosophical discourse on the one hand, and more popular, unreflexive genres on the other. From Hindu India we have the Sanskrit work of Abhinavagupta, along with pre-philosophical texts of visual contemplation; from Christian Europe we have the theology of Bonaventure and Richard of St Victor, along with popular vision texts in both Latin and the vernaculars; from Buddhism we have looked at meditation and the idea of the inner Buddha in the Mahāyāna. In the argument I am presenting, the popular works stand closer to each other, and Abhinavagupta stands closer to Bonaventure and Richard of St Victor than to a modern philosopher or late modernist world view. My claim is not that the content of these texts is the same—of course not; or that an extra textual, transcendent referent is the same; but rather that they share a structure of subjectivity in which an intensification of inwardness is understood as an internal journey to inner transcendence and the truth within: they share an inner cosmological world view. The realization of this inner truth is transformative such that the person is understood to have changed for the better, or even to have been 'saved' in some sense. In the Hindu case, this is to have realized that the indexical-I of common parlance is identical to the cosmic-I of the religion's transcendent focus. That is, the God within is intimately connected, and in the non-dualist Śaiva case identical to the self within. In the Christian case it is to have realized that the inner truth is truth of God's presence in the heart and his saving grace. There is a metaphysical variability of identification with the transcendent source in what we might call theistic traditions. In non-theistic traditions, such as Buddhism, where there is the rejection of a permanent self, the processes of transformation through the intensification of inwardness in meditation are the same, but the goal of the cessation of greed, hate, and delusion and realization that all is suffering, impermanent and not self in nirvāṇa, is distinct. The argument about process in the transformation of the human person through spiritual exercises is not a claim about the sameness or otherwise of a metaphysical goal, but it is necessitated by the examples we have presented.

In both the Christian and the Hindu cases the religious philosophers and popular devotees inhabited a symbolic world—a closed world, even if enormous—that each person both had a place within, and which was reflected in each person. But there are differences that reflect distinct ontological commitments. For the Śaiva philosopher Abhinavagupta, as we see in Readings 18, 19, and 22, the subjects and objects of consciousness are identical. In Reading 18 the Lord Maheśvara contains within himself all forms, and in Reading 19 the subject and object are contained only within consciousness. This could never be the case for Bonaventure or for Richard. The soul is God's image (Reading 5) that can be contrasted with Abhinavagupta's totalizing I-consciousness (Reading 22), although Abhinavagupta's view that all is contained within the Lord, within Maheśvara, would not be antithetical to Bonaventure's thinking that all is contained within Christ. Let us take two passages already cited, Readings 7 and 21, to bring out the differences between Abhinavagupta and Bonaventure, that also demonstrates their shared concerns.

In Reading 7 we find Bonaventure sketching out the idea of a path to God in which the mind perceives God as light above it. Through the mediation of Christ, who is described as the ladder and vehicle, the mind reaches God. Here we have a graded hierarchy of levels up which the soul or mind climbs. Indeed, Bonaventure reminds us, it only begins contemplation of the Lord at the sixth level. In complete contrast, Reading 21 shows a vision in which all distinctions are illusory, and objects of consciousness which appear to be distinct are, in truth, one's own nature. For Abhinavagupta, all talk of a graded hierarchy is ultimately illusory, and he offers the idea of a pathless path; the way to achieve the liberating gnosis is to realize the subject of language, the 'I', as the universal self or consciousness: a model of graded hierarchy versus a model of gnostic immediacy. Not only do we have different religions but different modes of understanding. And yet both share the idea of the truth within: but for Bonaventure this could not be a total dissolution of the self; for Abhinavaguta, it is.

In Reading 22, Abhinavagupta differentiates two kinds of 'I': one impure, the ordinary indexical-I in a condition of ignorance; the other pure and non-distinct from the universe. From the supreme perspective there is no distinction even at this level, but from the limited perspective of human life we can make this distinction. Although a long way from Abhinavagupta's monism, Bonaventure similarly makes a distinction in Reading 22 between our limited condition and the absolute condition of God that we can ascend into by the ladder of the universe. Bonaventure's distinction is between 'our position in creation' and God, which is related to the distinctions between material and spiritual, temporal and everlasting, outside and inside, darkness and light. The aim is to go from here to there by way of the ladder of ascent. Abhinavagupta has a parallel distinction between the impure within material power and the pure, which is the absolute light of consciousness, identical to the universe.

Thus both thinkers set up a binary opposition between limited human person and a transcendent God; but whereas for Bonaventure the cosmos is a ladder that takes us from here to there, for Abhinavagupta the universe is identical with the absolute I-consciousness, but we cannot perceive it as such because we see it as a determinate cognition. Thus, if A is the human condition and B is transcendence, for Bonaventure A does not equal B, whereas for Abhinavagupta A equals B. But what both agree on is the need for A to develop awareness of B, by light from God being received (Bonaventure) or realizing the innate light within (Abhinavagupta). We can diagram these as $A = B$ or $A \neq B$, where both are within the same plane or realm of discourse. For both Abhinavagupta and Bonaventure this realization is through inwardness: we must 'enter into (*intare*) our soul', which in Reading 22 is God's image, and in Reading 5 the I-consciousness found within the 'pellucid self'. Both metaphysical propositions concerning the identity or non-identity of the subject of experience with a transcendent absolute, although the inverse of each other, are found within the self, within interiority.

The truth is discovered for both Bonaventure and Abhinavagupta in inwardness. It is a precondition for the development of their metaphysical positions. For both thinkers, their theology is grounded in practice; and while the content of practice is different, both share in a general orientation towards interiority and both claim that the truth is within. While the nature of this truth is different, the structure is the same. Furthermore, we have in these readings the idea of participation in a greater reality than the ego-self.

In the readings on contemplative practice, again there is a variety of material that we have seen. The Buddhist account from the *Pratyutpanna-sūtra* in Reading 26 presents the image of a clear mirror as a representation of the mind purified through meditation, contemplation of which leads the practitioner to understand that the mind is empty of essence and ultimately that all is made of thought (*cittam*). This is the truth of inwardness that is the essence of consciousness yet devoid of self (Reading 27), a text that reflects Reading 20 by Abhinavagupta who says that in reality any separation of one consciousness from another is merely an appearance. Both of these readings can be contrasted with the Christian theologians, although even here there are resonances. Thus, in Reading 9, Richard of St Victor says that someone absorbed in contemplation ascends to 'sublime contemplation' from the mind, and this is all within a state of mental absorption—what Richard calls 'a dream rapture' (*somnium*). Now all three readings, while being unique, nevertheless convey a sense that contemplation is within a mental reality, the truth of which is so great that the Buddhist and Śaiva texts suggest that all of reality is like this: a mental representation. Again in Reading 8, Richard emphasizes the transcending of rational thinking by contemplation.

While these readings are so very different, they all convey the idea of an inner, mental world that reveals truth: the pellucid clarity of the mind or the truth of wisdom and intelligence. Through focusing on interiority a world of restriction is transcended. Two models are suggested by these readings. On the one hand, a model of stillness that through stilling the mind the truth is seen, as a reflection can be seen in a pool once it is calmed; on the other, a model of ascent, that the thought goes beyond itself in contemplation to a transcendent reality.

This notion of transcendence is also found in our pre-philosophical examples. In the Christian vision texts the visionary is taken beyond the body and world to purgatory and heaven. The vision of the other world in the Christian material often culminates in a vision of heaven as a bejewelled and crystalline palace, or Christ on a throne surrounded by shining angels (Readings 3 and 4). The cultivated vision of the Hindu texts presents the enthroned Śiva or Nārāyaṇa encircled by retinues of supernatural beings (Readings 10–14).

This idea of the perfected other world filled with light, crystal, and jewel structures, and brilliant other beings, is shared, and raises questions as to why such parallels should develop in distinct historical and cultural locations. One response to that question, the one developed here, is that both India and Europe shared a participatory view of the human person and cultivated practices of inwardness that come up with closely parallel structures. Direct historical influence is unlikely, and so we are left with the idea that similar social structures give rise to similar kinds of inwardness or, alternatively, that inwardness is quite independent of social structure and possibly linked to the very structure of the human brain or the universe itself.

The question about causality in the human sciences is contentious, but the development of parallel forms of inwardness in historically distinct locations within parallel time frames is something that requires explanation. I do not attempt an explanation here in the sense of arguing for a limited cause, but would simply observe that the specifications of the constraints operative in controlling events into their outcome are extremely complex. The cosmological world views of premodernity clearly inform the kinds of inwardness that people experience, and those cosmological imaginations inform judgements that result in effects or events in the world which, in turn, affect world view and the collective imagination. We will return to this in the last chapter.

Although the vision of the end, of the ultimate goal, is distinct in the Śaiva, Buddhist, and Christian traditions, for the Hindu, Christian, and Buddhist texts there is a totality that the mind can penetrate through spiritual exercises. There is a ladder or scale of perfection up which the inner self ascends to the vision of perfection and the truth within. Abhinavagupta has a graded hierarchy in the attainment of enlightenment that he summarizes from the ambient religious culture, and Bonaventure and Richard have a graded hierarchy to the attainment of the beatific vision. Similarly, the Buddhist stages of meditation form a graded hierarchy towards enlightenment with the qualification that a causal process cannot cause the uncaused state of nirvāṇa (Buddhist practice simply purifies the mind enabling enlightenment to be apprehended, but cannot cause enlightenment).

Furthermore, there is significant overlap in the cosmological psychologies presented. For Hindu, Buddhist, and Christian contemplative traditions the mind is understood to be wandering and uncontrolled in its nature and needs to be controlled through spiritual practices. In the popular prayer manuals we have referred to there is reference to 'putting away' idle thoughts and desires (see Chapter 2, note 75), and the identical sentiment is found in yoga manuals that emphasize control of the mind through concentration on a single point. Thus the Patañjali defines yoga as the cessation of mental fluctuation,[1] paralleling the Christian sentiment about the uncontrolled mind. The *Contemplations on the Dread Love of God* (quoted in Chapter 2, note 76) speaks of the

[1] For example, Patañjali, *Yoga-sūtras* 1.2: *yogaścittavṛttinirodhaḥ*.

need to find a clean and quiet place for prayer, a sentiment echoed in Hindu texts of the same period. Thus the *Jayākhya-saṃhitā* recommends the practitioner go to a lonely but charming and clean place to practise his ritual meditation on purifying the body.[2] An almost identical sentiment is expressed in the Buddhist *Sādhanamālā* that says, for example, that the sādhaka should wash and then practise in a meditation abode that is clean.[3]

In the Hindu, Buddhist, and Christian texts the human person is understood as participating in a total cosmos, and there is a structure of inwardness integrated into the structure of the cosmos that, on the one hand, means the person is bound by sin (for the Christian) and bound by action (*karma*) within the cycle of reincarnation (for the Hindu and Buddhist), but also that the structure of the cosmos allows for salvation. Christ as a cosmic figure mediates between the world and God the Father; Christ as *logos* is built into the very fabric of the universe. Śaiva liberation as realization of the totality of the cosmos is likewise built into its very structure, and that which binds can also be that which saves, a kind of homeopathic idea developed within the tantric traditions. The Mahāyāna Buddhist texts of the tathāgatagarbha tradition maintain that the truth of Buddhahood is within all beings, an idea that eventually results in the Zen doctrine that the everyday mind is the Buddha mind.

Participation is therefore common to the Śaiva, Buddhist, and Christian world view in the medieval period. In spite of wide theological differences—*creatio ex nihilo* versus a universe without beginning, one life versus reincarnation, final Judgement versus individual liberation, sin versus impurity through action—this means that the person is integrated into a symbolic system, and furthermore that there is variable indexicality of participation. That is, the referent 'I' is filled out with different content and its boundaries are variable depending upon the degree of cosmological participation. For Abhinavagupta, for example, the limited or indexical-I can be transformed into the cosmic 'I-ness' that is the totality of all that exists. 'I will' or 'I want' (*icchāmi*) is the primary linguistic act of each person that reflects the cosmic, divine 'I will' of the Lord expressing his spontaneous freedom (*svatantram*). The 'I' is an absolute subject, a complete I-ness (*pūrṇāntā*) that takes the form of the universe, just as the limited 'I' takes the form of the body.[4] The 'I will' (*volo*) in the Christian ascetic and mystical tradition ironically, or paradoxically, undermines itself so that God speaks and acts, as it were, through the person. The intentional object for Bonaventure, the Lord, comes to disappear as something distinct, in the end, as the deepest sense of the 'I' realizes its utter dependence on the greater will of God, a sentiment that echoes throughout the mystical

[2] *Jayākhya-saṃhitā* 10.1.

[3] B. Bhattacharya (ed.), *Sādhanamāmā* vol 1. (Baroda: Gaekwad's Oriental Series, 1925), 82, p. 156.

[4] Abhinavagupta, *Paramārthasāra* 49, 50.

tradition.[5] For Bonaventure, the indexical-I is transformed in varying degrees through participation in the life and cosmic reality of Christ. There are parallel structures of participation in both traditions, a claim that is not a claim about ontological identity of the object of practice (Śiva or Christ) but is a claim about what we might call an ontology of process. Similarly, in Buddhism the indexical-I is understood to be empty of essence through meditative practice: paying attention to the processes of awareness transforms awareness to the awakening of emptiness and not-self. There are directly parallel ways here in which human reality is integrated into the broader universe. We might say that the 'I will' expresses both Ricouer's *idem* (identity or sameness or self-constancy over time), and *ipse* (identity),[6] the unique capacity to initiate action that is linked to who one is in a network of relationships.

The 'I will' thus expresses identity through time and the particularity of action as free act and act constrained by the historical and cultural narratives that one finds oneself within. The 'I will' expresses an indexicality that varies in different contexts and in mystical settings finds itself expanded or stretched to conform to the structure of tradition. But this variability of indexicality is not precisely the same in the Indian and European texts. The vision texts in Latin and Middle English we have examined have a strong element of personal engagement. In the *Monk of Eynsham*, Edmund is insistent that his vision happened to him; there is a high degree of personal involvement and the consistent use of the first person pronoun indicates this. Such personal involvement is wholly lacking from the Sanskrit material we have looked at where the register is all in the third person. The visual contemplation genre of texts describes visualizations and there is an understanding that these are to be cultivated by practitioners, but there is no element of confession or narrative. The narrative dimension is minimized. While both the Latin and vernacular vision texts of medieval Christianity and the Sanskrit visual contemplation texts promote and assume a participatory model of the person in the broader cosmological scheme, the Hindu material has even less concern for personal narrative. But in spite of this difference, both genres understand the human person in cosmological terms, both understand the person as living within a symbolic universe, and both understand the person as a sign of a greater reality.

We can see this also in the very use of language. The Latin *interior homo* found in our medieval sources finds its equivalent in the Sanskrit *antarātman*, the inner self, and the metaphor of interiority is pervasive in the medieval Sanskrit sources. A search of medieval Sanskrit e-texts available to me reveals

[5] Thus Eckhart: 'I want God to want in place of my will wanting.' Cited in Michel de Certeau, *The Mystic Fable*, vol. 1: *The Sixteenth and Seventeenth Centuries*, trans. M. B. Smith (Chicago, IL: Chicago University Press, 1992), pp. 166–7.

[6] Paul Ricoeur, *Oneself as Another*, trans. Kathleen Blamey (Chicago, IL: Chicago University Press, 1992), pp. 2–3.

over ninety thousand occurrences of *antara-* and over five hundred occurrences of *antarātma-* in all genres of literature from that period. For example, in the *Jayākhya-saṃhitā* (12.117d) in the visualization of the throne in the inner worship that we have looked at, the Lord (Vāsudeva) dwells in the inner selves (*sa vasaty antarātmasu*). Abhinavagupta refers to the inner self (*antarātmā*) and often uses the term 'interiority' (*antaḥsthitatva*, literally 'inner-standing-ness') to denote the objects of consciousness that are not, in fact, distinct from the subject in his monistic world view.[7] There is also use of 'introversion' (*antarmukhaḥ*), 'facing inwards', in contrast to externality (*bahirmukhaḥ*), 'facing outwards',[8] terms that reflect the inner/outer container metaphor highlighted by Johnson[9] just as much, if not more than, European sources. The inner/outer metaphor is mapped onto an upper/lower metaphor that is part of a symbolic system where ascent and interiority are associated with purity and descent and externality with impurity. In the Buddhist material the idea of the truth within as enlightenment or Buddhahood is indicated by a number of terms, including the truth of the inner state of enlightenment (*pratyātmādhigamadharmaḥ*). It is not that these terms are identical in meaning, but rather that they indicate a turn to interiority to locate truth that we find in these contemplative traditions. These terms are analogues of each other.

Both medieval European and Indic world views are pervaded by the idea of a symbolic universe. Richard of St Victor sees the Bible as allegory and reads the very universe itself as a text, a view in which allegory is identified with symbol.[10] Similarly, the vision of Christ suffering (Readings 1 and 2) is a symbol that participates in the reality to which it points and invites the practitioner to participate in that reality. Abhinavagupta has a discussion of the symbol (*liṅgam*) that he understands in a hierarchical sequence. The unmanifest symbol is identified with God as the 'supreme essence of tranquillity' (*viśrāntihṛdayam param*) that, adds the commentator Jayaratha, is in fact the awareness of subjectivity (*ahaṃparāmarśam*). The manifest/unmanifest (*vyaktāvyakta-*) symbol is the body pervaded by the 'path' that is the cosmos, while the manifest (*vyakta-*) symbol is an external form (*bahīrūpam*), such as the icon of a deity or a mantra, conceptualized as a vibration of consciousness particularized in a form (*viśeṣaspandarūptam*).[11] Through focusing on the

[7] Abhinavagupta, *Īśvarapratyabhijñāvimarśinī* 1.5.1–2, 1.5.10. See Isabelle Ratié, *Le soi et L'autre: Identité, difference et altérité dans la philosophie de la Pratyabhijñā* (Leiden: Brill, 2011), pp. 307, 478.

[8] See Ratié, *Le Soi et L'Autre*, pp. 190–1.

[9] On the container metaphor as fundamental to human language, see M. Johnson, *The Body in the Mind: The Bodily Basis of Meaning, Imagination, and Reason* (Chicago, IL: Chicago University Press, 1987), pp. 30–7.

[10] See Jean Pepin, 'La notion d'allegorie', in Pepin, *Dante et la tradition d'allegorie* (Paris: Vrin, 1970), pp. 11–51; de Certeau, *The Mystic Fable*, p. 91.

[11] Abhinavagupta, *Tantrāloka* 5.117a and commentary.

forms of the manifestation of consciousness the practitioner conforms his mind to them and is thereby purified. Through visualizing the sufferings of Christ the disciple becomes one with Christ and achieves a more elevated state through that participation.

This participatory model of the human person that is shared by Hindu, Buddhist, and Christian religions in the premodern period is distinct from the sense of 'I' in modernity. If we were to imagine ourselves writing Edmund's text, if we try to put ourselves in his shoes through an imaginative act in which our sense of self is a formal indication of his own, then the difference would lie in the quality of indexical identification. The modern self has a sense of uniqueness and individualism that is absent in the participatory model of Edmund. It is not that people are not individuals with their own stories, their particular names and social relationships, as any modern person, but rather that the symbolic world view they inhabited entails a shared subjectivity in which there is great indexical identification with the cosmological world view. With the end of that symbolic world, which disintegrates at the end of the Middle Ages,[12] we have the rise of Protestantism in the West and the emphasis on conscience rather than participation. In India the model has continued down to modernity, at least at a popular level, although eroded by colonialism and rejected by India's intellectual elites probably since the eighteenth century. Indeed, the subcontinent acceded implicitly to the evolutionist scheme that saw individualism as the higher understanding of the person, that replaced participation.

INDIVIDUALISM

We have already examined the claim that the roots of individualism can be found in twelfth-century Europe (see 'The Idea of the Individual', pp. 37–42) and cited Simmel's essay on the topic. We now need to elaborate on the idea of the person in relation to individualism to bring into sharper focus our idea of a participatory, cosmological inwardness. Mauss and Dumont saw the individualism of modernity as the acme of an evolutionary, developmental process (as did others such as Jung). In his famous essay that builds on the work of his uncle Durkheim, Mauss argued that the concept of the self has been formed over a long history, of particular importance being a society's organization. For Mauss, a most significant time in the history of the self was ancient Rome when a person's role or mask (*persona*) became the locus of rights and obligations—that is, a legal citizen of the state. Christianity added to this the idea of a person with an

[12] De Certeau, *The Mystic Fable*, p. 91.

inner life that formed the foundation of the modern notion of the person as a being with a civic identity and a particular interiority characterized by conscience.

Mauss begins by limiting what his famous essay seeks to do: it aims at explaining how 'one of the categories of the human mind' ('une des catégories de l'esprit humain'), the notion of the person (*personne*) or self (*moi*), developed over the centuries, and provides a summary catalogue of 'the forms it has assumed'.[13] Beginning with the idea of 'the role' (*personage*), Mauss surveys his contemporary anthropological ethnography on the Pueblos, native Americans of the south-west, and aborigines in Australia, all of which present, in Nick Allen's summary, 'a bounded society consisting of totemic clans, each clan having a fixed stock of names transmitted by recognized procedures, the bearers of a name being reincarnations of their predecessors back to mythical times and dancing out the fact at rituals'.[14] These societies have developed the notion of 'role' (*personnage*), but not of the 'person' (*personne*) and 'self' (*moi*) that only came into being with the idea of the Latin *persona*. In contrast to China and India, Mauss argues, it was the Romans—or rather 'the Latins'—who came up with the notion of the person as a category of law, along with thing (*res*) and action (*actiones*). Originally the term *persona* meant 'mask' and can be etymologically explained as 'coming from *per/sonare*... the mask through which (*per*) resounds the voice (of the actor)'.[15] The Roman citizen, in contrast to the slave with no rights, had a civil *persona*, and some citizens also a religious *persona*; 'masks' as social actors which became synonymous with the true nature of the individual. The Stoics were important in this development, but it lacked a metaphysical foundation until the arrival of Christianity introduced the idea of the 'moral person' (*personne morale*), which ends up, in Cassiodorus' words as 'a rational substance, indivisible and individual' (*persona—substantia rationalis individual*).[16] The category undergoes a further transformation into the idea of the self (*moi*), gradually theorized by philosophers until Fichte formulated the idea that every act of consciousness is an act of self; 'a being possessing metaphysical and moral value'.[17]

[13] Marcel Mauss, 'A Category of the Human Mind: The Notion of Person; the Notion of Self', pp. 1–2, trans. W. D. Halls, in Michael Carrithers, Steven Collins, and Steven Lukes (eds.), *The Category of the Person: Anthropology, Philosophy, History* (Cambridge: Cambridge University Press, 1985), pp. 1–25. [French orig., Marcel Mauss, 'Une catégorie de l'esprit humain: La notion de personne celle de "moi"', in *Sociologie et anthropologie* (Paris: PUF, 1950), pp. 331–61.]

[14] Nick Allen, 'The Category of the Person: A Reading of Mauss' Last Essay', p. 33, in Carrithers et al. (eds.), *The Category of the Person*, pp. 26–45.

[15] Mauss, 'A Category of the Human Mind', p. 14.

[16] Mauss, 'A Category of the Human Mind', p. 20.

[17] Mauss, 'A Category of the Human Mind', p. 22.

Mauss aims at establishing the 'elementary form of the *personnage*' and contrasting this with the contemporary notion of the person.[18] His scheme is evolutionary in assuming the identification of 'primitive' with 'early' and in dismissing the significance of India and China. India, he notes, is the most ancient civilization where the notion of the self develops, but abandons the idea of the individual, as did China, where it ceased to evolve: although there were promising beginnings, only Christianity was able to fulfil the promise of the Latin category.

In spite of its brilliance, Mauss' essay is problematic in adopting such an overt evolutionary scheme. Sanderson and Elvin show that there was indeed a notion of the individual person in those civilizations, at least by the early medieval period,[19] and we therefore need to be cautious in accepting Mauss' developmental programme. But Mauss' essay raises a question for the current project concerning the relationship between inwardness, the person, and the individual. Although he does not discuss the term 'inwardness' or 'interiority', implicit in his scheme is the idea that non-literate societies have no inwardness, the person being defined wholly in terms of social role and inwardness identified with person only developing with more complex civilizations in which the person develops as an individual.

Building on his teacher's work, Dumont's distinction between holistic societies and the individual is useful. Dumont designates the term 'individual' to mean both 'the *empirical* subject of speech, thought, and will', and a value.[20] The empirical subject of speech is found in all societies, whereas 'the independent, autonomous and . . . non-social moral being'[21] is found in modern societies. Some societies emphasize the individual, which Dumont calls individualism, whereas other societies value society as a whole. Developing Mauss' point, Dumont illustrates this with reference to India, where he argues for a distinction between the renouncer as an individual-outside-the-world and the social being or individual-in-the-world, as we have seen (see 'The Person in Indian Religions', pp. 106–8). Contemporary Western societies are individualistic in orientation, in contrast to the tribal societies that Mauss opens his essay with, which are holistic.

This is arguably a useful distinction. Some societies have been more prototypical of holism, while others more prototypical of individualism. On Dumont's account, individualism has only developed in an extreme form in

[18] Allen, 'The Category of the Person', p. 31.

[19] See the essays by Elvin and Sanderson in Carrithers et al. (eds.), *The Category of the Person*: Mark Elvin, 'Between the Earth and Heaven: Conceptions of the Self in China', pp. 156–89; Alexis Sanderson, 'Purity and Power among the Brahmans of Kashmir', pp. 190–216.

[20] Louis Dumont, 'A Modified View of Our Origins: The Christian Beginnings of Modern Individualism', p. 94, in Carrithers et al. (eds.), *The Category of the Person*, pp. 93–122. See *Essays on Individualism: Modern Ideology in Anthropological Perspective* (Chicago, IL: Chicago University Press, 1986), p. 62.

[21] Dumont, *Essays on Individualism*, p. 62.

recent centuries, the project having been aborted in China and India. Dumont charts the shift from the idea of a social body as a whole with particular people as parts, the *universitas*, to a weakening of this conception in favour of partnership or *societas*.[22] Hindu *dharma*, Dumont observes, is akin to the medieval conception. Others have traced a similar trajectory from society integrated with a cosmos symbolized by kingship, to modern, individualistic society.[23]

We may accept the general argument that modern, Western, democratic societies of late modernity are distinct from the kinds of hierarchical societies of the past, and from some contemporary holistic societies; but we need to be cautious in accepting Mauss' evolutionary scheme, or accepting Dumont's characterization of holistic societies as non-individual, if by this we mean an absence of subjectivity or inwardness. Dumont and Mauss have identified an important theme of individualism as a *value* that is absent from premodern societies. While this is a forceful argument, and while one can see that post-medieval, industrial to post-industrial societies have a distinct idea of human flourishing, does this mean that holistic societies have an inadequate or attenuated conception of the human person? We need to distinguish a descriptive from a normative claim here. Restricting ourselves for the time being to the descriptive claim, if we take the premodern societies of the High Middle Ages and post-Gupta periods that we have examined, we can see that for them, the human person is integrated into a total social order that is considered sacred: each person is part of a cosmos.

But, as we have seen, this does not mean that there is no inwardness in these cultures. On Dumont's account the holistic societies of medieval Europe and India had the notion of the individual as a being outside of the social body, attempting to leave the social body, and that such an individual develops inwardness through meditation, asceticism, and so on. But, on the contrary, this is not the sense of an autonomous agent and carrier of the value of individualism. Rather, as we have argued, we have the intensification of subjectivity that is a form of inwardness: a form of inwardness that is shared and integrated into a sacred cosmos. Dumont's individual outside-the-world is not individual in the modern sense as a carrier of a particular value, but is a person within a world view who has developed a particular kind of inwardness or subjectivity that is nevertheless still shared. The inner path of the Christian monk to the beatific vision, or the path of the Śaiva renouncer to liberation, are prescribed by tradition—they participate in narratives that precede them, and although they are individual in the sense that particular persons walk along

[22] Dumont, *Essays on Individualism*, p. 63.

[23] The literature here is wide. Apart from Dumont, the shift is marked by Charles Taylor, *The Secular Age* (Cambridge, MA: The Belknap Press of Harvard University, 2007), pp. 56–75; Louis Dupré, *Passage to Modernity* (New Haven: Yale University Press, 1993).

these paths, they are not spontaneous outpourings of creativity or self-expression that we might associate with individualism.

Dumont and Mauss are therefore right in their highlighting that a shift has occurred from a holistic sense of the social body to a sense of individualism, but wrong in their implied rejection of inwardness from such societies. The inwardness is not individualistic but shared, an idea that has important ramifications in identifying the precursors of modern individualism or rejecting the idea of individualism from non-Western histories. So, to the question 'Can there be inwardness in holistic societies?' we can answer that there can be, but an inwardness that does not carry the values of individualism but distinct values of a cosmological human flourishing.

Lastly, we need to make that point that in emphasizing the sociological history of the person, Mauss and Dumont do not highlight the idea of transcendence that is crucial to understanding subjectivity. For the *sadhu* and monk, as well as for lay practitioners, the intensification of subjectivity through spiritual practice was in the service of inner transcendence; the journey beyond the world to the truth within that was also a higher realm. Inwardness is vertical ascent in the Hindu and Christian traditions, and from a traditional perspective not simply an ordering of hierarchical social relationships but an orientating of the soul towards a transcendent goal. Any etic account needs to bear this in mind and take the emic claim seriously. The human person is not simply a sociological entity. We can therefore identify two types of inwardness: the intensification of subjectivity that is an inner transcendence or vertical ascent within a total cosmos, and a type of inwardness that is the expression of individualism, characteristic of modernity.

INDIVIDUALITY

We need therefore to distinguish between individualism as a characteristic feature of modernity, and individuality, a property of all human persons. Presenting a thesis about inwardness as shared subjectivity does not, of course, entail that human beings are not distinct or unique, each person with their own story, nor that the actions of individual persons could not affect the wider social body. The cosmological psychology we have described is of persons with particular histories, desires, and goals. Thus, while individuality and individualism are coterminous in modernity, in premodernity they are not. Individuality is a property of persons, the particularity of each, which means that although there is a flow of events occurring in each person (a narrative flow), subjectivity is formed in ways constrained by the broader world view or tradition. The cosmological psychology is clearly of persons, but is shared. Thus individuality is a feature of persons, but this does not entail an isolated, self-contained entity; rather, it is a marker of particularity that signifies uniqueness and unrepeatablity. It does not deny relationship; indeed the ability to relate and form community is a fundamental feature of such individuality.

We can find an entry into this idea through the theorizing of a medieval thinker John Duns Scotus. Scotus argued that no two individuals, even if possessing the same qualities, are identical, and developed the idea of the particularity of each person.[24] Everything can be marked by the indexical 'this' (*haec*) as unique to itself. The doctrine of 'thisness' (*haecitas*) is an individuating principle. In terms of our thesis, the question is: 'How is the particularity of the person, the particular inwardness of the unrepeatable event of a unique person, related to the broader world view and collectivity?' (as I have argued it is). In speaking of a shared subjectivity, is this not a contradiction in terms? To respond to this we can turn to how the problem was theorized by Scotus. One of the main problems of medieval scholasticism was the relation between essence (*essentia*) and existence (*existentia*).[25] The Thomistic school claimed that in an actual being, the *what* of that being, is a second existent (*res*). Scotus, by contrast, disclaimed that these are two distinct realities. Rather than a real distinction between essence and existence, or between universal and particular, there is a formal distinction. This distinction is less objective than a real distinction and more objective than a virtual distinction. A formal distinction can pertain where there is no real distinction. For example, in two distinct objects—a book and a stone—there is a real distinction; but in one object with different aspects or properties, the distinction is not real but formal. Thus, in a human being sensible properties (the ability to experience a world through the senses) are distinct from rational properties (the ability to think coherently about the world), yet they both inhere within the same human being. The distinction is formal rather than real. It is also objective because it exists outside of the mind and its distinguishing activity.[26]

This helps us identify how individuality is formally distinct from individualism in so far as both inhere within a modern subject who is particular, yet embodies the values of self expression, autonomy, and self-assertion. Furthermore, this formal distinction between individuality and individualism allows us to understand and empathize with the premodern religious subject. Scotus'

[24] Allan B. Wolter (trans.), *John Duns Scotus—Early Oxford Lecture on Individuation*, Latin text and English translation (New York: St Bonaventure University, 2005).

[25] See M. Heidegger, *The Basic Problems of Phenomenology*, trans Albert Hofstadter (2nd edn, Bloomington and Indianapolis, IN: Indiana University Press, 1988), pp. 91–3.

[26] For a clear account, see F. Copleston, *A History of Philosophy*, vol. 2: *Medieval Philosophy* (London: Continuum, 1999 (first published 1950)), pp. 508–13. See also Antonie Vos, *The Philosophy of John Duns Scotus* (Edinburgh: Edinburgh University Press, 2006), pp. 255–9; Maurice J. Grajewski, *The Formal Distinction of Duns Scotus: A Study in Metaphysics Thesis* (PhD thesis, Catholic University of America, Washington, DC, 1944).

formal distinction is thus closely allied to Heidegger's formal indication that allows us to penetrate the phenomenology of historical appearances.

Individuality is linked to action in so far as action is unrepeatable and unique and has affects on history. Some actions, particularly the kinds we have been concerned with here—the constant acts of ritual, prayer, and fasting—are repeated over long periods of time; yet this is a non-identical repetition in that each performance of an action, although bearing similar properties, is unique to itself. The act is an index of the broader culture. The chain of actions that comprises a human life is the outer articulation of an inwardness that is both unique to itself and shared. The Monk of Eynsham has a particular story (born on Osney Island, becoming ill and so on), yet his story also conforms to the narrative of tradition: he becomes an index of the tradition, and at the same time his action—the events of his trance articulated through his composition written by his brother—has effects on history: his book reaches a broad audience in Latin and vernacular languages down to the present day. The inwardness of his life impacted on broader history.

Inwardness is thus both formed through cultural practices and discovered by them. Of particular importance here are spiritual practices or methods designed to discover the truth within that intensify a sense of inwardness. The repeated actions of liturgy, reading, and meditation channel the practitioner to a prescribed route and goal. The spiritual exercises of religions are both the formation of the self and the discovery of the self.

PRE-PHILOSOPHY AND THE FORMATION OF INWARDNESS

The participatory mode of subjectivity is expressed philosophically or theologically in the works of philosophers and theologians, but also has more popular expression, as we have seen, in non-philosophical genres of literature. These genres express and prescribe practices that are instrumental in the formation of inwardness in the traditions and creating a 'habit' within a group of people conducive to forming a life in a particular way. Mauss called the formation of such cultural habits 'techniques of the body' or the development of a habitus.[27] The human person is always within specific cultures that develop ways of carrying the body, ways of eating, ways of doing things, and ways of orientating the self in space and with others. The cultivation of the

[27] M. Mauss, 'Les techniques du corps', in *Sociologie et anthropologie* (Paris: PUF, 1950), pp. 363–86.

kind of inwardness I have been describing in Christianity, Hinduism, and Buddhism is not only an invisible inwardness but also the development of a specific habitus, a temporal and spatial orientation of the body. The cultivation of an intense inwardness is brought about through repeated, long practice. By focusing on the self I make myself an object for myself. But how is this to be done? Such an inner life is cultivated through spiritual exercises or practical techniques that shift the orientation of the person from the world and externality to God and internality. This turn to the self entails moral progress in the sense that the degree of intensification of inwardness lies in the development of a moral life, along with the 'techniques' of spiritual practices or exercises.

The adjectives 'spiritual' and 'religious' can no longer be used innocently, implicated as they are in a politics of representation that has seen fit to privilege a discourse about a referent or referents beyond the human and beyond the political realm in order to justify and uphold structures of power within that realm. But while we must be aware of the loaded histories of these terms, they are nevertheless central to our project in that religion cannot be simply understood in terms of cultural politics. There are kinds of practice formed within textual traditions that are not only constructions of a particular kind of subjectivity or experience of inwardness—the development of a religious imagination—but are also discoveries of a world; and these discoveries are generative of culture. In some ways this is to revisit the model of culture in which the 'hero' steals fire or some culturally advantageous product from the gods; and yet in other ways it is a distancing from cultural essentialism to a model of dynamic textuality in which the self is formed and reformed through the operation of the text working through particular kinds of cultural—namely 'spiritual'—practice.

These practices are in fact ways of life that have been prescribed by traditions, articulated in texts, and maintained and preserved through long historical trajectories. We might call these practices 'spiritual'. This is not simply another way of saying that socialization processes can be identified in religions—clearly they can be, and we cannot underestimate the force and truth-forming reality of such processes. But such truth-forming reality cannot be understood only in terms of socialization. While traditions form people in text and tradition-specific ways, there are degrees of intensification of inwardness that reveal truth about the world that needs to taken intellectually seriously; forms of practice are related to kinds of disclosedness. The creation of inwardness through spiritual practice is not simply construction but also discovery and the enabling of a skill for being in the world and the enabling of a skill for facing death. (We might even say that inwardness forming spiritual practice is a kind of wisdom.)

In terms of the phenomenology we have developed, we might say that inwardness in religions is a manner of givenness inseparably linked to the contents or intentional objects of consciousness. We have examined some of the contents of this givenness from Hinduism, Buddhism, and Christianity where we have seen how inwardness is formed as a cosmological psychology and corporate imagination that is quite distinct from individualism and inseparable from a sense of collectivity. The appearances to, or content of consciousness, comes forth *as* something—the appearance of an angel in the vision texts we have seen, the appearance of a sense of detachment or joy in the theological works we have seen—*for* a particular person for whom the appearance is meaningful. Indeed, this appearance to consciousness, this formation of inwardness, is the most meaningful and important event in the religious person's life. Inwardness occurs in a particular temporal and spatial location and the coming into view of a cosmological inwardness comes forth from a dimension that is hidden. The inner journey is a discovery, and the truth within manifests through the contents of consciousness from an unknown place. But this revealing of what lies hidden is not a random event; as we have seen, it is facilitated through spiritual disciplines—through the repeated acts of reading, meditation, asceticism, and liturgy. This is as true of the Christian and Buddhist monk as of the Hindu ascetic.

Hadot first drew our attention to the importance of spiritual exercises in the formation of the self in late antiquity and Christianity. For Hadot, the term 'spiritual exercises' (*exercitium spirituale*), that translated the Greek *askesis*, denotes a range of practices developed in late antiquity designed to confront the self with its true nature, to create habits of thought conducive to self-mastery and, ultimately, as training for death.[28] Such training for death was, for the ancient philosophers such as the Stoics and Epicureans, training for life and the practice of philosophy as 'a way of life'. While Hadot's characterization of the term 'spiritual' as indicating practices whereby 'the individual raises himself up to the life of the objective Spirit',[29] unnecessarily entails a truth claim about spirit, we can see the usefulness of the term in designating a range of practices that involve intellect, imagination, the development of moral sense, and techniques of inner change such as forms of asceticism. Indeed, Hadot's characterization of the spiritual exercises as comprising self-mastery, living in the present, dialoging with the self, and training for death, would seem to be shared in other cultures, particularly in India. While these general characteristics are important in cutting across cultural and historical divides, what makes spiritual exercises important is the way in which they form particular kinds of inner identity linked to social identity. We have seen this repeatedly in the medieval religions we have looked at.

[28] P. Hadot, *Exercices spirituels et philosophie antique* (Paris: Albin Michel, 2010), p. 51.

[29] P. Hadot, *Philosophy as a Way of Life*, ed. A. I. Davidson (Oxford: Blackwell, 1995), p. 82.

THE POLITICS OF INWARDNESS

Let us briefly summarize our discussion so far. I have argued that truth located in inwardness in the premodern sense of shared subjectivity is found in Indic and European religions, and that this inwardness is central to what they understood as human flourishing and completion—indeed, central to salvation. The concept of inwardness I have described is developed from the Latin *homo interior*, the inner man, and from the Sanskrit Hindu *antarātman* and a variety of Buddhist compounds using the phrase *pratyātma-*, the inner self; it is used in an etic sense in contrast to those emic terms. The *homo interior*, the *antarātman*, and *pratyātma-* must be understood within a cosmological world view and an understanding of the sacrality of the human person, and all three terms can be contrasted with the modern sense of inwardness that we are beings with inner depths, and also with the postmodern sense of the human as having no depth, only surface. Furthermore, human inwardness is important in the formation of history and must be understood as integral to the development of history, a point we shall develop in the final chapter. Lastly, we need to expand upon the potential critique of the idea of inwardness and its political dimensions.

In recent years there has been a general suspicion of seeing 'other' cultures through the lens of categories developed within a Western framework, and feminist critique has highlighted how women have been written out of history and historiography. To the potential criticism that 'inwardness', and indeed 'human person', are products of Western history, I have tried to show here that this is not the case and have circumvented this potential criticism by paying close attention to what the texts tell us, and to what shows itself through the textual material. This is a first level phenomenology, essentially descriptive in allowing what shows itself to be seen. I accept that description is in the service of theory in the selection of what is described, but I do not accept that all description is simply projection. Indeed, in any comparative project we must be careful to proceed carefully and with caution, paying attention to the particularity of text and language. I shall say more about this in Chapter 9.

But certainly in focusing on the representation of inwardness in Latin and Sanskrit sources of the medieval period (rather than the early modern period) we are inevitably receiving only a partial picture that excludes the illiterate, that mostly although not completely excludes women, and that excludes those on the margins of society such as the sick and disabled. This is clearly a problem. In medieval Christianity, women were excluded from the institutions of Latin learning (the universities of Paris and Oxford), although there were exceptions. The famous abbess and polymath Hildegard of Bingen knew Latin and expressed herself through writing in that medium. In the later Middle Ages, after about 1300 and into the beginnings of the Renaissance, we find an increase in women's voices and the writing out of subjectivity in vernacular languages, which came to replace the more narrowly technical Latin as the medium of self-expression.[30] We have already mentioned the Beguines in this regard, and others such as Julian of Norwich (*c.*1342–1416) who wrote in English and whose text, the *Revelations of Divine Love*, became widely copied before being printed in 1670. This work articulates a distinct sense of inwardness that is still part of the Christian cosmological world view, expresses, like Franciscan spirituality, identification with the poor and dispossessed, and describes particular inner visions.[31]

As with Christian Europe, in India it is only with the later, premodern devotional religion expressed in the vernaculars that we find a direct expression of women's spirituality and inner lives. For example, an older contemporary of Julian's, Lala Ded (1320–92), on a different continent in Kashmir, composed poetry in Old Kashmiri describing her inner journey to Śiva, that draws on the cosmological psychology of the Śaiva traditions of Kashmir we have discussed.[32] We can retrieve Lala Ded's poetry and read it through a postcolonial lens in offering resistance to dominant forms of power in Kashmir at the time, and to use Lala as a resource for a contemporary shaking off of the remnants of a colonial discourse. This is a legitimate and important enterprise, but it is one that I am not doing here. Rather, I seek to understand the world view that produced the forms of interiority that Lala and Julian inherit. Both Lala and Julian are articulating a devotion and an inwardness that is distinct to their own cultures, and the content of what they are saying is quite diverse; but what they share is the process of the cultivation of interiority, an interiority that is not controversial in their time and whose experience and writing carry authority for the religious communities of which they were a part and which flows from them.

There are therefore exceptions to an otherwise male dominated discourse about inner truth. These women's voices are distinct, and writing in the genre of interiority allowed them a vehicle for expression that they would otherwise not have. Can we then think of women's texts expressing inwardness as protest against the androcentric status quo? Can female mystical writing be read as protest? I think this would be far too simplistic a view. We cannot read these

[30] De Certeau, *The Mystic Fable*, p. 115. On the importance of vernacular literature in the development of the self in the Middle Ages, see Sarah Spence, *Texts and the Self in the Twelfth Century* (Cambridge, New York, Melbourne: Cambridge University Press, 1996).

[31] Julian of Norwich, *Revelations of Divine Love*, ed. Grace Chadwick (London: Methuen, 1901). For example, ch. 67, p. 167: 'And then our Lord opened my spiritual eye and shewed me my soul in the midst of my heart.'

[32] There is no critical edition or scholarship of her work to my knowledge since Grierson and Barnett's early efforts (George Grierson and L. D. Barnett, *Lalavakyani or the Wise Sayings of Lalla Ded* (London: Royal Asiatic Society, 1920)), although there is a useful book that presents and translates some of her verses by B. N. Parimoo, *The Ascent of the Self* (Delhi: MLBD, 1978). There is also a translation by the Indian poet Ranjit Hoskote, *I, Lalla: The Poems of Lal Ded.* (New Delhi: Penguin Classics, 2011).

women mystics simply in terms of protest. Firstly, in an Indic context there was no ecclesiastical authority ensuring orthodoxy, and so in a doctrinal sense there was nothing to protest against. Secondly, in a Western context, men were subject to ecclesiastical censure as much as women; thus Eckhart is put under suspicion of heresy, and many were tried and condemned, not only women; ecclesiastical authority tends to dislike mysticism because of the implied authoritative voice from within the self that could go against the external voice of the Church. Foucault has documented how human beings are subjected to power, and while we can see inwardness in terms of resistance to domination, so often inwardness has been in conformity to power and to hierarchical relationships in society. Foucault has analysed such conformity in terms of humans being complicit in their own subjection.[33]

THE CHALLENGE OF MODERNITY

This project has attempted to expound a sense of inner truth and inwardness that I believe to be fundamental to scriptural religions. This sense of inner truth can have extraordinary consequences in the transition to action, as we see with the life of the Buddha; and though the sense of inner truth for the vast majority of people has not been as historically significant individually, collectively it has had great historical impact. Indeed, traditions of inner contemplation and discipline continue to influence the modern world. Most people in scriptural religions have lived their lives within the boundary of tradition, trying to embody the tradition's values and to seek their highest value as the truth within, internalizing tradition in their own way, quietly and unobtrusively. Such lives have been made up of the particularities of daily living and following the liturgical pattern of tradition, attempting to live life in humility while struggling with the contingencies and difficulties of desire, other people, the cut and thrust of history, and natural disasters. Human life has been characterized by some sense of inwardness and self-reflection from ancient times, as we see from the narratives that have come down to us in Hebrew, Sanskrit, Chinese, and Greek. But the sense of inner truth accessed through interiority that has been our theme has been strongly challenged in the modern world.

The general argument I have presented is that the search for a truth within is characteristic of the premodern, cosmological religions of Europe and South

[33] See Kevin Thompson, 'Forms of Resistance: Foucault on Tactical Reversal and Self-Formation', *Continental Philosophy Review*, 36/2 (2003), pp. 113–38. Also Jeremy Carrette, *Foucault and Religion: Spiritual Corporeality and Political Spirituality* (London: Routledge, 2000). Of particular relevance is Carrette's idea of political spirituality, pp. 136–41.

Asia. I have described instances of this inner truth in terms of the cultivation of inwardness through the spiritual practices of those religions and have argued that what we find is a shared subjectivity and imagination in which the person shapes her life in accordance with tradition. There is an identification of the subject, the 'I', with the religion's account of reality and ideals of living it presents. The meaning of life becomes a question of where we are located in the cosmic scheme, and how we enact the goal and highest purpose of life. This highest purpose is conceptualized as being within the person: the truth within is sought through introspection and the techniques of inwardness developed in traditions of prayer and meditation, reading, and asceticism. This shared subjectivity, I have suggested, can be contrasted with the individualism of modernity that emphasizes individual rights and a distinct, non-repeatable and non-cosmological kind of interiority—a self with 'inner depth', to use Taylor's phrase, but a self set free from any cosmological moorings.

But we now need to see this binary distinction between shared and individual subjectivity in a more complex way. The religious person in the tradition who subjects herself to a bodily regime of transformation is not a collectivity but an individual person. Such a person is certainly embedded in a society and web of relationships, but also has reflectivity and self-narration that makes him or her distinct from others, and unique. Each person has their own unique qualities and personality that is nonetheless shaped and formed by tradition, and the religions we have looked at recognize human difference and the need to adapt practices to suit different human needs. But although, as human beings, we share much with our forebears, we are nevertheless constrained by the horizon of our history and world view we inhabit. The mode of human inwardness is arguably different in premodernity, shaped by religion, and directed to a goal that transcends the human condition and even transcends the world.

Charles Taylor has argued for the distinctiveness of the modern concept of the self. For Taylor, John Locke is a pivotal figure in the development of the modern notion of the individual and even the 'invention' of consciousness.[34] Our modern notion of inwardness, argues Taylor, is associated with disengagement and rational control, a theme whose origin is in Neoplatonism, although this legacy is lost by the time we reach Locke.[35] This idea develops through Locke to the Enlightenment, and Taylor calls it the 'punctual' self. With Descartes and then Locke we have moved from a medieval world where the cosmos is a self-manifesting order, to a view of a mechanistic universe that

[34] Etienne Balibar, *Identité et différence: L'invention de la consience* (Paris: Seuil, 1998), pp. 57–63. Also see Paul Ricoeur, *Memory, History, Forgetting*, trans. Kathleen Blamey and David Pellauer (Chicago, IL: Chicago University Press, 2004), pp. 102–9.

[35] Charles Taylor, *Sources of the Self* (Cambridge, MA: Harvard University Press, 1989), pp 159–76.

the self can be disengaged from because the self is no longer participatory in it. The disengagement begun by Descartes' *cogito* becomes turned towards the subject. There is a movement from the medieval idea of a meaningful order to a mechanistic universe that is non-teleological, to the idea of objectification both of universe and of experience. This leads to the disengaged self that has power and control. Locke, for Taylor, pushes the idea of disengagement to an anti-teleological view of human nature that we have no innate ideas but learn about the world through experience and understand it through rational thinking. The self can become disengaged from the world and from itself and so can reform the self: this is the power of the 'punctual' self, 'the power to objectify and remake'.[36] This ability to remake is the power of self-control in which our inner lives—our emotions and habits—can become objects of our inquiry. It is a view of the self from a third person perspective that is actually turned into a first person account such that 'radical objectivity is only intelligible and accessible through radical subjectivity'.[37] The third person view of the self necessitated by disengagement from the world is turned to the self, and so a first person account is necessitated that is nevertheless still a third person account in essence. The self and its emotions and inner states are objectified and opened for rational explication, just like the external, mechanistic world.

This reading of Locke has not gone unchallenged. Siegel questions what he regards as Taylor's nostalgia 'for a lost Aristotelian cosmos'[38] with a reading of Locke that sees him as paying close attention to both reflective and non-reflective aspects of consciousness that challenged the very stability of the self, let alone seeing it as an embodiment of reason. On Seigel's account, Locke cannot see the self as having the power to remove itself from time and circumstance, although he certainly foreshadows modern individualism. I leave it to Locke scholars to adjudicate this disagreement, but the broader point that Taylor wishes to stress is apposite: that the meaningful cosmos of the Aristotle-inspired scholastic world has gone by the time we reach Locke, and the mechanistic universe that replaces it brings with it a certain understanding of the self. This understanding is one of objectification and the ability to see world in a disengaged way, a kind of gaze that can be turned to the self. That Locke understands the self as a *tabula rasa* is not in dispute, but the disagreement seems to be over the contents of the self and its mode of operating in that objective world.

In the broader picture, the contrast that Taylor is making is surely correct. The kind of inwardness that Locke has created that allows us to perceive a 'consciousness', where Descartes had posited a *cogito*, is a new move in philosophy. This is a kind of inwardness that, while being reflective, is not reflective in

[36] Taylor, *Sources of the Self*, p. 171. [37] Taylor, *Sources of the Self*, p. 176.

[38] Jerrold Seigel, *The Idea of the Self: Thought and Experience in Western Europe Since the Seventeenth Century* (Cambridge and New York: Cambridge University Press, 2005), p. 43.

the ancient and medieval sense that we have been examining here. The inwardness of Locke is not that of Bonaventure or Abhinavagupta. The truth within in our medieval Latin and Sanskrit sources is a truth of the self that is intimately linked to a non-mechanistic universe, a cosmos populated with supernatural agencies in which the self is intimately engaged. Even in a radically anti-metaphysical Theravāda Buddhist perspective where there is no self, the person is embroiled in an enlivened cosmos that can be experienced through introspection, even to the extent that meditation can lead to relocation within it (that is, through meditation we can experience different worlds on this account).

The modern senses of the self that are contingent upon the massive shift from a cosmos to a scientific and mechanistic world view are different to the shared subjectivity of the earlier centuries. Yet this shift brings with it renewed inquiry into the self and problematizes inwardness. Locke is clearly no philosopher of interiority, yet he is pivotal in the modern understanding of self and consciousness. From Locke we can trace a history of the inner life in a number of ways: one British trajectory goes into Hume and empiricism along with concern for questions of personal identity in analytical philosophy, a concern not so much with the inner life as what constitutes a human person persisting through time; a tradition of German romanticism rejects the empirical perspective in favour of a focus on interiority and longing (as we find in Novalis' young Heinrich longing for the blue flower), that leads into the existentialism of the twentieth century via Kierkegaard and Nietszche; another route stems from Kant into phenomenology and an attempted science of the self; while yet another, related to German romanticism, develops into the psychoanalysis of Freud and psychotherapy of Jung, through to Lacan, and so to Kristeva and Irigaray. Other philosophers have simply not been particularly interested in inwardness: Marx, in particular, seeing bourgeois individualism as a kind of false consciousness that needs to be overcome by the objective historical consciousness of the proletariat revolution. On this view, inwardness is the product of historical process and, in the end, has to be deconstructed in the name of historical truth. Inwardness on this account has only historical status and not ontological status. While there are many examples of new forms of inwardness, let us take two to provide a contrast with the material we have presented.

TWO EXAMPLES: KIERKEGAARD AND KRISTEVA

Kierkegaard's idea of inwardness must be distinguished from the earlier thinkers we have seen, and from the premodern world view. For Kierkegaard, inwardness is the mode of being that begins with alienation and is both a designation of our condition and a task to be realized.[39] Kierkegaard identifies truth with subjectivity and subjectivity with inwardness as the fundamental message of Christianity. In becoming subjective we intensify the reality of our existence, experiencing the contingency and fragility of life and so realizing through faith the qualitative distinction between our finitude and God's eternity. For Kierkegaard, this inwardness is not participation in a great cosmic structure or a journey into God in a way we have seen with Bonaventure, and although he does have the developmental stages through time of the aesthetic, the ethical, and the religious, this is less a ladder of interior ascent than moral progress towards faith as passionate engagement and commitment to a transcendent being wholly outside our understanding. Such passionate commitment is love. Not the love of friends or erotic love, but the love of the commandment 'you shall love'.[40]

With Kierkegaard we have a precursor to the postmodern critique of grand narratives.[41] Far from the medieval world of inwardness and the discovery of the 'inner man' as cosmological participation, with Kierkegaard we have an almost unpredictable spontaneity that is essence of truth. It is not so much spiritual practices that develop an inner journey that is also a journey through the cosmos, but the realization of conscience and the inner leap of faith. This is also a question about to what extent truth can be learned and how eternal happiness can be based on the merely historical.[42] Of course, truth cannot be learned on this view but needs to be realized as inwardness that responds in an act of will to the commandment to love. Indeed, for Kierkegaard, the cultivation of habit—such as the habitual patterns of the liturgical day of the religious practitioner that we have described—is antithetical to love. Habit is like a predatory creature that sucks blood from a sleeper while fanning him to make his sleep more pleasant.[43] What is required is that one obeys the commandment 'you shall love', and this means love of neighbour by the individual. Kierkegaard writes: '*You* shall, *you* shall love the neighbor. O my listener, it is not you to whom I am speaking; it is *I* of whom eternity says: You shall.'[44] The demand is emphatic. It is not a general command but a direct address to me, the individual, who stands before eternity. And rather than asceticism, prayer, reading, and the liturgical, participatory life, it is conscience that matters, and conscience is a synonym for the individual. The command to love is an injunction for the individual to stand before God and is a 'most dreadful

[39] For a good introduction, see George Pattison, *The Philosophy of Kierkegaard* (Montreal and Kingston; Ithaca, NY: McGill Queens University Press, 2005). Also Alastair Hannay, *Kierkegaard: A Biography* (Cambridge: Cambridge University Press, 2001).

[40] Soren Kierkegaard, *Works of Love*, ed. and trans. Howard V. Hong and Edna Hong (Princeton, NJ: Princeton University Press, 1995), pp. 17–43.

[41] George Pattison, *Kierkegaard's Upbuilding Discourses: Philosophy, Theology, Literature* (London: Routledge, 2002), p. 9.

[42] Hannay, *Kierkegaard*, p. 394.

[43] Kierkegaard, *Works of Love*, p. 36.

[44] Kierkegaard, *Works of Love*, p. 90.

responsibility'.[45] While 'purity of heart' is a category Kierkegaard uses, he means by this the single individual's responsibility as act of will towards God, rather than the early Christian idea of moral purification and inner illumination. The individual rather than 'the crowd' is what counts, and the inner voice of conscience over the voice of the majority.[46]

This inwardness as the central characteristic of human life must be translated into action. There needs to be a movement (kinesis) from intention to action that thereby expresses the fundamental existential orientation of our existence as becoming. Truth involves the movement from potentiality to actuality. As a recent commentator writes: 'For Kierkegaard truth implies actualization: an idea of possibility being brought into existence, as in repetition, rather than the transition from existence to idea that occurs in recollection ('the same movement, only in opposite directions').'[47] Not recollection but repetition is important, where repetition means motion towards actualization and so is future orientated. Recollection, by contrast, is remembrance and an attempt to reconstruct or dwell on the past. This is a modern understanding where temporality takes precedence over cosmological structure. Kierkegaard's inwardness is a radical departure from the traditional inner journey, focused on conscience, responsibility, and spontaneous love of God. Of course, his is a Christian view, but one that has developed in a world where cosmology has retreated from science and individualism has developed as a social value over the collective. Although a religious perspective, Kierkegaard's is a modern understanding that, while developing the logical historical outcome of Luther, is thoroughly modernist in its refusal of authority and emphasis on individual will.

Yet in many ways the Kierkegaardian perspective does not do justice to the full potential of inwardness. Standing in a different although related philosophical trajectory, a semiotic lineage from Nietzsche through Freud to Lacan, Julia Kristeva criticizes the 'phenomenology' of Kierkegaard, firstly for isolating the subject from natural and historical processes and secondly for his 'failure' to found a thesis of kinesis. The first criticism could pertain more generally to phenomenology, but the force of the second is not so clear. Kierkegaard in *Repetition* did develop a thesis about kinesis, but its inadequacy, on Kristeva's reading, lies in the neglect of desire. Kierkegaardian kinesis as the expression of inwardness moving towards actualization resonates

[45] See Jamie Ferreira, *Love's Grateful Striving: A Commentary on Kierkegaard's Works of Love* (New York: Oxford University Press, 2001), p. 89.

[46] Ferreira, *Love's Grateful Striving*, pp. 87–8.

[47] Clare Carlisle, *Kierkegaard's Philosophy of Becoming: Movements and Positions* (Albany, NY: SUNY Press, 2005), p. 73.

with the idea of care (*cura*). Movement is care as the fundamental attitude of human existence towards itself in the condition of becoming, and as such is related to desire. Care is the articulation of desire, but Kierkegaard, in Kristeva's view, does not develop this, and so desire is fundamentally and glaringly absent from Kierkegaard's account of inwardness. In defense of Kierkegaard, one might say simply that desire is not a category he uses, speaking rather in broader terms of love and introducing the new idea of repetition; and this is certainly true. But Kristeva has a point when she identifies the lack of desire in Kierkegaard's oeuvre. The truth within for Kierkegaard is subjectivity that is orientated towards the transcendent other, towards God who, while outside of gender, is nevertheless articulated in the gendered language of Protestant Christianity. For Kristeva, on the other hand, the truth within is a nostalgia for the lost mother who we must experience in abjection if we are to grow. In her view we must abandon the inner mother (and so the realm of the semiotic) in order to approach the (good) father and enter into the realm of the symbolic, the male realm of language and self-assertion.

Although Kristeva is critical of Kierkegaard's lack of understanding, the dynamic nature of self-development and what she sees as his failed thesis of motility, they nevertheless share common ground in laying claim to self-transformation as the transgressing or transcending of limitation. For both thinkers, the human person has to confront the truth within in a dynamic process of discovery: the leap of faith that bridges the qualitative disjunction between temporality and eternity for Kierkegaard, the abjection that separates us from the (bad) mother, from the maternal body, and opens us to the inner, loving father who is identified with the stranger within.[48] And both Kierkegaard and Kristeva are concerned with the power of becoming. The goal of life is transition from limitation, understood as sin by Kierkegaard and as the crippling effect of the failure of transition from the semiotic to the symbolic realms, from the bad mother to the good father, for Kristeva. These goals are not, of course, the same, but the point I wish to make is that in Kierkegaard and Kristeva we are confronted with a modern view of interiority as temporal process. In both we see self-reflection and in both we see narratability, particularly in Kristeva for whom the realm of the symbolic, the realm of language (and so narration) is so important for self-integration and psychic health. With Kristeva, inwardness is linked to unconscious drives in a way that could not have occurred in Kierkegaard, nor in the earlier thinkers and texts we have examined, because of the relatively recent discourse about it.

[48] Julia Kristeva, *Black Sun: Depression and Melancholia*, trans. Leon S. Roudiez (New York and Chichester: Columbia University Press, 1989), pp. 69–94.

CONCLUSION

The texts and histories of Christianity, Hinduism, and Buddhism described in Part I showed us the context and history-specific nature of inwardness, but claimed that the inwardness between these religions in premodern times is closer than the contrast between the modern and the premodern. The phenomenology of inwardness has allowed us to render this more complex and to see that there are, in fact, continuities between the premodern and the modern that allow us to recognize those earlier forms of inwardness as inwardness. In a recognizably inward looking poem by Wallace Stevens we could begin to articulate a number of characteristics of inwardness—such as temporality, reportability, and self-reflection—that are key elements to inwardness also found in the premodern religions.

On the one hand, there are parallels to be seen through the widespread history and texts we have encountered (and I would not wish to overemphasize the premodern/modern distinction); but on the other, Abhinavagupta and Bonaventure live within a cosmos with a redemptive ideology that is not shared by the modern thinkers. Kierkegaard, although the redemption of the individual through grace is his ideal, could only have developed his ideas in his particular historical location. Kristeva, likewise, could only have developed the idea of abjection in a post-Freud world. We are constrained by the histories within which we find ourselves. And yet, as the search for the truth within shows, we share much over the centuries and between continents; if not the truth, then we share the processes of interiority and the search within. We are all seekers.

8

The Phenomenology of Inwardness

In sharp contrast to the historical material so far presented, let us begin with a modern account of inwardness implied in Wallace Steven's 'Re-statement of Romance':

The night knows nothing of the chants of night
It is what it is as I am what I am:
And in perceiving this I best perceive myself

And you. Only we two may interchange
Each in the other what each has to give.
Only we two are one, not you and night,

Nor night and I, but you and I alone,
So much alone, so deeply by ourselves,
So far beyond the casual solitudes,

That night is only the background of ourselves,
Supremely true each to its separate self,
In the pale light that each upon the other throws.[1]

In this remarkable poem, Stevens presents us with a sense of inwardness that is illuminated through the other person. The humanity of each necessitates their distinction from an ambient darkness that surrounds them and threatens to engulf them. In the intimacy of co-presence each comes into view only 'in the pale light that each upon the other throws'. The poem highlights a sense of identity formed through reflection upon a relation to another self and in relation to the surrounding world ('the night') in which the two lovers find themselves. Here we have a sense of subjectivity arrived at *through* the other, an understanding that entails both intimacy and relationality. The distance between self and other in Stevens' poem is simultaneously extremely close, one might even say painfully so, and infinitely distant—an intimacy that opens out the solitude of the relation of subject to subject and self to other. I know myself through the other against whom I am defined more than against the backdrop

[1] Wallace Stevens, 'Re-statement of Romance', *Collected Poems* (London and Boston, MA: Faber and Faber, 1954), p. 146.

of the surrounding world. In Stevens' poem we have inwardness as both intimacy and alienation, a sense of the subject as most intensely true to him or herself in its unique solitude, a solitude highlighted in relation to the other; most importantly the human other, but also the other of the night. This inwardness is clearly a form of knowledge, a knowledge that is only opened up through the poetic space of the poem, through the poem's imaginaire.

THE POWER OF PRONOUNS

Stevens' poem rings true to modern, Western ears because in it we can see the intensification of subjectivity that is inwardness, sketched in stark and minimal terms. The subject is confronted with another, and that very face-to-face encounter opens up simultaneously a vast distance and close proximity. The other in the poem, or more precisely and more intimately the 'you', addresses a question to 'me' about who I am and where I stand in the world. At one level the narrator of the poem stands 'here' in contrast to the 'there' of the 'you'. The deixic language, which generally requires specificity in space to be meaningful, has specificity here only in the space of the imagination, although each reader of the poem will specify the narrator more precisely as 'myself'. 'I' as the reader of the poem come to be identified with the 'I' as narrator of the poem, which means the poem succeeds because of its ability to complete a sense that the 'I' of the text is recognizable in the extra-textual 'I'. The deixic language of the narrator invites the identification of the extra-textual or 'indexical-I' with the intra-textual 'I of discourse', to use Greg Urban's phrase again.[2] In other words, the poem works through the power of pronouns. The floating signifier of the first and second person pronouns allows the identification of myself, as the user of the first person, with the narrator's use. I can identify 'myself' with the narrator and the 'other' with 'you', through the floating signifiers.

The second distance that opens up is between self and other as the ambient darkness. We might take darkness to be the world or perhaps nature. Indeed, 'the chants of night' indicate culture and a cultural attempt to comprehend the night, and the narrator seems equally alienated from both the culture that shapes the world or nature and the world or nature itself. We have an implicit theme here that echoes the theme of escape and inner flight, usually from nature although often from others, that we have come across in the religious literature we have described. Inwardness can mark an unbridgeable distance between humans and the world or universe, as we see here. The intimacy that

[2] I have often cited this very insightful paper: Greg Urban, 'The I of Discourse', in Benjamin Lee and Greg Urban (eds.), *Semiotics, Self and Society* (Berlin and New York: Mouton de Gruyter, 1989), pp. 27–51.

allows inwardness to show itself, all too briefly and with great fragility, is confined to the human world and does not thrive in nature, in the ambient darkness around the lovers.

Inwardness implies distance from the other yet is also constructed through language and so formed within a cultural system. Indeed, inwardness needs language to be publicly accessible. In the poem, the power of pronouns governs the identification process. This structure, the power of pronouns or the ability for deixic identification, is in language itself and is probably a universal property of all languages,[3] although the imaginative space in which deixis occurs is culture-specific. While Stevens' poem could only have been written at a particular historical juncture in the history of the West, it nevertheless contains the potential for universal understanding through the linguistic property of deixis. This idea of potential understanding means that a host of cultural presuppositions must be assumed before such identification can successfully take place—such as recognition of the poetic genre, recognition of the intimacy of lovers, and recognition of intellectual history in which Nietzsche has declared the 'death of God'. Indeed, the subjectivity of 'Re-statement of Romance' is particularly modernist, and while it contains universal properties of inwardness—the power of pronouns in the process of identification, intimacy, self-knowledge, and otherness—it can be contrasted with a traditional view of inwardness of the kind we have seen, in which the self is oriented in quite a different imaginative space.

A PRELIMINARY PHENOMENOLOGICAL ACCOUNT

Beginning with Wallace Stevens' poem allows us to discern general features of inwardness amenable to phenomenological inquiry, features that are arguably shared across cultures and histories. Although we have been arguing for the distinctiveness of premodern, cosmological inwardness, there is a commonality that allows us to identify general features of inwardness that cut across cultures and identify the premodern expression that we have been focusing on as 'inwardness'. We will need to develop further our thesis presented in the last chapter through focusing on a general phenomenology of inwardness. Each of these general features will need to be examined in more specificity. Our preliminary inquiry therefore suggests the following theses:

[3] On the universality of deixis see Stephen C. Levinson, *Pragmatics* (Cambridge: Cambridge University Press, 1983), pp. 68–73; A. Wierzbicka, *Semantics: Primes and Universals* (Oxford and New York: Oxford University Press, 1996), pp. 35–43.

1. Inwardness is self-reflection. But a theory of inwardness is not a theory of consciousness, although (i) inwardness does entail consciousness in a phenomenal as opposed to a psychological sense; (ii) as a phenomenal concept it cannot be the direct object of consciousness but is reflectively perceived when consciousness has specific kinds of content (phenomena) related to cultural forms such as 'text', although we can expand the notion of text to include painting, music, or ritual; (iii) as a phenomenal state, inwardness therefore entails a cultural content that can be described as a moral space. Forms of inwardness or kinds of moral space generated through religious traditions are distinct from other kinds of inwardness generated through, for example, aesthetic experience, although the mode of apprehension is directly parallel, that is, an indirect or mediated mode.
2. Inwardness is reportable. Because inwardness is characterized by reflectivity, it is not the basic mode of being human that has been subjected to phenomenological analysis that we might call pre-reflective awareness. Inwardness therefore enters into language and so enters into culture, and thereby is open to or demands not only phenomenological but semiotic analysis.
3. Inwardness is related to time and consciousness of time because inwardness as a shared subjectivity that we have been discussing involves a kind of temporal collapse between text and self. We might say that inwardness is generated by the encounter of self and other, where 'other' could be a person, object, or text.
4. Therefore: Inwardness entails narrative, the story of a life moving from birth to death, and in the case of traditional religions, the idea of life as an inner journey.
5. Inwardness is therefore historical and cultural. Inwardness is formed in tradition-specific ways at particular times in history. Yet there is also a sense in which inwardness is discovered or, in phenomenological terms, discloses itself.
6. The disclosing of inwardness is through signs or a system of signs.

Let us look more closely at each of these theses.

INWARDNESS IS SELF-REFLECTION

To use phenomenological language, inwardness is not directly perceived as an object of consciousness but is subjective, indirectly perceived through the objects of consciousness. This is self-reflection where 'reflection', in contrast to 'reflexivity', is intentional and purposeful. Seigel has drawn our attention to this distinction. A reflex, he observes, is 'an automatic or involuntary action', something that reinforces its origin like a reflection in a mirror. Reflection, by contrast, is not an unwilled response but is self-directed and intentional.[4] As such, inwardness is both *formed* through its objects and yet is also *discovered* in the process of reflection. A theory of inwardness is not in itself a theory of consciousness, as inwardness is a particular mode of consciousness but cannot be identified with consciousness *tout ensemble*: there are kinds of consciousness that are not inward—certain kinds of collectivity in battle or sport might be examples. But inwardness does entail consciousness.

We need here to distinguish between phenomenal consciousness and psychological consciousness. This distinction from the philosophy of mind is useful in allowing us to see the distinctive nature of inwardness as a particular mode of consciousness. The phenomenal concept of mind is of the mind 'as conscious experience, and of a mental state as a consciously experienced mental state', as opposed to a psychological concept of mind 'as the casual or explanatory basis for behaviour'.[5] A psychological property may or may not be conscious, whereas a phenomenal property is conscious and accompanies a psychological property but cannot be equated with it. The phenomenal property is the experience that tends to accompany the psychological state. These two are logically distinct. Chalmers gives the example that a Rolls-Royce icon is generally found on Rolls-Royce cars 'but this does not mean that to be a Rolls-Royce icon is to be a Rolls-Royce car'.[6] There are various kinds of psychological consciousness—Chalmers lists awakeness, introspection, reportability, self-consciousness, attention, voluntary control, and knowledge[7]—that are functional notions but they also have a phenomenal quality. Awareness, for example, is a state 'wherein we have access to some information, and can use that information in control of behaviour'.[8] Awareness is a psychological fact that accompanies consciousness but in itself might not be conscious, as we see in the awareness of a fact without any accompanying conscious experience.

Inwardness is a phenomenal experience characterized or re-described as self-reflection, introspection, awareness of internal objects or thoughts, and so on. But inwardness cannot be the direct object of consciousness. It rather emerges through different kinds of objects of consciousness. These objects are the content of consciousness, the content of intentionality, which are formed through and in culture. The category 'text', for example, might form a culture-specific content of consciousness—Proust reading a novel in his hedge while

[4] Jerrold Seigel, *The Idea of the Self: Thought and Experience in Western Europe Since the Seventeenth Century* (Cambridge and New York: Cambridge University Press, 2005), pp. 12–13.

[5] David J. Chalmers, *The Conscious Mind: In Search of Fundamental Theory* (Oxford: Oxford University Press, 1996), p. 11.

[6] Chalmers, *The Conscious Mind*, p. 23.

[7] Chalmers, *The Conscious Mind*, pp. 26–7.

[8] Chalmers, *The Conscious Mind*, p. 28.

his mother looks for him, or the monk's silent recitation of the Psalter—and these variable contents entail different kinds of inwardness although the process of inwardness is shared, as we have argued. Music or the plastic arts might similarly form objects of intentionality that evoke particular kinds of inwardness, particular kinds of phenomenal awareness. There is a dependence relation on the kind of content or object of consciousness and the kind of inwardness that emerges that we might describe both as construction and disclosure.

There are many ways into this issue, but let us formulate the nature of inwardness, or rather these two aspects of construction and disclosure, through phenomenology, which has been so concerned with consciousness and subjectivity. We need further leverage on the notion of subjectivity to develop a phenomenological account. Phenomenology has been the philosophical tradition that has concerned itself above all with selfhood, subjectivity, and consciousness. As Steinbock observes, phenomenology 'is a type of reflective attentiveness attuned to givenness that occurs *within* experiencing itself'.[9] For an initial formulation we can turn to that pivotal figure, Edmund Husserl. With Husserl we find an account of consciousness that seeks initially to describe the processes of being aware and consequently to account for the arising or genesis of those processes. A second phenomenology of Heidegger reviews and critiques the Husserlian formulation, revealing problems involved with the subjectivist view and complexifying the question of the subject, replacing subjectivity with *Dasein* ('being-there') as the primary mode of being in the world. While Heidegger develops an account of ontology, which implicitly raises questions about the primacy of inwardness, his account is important in opening inwardness as a mode of discovery or disclosure. Yet Heidegger's account is arguably insufficient in the development of an ethical and narrative dimension. Having formulated these two phenomenological accounts we will then be in a position to develop relevant moral and narrative descriptions, particularly through Ricoeur's work. With narrative accounts of subjectivity we can discuss the interface between narratives of the self and macro-narratives of traditions in history, and so we will have a more thorough understanding of what we mean by inwardness, how this concept relates to the past, and why it is so important.

Intentionality for Husserl

During his life Husserl developed a number of strategies and methods that he considered to be at the heart of phenomenology, the most important of which

[9] Anthony J. Steinbock, *Phenomenology and Mysticism: The Verticality of Religious Experience* (Bloomington, IN: Indiana University Press, 2007), p. 3.

for the study of religions has been the first phenomenological reduction, the method of bracketing or the suspension of the question of the being behind appearances to consciousness, and the eidetic reduction, the intuition of the essence of what appears.[10] The first assumption of phenomenology is that consciousness is intentional, which means that consciousness is *of* something; there is always an object of consciousness that comprises the two poles of the 'I think' (*ego cogito*) and the thought (*cogitatum*), which is the intentional object. In summary, as expressed in the introduction to phenomenology that Husserl wrote for a French audience, the *Cartesian Meditations* (thereby acknowledging and referencing Descartes, who first argued in a sustained way for the modern ego as centre of consciousness), *cogito ergo sum.* Husserl turned Descartes' doubt into 'bracketing' the being behind appearances (the *epoché*) and turned the 'I think' (*ego cogito*) into 'I think what is thought' (*ego cogito cogitatum*).[11] That is, he identified consciousness as being intentional, as always being 'consciousness of', as always having an object. While the question concerning the being behind the objects of consciousness (and anything could in principle be an object of consciousness: a tree, an emotion, or a god) is suspended, the bare fact of consciousness, the pure ego in itself, cannot because it is an irreducible given: a transcendental ego that is the subject of experience. This transcendental ego is pure subjectivity and inwardness, and although such inwardness goes back centuries—Husserl quotes Augustine that the truth lies in the inner man[12]—it is Husserl who understood it in this way as the subject for whom appearances show themselves or are given.

The phenomenological method entails a shift from the 'natural attitude' of assuming the material existence of the world or the reality of the flow of appearances, to the suspension of the question of the reality behind appearances to consciousness. This method of bracketing the being behind appearances, or the *epoché*, in the first instance, takes phenomena or objects that appear in the flow of conscious awareness (*cogitationes*) simply as phenomena in order to thoroughly investigate the appearances in the spirit of detachment of true science. Phenomenology as conceived of by Husserl was in the first instance descriptive, which he called the static phenomenology. This was an extremely important move and marked the main feature of phenomenology. Many phenomenologists of religion, for example, have restricted their activity to this descriptive level. From this descriptive phenomenology the second reduction to the essence (*eidos*) of appearances can be performed—the imaginative intuition of the abstraction from the objects of intentional

[10] For an account of this with regard to the study of religions see my *Beyond Phenomenology: Rethinking the Study of Religion* (London: Cassell, 1999), ch. 5.

[11] E. Husserl, *Cartesian Mediations*, trans. Dorion Cairns (Dordrecht: Kluwer, 1950), pp. 18–21; Joseph J. Kockelmans, *Edmund Husserl's Phenomenology* (West Lafayette: Purdue University Press, 1994), pp. 16–18.

[12] Husserl, *Cartesian Meditations*, p. 157.

consciousness. Indeed, many thinkers, including the inheritors of the phenomenological tradition such as Merleau-Ponty, rejected the eidetic reduction as too Platonic, although Husserl arguably avoids this accusation through the claim that the essences are still within the intentional structure and are simply objects of a different order.[13]

To simplify Husserl's complex account, subjectivity is the I-pole of the intentional structure of consciousness. But the 'I' itself cannot be subjected to the *epoché* as it cannot be an object (*Gegenstand*) of itself[14]—as Welton observes, 'to the extent that it is an object, it ceases to be capable of providing the ground for any object whatsoever'.[15] Furthermore, 'rendering consciousness thematic in reflection turns it into an object (of analysis), a procedure that already assumes that I am acquainted with consciousness'.[16] While cognition can fall under the gaze of the phenomenologist, the subject of cognition is illusive and evades direct apprehension and yet is crucially implicated and revealed through the phenomenological method. As Donn Welton in his groundbreaking study of Husserl explains, Husserl identifies a fourfold structure of intentionality, namely the *as-*, *for-*, *in-*, and *from-* structures.[17] That is, all objects of consciousness come forth *as* something, the 'what' of the phenomenon prior to the work of interpretation. These objects come forth *for* someone. The for-structure is the object's significance for the one *for* whom it has meaning. Indeed, as Welton puts it, the for-structure is the condition of the as-structure's being; 'The "What" of the object is internally tied to the "How" of its appearing which, for its part, owes its being to the modalities of the for-structure.'[18]

This is really another way of saying that consciousness is intentional. The appearances come into view *as* something *for* someone. Thus in any conscious act there is the subject pole and the intended object. Furthermore, phenomena appear 'in a certain clearing that allows them to come forth', the dimension wherein appearances take place, and they come *from* a dimension that is hidden, 'that is not cleared'.[19]

In terms of the Wallace Stevens poem cited above, we might say that the poem's narrator, the 'I of discourse', has the other person as intentional object, and through that other, reflectively the self, which can only be apprehended indirectly. Subjectivity, the I-pole of the intentional structure, only comes into view through the intentional objects. The understanding or intuition of the

[13] E. Husserl, *Ideas Pertaining to a Pure Phenomenology and to a Phenomenological Philosophy*, trans. R. Rojcewicz and A. Scuwer (Dordrecht: Kluwer, 1989), p. 9.

[14] Husserl, *Cartesian Meditations*, pp. 25–6.

[15] Donn Welton, *The Other Husserl: The Horizons of Transcendental Phenomenology* (Bloomington and Indianapolis, IN: Indiana University Press, 2000), p. 72.

[16] Welton, *The Other Husserl*, p. 248.

[17] Husserl, *Ideas I*, pp. 332, 339, expounded by Welton, *The Other Husserl*, pp. 22–3.

[18] Welton, *The Other Husserl*, p. 26.

[19] Welton, *The Other Husserl*, p. 26.

pure 'I', that Husserl calls the transcendental reduction or intuition, is certainly apprehended, but only because it is aware of something. The ego on this account cannot be directly apprehended, for then it would be an object of consciousness and not the subject of consciousness. The second reduction, the intuition of the self as transcendental ego, takes place at a different level. There are many problems with such a formulation of intentionality, however, such as the question of whether all conscious states are intentional and Heidegger's question of 'how can this ego with its intentional experiences get outside its sphere of experience and assume a relation to the extant world?'[20] This problem is clearly central to the accusation of idealism and a too great epistemological certainty levelled against Husserlian phenomenology, but for our current purposes we do not need to pursue the problem at this juncture as our initial formulation is about the relation of inwardness to subjectivity and the intentional structure of consciousness.[21] But for Heidegger, Husserl's formulation of intentionality is merely preliminary.

Self-Disclosure for Heidegger

For Heidegger, Husserl's formulation of intentionality, predicated as it is on the subject–object distinction, is only a surface formulation that avoids the deeper question of the nature of being. Indeed, the subject–object distinction is constructed, or rather is one of the modes of being-in-the-world, but is not foundational. The erroneous subjectivizing of intentionality leads to irresolvable problems about the relation of self to world. (How is the self connected to the world? How can the self know that which is outside of it?) On this view we have the ego or the sphere of the ego having intentional experiences directed towards a transcendent realm beyond. This, for Heidegger, is too crude, and rather than intentionality being a modality of the subject, the subject is determined by intentionality. That is, intentionality is part of the comportment (*Verhaltung*) of the *Dasein* and as such is neither subjective nor objective. The *Dasein* comports towards extant beings but not towards subjectivity as such. In his lectures on the problems of phenomenology Heidegger introduces the notion of *Dasein* in relation to intentionality, that intentionality 'must not be misinterpreted on the basis on an arbitrary concept of the subject and ego and subjective sphere and thus taken for an absurd problem of

[20] Heidegger, *The Basic Problems of Phenomenology*, trans. Albert Hofstadter (2nd edn, Bloomington and Indianapolis, IN: Indiana University Press, 1988), p. 61.

[21] For a survey and development of the idea of intentionality in mainly analytic philosophy (Quine, Dennett, Churchland), see William E. Lyons, *Approaches to Intentionality* (Oxford: Clarendon Press, 1995). On mainstream philosophical understanding, see pp. 10–39. Husserl's formulation of intentionality arguably pervades *Being and Time*, although it is not explicitly thematized.

transcendence...'[22] Intentionality is one of the basic constitutions of the *Dasein*, which cannot be explained in terms of self-consciousness or self-understanding, but rather self-understanding must be explained by an adequate account of existence itself.[23] Inwardness on this view is therefore not a primary mode of existence, in contrast to externality. Rather, inwardness must be seen as a modality of the *Dasein*.

One of the features of *Dasein* is self-disclosure, a primary character of assertion (*apophansis*), that the *Dasein* lets itself be seen as it is in itself.[24] In this sense, inwardness (not a term that Heidegger uses) might be seen as a mode of the self-revealing of the *Dasein* and so akin to discovery. In contrast to the Husserlian model of intentionality in which a subject intends an object, here both subjectivity and objectivity are modes of self-revealing—of being-there. Intentionality is fundamental to *Dasein* as self disclosure.

The difference between these two phenomenologies—the Husserlian and Heideggerian—is wide. But both contribute to our project in that, in the first instance, an initial description of inwardness must entail an account of intentionality, that consciousness has an object, and that self-consciousness arises through reflection in which it itself is constituted as its own object, a reflection fundamental to a sense of inwardness, but only apprehended indirectly. While Heidegger may be right that the subject–object distinction is a crude formulation that does not approach the nature of being itself, it is nevertheless important in so far as the distinction must be assumed by various accounts of inwardness that have developed. A deeper formulation of inwardness in terms of being itself is not necessary at this initial level of description. But we need to take from Heidegger the possibility of self-disclosure—that inwardness is not only the construction of inner space through text, but is also a revelation, an opening out or discovery of a world. We shall return to this important theme in due course.

We might say then that inwardness, like subjectivity itself or the pure 'I' (that answers to the question 'who?'), is not an object of consciousness in any direct sense, but rather a manner of givenness reflectively perceived when consciousness has a certain kind of content—a content that has the effect of making consciousness turn in on itself. The content that precipitates a sense of inwardness can be described, but not inwardness itself. Thus, 'Re-statement of Romance' as a poem is the object of the reader's consciousness, which precipitates a particular kind of inwardness in the reader in the way we have described. The *as*-structure, the 'fold' in phenomena that allows them to appear,[25] is the poem itself that simultaneously entails the *for*-structure, the one for whom the poem has meaning. Thus the reader perceives a sense of

[22] Heidegger, *The Basic Problems of Phenomenology*, p. 64.
[23] Heidegger, *The Basic Problems of Phenomenology*, p. 174.
[24] Heidegger, *The Basic Problems of Phenomenology*, p. 209.
[25] Welton, *The Other Husserl*, p. 22.

inwardness indirectly through the poem as object of consciousness and through a structurally higher cognition or intuition in which awareness becomes aware of itself with the poem as its object. We might say that inwardness is perceived through the content of consciousness or the intentional object being filled by the text. We might even go further and say that inwardness comes into view in the 'clearing' or the *in*-structure within which the *as*- and *for*- structure of intentionality appear. The text, then—in this case the poem—becomes integral to the perception of inwardness. Indeed, we could replace the poem with any number or kind of texts, including the ones we have read in Part I, and even include music and painting, and the effect would be reflective awareness via its object. Standing before the 'text' of Manet's Bar at the Folies-Bergère at the Courtauld Institute, which might be taken to be a 'text' as object of consciousness, precipitates a sense of inwardness in which reflective awareness is integral to the aesthetic act. Inwardness comes into view indirectly through the 'text', in this case the painting: the subjectivity of the painter fused with the subjectivity of the model, and this complete text involved in a temporal collapse into the present field of meaning for the beholder in which the painting becomes a trigger for the beholder's own sense of inwardness.

In a parallel way, a religious inwardness might be triggered through ritual as the 'object' of consciousness as we have seen in our Hindu and Christian examples. The sustained, regular attendance at an Orthodox liturgy for the practitioner might create a kind of inwardness through the same mechanism of identification, although the content is quite different. The repeated action of the liturgical process over a sustained period enables an inwardness to develop that is in complete consonance with the tradition. Although quite different from the Wallace Stevens poem, the mechanism of the production of inwardness is parallel whereby the self becomes identified with the self or implied reader of the text. An important difference between simply reading a poem and the formation of a religious inwardness is that the latter is formed through repeated actions of a liturgical process, through the sustained effort of a discipline, often over many years. This subordinating oneself to an objective discipline is, one might say, to place one's life under the religious question. Wallace Stevens' poem might move us, make us reflect, momentarily create an inner space of reflection, formulate a sense of inwardness, but does not affect the deeper structures of the self in the way that the internalization of the religious text through spiritual practice does.

Moral Space for Taylor

If subjectivity is the answer to the question 'Who?', as Paul Ricoeur suggests,[26] then part of this answer is historical, cultural, and philosophical location.

[26] Paul Ricoeur, *Oneself as Another*, trans. Kathleen Blamey (Chicago, IL: Chicago University Press, 1992), pp. 57–62.

Charles Taylor has argued that to answer the question 'Who?' is 'to be oriented in moral space'.[27] Whether Bonaventure or Abhinavagupta could have understood Wallace Stevens is, of course, impossible to say, but what is certain is that any such cross-cultural, transhistorical understanding would involve a learning process and, if not, a reorientation in moral space, then an empathy for the moral space of the other that can be described in terms of Heidegger's formal indication. The pronouns are formal indicators that enable understanding. Even though the moral space assumed by the narrator of the Stevens poem is distinctly modern and distinct from the cosmological moral space of premodern traditions, both East and West, the formal indication of the pronouns facilitates an understanding across cultural, historical, and linguistic barriers. The very use of the term 'I' in Edmund's text, or Abhinavagupta's discussion of the term 'I' (*aham*), allows some identification between reader and text. The very use of the first person pronoun also entails some notion of honesty in relation to the contents of inner truth and its declaration. True inwardness must involve the honesty of witnessing inner events (self-reflection) and in their articulation (narration). This process of deixic identification whereby a person can understand and identify with the subject of a text is arguably shared. The narrative of the self, the story of my life, can come to be identified with the narrative of tradition, the historical story, through processes of linguistic identification. While the self of modernity is largely bereft of religious cosmology, the self of the religious traditions we have examined is strongly formed in cosmological terms. The disenchantment characteristic of modern culture, as Taylor observes, undermines traditional frameworks which people thought to be coterminous with reality: 'people saw their frameworks as enjoying the same ontological solidity as the very structure of the universe'.[28]

In his famous book on the identity of the modern self, Charles Taylor argues for human beings as having a visceral moral sense that is articulated in terms of frameworks or orientations, and he traces the history of this moral sense into the formation of modern identity and a sophisticated understanding of inwardness; that we are beings with 'inner depths' alongside the idea that we are beings with a procedural rationality who construct a picture of ourselves and the world through disengaged reason. Although Taylor has argued for the continuity between the inwardness of modernity and the premodern self, we have seen that there is a greater disjunction between the two in so far as, in contrast to modern 'inwardness' and the 'procedural self', the premodern religious self offers a vision closely linked to a cosmic and moral order revealed from a transcendent source and perpetuated through tradition, text, and hierarchical social order. The traditional cosmological psychology has little

[27] Taylor, *Sources of the Self* (Cambridge and New York: Cambridge University Press, 1989), p. 29.

[28] Taylor, *Sources of the Self*, p. 26.

place in mainstream modernity.[29] While both modern inwardness and procedural rationality have their roots in such a traditional world view, the traditional self is in many ways at odds with the self of late modernity, not only on grounds of technological development but on grounds of fundamental orientation in the world. But Taylor is surely right in highlighting that we understand our lives as an unfolding story and 'you know what you are through what you have become'.[30] These stories are themselves part of a broader cultural and historical picture, and to know oneself is to know where one stands within the broader moral framework.

While the process of inwardness—the way in which a religious identity is formed through prayer, asceticism, and reading, which entails intimacy, narrative, temporality, orientation in moral space, and otherness—might be common, the content of that inwardness—the kind of moral space we inhabit, the location of the self—is inescapably historical. But it is precisely here in common human processes functioning in particular historical and cultural circumstances that we find a deep sense of inwardness as being central to understanding a universal human condition. On the one hand, inwardness is formed through cultural practices—the development of the *habitus*; on the other, the *interior homo* is discovered.

INWARDNESS IS REPORTABLE

So far we have characterized inwardness as being phenomenal consciousness, a mode of reflective awareness of the self that is indirect: the *homo interior* is constituted as reflective awareness, but this awareness can never have inwardness as its object. Inwardness is the subject of consciousness in a fundamental sense that is evoked by various kinds of content or object of consciousness; inwardness is always mediated. Yet inwardness is within the realm of reflectivity and so is open to linguistic commentary. What Chalmers has called 'reportability' (see 'Inwardness is Self-Reflection', p. 225) is a characteristic of inwardness. Even if an inner experience is outside of language, it is brought into language through being reported or narrated. That is, even absorption in a mystical awareness or absorption in music is not ineffable once reflection begins: inwardness as reflection is therefore not bare experience in which the self is undifferentiated from its objects and which is not an object for me. Phenomenology, partly in reaction against Husserl's Cartesianism, has highlighted a pre-reflective realm

[29] There are exceptions. Jung might be understood in terms of cosmological psychology, and even Freud adhered to the idea that ontogeny recapitulates phylogeny, so in that sense his psychology is cosmological.

[30] Taylor, *Sources of the Self*, p. 49.

of existence that is prior to language, and so prior to semiotic system. Merleau-Ponty has been particularly important here in stressing the primacy of bodily perception and latterly the idea of the flesh as embedded in world that comes into view as 'reversibility', the chiasm, where body/world and the visible/invisible are inseparably intertwined.[31] Merleau-Ponty famously rejects Husserl's Augustinian motto claiming that 'there is no inner man' for 'man is within the world'.[32] We are embodied and embedded within the world that is meaningful prior to our entry into it. The primordial fabric of our life, the flesh (*la chair*), precedes what becomes bifurcated into the opposing categories of subject/object and the Sartreian *en soi/pour soi* which are not part of primary experience but superimposed a priori. This is illustrated by the touch. Between what I touch and the movements of touching there is a relationship that opens up a tactile world and this occurs because my hand is both felt from within and accessible from without when, for example, touched by my other hand. In touching and being touched the hand opens to a tangible being. At Merleau-Ponty puts it: 'Through this criss-crossing within it of the touching and the tangible, its own movements incorporate themselves into the universe they interrogate, are recorded on the same map as it; the two systems are applied to one another, as the two halves of an orange.'[33] Thus the body is 'a being of two leaves, from one side a thing among things and otherwise what sees and touches them'.[34] Here the Cartesian *cogito* is brought into question by the flesh, by the two hands that exemplify the fundamental reversibility and ambiguity of existence. This 'wild being' (*l'être sauvage*) is primary to culture and system, prior to language, and prior to any subject/object dichotomy.[35]

This view supports a trajectory within feminist scholarship that emphasizes the fragmented and decentred nature of the 'I'. Following Merleau-Ponty later post-structuralist thinkers wish to erase or deconstruct subjectivity, arguing for the interplay of language and signs on the surface of culture, the disengagement of the signifier from the signified. Other feminist thinkers, notably Fionola Meredith and Pamela Anderson, have defended the notion of

[31] Maurice Merleau-Ponty, *The Visible and the Invisible*, trans. Alphonso Lingis (Evanston: Northwestern University Press, 1968), pp. 130–55. See Fred Evans and Leonard Lawlor (eds.), *Chiasms: Merleau-Ponty's Notion of Flesh* (Albany, NY: SUNY Press, 2000).

[32] M. Merleau-Ponty, *The Phenomenology of Perception*, trans. Colin Smith (London: Routledge, 1962), p. xii.

[33] Merleau-Ponty, *The Visible and the Invisible*, p. 133. *Le visible et l'invisible* (Paris: Gallimard, 1964), p. 175: *Par ce recroisement en elle du touchant et du tangible, ses mouvements proper s'incorporent à l'univers qu'ils interrogent, sont reportés sur la meme carte que lui; les deux systèmes s'appliquent l'un sur l'autre, comme les deux moitiés d'un orange.*

[34] Merleau-Ponty, *The Visible and the Invisible*, p. 137. *Le visible et l'invisible*, p. 178: *un être à deux feuillets, d'un côte choses parmi les choses et, par ailleurs, celui qui les voit et les touché.*

[35] This issue of the flesh as prior to culture is related to the question of the gendered and sexualized body. Some feminist thinkers have taken Merleau-Ponty to task for his non-recognition of sexual difference and the importance of gender. See Cecelia Sjoholm, 'Crossing Lovers: Luce Irigaray's Elemental Passions', *Hypatia*, 15/3 (2000), pp. 92–112.

subjectivity. Meredith, for example, argues that the response to the questions 'Who is speaking? Who is writing?' is insufficiently addressed by the post-structuralist claim, and that there is indeed a singularity to respond to the question 'Who?'.[36] Anderson similarly upholds the idea of self as possessor of virtues that can be developed in a transformed context beyond the masculinist myth.[37] In the light of these considerations it seems to me that we must distinguish two senses of the subject: one is the pre-reflective awareness highlighted by Merleau-Ponty that seems to be developed by post-structuralist thinking—such as Kristeva; the other is a formulated sense of the first person that not pre-cultural although organically linked to the pre-cultural sense of being, of self-awareness.

Although clearly there is subjectivity involved in Merleau-Ponty's flesh as the being of two leaves, in the sense that the lived body is one side of the chiasm, this sense of self is not pre-reflective, corporeal awareness but rather a stage beyond this layer of human existence.[38] The pre-reflective sense of the being of two leaves may not even be gendered, but a more primitive awareness. Inwardness, however, entails self-reflection, language, and so culture, although it is not necessarily highly articulated as we have seen with the vision literature we have examined. The phenomenology of inwardness is therefore connected with a phenomenology of culture and religion in that the forms of inwardness are particular, although built up, as it were, upon the pre-reflective flesh. The pre-reflective flesh is the carrier or precondition for the self-reflective subject of first person predicates.

[36] Fionola Meredith, 'A Post-Metaphysical Approach', in Pamela Sue Anderson and Beverley Clack (eds.), *Feminist Philosophy of Religion* (London: Routledge, 2004), pp. 54–72. On the post-structuralist critique of subjectivity, see E. Cadava, P. Connor, Jean Luc Nancy (eds.), *Who Comes After the Subject?* (London, Routledge, 1994).

[37] Pamela Anderson, *A Feminist Philosophy of Religion: The Rationality and Myths of Religious Belief* (Oxford: Blackwell, 1998).

[38] There have been other phenomenologists, of course, who have critiqued the Husserlian position: most famously Levinas, but also Michel Henry. In a similar way to Merleau-Ponty, Michel Henry has argued for the primacy of life in a radical inner ontology that identifies the essence of the human self with the essence of God. In doing this, he perceives the world to be essentially impotent and the realm of untruth in contrast to the truth of inner transcendence. This inner truth is still embodied. But this position has been criticized for its potentially gnostic leanings in presenting an essentially negative appraisal of the world. See Michel Henry, 'Le cogito et l'idée de phénoménologie', in Henry, *Phénoménologie de la vie*, vol. II *De la subjectivité* (Paris: PUF, 2003), pp. 57–72. Henry observes that 'knowledge of the soul' ('la connaissance de l'âme') and 'knowledge of the body' ('la connaissance du corps') are two ways of speaking that cannot be reduced to each other (p. 63). For a critique of the gnostic leanings in Henry, see Kevin Hart, '"Without World": Eschatology in Michel Henry', in Neal DeRoo and John P. Manoussakis (eds.), *Phenomenology and Eschatology: Not Yet in the Now* (Burlington, VT: Ashgate, 2009), pp. 167–92; also, Joseph M. Rivera, 'Generation, Interiority and the Phenomenology of Christianity in Michel Henry', *Continental Philosophy Review*, 44/2 (2011), 205–35. For a good account of the phenomenology of the body in general, see George Pattison, *God and Being: An Enquiry* (Oxford: Oxford University Press, 2012), pp. 238–56.

INWARDNESS IS TEMPORAL

Our preliminary account proposed that inwardness is formed through particular kinds of contents of consciousness that generate reflective awareness, as in an aesthetic response to a painting or participation in a religious ritual. The self apprehends the text and inwardness is formed through the identification process of the self with the text through the function of the floating signifier, the 'I' in the case of written text but through a non-linguistic mode of identification with a 'non-language' text such as a painting or piece of music.

But there is a deeper level of exposition to this initial formulation of the thesis—namely, the idea of temporality. The deixic process of identification of self with text entails a diachronic dimension in which there is a temporal collapse between the source of generation of the text and the present apprehension. The text from the past is apprehended as an object of contemporary consciousness and the resulting sense of inwardness is generated through the collapse of the past into the present. In apprehending Manet's barmaid, the subjectivity of the beholder conflates with the subjectivity of the painting from the past. Similarly in a liturgical setting, the rite generated in past centuries is internalized by practitioners and a particular sense of inwardness opens out for them, a sense generated by and anticipated within the rite itself. In the cosmological religions we have examined, to internalize ritual is to locate oneself within a community and to realize a subjectivity that is collective. We need to examine this temporal collapse in a more systematic way. If what we have offered so far is a first-level phenomenological description, we need to move on to a deeper level of phenomenological analysis, the genesis of appearances.

As Welton observes, Husserl reworked his theory of inner time-consciousness throughout his life,[39] but the important point is that it goes beyond the static analysis of the first phenomenological reduction to a genetic phenomenology, which identifies the basis of the intentionality structure. The problem to be accounted for is that conscious life falls away into the past at every moment, and yet the self is always self-aware. This is crucial for Husserl, for through the laws of time-consciousness we understand the laws of genesis. Husserl's argument in the *Phenomenology of Internal Time Consciousness* is that two aspects of retention and protention are crucial to inner time-consciousness. Consciousness retains what has just been and is not merely conscious of the now-point.[40] Consciousness is consciousness of appearances that are its objects. These objects are 'immanent' objects in that they are within the field of consciousness as time-bound and appear in a 'now' and then in a

[39] Welton, *The Other Husserl*, p. 248.

[40] E. Husserl, *The Phenomenology of Internal Time Consciousness*, trans. James Churchill (Bloomington, IN and London: Indiana University Press, 1966), pp. 53–4.

'past'. Husserl speaks of these modes of temporal orientation as 'running off phenomena' (*Ablaufsphänomene*) which are 'a continuity of constant transformations which form an inseparable unit, not severable into parts which could be by themselves nor divisible into phases, points of continuity, which could be by themselves'.[41] Time is therefore not an intentional object in the sense of phenomena, observed by a detached consciousness, but rather consciousness and time are without gap: there can be no consciousness outside of time which appears before it. This understanding that consciousness cannot be separated from time itself is in fact the consequence of bracketing 'normal' time and the sense that it is external to consciousness.[42] Bracketing for Husserl allows us to see that consciousness and time are coterminous. There is, then, a continuity of these phases of running off in which each new 'now' is changed into a past, and so the running off of these pasts 'moves uniformly downwards into the depth of the past'.[43] The series of running-offs move into the past and are no longer a 'now', while the future holds the potential for further series of nows which might be filled out with new objects or content. These running-offs into the past become retention as primary remembrance and recollection or secondary remembrance. Retention therefore pertains to the running off of objects that are no longer 'now', while protention is projection into the future from out of the running off phenomena. Every new appearance to consciousness develops from past appearances; thus 'everything new reacts on the old; its forward moving intention is fulfilled and determined thereby, and this gives the reproduction a definite colouring'.[44] We have, then, not simply the flow of consciousness within the horizon of temporality, but the protention of one moment of consciousness out from the other. The genesis of consciousness lies in temporality in so far as one moment is the basis of the next; one act of consciousness, as it were, flows from the previous, and we have a pattern of protention, the now-phase of the object or primal presentation, and retention.[45]

Extending this kind of Husserlian account we might say that inwardness entails a diachronic flow of awareness, conscious of itself through a content in which the temporality of the object becomes one with an inner time-consciousness. Indeed, Husserl speaks of the time-constituting flow of absolute subjectivity; the continual flow of time creates a 'form-now' in which the flow itself is apprehended as a unity.[46] Indeed, the flow itself has a reflective

[41] Husserl, *The Phenomenology of Internal Time Consciousness*, p. 48.

[42] Paul Ricoeur, *Memory, History, Forgetting*, trans. Kathleen Blamey and David Pellauer (Chicago, IL: Chicago University Press, 2004), p. 110.

[43] Husserl, *The Phenomenology of Internal Time Consciousness*, p. 50.

[44] Husserl, *The Phenomenology of Internal Time Consciousness*, p. 78.

[45] For a clear exposition, see Dan Zahavi, *Subjectivity and Selfhood: Investigating the First Person Perspective* (Cambridge, MA: MIT, 2005), pp. 55–8.

[46] Husserl, *The Phenomenology of Internal Time Consciousness*, p. 112.

mode of appearing in so far as awareness of temporal flow must appear within the flow itself. In this deeper analysis, Husserl discovers that the ground of intentionality itself is constituted within the temporal flow. Reflectivity as a feature of temporal flow is built into the very structure of being aware, and being aware is always bounded by time. Temporality is the horizon or generative power of awareness, and to provide an account of temporality, as Husserl tries to do, is to present a genetic phenomenology which goes beyond the static phenomenology of mere description. Perhaps in Augustinian terms we might say that in inwardness the present of the past merges with the present of the present, or even that, in some instances of anticipation of the future, the present of the future falls into the present of the present.

INWARDNESS ENTAILS NARRATIVE

An integral part of the experience of inwardness is the ability to represent inner states or objects of attention—to report experience. The ability of events to be reported, or reportability that we have discussed above, always occurs in time. In Husserl's account of genetic phenomenology, internal time-consciousness is at the heart of understanding subjectivity; it is the horizon within which all activity occurs. Although the later Husserl did develop the idea of the lifeworld as the horizon of possibility within which intersubjective consciousness operates, particularly in the fifth *Cartesian Meditation*, he did not develop the idea of narrative. But temporality is deeply implicated in the very nature of being aware—characterized as running-off phenomena—and so provides the coherence necessary for identity and for the answer to the question 'Who?'. Indeed, we might say that the identity of a life is the coherence of the running-off phenomena understood in terms of events that can be narrated or reported. Inwardness occurs within temporal flow, and the nature or quality of that temporality can be reported in narration. But reportability and narration are always after the event; even in spontaneous narration—as in a running report of an inner state, for example—there is a temporal gap between awareness and report, between the event of the story and its narration. The analysis of the temporal nature of inwardness provides a structure for narratability, and that ability to be narrated is itself inseparable from temporal structure.

This ability to be narrated is developed by Ricoeur who extends Husserl's analysis of duration as an extended present comprising three components of memory, attention, and expectation. In examining the problem of objective or cosmic time and inner time, or the 'time of the soul', Ricoeur, in *Time and Narrative*, formulates a corrective thesis to both Husserl and Heidegger. Heidegger critiques and corrects Husserl's emphasis on consciousness with an emphasis on being and its temporal structure, and Ricoeur offers a corrective to Heidegger in introducing the dimension of narrative to human life. That is, neither intentionality nor the *Dasein* can be understood without the narrative dimension that brings time into relation with human life, that gives meaning to human life, and that accounts for the intersection between an individual life and the life of the community or nation—that is, narrative identity at the level of the person intersects with the narrative identity of history. As Ricoeur says, 'time becomes human to the extent that it is articulated through a narrative mode, and narrative attains its full meaning when it becomes a condition of temporal existence'.[47] That human life can be narrated is a central feature of human existence, and Ricoeur specifies this in relation to three levels of narration or 'imitation' (*mimesis*) that might be summarized as the anticipation of action in the world or emplotment, opening the kingdom of 'as if' in imagination, and the way the world intersects with text. The first level of mimesis, emplotment or the organization of events that Aristotle identifies as *mythos*, is the distinguishing of a domain of action through a conceptual framework, which is also a symbolic resource and the recognition of the inherent temporal structures in life (the extended duration of the present) that call for narration. That human life and action can be narrated is because it is already codified in a symbolic or sign system with rules and codes: action is narratable because it is embedded within culture. The second level of mimesis shows how action is parallel to text in being organized in certain ways, particularly in terms of fiction and the writing of history. History and fiction are brought into close proximity through mimesis 2, which develops the close link between the story lived and the story told. Lastly, mimesis 3 is the interaction of the world of the text with the world of the reader; in a sense, this is the way the text meets the world.[48]

That subjectivity is irreducibly temporal and narratable means that the self is embedded, and embodied, within a narrative structure that minimally entails being born and dying.[49] Indeed, the narrative structure of human life entails not only one who is born and dies, but a whole network of relationships that form a person's life and a complex of other intersecting narratives. The story of my life is also the story of other lives, and this fundamental point entails a moral dimension to the nature of subjectivity and highlights the absolute centrality of body—moreover, a body partly formed in and by culture. To repeat a point previously made, if subjectivity is the response to

[47] Paul Ricoeur, *Time and Narrative*, vol. 1, trans. Kathleen McLaughlin and David Pellauer (Chicago, IL: Chicago University Press, 1983), p. 52; *Temps et récit*, tome 1: *L'intrique et le récit historique* (Paris: Seuil, 1983), p. 105: *le temps devient humain dans la mesure où il est articulé sur un mode narratif, et que le récit atteint sa signification plénière quand il devient une condition de l'existence temporelle.*

[48] Ricoeur, *Time and Narrative*, vol. 1, pp. 54–71.

[49] A. MacIntyre, *After Virtue: A Study of Moral Theory* (London: Duckworth, 1985), p. 216.

the question 'Who?', then this immediately opens into a range of other questions, as Ricoeur observes, such as 'Who is speaking of what? Who does what? About whom and about what does one construct a narrative?'[50] In Taylor's terms, to answer this question is to orientate oneself in moral space,[51] and in MacIntyre's terms this is to develop a narrative identity.[52] To be orientated in moral and cultural space is to see one's life in terms of a particular narrative and a particular journey. For religious practitioners this journey, we might generalize, is not simply from birth to death, but from limitation to a fulfilled or completed state. And while it might entail a subject—the one who is born and the one who dies—such a journey, while being my own, entails others, and a community 'journeying' through time.

The collective subjectivity of the cosmological religions is an example of this kind of narrative identity formation, distinct from modernist formations (although we still find echoes of this in the contemporary world). To perceive life as a journey that can be narrated entails a sense of inwardness and the structure described above, namely that inwardness is a kind of reflectivity that discloses itself when 'text' is the intentional object of the self. When Dante writes 'halfway through the journey of this life I woke to find myself in a dark wood, for I had wandered from the straight path' he is articulating a reflective inwardness that sees his life as a fundamentally Christian journey. Bunyan similarly saw the journey to God as an inner journey beset with obstacles that can be overcome with the correct virtues, although perhaps unlike Dante, for him the journey is metaphorical. For our earlier thinkers, the Monk of Eynsham to Richard of St Victor, the inner journey is less metaphorical and more existential, entailing the inner travelling to objectively real places in the pre-Copernican world. Inwardness is intimately linked with this sense of life as quest and journey, an idea that is very ancient, and which is textually structured in tradition-specific ways. Inwardness is representable and narratable, as we have seen in all of our examples. Bonaventure's journey is the narration of inwardness, as is Richard of St Victor's narrativizing inner states in terms of a biblical story. Likewise, Abhinavagupta's emphasis on inner experience is set within the narrative frame of a journey to enlightenment that is both personal and collective. The vision texts from Europe are heavily narrativized, although with the Indian material ornate narrativization is minimal, being substituted for a visual description of an inner world, and an emphasis being on inner space rather than inner time.

We have then a cluster of interrelated concepts that are mutually entailing: time, narrative, inwardness, consciousness, and subjectivity. To be conscious is

[50] Ricoeur, *Oneself as Another*, p. 19, cited in Gavin Flood, *The Ascetic Self: Subjectivity, Memory and Tradition* (Cambridge: Cambridge University Press, 2004), p. 18.

[51] Taylor, *Sources of the Self*, p. 28.

[52] MacIntyre, *After Virtue*, pp. 215–19.

to be temporal, and to be temporal is to live a narrative that, for any human being, entails inwardness. Narrative establishes a moral identity for the person, and the intensification of inwardness occurs within the moral space generated through narrative sequence. The totality of narrative sequences forms history.

INWARDNESS IS HISTORICAL AND CULTURAL

Phenomenology has pursued the analysis of subjectivity down different avenues of inquiry. Husserl drew our attention to the foundational features of human experience in intentionality, and while other phenomenologists have justifiably criticized Husserl's emphasis on consciousness, Merleau-Ponty's emphasis on pre-cognitive experience of the flesh or Levinas' privileging of the other, it nevertheless seems to be the case that inwardness entails a subject–object structure of experience, a structure moreover that is inextricably located within temporal flow and the causal chain of events. There are then two problems that face this kind of account, the first being how the inwardness of a particular person relates to the inwardness of others.[53] We have indirectly addressed this problem through showing how, in the cosmological traditions, inwardness is collective or shared such that my interiority or inner journey is in fact the same as everyone else's. The second problem is the relation between inwardness and the causal flow of events, the flow of history; the relation between the time of my life and the time of the group or nation or world. This has been posited as a problem in that the person's life is formed in the historical tradition and yet contributes to historical time.

Ricoeur offers a fine analysis of how individual time relates to broader historical time, or how subjectivity is related to history. In *Memory, History, Forgetting*, Ricoeur offers an account of memory as individual and collective. As individual, memory is formed in a person's life as the way her past is represented in the present. But this representation is always formed in the context of collective memory. Our lives are formed not only from the memories of our own past, but these memories are shaped by the collective memory of familial discourse into which we are born. Individual memory—someone witnessing an event—in turn affects or contributes to group memory. The testimony of people is shared knowledge and common bond that in turn is translated into history and collective memory. The writing of history is itself both a support and corrective to collective memory. In this way, individual memory relates and contributes to collective memory. Thus there is a transformation from individual memory as testimony, to archive as repository of

[53] See A. Steinbock, *Home and Beyond: Generative Phenomenology After Husserl* (Evanston, IL: Northwestern University Press, 1995), pp. 57–60.

collective memory. The historian's task—the historiographical operation—is the explanation or interpretation of documents and artefacts and presenting an account of how they are related. Such accounts in turn become objects of an archive.[54] Inwardness, then, is related to broader society and history because of its propensity to be narrated. Although phenomenology has attempted to map the processes of inner perception and the way in which people are in themselves and with others, sociological and semiotic discourses has emphasized the way in which we, as subjects of experience, are embedded within broader historical and social webs of meaning. That is, inwardness is inevitably cultural and historical: the kind of inwardness experienced will depend upon the ambient culture and longer temporal forces. But, arguably, the formation of inwardness in the context of a broader historical and social context means that we must understand inwardness and the 'I' as carrier of social values in relational terms, and if we are to do that, we need to understand the semiotics of inwardness.

INWARDNESS IS DISCLOSED THROUGH SIGNS

The specificity of inwardness is culturally mediated, as we have seen in our Hindu, Christian, and Buddhist examples. Spiritual exercises—asceticism, meditation, reading—give rise to the specificity of inwardness in the traditions although, as we have argued, the forms of inwardness in medieval religions of India and Europe are proximate in both emphasizing a cosmological inwardness that is collective. Both the formation of inwardness and its expression is therefore through systems of signs—above all, through the internalization of the texts, the stories they tell, and the practices they describe. Inwardness is mediated through cultural forms; thus, as we have seen, visualization techniques generate a Śaiva inwardness that, although experienced by a specific person, is nevertheless participatory. Similarly, the Christian monk cultivating inner vision through reading and contemplating texts is participating in a shared subjectivity. There is therefore a complex relationship between inwardness as the intensity of subjectivity, the mediation of signs or the way in which inwardness is disclosed, and action that manipulates signs and generates forms of inwardness.

Earlier we have suggested that inwardness is self-reflection and that the pre-reflective flesh is the carrier or precondition for the self-reflective subject. The self-reflective subject, because a linguistic entity, is embroiled in a system of signs. But the question still remains as to whether the pre-reflective flesh, to

[54] Ricoeur, *Memory, History, Forgetting*, pp. 166–76.

use Merleau-Ponty's terminology, is within a system of signs? Is there a bare, biological stratum of the body that is outside of culture? I suspect not: that even the prelinguistic level of bare experience is within a web of cultural signification. We are born into a web of meanings that precede us and that precede language. Inwardness then entails self-reflection (and so is linguistic) on pre-reflective experience (that is somatic), but even this somatic experience is itself embedded within a system of signs.

The relationship between the pre-reflective flesh and the self-reflective awareness is complex. Self-reflection upon pre-reflective flesh entails a triangular relationship between subjectivity, sign, and bodily act. Bodily act is within a system of signs and reflected upon in subjectivity through a system of signs. A Carthusian monk reciting the psalter in his cell, for example, experiences a particular kind of inwardness that he might describe as striving for God or being in the presence of God, which is mediated through the recited text. Moreover, the recitation of the text, even with eyes closed in silence, is an action that serves to generate the particular kind of subjectivity. Opening the *Guhyasamāja-tantra* randomly we read that the practitioner should perform the imposition of mantras upon the body and visualize himself situated in the moon, which is imagined within his heart.[55] Here we have awareness cultivated within subjectivity in which the sign system—the self in the moon in the heart—is enacted in the body. Subjectivity, sign, and bodily act are entailed in this performance of inner meditation.

It is action that fosters inwardness and inwardness in turn is expressed through action, particularly through the action of writing or composing text, through speech, and through other cultural mediations such as music or even mundane action such as walking. The monk from Eynsham, Edmund, expresses an inner vision through the medium of the written word and presents his interiority to the world through language. Edmund shapes his inwardness in conformity to tradition through the act of writing or, more precisely, through dictation to his brother who writes. Action—the act of dictation and writing—is the result of this inner vision and action in the form of prayer is the facilitator.

As I have written elsewhere, there are fundamentally two kinds of religious action: the unrepeatable moral act and the non-identical repetition of the ritual act.[56] Ordinary actions in their particularity are unrepeatable, once and for all events, while ritual actions are repeated through time, although never completely identical. The repeating of action through time in the ritual context

[55] *Guhyasamāja-tantra* ch. 8, p. 33: *ākāśadhātumadhyasthaṃ bhāvayed jñānasāgaram / ātmānaṃ candramadhyasthaṃ bhāvayed hṛdaye punaḥ* // 'He should meditate on the ocean of knowledge situated in the element of space. He should meditate again on the self located in the moon in his heart.'

[56] Gavin Flood, *The Importance of Religion: Meaning and Action in Our Strange World* (Oxford: Wiley-Blackwell, 2012), pp. 60–5.

is the repetition of a system of signs that is formative of communities and individuals.

This is an important theme in understanding inwardness. It is not that there is a pristine kind of interiority, a self-enclosed sphere outside of semiosis, but rather the somatic experience is already embedded within a system of signs that becomes articulated in self-reflection—the languages of interiority—and so is constitutive of interiority. The level of the flesh, the prelingusitic somatic experience, is reflected upon and articulated in language: it becomes narrated or reported and so becomes inwardness. There is a translation of bodily experience into self-reflection, and in that transition inwardness occurs.

In an interesting book, Anthony Steinbock examined religious experience as given, and what he calls 'verticality'. Verticality has various modes of givenness including 'epiphany' that is religious experience. Such givenness takes us beyond a subject and object distinction and so is open to phenomenological analysis.[57] Such vertical givenness can only be described as inwardness in so far as it becomes narratable and brought into the realm of language. In our terms, vertical experience is within the realm of the flesh, within somatic experience, and becomes inwardness through its articulation and narratability.

But it is even questionable as to what extent this verticality itself is wholly outside of language. We have seen this in the medieval context of Hindu, Christian, and Buddhist traditions. Here we see how the words of scripture—the Old Testament or the Tantras—play a role in forming the inner landscape. Bonaventure's *Itinerarium* is peppered with scriptural quotation, as is Abhinavagupta's *Tantrāloka*, illustrating how forms of inwardness are not simply interchangeable but are specifically located. It is not the content that is common but the process, and this process is a way in which signs are mediated. This process, that is shared by both Hindu and Christian, is that the mind takes on the forms of its object, and so the object mediates the kind of interiority that it discloses.

The system of signs is constitutive of interiority, which means that the truth within in religions is partially constituted by the world view the practitioner inhabits. This is not a constructivist argument—along the lines of Steven Katz in the 1970s and 80s, that mystical experience is constructed through language and culture—but rather that the languages of interiority are given rise to within specific cultures that are available for self-reflective use. The Śaiva practitioner cultivating a vision of Bhairava, the Eynsham monk cultivating a vision of the other world, the Buddhist cultivating the inner sign for absorbed meditation, are all using language to reflect upon non-discursive, somatic experience. As we have discussed, there is a level of human experience

[57] Steinbock, *Phenomenology and Mysticism*, p. 4.

that is prelinguistic and corporeal, the realm of the flesh, but which nevertheless is still semiotic and within culture. Inwardness occurs at a level beyond this in reflection upon experience and in its narration. Intense forms of inwardness in meditative trance or ritual can be so described because they are within language and develop a language of reflection. Absorption in trance itself is not inwardness because it is pre-reflective and at a stage prior to interiority of bare awareness or somatic transition.

Returning to our opening poem by Wallace Stevens we might say that here too inwardness is mediated through the other and only comes into view because of the other. The system of signs—the metaphors Stevens uses, the theme of dark, light, and twilight—serves to articulate inwardness, an inwardness that is in fact constituted by the language of the poem. There is no inwardness in this particularity outside the language of the poem, and yet the particularity speaks to something shared by all people. This something shared is interiority, an interiority that is always and only formed in relationship and in dialogue. The other person allows the subjectivity of the self to come through by throwing a pale light onto the self; and this glimpse of both self and other is the best that can be achieved in Stevens' modernity.

CONCLUSION

Our analysis of inwardness in abstraction has shown that we can identify features that cut across cultures and times and that allow us to understand premodern concerns about the self as concerns about inwardness. Inwardness is characterized by particular phenomenological features such as self-reflection, reportability, temporality, narrative, and mediation by signs. The experience of inwardness is therefore always indirect through reflection, through language, and through the narration of experience. Inwardness cannot be identified with pure, somatic experience, but as reflection is after the event. It is concerned with reporting experience and relating experience to a narrative that gives inwardness coherence. The temporal structure identified by Husserl—of retention, present awareness, and protention—is the way through which narrative that constitutes inwardness works.

This general pattern or structure can be identified in the texts of the religions we have seen. The Monk of Eynsham's vision is in the first person singular, concerned with his inner vision, and is an inwardness that is reportable. Edmund narrates his experience that exemplifies broader cultural concerns and reflects the symbolic order of the world he inhabits. Similarly, the vision texts of the tantric traditions are instructions that express how the practitioner is self-reflective and temporal. That these qualities of self-reflection, reportability, and narrative can be found in modernist poetry, such as Wallace Stevens, illustrates the idea that inwardness has retained some of its qualities into modernity. While there are clearly differences, there is nevertheless continuity in accounts of inwardness across the centuries and across cultures. It could be that inwardness as described in these terms is a feature of a common humanity.

9

The Historical Self and Comparative Religion

We have now come to a point where we need to discuss the broader theoretical assumptions behind a project such as this, namely the assumed legitimacy and importance of comparative religion. We need therefore to present a case for comparative religion and to examine the importance of subjectivity as a universal value that legitimates the enterprise. There are at least two levels of complexity here: firstly, the historical place of the science of religion within the broader human sciences and the relation of comparative religion to theology; and secondly, the way macro-history relates to subjectivity. Both problems are connected in that any account of subjectivity across cultures and times, as here, entails the legitimacy and importance of comparison. In the current chapter we need to argue for the legitimacy of comparative religion and to argue that the broad sweep of history on its own is insufficient to understand the importance of religion for human communities. We also need to understand subjectivity and religious action. A number of terms that designate a non-theological account or explanation of religion have arisen in the course of the last 150 years or so—'comparative religion', 'the science of religion' (particularly its German equivalent as *Religionswissenschaft*)—which have sometimes been regarded as synonymous with 'religious studies', and the 'phenomenology of religion'. I do not intend to present a history of these developments[1] but wish rather to promote

[1] For a good history of religious studies, see Walter H. Capps, *Religious Studies: The Making of a Discipline* (Minneapolis, MN: Fortress Press, 1995). For a good survey of the phenomenology of religion that covers some of the same ground, see James Cox, *A Guide to the Phenomenology of Religion* (London and New York: Continuum, 2006). For a more philosophical orientation, see Jonna Bornemark and Hans Ruis (eds.), *Phenomenology and Religion: New Frontiers* (Stockholm: Södertön University Press, 2010). Also see Eric Sharpe, *Comparative Religion: A History* (London: Duckworth, 1975). For a history of the science of religion, see Guy Stroumsa, *A New Science: The Discovery of Religion in the Age of Reason* (Cambridge, MA: Harvard University Press, 2010). Also J. S. Preus, *Explaining Religion: Criticism and Theory from Bodin to Freud* (Atlanta, GA: Scholars Press, 1996). For a critical review and strong case for a science of religion distinct from theology, see Donald Wiebe, *The Politics of Religious Studies* (New York: St Martin's Press, 1999), pp. 3–50. See also J. S. Jensen, *The Study of Religion in a New Key: Theoretical and Philosophical Soundings in the*

an argument for comparative religion as a hermeneutical–phenomenology that has absorbed its critique, and to present an argument for the importance of inwardness in understanding religion. We may have already raised the hackles of potential criticizers by our use of the terms 'comparative', 'religion', and 'phenomenology'; and indeed they are problematic terms that, according to some, hide a somewhat sinister (because unconscious) will to power.

The Western academy has been changed by the critique of Enlightenment values and methods with the postmodern turn, and the place of religion within these developments has been ambiguous. On the one hand, religion and its sympathetic study have been subjected to critique from a genealogical and critical theory perspective; on the other, there have been lively developments in theology that have positively responded to the shift in gear in the humanities. In particular, scriptural reasoning and comparative theology have offered onstructive ways of engaging diverse religions in a common conversation, both accepting the problematic nature of an earlier comparative religion. Comparative religion has had a bad press in recent years because of its ethnocentric and androcentric bias in the past, and the very endeavour has been criticized for being in thrall to colonialism (see 'Comparative Religion', pp. 251–2). Post-liberal theology, and other forms of Christian intellectual engagement with non-Christian religions, has similarly cast a sceptical eye on comparative religion because of what it perceives to be implicit Enlightenment values that actually cover a hidden ontology of violence. We need therefore to say something about comparative religion before assessing some of these critiques.

COMPARATIVE RELIGION

Comparative religion—or its synonym the science of religion—has been deeply neo-Kantian, as Gillian Rose argued with regard to both Weberian and Durkheimian sociology. Rose argues that although we usually see the classical sociology of Durkheim and Weber in terms of two competing models of explanation (*Erklaren*) and understanding (*Verstehen*), both are founded upon a neo-Kantian paradigm.[2] By neo-Kantian she means that the early sociologists and philosophers of the Marburg School, whose concern was 'logical idealism', and the Heidelberg School, concerned with 'logical value theory', read Kant to be referring to objective validity (*objektive Gültigkeit*) or a judgement's empirical meaningfulness. To paraphrase Rose paraphrasing

Comparative and General Study of Religion (Aarhus University Press, 2003), Carl Olson, *The Allure of Decadent Thinking: Religious Studies and the Challenge of Postmodernism* (Oxford and New York: Oxford University Press, 2013), and Manuel A. Vasquez, *More than Belief: A Materialist Theory of Religion* (Oxford and New York: Oxford University Press, 2011).

[2] Gillian Rose, *Hegel Contra Sociology* (London and New York: Verso, 2009 (first published 1981)), pp. 1–3.

Kant, she tells us how Kant distinguished questions of fact (*questio quid facti*) from questions of right (*questio quid juris*), the way a concept is acquired through experience and the way concepts relate to objects a priori. Objective validity pertains to what can be represented to us as an object, as something that appears to us, within the limits of our sensibility. The objective validity of experience needs to be justified, which is to demonstrate how subjective conditions of thought possess objective and not merely subjective validity. We can do this, we can justify how subjective conditions of thought possess objective validity, through a priori rules that make empirical knowledge possible; these are rules for 'the synthesis of perceptions into objects of experience', and these rules or synthetic judgements in relating to experience entail 'the objective validity of their synthesis'.[3] That is, the objective validity of knowledge arises when the concept in my subjective perception is linked to an object, and different objects of perception are linked through rules or categories such as causation. Rose cites Kant's example 'when the sun shines, the stone is warm' as a judgement that joins two perceptions. 'But if I say the sun warms the stone, the concept of cause proper to the understanding is added to the perception, and connects the concept of warmth with the concept of sunshine. The synthetic judgement becomes necessarily universally valid, consequently objective, and is converted from a perception into an experience.'[4] Objective validity therefore is established by what can be presented to the self as an object.

Although the science of religion partly stems from Hegel, particularly the historicist idea of developmental stages, the Kantian objective validity has been important in a science of religion as an objectively valid enterprise that could map the development of religion and inquire into its arising in human experience. The new science of comparative religion, as initiated by Max Müller, operated within the neo-Kantian paradigm of objective validity. In his first lecture on the science of religion (1870), Müller claims that it is divided into what he calls 'comparative theology', which is the historical forms of religion, and 'theoretical theology' that 'explains the conditions under which religion . . . is possible'.[5] Müller thinks that we should not take up the concerns of theoretical theology until all the data for the history of religions has been gathered, but that such an enterprise is possible and desirable he was in no doubt. Indeed, the passage where he makes this distinction between comparative and theoretical theology comes immediately after a short discussion of Kant and the possibility of a human faculty for apprehending the infinite. The Kantian paradigm can also be seen entering the science of religion through

[3] Rose, *Hegel Contra Sociology*, p. 3.

[4] Rose, *Hegel Contra Sociology*, pp. 3–4, quoting Kant, *Prolegomena to any Future Metaphysics*, sec. 20.

[5] Max Müller, 'The Science of Religion: Lecture One (1870)', p. 114, in Jon R. Stone (ed.), *The Essential Max Müller: On Language, Mythology and Religion* (New York: Palgrave Macmillan, 2002), pp. 109–21.

Husserl and the *epoché* that draws on the distinction between appearance and the thing in itself, or the being behind appearances, the question of whose validity must be bracketed (see the last chapter). The objective validity of religious experience, on this view, is provided by the constancy of religious appearances intersubjectively agreed upon. A further step of having presented an account of religious experiences is their classification into types, an enterprise undertaken in the Dutch school of the phenomenology of religion, and also in the sociology of religion by the doyen of that art, Max Weber.

That comparative religion in both its phenomenological and sociological forms should be neo-Kantian is not self-evidently a criticism but simply a descriptive argument. However, Rose wishes to show (and support) how Hegel anticipates and critiques the Neo-Kantian endeavour and thereby to offer a critique of classical sociological thinking. By extension, the Hegelian stance is also the basis for critical theory's critique of religion and much post-colonial critique. Rose presents Hegel's criticism that accepts the idea of transcendental inquiry, but rejects Kant's conclusions from this—namely that we can distinguish between the thing in itself, which remains unknowable, and appearance that can be known. How can the unknowable be called a 'thing', and how can its relation to appearance be specified? If the relation is a causal one, then the thing cannot be unknowable because we know the cause.[6] In both the phenomenology of religion and in Durkheimian sociology of religion, the category of the sacred, as things set apart from the profane, took a privileged place as defining the realm of the religious. The task of this phenomenology came to be the mapping of appearances of the sacred and organizing these appearances into types. For example, Joachim Wach discussed types of religious experience, primarily Christian and non-Christian; Mircea Eliade, basing his work on the key idea of the manifestation of the sacred, distinguished types of religious phenomena—sacred trees, sacred space and so on; and Ninian Smart categorized different dimensions of religion.[7] Much of the scholarship of these old scholars is good, yet the whole project that they were engaged in has come under critical review in recent years on a number of grounds that stem from either a theological or philosophical root.

The criticism of comparative religion has been explicit and implicit. On the one hand we have a theological response to cultural pluralism and Enlightenment reasoning that positions itself in consonance with postmodern thinking and with premodern theology, that has implicitly critiqued the comparative study of religion. On the other we have an explicit, critical, philosophical response from either a Hegelian or a Nietzschian perspective. One group of scholars in particular has been vehement in their critique, a critique generally coming from the political left and an indirect Hegelian inheritance. Another

[6] Rose, *Hegel Contra Sociology*, p. 5.

[7] Ninian Smart, *Dimensions of the Sacred: An Anatomy of the World's Beliefs* (London: Harper Collins, 1996), pp. 8–25.

critique has come from post-colonialism. I cannot review all of this scholarship here, but some of the arguments against comparative religion have been that the category 'religion' has arisen in the (fairly recent) history of the West closely linked to the separation of the religious from the secular and the relegation of religion to the private sphere and governance to the public sphere.[8] The imposition of religion upon the colonized 'native others' firstly created a realm of 'religion' that Christianity could be related to as the 'true religion' in contrast to the other false religions, and secondly depoliticized the 'native others' in the service of Western colonial powers that wished to see them subservient and compliant. Apart from Fitzgerald, David Chidester has written on the formation of comparative religion in South Africa in precisely this context,[9] and McCutcheon, Masuzawa, King, Asad, and Mandair have offered related critiques.[10] There is also the partly persuasive view put forward by Hausner and Gellner that religion is not an exclusive category, and that as a social reality many people participate in more than one religion.[11]

Chidester presents an engaging, if dismaying, account of how comparative religion was linked to colonial oppression and conducted on frontier battlefields. Some well-meaning missionaries, such as John Colenso who became Bishop of Natal in 1853, identified what he believed to be Zulu beliefs in a supreme being and thereby a Christian truth in a non-Christian religion; while others, such as Robert Godlonton, claimed that the Xhosa had no religion, or rather just the superstitious remnants of a religion degenerated from their forefathers, thereby justifying the imposition of Christianity and its accompanying colonial power upon them.[12] Arvind-Pal Mandair has developed a Post-colonial critique of the

[8] Tim Fitzgerald, in particular, has put forward forceful arguments against the category religion (*The Ideology of Religious Studies* (New York: Oxford University Press, 2000)) and that it can only be understood in the context of the history of its distinction from the secular (*Discourse on Civility and Barbarity: A Critical History of Religion and Related Categories* (Oxford and New York: Oxford University Press, 2007).

[9] David Chidester, *Savage Systems: Colonialism and Comparative Religion in Southern Africa* (Charlottesville, VA: University Press of Virginia, 1996).

[10] For example, R. McCutcheon, *Manufacturing Religion: The Discourse on Sui Generis Religion and the Politics of Nostalgia* (New York and Oxford: Oxford University Press, 1997); T. Masuzawa, *The Invention of World Religions or How European Universalism was Preserved in the Language of Pluralism* (Chicago, IL: Chicago University Press, 2005); Richard King, *Orientalism and Religion: Postcolonial Theory, India and 'The Mystic East'* (London: Routledge, 1999); Talal Asad, *Genealogies of Religion: Discipline and Reasons of Power in Christianity and Islam* (Baltimore, MD and London: Johns Hopkins University Press, 1993), Arvind-Pal S. Mandair, *Religion and the Specter of the West: Sikhism, India, Postcoloniality, and the Politics of Translation* (New York: Columbia University Press, 2009).

[11] Sondra L. Hausner and David Gellner, 'Category and Practice as Two Aspects of Religion: The Case of Nepalis in Britain', *Journal of the American Academy of Religion*, 80/4 (2012), pp. 971–97. I say 'partly persuasive' because although it is useful to understand religions in terms of the two aspects 'category' and 'practice', and people can clearly participate in the practice of different religions, nevertheless religions as historical forms are necessarily constrained by high degrees of boundary protection that ensures their continuance through the generations.

[12] Chidester, *Savage Systems*, pp. 100–1, 129–40.

formation of Indic religion, particularly Sikhism. There is no space here for a full description of Mandair's interesting book, but in short, in the spirit of Hegel, through constructing and historicizing 'Indian religions', the West was able to compare religions and to place the colonized in a subordinate position. Sikhism is a good illustration of this; a Sikh symbolic order being formed initially by the colonizers and then appropriated by native elites.[13] Thus, rather than a Neo-Kantian paradigm, a Hegelian paradigm is more dominant in Mandair's view.

Post-colonial studies forcefully argue for the link between religion as a comparative category and colonialism: comparative religion developed within the colonial period, at times serving to legitimize colonial power and show how other religions were inferior to Christianity. The force of this critique is palpable, but are we then to reject the practice of comparative religion as inevitably bringing with it colonialist assumptions and so being now redundant in a post-colonial period? I would think not, but rather this critique sharpens the practice of comparative religion, rendering it sensitive to problems of translation, the imbalance of power in Western scholarship dealing with 'non-Western' communities and ideas, and more reflexive in recognizing the necessarily theoretical apparatus for responsible comparison. That comparative religion has been done badly is not sufficient reason to abandon it.

There have been some attempts to defend comparative religion against postmodern relativism. A volume of essays edited by Patton and Ray[14] defends comparative religion broadly on the ground of a universal human nature and contemporary globalization and multiculturalism. As William Paden points out in that volume, there is 'no study of religion without cross-cultural categories, analysis and perspective'.[15] Assuming that the category 'religion' is one that has relevance across cultures,[16] as I think we must, the study of religion is a legitimate and important field of study that can only be done through comparison. Indeed, all academic study—which is simultaneously detached and participatory—implicitly assumes comparison. Indeed, other disciplines develop through comparison and the question of the legitimacy of that pursuit hardly arises: thus we have comparative linguistics, comparative literature, comparative sociology, comparative politics, and so on. Another important

[13] Mandair, *Religion and the Specter of the West*, pp. 106–71.

[14] In particular, Kimberley C. Patton and Benjamin C. Ray (eds.), *A Magic Still Dwells: Comparative Religion in the Postmodern Age* (Berkeley, CA: California University Press, 2000). This book responds or takes up the comparativist project as outlined in J. Z. Smith's article 'In Comparison a Magic Dwells', in J. Z. Smith, *Imagining Religion: From Babylon to Jonestown* (Chicago, IL: University of Chicago Press, 1982), pp. 19–35.

[15] William Paden, 'Elements of a New Comparativism', p. 182, in Patton and Ray (eds.), *A Magic Still Dwells*, pp. 182–92.

[16] For an argument for religion as a cross-cultural category, see my *The Importance of Religion: Meaning and Action in Our Strange World* (Oxford: Wiley-Blackwell, 2012), pp. 12–16.

and innovative development has been the Comparative Religious Ideas Project by the process theologian Robert Neville, who edited three volumes on comparative religion. Drawing on Peirce, Neville develops the notion of 'vagueness' in comparison—that vague categories can allow comparison that respects difference and diversity. This is a positive development for the comparative philosophy of religions that is able to recognize contradictory ideas within the same area of inquiry. For example, 'all swans are black' contradicts 'all swans are white', but both are subsets of the vague category 'all swans are coloured'.[17]

REFUSING TOTALITIES

What the post-colonial and postmodern critiques of comparative religion share is a commendable desire to refuse totalities in the conviction that totalizing claims can lead to oppression and even violence. In this sense these positions advocate indeterminacy, and are anti-foundationalist and anti-universalist. Perhaps we can even see this as a neo-Hegelian critique of a neo-Kantian science of religion. In this respect, the secular, implicitly atheistic critique of comparative religion from a post-colonial and postmodern perspective is ironically close to some contemporary theological developments. Post-liberal theology that developed out of the Yale School and George Lindbeck's 'cultural turn' is in consonance with post-colonialism in emphasizing the narrative dimension of religion, or rather of Christianity.[18] The refusal of universals, the refusal of a Kantian foundation to knowledge, pushes us into the recognition of narrative (and history) and also textual revelation. Theologians need to read Christian scripture in a way that is relevant to a community of reception where doctrines are 'communally authoritative rules of discourse'.[19]

What these movements underline is the problematic nature of the Kantian or Enlightenment project that seeks the objective knowledge of the transcendent knowing subject. John Milbank's radical orthodoxy stems from his critique of social theory and argues for a theology that is politically relevant and avoids the metaphysics of violence he claims is implicit in secular social

[17] Robert C. Neville (ed.), *Religious Truth* (Albany, NY: SUNY Press, 2001), pp. 203–18. The other two volumes in the trilogy are *Ultimate Realities* (Albany, NY: SUNY Press, 2001) and *The Human Condition* (Albany, NY: SUNY Press, 2001).

[18] For example, Hans Frei, 'The Literal Reading of Biblical Narrative in the Christian Tradition: Does it Stretch or will it Break?', in Peter Ochs (ed.), *The Return to Scripture in Judaism and Christianity: Essays in Postcritical Scriptural Interpretation* (Mahwah, NJ: Paulist Press, 1993), pp. 55–82.

[19] George Lindbeck, *The Nature of Doctrine: Religion and Theology in a Postliberal Age* (Westminster: John Knox Press, 1984), p. 18.

theory.[20] Oliver Davies' transformation theology likewise comes out of a critique of secular discourse, although it does embrace universalist aspirations that it claims we can identify in human communities.[21] In consonance with this post-liberal turn is scriptural reasoning, founded by the Jewish philosopher Peter Ochs along with David Ford and Dan Hardy, that is now a worldwide practice that seeks interreligious encounter through groups of Jews, Christians, and Moslems reading their sacred texts together. Through reading texts with semantic density, textual meanings are accessed that would normally remain hidden, and creative reasoning produced—or abductions—that are relevant to a particular context or situation. The intellectual foundation of the practice is a kind of rationality, but a reasoning that emerges in the group context and, moreover, reasoning based on friendship formed through the practice that does not necessarily seek agreement or consensus, but rather a recognition of deep differences.[22] What emerges from the group is a collective or shared *cogito* that is non-teleological. This practice claims to be a non-foundational and non-totalizing reading that is simultaneously world-disclosive and a resource for solving problems.[23] In the sense that it claims to be world-disclosive it is close to phenomenology, and in the sense that it refuses finality or closure it is close to hermeneutics and semiotics. As an intellectual practice it is emergent from the theologies of different traditions and yet still fundamentally theological in honoring what it regards as the sacred nature of the texts and the legitimacy of religious readings.

Another practice based on reading is comparative theology developed by Frank Clooney. Assuming the general 'Anselmian' understanding of theology as Faith Seeking Understanding, comparative theology seeks 'deep learning across religious borders' and assumes the foundation of a faith tradition from which to 'venture into learning from one or more other faith traditions', thereby combining 'tradition-rooted theological concerns with actual study of another tradition'.[24] In a number of fascinating book-length studies,

[20] John Milbank, *Theology and Social Theory* (Oxford: Blackwell, 1990), on the implicit ontology of violence, pp. 278–85.

[21] Oliver Davies, Clemens Sedmak, Paul Janz (eds.) *Transformation Theology: A New Paradigm of Christian Living* (London: T and T Clark, 2007).

[22] David Ford, 'An Interfaith Wisdom: Scriptural Reasoning Between Jews, Christians and Muslims', p. 5, in David F. Ford and C. C. Pecknold (eds.), *The Promise of Scriptural Reasoning* (Oxford: Blackwell, 2006), pp. 1–22. See also David F. Ford, *Christian Wisdom: Desiring God and Learning in Love* (Cambridge: Cambridge University Press, 2007), pp. 273–303.

[23] Nicholas Adams, *Habermas and Theology* (Cambridge University Press, 2006), p. 244.

[24] Francis Clooney, *Comparative Theology: Deep Learning Across Religious Borders* (Oxford: Wiley-Blackwell, 2010), p. 10. There has been a flurry of comparative theology spawned by Clooney's project, much of which is engaging. Often Rāmānuja is the Hindu theologian of choice for comparison, and there have been many studies over the years. For more recent work, see J. P. Synor, *Ramanuja and Schliermacher: Toward a Constructive Comparative Theology* (Cambridge: James Clarke and Co., 2012); R. M. Ganeri, *The Vedāntic Cosmology of Rāmānuja and its Western Parallels*, DPhil thesis, University of Oxford, Oxford, 2004; but from earlier

Clooney has performed comparative theology with Hinduism and Christianity, offering cross-readings of texts, and bringing to bear his own significant scholarship on the Tamil and Sanskrit sources. The point is that theology is a kind of detailed reading that takes place in 'a shared space'; the object is a kind of theological enrichment without reducing the claims of the 'other' tradition, but without being prevented from high-level dialogue by divergent (and incompatible) metaphysical assumptions. Like scriptural reasoning, comparative theology has a connection to living religious communities and rests on the authority of those communities. There have been Hindu theological responses to Clooney's work, generally sympathetic and acknowledging the validity of the enterprise and the desire to redress any imbalance of power that has accompanied Hindu–Christian relations in the past.[25]

If we accept the argument of post-colonial, theological, and scriptural/semiotic critics against an Enlightenment project in comparative religion on the grounds of the critique of neo-Kantianism—namely that we cannot separate appearance from the thing in itself, and that we cannot arrive at apodictic, objective value because of the historical location of subjects of experience, and that what was taken to be objective knowledge was actually from the perspective of the dominant power—then must we abandon comparative religion altogether? I would wish to argue that we cannot and should not abandon comparative religion for both intellectual and political reasons concerning the importance of religion in the contemporary world. Religion has high stakes in many parts of the world where it can cost one's life. Rather than characterizing comparative religion in negatives—non-foundation, non-totality, non-hegemony, indeterminacy—as some post-liberal theology tends to represent itself, we can represent comparative religion positively. We

years, of note is, A. Hunt-Overzee, *The Body Divine: The Symbol of the Body in the Works of Teilhard de Chardin and Rāmānuja* (Cambridge, New York, Melbourne: Cambridge University Press, 1992). For one of the few studies comparing Christian theology with Śaivism, see N. Bamford, *Converging Theologies: Comparing and Converging Terms within the Byzantine and Pratyabhijñā (Kahmir Śaivitie) Traditions within a Space for Convergence* (Delhi: ISPCK, 2011). Comparative theology has some overlap with the distinct project of comparative philosophy. For recent exemplary work here, see Jessica Frazier, *Reality, Religion, and Passion: Indian and Western Approaches in Hans-Georg Gadamer and Rūpa Gosvami* (Aldershot: Ashgate, 2008). Also, for more recent attempts at comparative philosophy, see Joachim Lacrosse (ed.), *Philosophie Comparée, Grèce, Inde, Chine* (Paris: Vrin, 2005). One of the aims, notes Lacrosse, is not to see whether a thought is intrinsically philosophical, but rather to see what type of work is needed to see whether two thoughts can be rendered philosophically commensurable. Lacrosse, 'La philosophie greque à l'éreueve dela Chine et de l'Inde', p. 10, in Lacrosse, *Philosophie Comparée* , pp. 7–20.

[25] Parimal Patil, 'A Hindu Theologian's Response', in Frank Clooney (ed.), *Hindu God, Christian God: How Reason Helps Break Down the Boundaries Between Religions* (New York: Oxford University Press, 2001), pp. 185–95. See also C. Ram-Prasad, 'Finding God with—and Through—the Other', *Harvard Theological Review*, 105/2 (2012), pp. 247–55.

cannot develop this argument here, but I would wish to list to following points for the performance of any new comparative religion.

1. Religion is of vital importance in understanding contemporary global human communities and therefore is a legitimate focus of inquiry (in a way that economics, social structures, or political institutions are legitimate foci of academic inquiry).
2. Understanding religion from any perspective entails a) comparison and b) the refusal of totalities, c) indeterminacy and the finality of non-closure in human reality, and d) the possibility of making normative claims.
3. Comparative religion is therefore dialogical and not totalizing, which entails careful reading, listening, and hearing the voice of the other, and in this way is close to scriptural reasoning and comparative theology.
4. But comparative religion should be theory driven (even weak theory) and in this way is close to social science and close to the broader Enlightenment project. Indeed, comparative religion could be rooted in sociology, drawing on Weber, or in phenomenology, drawing on Husserl.
5. Comparative religion entails a number of levels, the first of which is phenomenological description or the mode of showing, which entails the rigour of philology in textual inquiry and the rigour of thick description in ethnography for fieldwork inquiry.

This at last leads us onto our current project. In this book we have argued that inwardness is a crucial theme for understanding religions and that this can be demonstrated through a concrete comparison, here between medieval Hinduism, Buddhism, and Christianity. Through a broad but selective reading of medieval texts across traditions I have argued that the idea of transcendence being found within the self, which is conceptualized as a cosmological journey, is common. This cosmological subjectivity or inwardness can be contrasted with modernist understandings or senses of inwardness, as we have seen. We need to relate our discussion about method and methodology to our discussion about inwardness, how the phenomenological method reveals that inwardness, and what the implications of this are for understanding how subjects relate to history in what I shall call 'act theory'.

PHENOMENOLOGY AND COMPARATIVE RELIGION

We have dealt summarily with the phenomenological method. We now need to return to it, firstly in defence of a new comparative religion in religious studies, and secondly to examine the relation between subjectivity and religious history. In our opening chapter we referred to Heidegger's early lectures on the phenomenology of the religious life and his idea of the formal indication. That is, the structures of the everyday self, the patterns of the *Dasein*, provide a formal indication of the meaning of being or, more prosaically, the meaning of appearances that show themselves. The fact that I am a human being allows me access to understanding human beings, their practices and their texts, and this is a fact acknowledged by the formal indication. The texts and topics of comparison are brought together in the scholar's imagination,[26] although comparison is not purely subjective. Within this general approach we can identify a number of levels of phenomenological inquiry. John Bowker has usefully identified a first level of description and a second level of ontological inquiry necessitated by the pressure of data in the first.[27] Paul Ricoeur also identifies levels of phenomenological analysis close to Bowker's: namely, a descriptive level, the transcendental constitution, by which he means the extension of the intentional method to the will where the power that constitutes consciousness can be interpreted in terms of the voluntary and the involuntary, and the threshold of ontology.[28] This last moment Ricoeur calls a 'second reflection', which enables the passage from a transcendental phenomenology to a truly ontological phenomenology in which, for Ricoeur, the ontological preoccupation is 'decentred' from the self. Although I would generally support this phenomenological trajectory, we must be cautious in adapting such a methodological recommendation uncritically. Drawing on Ricoeur's typology of levels we can argue that phenomenology as method entails a level of description, an account of subjectivity in terms of intentionality, and an ontology of the self that takes us out of the realm of comparative religion into a comparative philosophy of religion.

A comparative religion could be sociological, comparing institutions, legal systems, and formal political arrangements, or it could be phenomenological comparing understandings of subjectivity, religious experience, and the way the human person interfaces with broader social and historical institutions that could be described in a sociology. It is clear that a phenomenology of some kind is needed in the comparative explication of inwardness across cultures, and that this firstly requires a level of description and secondly an account of what lies behind or beyond description.

[26] Doniger makes a similar point about the reality of comparison in a Pericean 'third thing' of semiotic realism. Wendy Doniger, *The Implied Spider: Politics and Theology in Myth* (New York: Columbia University Press, 1998), p. 36.

[27] John Bowker, *The Meanings of Death* (Cambridge: Cambridge University Press, 1991), pp. 28–9.

[28] Paul Ricoeur, 'Méthode et tâches d'une phenomenology de la volonté', in Ricoeur, *A l'école de la phenomenologie* (Paris: Vrin, 2004 (first published 1986)), pp. 65–92.

Description

Ricoeur describes this as the patient descriptive analysis applied to the functioning of consciousness. It is what Husserl spoke of in *Ideas*, and what is generally taken to be the main thrust of phenomenology: the description of appearances to consciousness while simultaneously suspending the question of being behind appearances—that is, bracketing. As Ricoeur observes, later phenomenologists have tended to neglect this important aspect of Husserl's work, concentrating instead on the emphasis on the lifeworld in the *Crisis*. In relation to the phenomenology of religion, the thrust of criticism has been that neutral description of the kind supposedly facilitated through the *epoché* is impossible; there can be no view from nowhere as all epistemology comes from particular viewpoints and is invested with pre- or un- conscious forces: we are blinded by the ideologies we live within that make description and the assumed distance between Cartesian self and object of consciousness highly questionable. Indeed, the self-identity required for such a perspective has been the general topic of criticism from post-structural and feminist perspectives for a number of years.

To bring the issue into sharp focus, let us summarize an argument of Julia Kristeva. In her first major work, *Revolution in Poetic Language*, Kristeva begins with language and raises the problem in Husserlian terms. The phenomenological method of Husserl is a theory of meaning that can be distinguished from the semiotic. For Husserl, writes Kristeva, meaning is constituted by the bracketing of real objects (as we have seen) so that intentional experience is revealed for the ego.[29] But the subject and object of experience—or, more technically, the process of knowing (*noesis*) and object of knowledge (*noema*)—are already constituted prior to consciousness, prior to intentionality, within 'matter' (*hyle*), a 'universal medium which in the last resort includes within itself all experiences'.[30] Thus, at a deeper level, there is no absolute distinction for Kristeva between subject and object questions—this ability to separate so clearly the *noema* from the *noesis*. In a good summary of her thinking about subjectivity she writes:

> The subject is thus not a fixed system, prone to the occasional outburst of incomprehensible and irrational displacement, the odd outlay thought or image crossing the boundary fence from the unconscious to the conscious. It is incomplete and unresolved nature permanently accompanies it. In fact subjectivity never quite forms. The boundary fence is never finished. Yet it is important to emphasize that the dramatic nature of this subjectivity is experienced as an intense ambivalence. The subject never feels itself to be ordered and knowable.

[29] Julia Kristeva, *Revolution in Poetic Language*, trans. Margaret Waller (New York: Columbia University Press, 1984), p. 33.

[30] Kristeva, *Revolution in Poetic Language*, p. 33.

> It is always under threat, in an unresolved state that is exciting as well as dangerous, 'as tempting as it is condemned'.[31]

Subjectivity is never stable, and for Kristeva, following Freud and Lacan, is constantly under pressure from unconscious drives. The implications of this position are that what we know and what we experience is always constrained by that which is outside of language and the forces that make us who we are. True objectivity is elusive on this account, and the phenomenological desire to bracket the question of being in order to get at the truth is an illusion founded on the neo-Kantian paradigm of the transcendent subject.

On this account, comparative religion in any objective sense is doomed to failure because of the constantly shifting ground of subjectivity driven by unconscious drives and constrained by forms of external culture. There is great force to this criticism. How can any comparative method be assured of some objectivity and that we do not simply project ourselves, our values, our ideologies, our unconscious prejudice onto others? A response to Kristeva's challenge must look something like this: that a first phenomenological description is a valid enterprise because some objectivity is assured through methods that are generally scientific—namely philology and fieldwork—and that there is an initial trust in what shows itself (even if this is later interrogated).

If we are engaged in historical and comparative inquiry through the study of texts, as here, the first strategy in any descriptive enterprise must be philology. Of course, philology—or rather a particular philological reading of a text—is an argument supported by a body of evidence (variant readings and so on), but the system of grammar assumed in philology goes some way to eliminating subjectivity. The showing of the texts is facilitated by the philological method. There are problems with this method—in the distinction between 'work' and 'text', for example, that philology generally implies (actual texts are witnesses to the notional work[32])—but if any comparative enterprise is to be undertaken, we must begin here. In the texts selected for this study, I have tried to use editions that have gone through a philological process. Of course subjectivity is involved in the selection of texts, but philology does allow the texts themselves to shine through (and so allows us to understand something of the subjectivities that produced them). The phenomenological method does assume a subject, the indexical-I, that itself is questionable as a self-identical entity on Kristeva's account; but we must assume some subject—or rather a lifeworld of subjects—for a description of appearances to consciousness to take place. Indeed, even if we were to accept the fragmented nature of the

[31] Julia Kristeva, *Powers of Horror: An Essay on Abjection*, trans. Leon S. Roudiez (New York: Columbia University Press, 1982), p. 1. For Kristeva, subjectivity is formed through separation from the mother, the experience of abjection, and the discovery of the 'good' father and the move from the pre-Oedipal semiotic realm to the symbolic realm of language.

[32] See D. C. Greetham, *Theories of the Text* (Oxford: Oxford University Press, 1999), pp. 44–9.

subject, then this does not entail that the phenomenological method will always produce distorted results.

More in consonance with Kristeva's problematic is a sense of phenomenological description, different from Husserl's, provided by Heidegger. He bypasses the Husserlian problematic of intentionality by focusing rather on what appears, on what shows itself, and 'letting an entity be seen from itself' in this way avoiding any implicit Cartesian duality between subject and object of consciousness. Heidegger describes the task of phenomenology in the following terms:

> Thus 'phenomenology' means *apophainesthai ta phainomena*—to let that which shows itself be seen from itself in the very way in which it shows itself from itself. This is the formal meaning of that branch of research which calls itself 'phenomenology'. But here we are expressing nothing else than the maxim formulated above: 'To the things themselves.'[33]

Phenomenology is 'letting be seen' and so a kind of 'showing'. Heidegger thinks that this is the true phenomenological method that does indeed reach 'the things themselves', in contrast to Husserl for whom, although he coined the phrase, 'the things' are still appearances to consciousness; Husserl's method, while trying to free philosophy from both idealism and materialism, falls back into idealism. For Heidegger, phenomenology is not defined as a method or by its object in the way that theology could be described as defined by a *theos*, but is 'the *how* with which *what* is to be treated in this science gets exhibited and handled'.[34] This is a formulation of phenomenology conducive to the showing itself, rather than an emphasis on a Cartesian subject of knowledge, the problematic *cogito*, and its flow of *cogitationes*. And what is it, asks Heidegger, that phenomenology is to let us see? This is precisely what does not show itself or remains hidden, namely being itself.

After Description

After description we are left with the task of theorizing what shows itself to us. This second level is to understand phenomenology in hermeneutical and dialogical terms, and it turns comparative religion into a hermeneutical enterprise. The generation of theory at this level is not so much an objective science as a dialogical science that recognizes the historical situatedness of inquiry and the provisional, open-ended nature of its results.[35] But

[33] Martin Heidegger, *Being and Time*, trans. John Macquarrie and Edmund Robinson (Oxford: Blackwell, 1962), p. 58.

[34] Heidegger, *Being and Time*, p. 59.

[35] See my *Beyond Phenomenology: Rethinking the Study of Religion* (London and New York: Cassell, 1999), pp. 143–68.

recognizing indeterminacy and resisting totalities does not entail that theoretical or normative claims cannot be made in religious studies. Indeed, our thesis about inwardness as collective subjectivity is such a claim.

So far then we have argued that comparative religion, grounded in a hermeneutical phenomenology (phenomenology because concerned with what shows itself, and hermeneutical because always historically located and understood from a perspective), can generate theory and normative claims about the human person across traditions. We have tried to demonstrate through a thick textuality that Hinduism, Buddhism, and Christianity share a view about inwardness as collective subjectivity, and we have argued this through textual examples (see Chapters 2 to 5). Furthermore, we have developed a normative claim based on this material in Chapters 6 and 7. But the question still remains about the ground of comparison and its justification. Arguably something universal (by which I mean common to human beings) is required, such as the body, the narrative of life from being born (we all come from a human female body) to dying (we all return to the elements), or something more abstract such as moral response to the face of the other (as Levinas argued). The pressure of evidence from this study alone suggests that we have to accept some universality to the human condition. Indeed, not to do so, to concede to a strong cultural relativism, would be a relegation of responsibility as comparativists.

In an old-fashioned language this is to raise the problem of whether there is a common human nature, a problem that can be approached from an ontological or a moral angle. While there is evidently strength in the relativist position that human reality is greatly (although probably not infinitely) variable, and we need to be anthropologically committed to difference as the many kinds of society and incompatible world views demonstrate, this must be soft relativism because of the strength of evidence for shared human features. But let us not override difference in the rush towards common human features. There is danger that we project modernist conceptions of the self onto other societies and onto the past, a danger that is hopefully alleviated by the method I have advocated of careful reading at a first phenomenological level.

But at this second level we are faced with the difficulty of reconciling a resistance to totalizing claims, a resistance to foundational claims, alongside the necessity to expose or make explicit the ground of comparison. If we are to engage in a comparative enterprise, what is its ground given the force of the critique of the philosophy of consciousness from the perspective of the philosophy of the sign? To substantiate a thesis about inwardness, what do we need to presuppose about the world and the human person? We have already mostly addressed this question in the last chapter in our account of the phenomenology of inwardness and the account of general features of subjectivity as the shared ground that enables comparison. What we did not do there was to present an account of the relation between inwardness and the long sweep of history, and to this task we need, finally, to turn. This relationship can be usefully accounted for in terms of what might be called 'act theory'.[36]

ACT THEORY

From the comparative material from the traditions we have seen, we need to develop an account of the relationship between inwardness and history, the narratives formed through historical sequence. Firstly, we need to say that inwardness impacts on history through action. Although interiority is by definition invisible in itself, we are here concerned about the ways in which it comes into view and shows itself. This must be through action—through the unrepeatable moral act, through the non-identical repetition of the ritual act, and through the act of writing. A characteristic feature of human reality is action, and it is only action that forms historical events. The relevance of this for our thesis of inwardness is that the act is intimately related to subjectivity as the articulation of intention, imagination, and judgement. Intention, imagination, and judgement are inseparably linked functions within subjectivity, intention referring to the direction of thought informed by imagination, and judgement to the curtailing of thought or making it concrete in act.[37] An act is a movement in space and time, as Davies points out,[38] preceded by a judgement, to affect a certain outcome. What we might call act theory shows how the realm of subjectivity is related to the realm of world, and how subjectivity affects—or rather creates—events that form history. The sequence can be delineated in the following terms:

1. Intention and imagination produce judgement that is followed by physical movement to produce an effect that we can call an event.
2. The event produces, or is the cause of, further events, thus possibly instituting a chain of events. This causally linked chain of events we call history that can be described as a narrative sequence.

[36] I use the term 'act theory' to denote action from background or ambient activity of human life, such as just being, breathing, and moving. It directly parallels 'thing theory', developed by Brown from Heidegger's demarcation of thing from background. See Bill Brown, 'Thing Theory', *Critical Inquiry*, 28/1 (Autumn 2001), pp. 1–22.

[37] I do not distinguish between 'act' and 'action'. For a survey of the burgeoning field of human action studies, see Ezequiel Morsella, John A. Bargh, and Peter M. Gollwitzer (eds.), *Oxford Handbook of Human Action* (New York: Oxford University Press, 2009).

[38] Oliver Davies, *Love in Act: Transforming Theology* (forthcoming).

3. Events constrain, although do not determine because of the radical freedom entailed by subjectivity, future judgements. The effects of our actions constrain whether we will perform such action again.
4. Apart from event, world view or ideology is a constraint upon judgement. World view also affects movement or, more precisely, the style and genre of movement, and world view affects the event as the result. The event is the result of action that is the result of judgement performed within the constraints of a particular world view or ideology. In this view, the event is not seen in contrast to process but is part of process, the result of the way the human person meets world or, perhaps more accurately, the way inwardness encounters that which is external to itself.

This, then, is the sequence of the act that can be diagrammed in Figure 1.

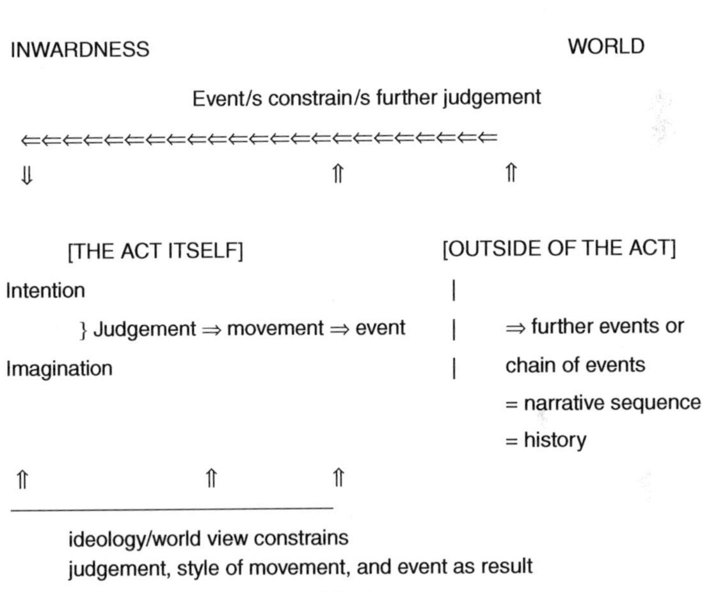

Fig 1.

Imagination, intention, and judgement are within subjectivity, while movement and the event are within the world. Of course, in one sense subjectivity is within the world—there is no living human person outside of the world—but here the subjectivity/world dichotomy roughly maps onto the internal/external dichotomy. Judgement and intention are internal to the self and are not spatial, while movement is bodily and observable occurring through space and time. Event, likewise, is spatial and temporal and more specifically entails location and probably other persons. The movement that results in event is in the world. This structure represents *the act itself*, although the event can cause further events that would be outside of the act itself and this chain of events we call narrative sequence or history. The event (within the act itself) and the chain of events (outside of the act) in turn constrain further judgements. The act itself is furthermore constrained by an ideology or world view: it affects judgement, it affects the style of movement, and it affects the event when seen as the result of action. On another view we could replace ideology/world view with truth (as Badiou might wish to do), but this would not be justified in that world view or ideology affect judgement, whether that world view is true or not. As a comparativist I cannot adjudicate on matters of supreme truth. A world view makes claim to truth, of course, but the comparative analyst needs only to recognize that meaning for a particular world view makes such a claim. This is to implicitly concede to Heidegger's separation of philosophy as world view (which we might say is the object of the comparativist's work) from philosophy as ontology.[39]

We can illustrate act theory with examples. Drawing on the traditions we have already described, the intention of Edmund, the Monk of Eynsham, was to convey the vision of God he had received and so make the judgement to dictate the story, a movement that produces the event of the text itself. This event leads to further events, such as the translation of the text into vernacular languages several hundred years later; and this chain of events forms a narrative sequence or history. The event of the written text itself constrained further judgements in Edmund, and the act was constrained by the world view within which he lived, of purgatory and paradise, Fall and redemption. On a broader scale we might say that the Buddha made a judgement, based on his intention to become enlightened, to sit beneath the banyan tree that led to the event of his enlightenment. This event led to further events and a whole narrative chain of events that we call Buddhism. The Buddha's act was constrained by his world view—such as reincarnation, the belief that life is suffering, that detachment leads away from suffering, that this is achieved through meditation, and so on—and the event of his enlightenment led to further judgements on the Buddha's part, such as going to teach the five ascetics he had previously been with and establishing the *saṅgha*. Abhinavagupta's philosophy of consciousness entails that unconscious impulses (*saṃskāraḥ*) give rise to particular conscious experience that results in the performance of action (*karma*), which in turn produces further impulses that come to fruition at a future date (see 'The Flow of Experience', pp. 150–1). For him, individual judgement is severely constrained by the past until liberation ensures the free spontaneity of all acts.

[39] M. Heidegger, *The Basic Problems of Phenomenology*, trans. Albert Hofstadter (2nd edn, Bloomington and Indianapolis, IN: Indiana University Press, 1988), pp. 8–11.

This structure of judgement (accompanied by particular reasons), plus movement, constitutes the historical act. Such an account recognizes that the human subject is embedded within the world and is part of the flow of events, and while being the consequence, also has the capacity to affect that flow. On the subjectivity side, the self as unique and unrepeatable is also universal—perhaps akin to what Badiou has called the 'universal singularity'[40]—although used as a descriptive term does not entail the emancipatory idea that Badiou intends. We need here to distinguish between the act as a movement following a judgement, from event that lacks the dimension of intentionality—such as a natural event or a historical event that I simply find myself within. The model presents us with a minimal view of human subjectivity in relation to world that is always filled with culture-specific contents. This structure is also applicable to collective bodies, such as traditions or political parties, which can come to collective judgements and collection actions. The crusades, for example, might be understood as a collective judgement that resulted in a movement of armies, and the event of the crusades themselves that had further consequences reverberating through history. Going to war might be the collective judgement of a parliament followed by the act of the mobilization of armed forces, and so on. Not all judgements create such strong events, of course, and most acts do not.

The substitution of the word 'event' for 'effect' is important in highlighting the potential historical significance of the effect. The Buddha's enlightenment is the effect of his meditative efforts, but the significance of the effect is captured more precisely by the term 'event'. The idea of the event is controversial in philosophy, but it seems generally agreed that events can be distinguished from objects in so far as objects are clearly spatially bounded but not clearly temporally bounded, whereas events are temporally bounded but not clearly spatially bounded. Event, which is diachronic, can also be distinguished from structure, which is synchronic.[41] Furthermore, different types of events can be distinguished that Casati and Varzi classify, following Rorty, into four types: activities, accomplishments, achievements, and states, although accomplishments and achievements are grouped together as performances.[42] In our sense then, an event can thus be the product of movement

[40] Alain Badiou, *Saint Paul, the Foundation of Universalism*, trans. Ray Brassier (Stanford, CA: Stanford University Press, 2003), p. 13.

[41] Reinhart Koselleck, *The Practice of Conceptual History: Timing History, Spacing Concepts*, trans. T. S. Presner et al. (Stanford, CA: Stanford University Press, 2002), pp. 123–6.

[42] Roberto Casati and Achille Varzi, 'Events', *The Stanford Encyclopedia of Philosophy* (Spring 2010 edition), ed. Edward N. Zalta <http://plato.stanford.edu/archives/spr2010/entries/events/>, accessed 3 July 2012. The philosophical literature on events is large and a growing area of interest. See Casati and Varzi's online bibliography, *50 Years of Events: An Annotated Bibliography 1947 to 1997* <http://www.pdcnet.org/pages/Products/electronic/events.htm>, accessed 3 July 2012.

(for instance, the event of winning a race is the product of the movement of running) or an event can be coterminous with the movement (going for a run is coterminous with the movement). Some events are relatively insignificant in a person's life (wearing a blue or white shirt), whereas other events are deeply significant (birth, marriage, death). Furthermore, some events are of historical significance that goes far beyond the boundaries of the person's biography (Caesar crossing the Rubicon, and so on).[43]

Ricoeur made the point that the effects of action exceed the intentionality of the actor, and in this sense actions are like speech acts. An action can be identified by its illocutionary force and, as a text, can be detached from its author. In terms of our model, judgement followed by movement results in event can be related to speech acts. Thus an act may be identified by its illocutionary force in that actions have consequences of their own, detached from their authors. Caesar crossing the Rubicon has historical consequences beyond the intentional act. 'History', writes Ricoeur, 'is this quasi-"thing" *on* which human action leaves a "trace", puts its mark.'[44] We put our mark on history through this process of movement following judgements, which are constrained by intentions within a particular world view. The events we perpetrate can generate further events, and social actors 'read' the past in ways that go beyond the original frame and intention of the act. In Ricouerian terms, an action can exceed ostensive reference and go beyond the social conditions of its immediate production, and, like a text, address an indefinite number of possible 'readers'.

When we study comparative religion we study particular traditions (and so comparative religion is historicist in one sense); yet we also implicitly assume a universal history of the human species that thereby allows meaningful comparison. But we need not assume a developmental Hegelian model of history in which history progresses to a final telos, a view that has supported the hegemonic power of the West over the rest of the world. As Riceour points out, consciousness exposed to the efficacity of history offers an alternative to sovereign consciousness transparent to itself.[45] Yet as we have rejected the

[43] Related to this question, that I cannot address here, is the problem of the degree to which the human subject is overwhelmed by the inexorable flow of events, and the degree to which the subject has agency and can affect that flow. Of importance here is Heidegger's later philosophy in which he reflects on the importance of the idea of the event (*Erreignis*). The event is that which comes into view and has an imperative demand upon us as evoking concern or care. The event is a grounding of Dasein, whose basic disposition is restraint. Martin Heidegger, *Contributions to Philosophy (Of the Event)*, trans. Richard Rojcewicz and Daniela Vallega-Neu (Bloomington and Indianapolis, IN: Indiana University Press, 2012), p. 27.

[44] Paul Ricoeur, 'The Model of the Text: Meaningful Action Considered as a Text', p. 207, in Ricoeur, *Hermeneutics and the Human Sciences*, trans. J. B. Thompson (Cambridge: Cambridge University Press, 1981), pp. 197–221.

[45] Paul Ricoeur, *Time and Narrative*, vol. 3, trans. Kathleen Blamey and David Pellauer (Chicago, IL: Chicago University Press, 1988), p. 219.

Hegelian totalization of history so, Ricoeur goes on to argue, we also need to reject pure localization or relativism. This is a position that allows historical grounding within tradition while being open to anticipation of the future. Comparative religion has to be like this. As comparativists we need to be cautious of historical claims that see progress in terms of one history supplanting another, in terms of the West's cultural and, until recently, political domination of the world; but similarly, we have to reject a purely relativist or historicist position that we are locked into our innumerable, distinct histories. Act theory assumes a shared human constitution and assumes that history as the causal sequence of events functions in parallel ways in different cultures and traditions, in particular, as I have argued here, that subjectivity impacts on world through the structure of judgement, movement, and event.

GLOBAL HISTORY

Yet this opens up a further problematic that cannot be addressed here: namely, whether we can speak of global history. And so we revert back to one of our opening problems concerning the justification of comparing religious histories and for choosing examples from what might be called 'scholastic religions' or 'cosmological religions'. More than that, the examples and readings discussed are simply present in my consciousness as author; the claim of the book is that these examples tell us about a shared understanding of inwardness and the nature of the human person in the histories of Christianity, Hinduism, and Buddhism. During a parallel time frame—the High Middle Ages in Christianity; the generally post-Gupta period in South Asian religious history—a similar story can be told about the formation of inwardness through religious practices of prayer, asceticism, liturgy, and reading. I hope the examples given demonstrate the parallelism. I have not addressed the broader reason for the parallelism other than in terms of a shared subjectivity or imaginaire. In one sense I have offered a historical description and an argument for characterizing inwardness in this way, rather than a historical explanation.

But what would an explanation of parallel religious forms in different areas within a common time frame look like? That there are such parallels, as I have shown, is surely significant. There could have been historical forces at work across continents through trade, and there was some missionary activity on the part of Christianity and Buddhism, but this is a currently thin, inadequate account and could not explain the deep parallel structures I have identified. The specification of constraints is so complex, as Bowker reminds us, that a sufficient account of why these parallels occur is outside the boundary of the present project; but, nevertheless, we do need to confront this problematic.

Going back to an earlier age, Karl Jaspers and others after him posited the idea of the axial age to account for a parallel shift in world civilizations to an emphasis on moral being.[46] Axial theorists argue that Confucius, Moses, Yajñavalkya, the Buddha, and even Jesus and Mohammad are axial thinkers who changed the world. But even if we accept the idea of the axial age—and there are problems in accepting it as it spans such a wide period of history, from the Buddha to Mohammad—it is not clear that it is an explanation. It seems rather to be a description. An explanation would presumably have to be in terms of a historical purpose, but such a teleological account of history that itself entails problematic metaphysical assumptions of a Hegelian nature.

In positing a parallelism in the histories of Christianity, Hinduism, and Buddhism we are faced with the same problematic. Leaving aside the question of explanation in history, we arguably can speak of global history now in the twenty-first century. Indeed, this is related to the development of a new comparative history that questions the older (and deep) link between the discipline of history and nationalism; a link that new generations of historians can transcend in an interdisciplinary spirit.[47] This project has simply identified some of the streams that have flowed into the global present and contrasted the modernist understanding of inwardness with the cosmological understanding found across premodern civilizations. Even an account along Dumont's lines in terms of a shift from a holistic society to an individualist one is not so much an explanation as a redescription. But the interrogation of this problematic will need to wait for another day.

CONCLUSION

When we study the history of religions we primarily study tradition and how tradition has changed through time. We bring contemporary questions to bear on the past, and we also question the present through the past. Collective subjectivity in premodern religions questions modernity and models of the self in late capitalism. Yet modernity would also question collective subjectivity. While the self in modernity might well be 'buffered' (to use Taylor's term

[46] On recent treatment and use of the axial age, see Robert Bellah, *Religion in Human Evolution: From the Paleolithic to the Axial Age* (Cambridge, MA: Belknapp Press, Harvard University Press, 2012), pp. 474–80.

[47] On new comparative history see the inaugural lecture by John H. Eliot, *National and Comparative History: An Inaugural Lecture Delivered Before the University of Oxford on 10th May 1991* (Oxford: Clarendon Press, 1991). Also see Marcel Detienne, *Comparing the Incomparable*, trans. Janet Lloyd (Stanford, CA: Stanford University Press, 2008), especially pp. 23–56.

again), and contemporary communities are fragmented,[48] the conditions of the majority of human beings in Western democracies have considerably improved from the medieval world we have discussed. The inwardness that we have described was the pursuit of a minority, articulated in literary genres that were simply closed to the majority of people: closed to most women, to agricultural workers (many of whom were virtually slaves), and to other minorities such as lepers and the disabled. In South Asia, the avenues of philosophical and literary self-expression we confined in the earlier medieval period to the Brahmins, and lower castes, along with women, were strictly excluded. Modernity can offer critique of the world view I have been describing from an emancipatory perspective.

Of course, life after the Second World War in the Western world is materially better for most of its citizens—many diseases are eliminated, life is longer, there is education for more people, and so on; yet the collective subjectivity of the cosmological religions offers a potentially forceful model for human solidarity in the future. While I would resist any nostalgia for a world now gone in which meaning was ensured by understanding one's place in the cosmological scheme, we should welcome the questioning of contemporary social fragmentation that cosmological subjectivity suggests. Perhaps it is asking too much for the human future to reinstall the sacrality of the human person while simultaneously rejecting any totalizing claims, but as human subjects we have for long held in tension the desire for completion and resolution—the utopian dreams of our forefathers—with the reality of contingency, the reality of the precarious nature of life, and the inevitable truth of finitude. We must try to live successfully with our need for completion, along with the necessity of accepting 'the finality of non-resolution'[49] and the aleatoric nature of our fates.

[48] For example, Rowan Williams, *Lost Icons: Reflections on Cultural Bereavement* (Edinburgh: T. and T. Clark, 2000), pp. 166–7.

[49] This phrase is from Paul D. Janz, *God, the Mind's Desire: Reference, Reason and Christian Thinking* (Cambridge and New York: Cambridge University Press, 2004), pp. 21–2.

Epilogue

What does this inquiry about the truth within teach us? Although the histories of the religions are so different, I have tried to make a case for a certain commonality in the realm of interiority—that there is a truth within human beings, the realization or knowledge of which is the guiding telos of life. What the kinds of inwardness in Christianity, Hinduism, and Buddhism share is a hierarchical order of being (even though this hierarchy is sometimes subverted) along with the idea of the human person as sacred. This sacrality of the human person, however, lies not in individualism but in participation in the order of being. The kinds of inwardness I have described are developed over a long period of time, throughout a lifetime in the non-identical repetition of ritual and meditative act, by developing a certain habitus, a certain way of life that aligns the being of the person with forms and forces greater than the self. To view the person as sacred is to view the person as having a life whose meaning is legitimated by, and imbued with, a transcendent order. This idea of the sacrality of the human person that is entailed by a participatory model of being in which forms of subjectivity are intensified through spiritual practice is generally antithetical to secular modernity because it posits a truth deeper than the satisfaction of desire.

A contemporary response could well be that it is surely a beneficial thing that the kind of inwardness we have encountered here has disappeared or is relegated to a minority interest in modern societies. The secular individual embodies values that emphasize the importance of the individual person over any collectivity. And the contemporary secular person embodies human rights that were absent in earlier societies that cultivated the forms of inwardness I have described. In all of these holistic societies the emphasis on the shared social order entailed the oppression of women, gay people, and the disabled. There is truth in this, and we can never return to the sacrality of the social body entailed by those kinds of hierarchical systems. Yet there is also a sense in which contemporary life has lost something significant in relegating religious inwardness to history or seeing it as a historical leftover in monastic institutions. Surely a sense of inwardness is important that goes beyond merely ephemeral feelings? We can appreciate traditional forms of inwardness to a greater degree now that we have surpassed a view of the world as a purely mechanistic entity set against the freedom of the mind. We now know that we inhabit a complex materiality in which subject and object are mutually implicated and in which subjectivity emerges from complexity in relation to others. There is a case for the presence of religious inwardness in the contemporary world that may take on different forms—collective experiences of art are, perhaps, close to it—and there is an ethics that can be abstracted from the religious inwardness we have encountered. Firstly, inwardness is antithetical to evil. Evil is exterior, whereas the cultivation of the good is an inner cultivation within a social context (as the Greeks knew). Secondly, there is an imaginative space opened up by religious inwardness in which forms of love are cultivated that take us beyond our personal desires and in which awareness of death is our companion. We began with Gerard Manley Hopkins' mountains of the mind, the particularity of the inscape of each, and we can end with his gentle awareness (perhaps more factual than melancholic) that inwardness ends at the close of the day: 'all/ Life death does end and each day dies with sleep'.[1]

[1] Gerard Manley Hopkins, 'Terrible Sonnets 65', *Poems of Gerard Manley Hopkins* (London, New York, Toronto: Oxford University Press, 1948), p. 107.

References

Primary Sources and Translations

Christian Texts

Aquinas, Thomas, *Summa Theologica*, 8 vols (Rome: Barri-Duccis, 1877); trans. Fathers of the English Dominican Province as *The Summa Theologica of St Thomas Aquinas* (London: Burns, Oates and Washbourne, 1920).

Aquinas, Thomas, *Questions on the Soul (Questiones de Anima)*, trans. J. H. Robb (Milwaukee: Marquette University Press, 1984).

Augustine, *De Civitate Dei*, in B. Dombart (ed.), *Santi Aurelii Augustini Episcopi De Civitate Dei,* vol. 1, (Bibliotheca Scriptorum Graecorum et Romanorum Teubneriana, 1877); ed. and trans. R.W. Dyson as *Augustine: The City of God Against the Pagans* (Cambridge: Cambridge University Press, 1998).

Augustine, *Confessiones*, in Paul Migne (ed.), *Patrologia Latina*, vol. 32, col. 659–868, electronic database <http://pld.chadwyck.com>; trans. R. S. Pine-Coffin as *Saint Augustine Confessions* (London: Penguin, 1961).

Augustine, *De Genesi ad Litteram*, in Paul Migne (ed.), *Patrologia Latina*, vol. 34, col. 219–45, electronic database <http://pld.chadwyck.com>; trans. J. Teske as *On Genesis: Two Books on Genesis Against the Manichees and On the Literal Interpretation on Genesis: An Unfinished Book* (Washington, DC: Catholic University of America, 1990).

Avril, Henry, *The Pilgrimage of the Lyfe of the Manhode, Translated Anonymously into Prose from the First Recension of Guillaume de Deguilevile's poem Le Pèlerinage de la Vie Humaine* (Oxford: Early English Text Society, Oxford University Press, 1988).

Bede, *Historia Ecclesiastica*, in James Campbell (ed.), *Bede: The Ecclesiastical History of the English People and Other Selections* (New York: Washington Square Press, 1968).

Bonaventure, *Itinerarum mentis in deum*, in Q. Muller (ed.), *Opera Omnia*, vol. 5 (Florence: Quaracchi, 1957); trans. Ewart Cousins as *Bonaventure*, Classics of Western Spirituality (New York: Paulist Press, 1978).

Caxton, William, *Here Begynneth a Lityll Treatyse Short and Abrydgyd Spekynge of the Art and Crafte to Knowe Well to Dye* (London: Emprynted by Richarde Pynson, 1495).

Cisterciensis, Thomas, commentary on the *Cantica Canticorum* Book 1, in Paul Migne (ed.), *Patrologia Latina*, vol. 206, col. 21B–86B, electronic database <http://pld.chadwyck.com>.

The Cloud of Unknowing, in Phyllis Hodgson (ed.), *The Cloud of Unknowing and the Book of Privy Counselling* (Oxford: Oxford University Press, 1944).

Dionysius the Pseudo-Areopagite, *Mystical Theology and the Celestial Hierarchies*, trans. The editors of the Shrine of Wisdom (Godalming: Shrine of Wisdom, 1949).

Duns Scotus, John, *De principio individuationi*, trans. Allan B. Wolter as *John Duns Scotus—Early Oxford Lecture on Individuation*, Latin text and English translation (New York: St Bonaventure University, 2005).

Edmund Leversedge, in W. F. Nijenhuis (ed.), *The Vision of Edmund Leversedge: A Fifteenth Century Account of a Visit to the Other World edited from BL MS Additional 34, 193 with an Introduction, Commentary and Glossary* (Nijmegen: Katholieke Universiteit te Nijmegen, 1990).

Evagrius, *Kephalaia Gnostica*, in A. Guillaumont (ed.), *Les Six Centuries des 'Kephalaia Gnostica' d'Evagre le Pontique. Edition critique de la version syriaque commune et édition d'une novelle version syriaque, intégrale, avec une double traduction française*, Patrologia Orientalis, vol. XXVIII, fasc. 1 (Paris: Frimin Didot, 1958).

Ficino, Marsilio, *Platonic Theology*, vol. 1, trans. Michael J. B. Allen, Latin text ed. James Hankins (Cambridge, MA, London: Harvard University Press, 2001).

Handlying Sinne, in R. Furnivall (ed.), *Robert of Brunne's Handlying Sinne* AD *1303 with those Parts of the Anglo-French Treatise on which it was Founded* (Oxford: Early English Text Society, 1901).

Hugh of St Victor, *De arca Noe morali*, in Paul Migne (ed.), *Patrologia Latina*, vol. 176, col. 617–680D.

Jacob's Well, in Arthur Brandeis (ed.), *Jacob's Well: An English Treatise on the Cleansing of Man's Conscience, Edited from the Unique MA about 1440 in Salisbury Cathedral* (London: Early English Text Society, 1900).

Julian of Norwich, *Revelations of Divine Love*, ed. Grace Chadwick (London: Methuen, 1901).

Lactantius, *Liber tertius et Falsa Sapientia Philosophorum*, ch. 20, in Paul Migne (ed.), *Patrologia Latina*, vol. 6, 347C–446B, electronic database <http://acta.chadwyck.com>.

Magna Vita, in Decima L. Douie and Dom Hugh Farmer (eds.), *Magna Vita Sancti Hugonis: The Life of St Hugh of Lincoln*, 2 vols (reprinted with corrections, Oxford: Oxford Medieval Texts, 1985).

Mechthild of Magdeburg, *Das fliessende Licht der Gottheit*, ed. Gisela Vollmann (Frankfurt am Main: Deutscher Klassiker Verlag, 2003); trans. Lucie Menzies as *The Revelations of Mechthild of Magdeburg (1210–1297) or The Flowering Light of the Godhead* (London: Longmans Green, 1953).

Monk of Eynsham, in Robert Easting (ed.), *The Revelation of the Monk of Eynsham* (Oxford: Oxford University Press for the Early English Text Society, 2002).

Richard of St Victor, *Benjamin Major*, in Paul Migne (ed.), *Patrologia Latina*, vol. 196, col. 63B–202B, electronic database <http://pld.chadwyck.com>; ed. and trans. (French) Jean Châtillon and Monique Duchet-Suchaux as *Richard de Saint-Victor: Les Douzes Patriarches ou Beniamin Minor* (Paris: Cerf, 1997); trans. (English) Grover A. Zinn as *The Twelve Patriarchs; The Mystical Ark; Book Three of the Trinity* (New York: Paulist Press, 1979).

Richard of St Victor, *Benjamin Minor*, in Paul Migne (ed.), *Patrologia Latina*, vol. 196, col. 1A–64A, electronic database <http://pld.chadwyck.com>; trans. S. V. Yankowski as *Benjamin Minor* (Ansbach: E. Koomeier and E. G. Kostetzky, 1960).

Richard of St Victor, *Benjamin Minor*, trans. Dick Barnes as *Richard of St Victor's Treatise of the Study of Wisdom that Men Call Benjamin: As Adapted in Middle*

English by the Author of the Cloud of Unknowing (Lewiston, Queenston, Lampeter: Edwin Mellen Press, 1990).

Richard of St Victor, *De Eruditione Hominis Interioris Libri Tres*, in Paul Migne (ed.), *Patrologia Latina*, vol. 196, col. 1229D–1366A, electronic database <http://pld.chadwyck.com>.

Richard of St Victor, *De Statu Interioris Hominis*, in Paul Migne (ed.), *Patrologia Latina*, vol. 196, col. 1115C–1160B, electronic database <http://pld.chadwyck.com>; trans. (French) J. Ribaillier as 'De statu interioris hominis de Richard de Saint Viktor', *Archives d'histoire doctrinale et littéraire du Moyen Âge*, tome 42, 1967, pp. 7–128.

Richard of St Victor, *Tractatus de Gradibus Charitatis*, in Paul Migne (ed.), *Patrologia Latina*, vol. 196, col. 1195A–1208B, electronic database <http://pld.chadwyck.com>.

Tundale, in Jean-Michel Picard (ed.), *The Vision of Tnugdal* (Dublin: Four Courts Press, 1989).

Victorinus, Marius (4th cent.), *Adversus Arium*, in Paul Migne (ed.), *Patrologia Latina*, vol. 8, col. 1039B–1138B, electronic database <http://acta.chadwyck.com>.

Hindu Texts

Āgamaḍaṃbara, in Jayantha Bhatta, V. Raghavan, and A. Thakur (eds.), *Āgamaḍaṃbara, Otherwise called Ṣaṇmataṇātaka of Jayantha Bhaṭṭa* (Darbhanga: Mithila Institute, 1964); trans. Csaba Dezso as *Much Ado About Religion* (New York: New York University Press, 2005).

Īśānaśivagurudevapaddhati, ed. M. M. T. Ganapati Sastri with an introduction by N. P. Unni, 4 vols (Delhi and Varanasi: Bharatiya Vidya Prakashan, 1988).

Utpaladeva, *Īśvarapratyabijñākārikā*, ed. M. S. Kaul (Śrīnagara: Kashmir Series of Texts and Studies, 1921); trans. Raffaele Torella as *The Īśvarapratyabhijñākārikā of Utpaladeva with the Author's Vṛtti: Critical Edition and Annotated Translation* (Rome: Istituto Italiano per il Medio ed Estremo Oriente, 1994).

Abhinavagupta, *Īśvarapratyabijñāvimarśinī*, ed. and trans. R. C. Dwiwedi, K. C. Pandey, and K. A. Subramania Iyer as *Bhāskarī*, 3 vols (Delhi: Motilal Banarsidass, 1986 (first published 1938, 1950, 1954)).

Jayākhya-saṃhitā, in E. Krishnamacharya (ed.), *The Jayākhya-saṃhitā of the Pāñcarātra Āgama* (Baroda: Gaekwad's Oriental Series, 1931).

Ādinātha, *Khecarīvidyā*, in James Mallinson, *The Khecarīvidyā of Ādinātha: A Critical Edition and Annotated Translation of an Early Text of Haṭhayoga* (London: Routledge, 2007).

Mālinīvijaottara-tantra, ed. M. S. Kaul (Śrīnagara: Kashmir Series of Texts and Studies, 1922).

Netra tantra, in M. S. Kaul (ed.), *The Netra-tantra with uddyota by Kṣemarāja*, 2 vols (Śrīnagara: Kashmir Series of Texts and Studies, 1926 and 1927).

Aghoraśivācārya, *Pañcāvaraṇastava*, in Dominic Goodall, N. Rout, R. Sathyanarayanan, S. A. S. Sarma, T. Ganesan, and S. Sambandhasivacarya (eds.), *Pañcāvaraṇastava of Aghoraśivācārya: A Twelfth-Century South Indian Prescription for the Visualisation of Sadāśiva and his Retinue* (Pondichéry: Institut Français de Pondichéry, 2005).

Parākhya-tantra, in D. Goodall (ed. and trans.), *The Parākhya Tantra: A Scripture of the Śaiva Siddhānta* (Pondichéry: Institut Français de Pondichéry, 2004).

Abhinavagupta, *Paramārthasāra*, in Lyne Bansat-Boudon and Kamaleshadatta Tripathi, *Introduction to Tantric Philosophy: The Paramārthasāra of Abhinavagupta with the Commentary of Yogarāja* (London and New York: Routledge, 2011).

Abhinavagupta, *Parātriṃśikālaghuvṛtti*, ed. and French trans. André Padoux as *La Parātriṃśikālaghuvṛtti: Texte traduit et annoté* (Paris: de Boccard, 1975).

Pratyabhiñāhṛdāya by Kṣemarāja, ed. J. C. Chatterji (Srinagar: Kashmir Series of Texts and Studies, 1911).

Ṛg-veda, in Ralph Griffith, *Hymns of the Rigveda* (Benares: E. J. Lazarus, 1889–92).

Sāṃkhya-kārikās, in Har Dutt Sharma, (ed. and trans.), *The Sānkhyakārikā: Īśvarakṛṣṇa's Memorable Verses of Sāṃkhya Philosophy with the Commentary of Gauḍapāsācarya* (Poona: Oriental Book Agency, 1925).

Sarvajñānottarāgamaḥ vidyāpāda and yogapāda, ed. K. Ramachandra Sarma, rev. R. Thanasvami Sarma, in *Adyar Library Bulletin*, 62 (1998), 181–232.

Somaśambhupaddhati, ed. and French trans. Hélène Brunner, 4 vols (Pondichéry: Institut Français de Pondichéry, 1963, 1968, 1977, 2000).

Kṣemarāja, *Spandanirṇaya*, ed. and trans. M. R. Śāstrī (Śrīnagara: Kashmir Series of Texts and Studies, 1925).

Abhinavagupta, *Tantrāloka* with the *viveka* by Jayaratha, vol. 1 ed. M. S. Śāstrī, vols 2–12 ed. M. S. Kaul (Śrīnagāra: Kashmir Series of Texts and Studies, 1918–38); chapters 1–5 French trans. A. Padoux as *La Lumière sur les tantras* (Paris: CNES, 1998).

Abhinavagupta, *Tantrasāra*, ed. M. S. Kaul (Śrīnagāra: Kashmir Series of Texts and Studies, 1918).

Nārāyaṇa, *Tantrasāra-saṃgraha*, critically ed. M. Duraiswami Aiyangar (Madras: Government Oriental Manuscripts Library, 1950).

Vijñānabhairava tantra, in M. Śāstrī (ed.), *The Vijñāna-bhairava: With Commentary called Kaumadi by Ānanda Bhaṭṭa* (Śrīnagara: Kashmir Series of Texts and Studies, 1918); French trans. Lilian Silburn as *Le Vijñānabhairava: Texte traduit et commenté* (Paris: de Boccard, 1961).

Vijñānabhairava-vivṛti, in *Vijñānabhairavatantra with Commentary (-uddyota) by Kṣemarāja Surviving on Verses 1 to 23 Completed by the Commentary of Śivopādhyāya (-vivṛti)*, ed. Mukund Ram Sastri (Srinagar: Kashmir Series of Texts and Studies, 1918).

Patañjali, *Yoga-sūtras*, in Swami Hariharananda Aranya, *The Philosophy of Patañjali*, trans. P. N. Mukerji (Albany, NY: SUNY Press, 1988 (first published1963)).

Buddhist and Jain Texts

Caṇḍamahārośana-tantra, in C. S. George (trans.), *The Caṇḍamahārośana-tantra*, Chapters II–VIII (New Haven: Oriental Society, 1974).

Caryamelapakapridipa, in Christian K. Wedemeyer (ed. and trans.), *Aryadeva's Lamp that Integrates the Practices (Caryamelapakapridipa): The Gradual Path of Vajrayana Buddhism According to the Esoteric Community Noble Tradition* (New York: Columbia University Press, 2007).

Guhyasamāja-tantra, in Benoytosh Bhattacharya (ed.), *Guhyasamāja Tantra or Tathāgataguhyaka* (Baroda: Oriental Institute, 1967).

Hevajra-tantra, in David Snellgrove, *The Hevajra Tantra*, vol. 1 (London: Oxford University Press, 1959).

Laṅkāvatāra-sūtra, in Buniyiu Nanjio (ed.), *The Laṅkāvatāra Sūtra* (Kyoto: The Otani University Press, 1923); trans. D. T. Suzuki as *The Laṅkāvatāra Sūtra* (London: Routledge and Kegan Paul, 1932).

Mahāparinibbāna-sutta, in Trevor Ling (ed.), *The Buddha's Philosophy of Man* (London: J. M. Dent, 1981), pp. 139–213.

Mañjuśrīmūlakalpa, in T. Gaṇapati Śāstrī (ed.), *The Āryamañjuśrīmūlakalpa* (Trivandrum: Government Press, 1920–5). A diplomatic edition of this text is in preparation by the Early Tantra Project—see <http://www.tantric-studies.uni-hamburg.de/projects/manjusrimulakalpa/>.

Pratyuttpana-sūtra, in Paul Harrison (trans.), *The Samādhi or Direct Encounter with the Buddhas of the Present: An Annotated English Translation of Tibetan Version of the Pratyuttpana-Buddha-Saṃmukhāvasthita-Samādhi-Sūtra* (Tokyo: The International Institute for Buddhist Studies, 1990); trans. Paul Harrison as *The English Tripiṭaka: The Pratyuttpana Samādhi Sūtra, The Śūraṅgama Samādhi Sūtra* (Berkeley, CA: Numata Center, 1998).

Ratnagotravibhāga, in Jikido Takasaki, *A Study on the Ratnagotravibhāga (Uttaratantra), Being a Treatise on the Tathāgatagarbha Theory of Mahāyāna Buddhism* (Rome: Istituto Italiano per il Medio ed Estremo Oriente, 1966).

Sādhanamālā, in B. Bhattacharya (ed.), *Sādhanamāmā*, vol. 1 (Baroda: Gaekwad's Oriental Series, 1925).

Saṃdhinirmocana-sūtra, in E. Lamotte (trans.), *Saṃdhinirmocana sūtra, l'explication des mys mystères* (Louvain: Bureaux du recueil, Bibliothèque de l'Université, 1935).

Śūraṃgamasamādhisūtra, in E. Lamotte, *Śūraṃgamasamādhisūtra: Concentration of Heroic Progress: Early Mahāyāna Buddhist Scripture*, trans. Sarah Boin-Webb (London: Curzon Press, 1998).

Vajracchedikā Prajñāparamitāsūtra, trans. Conze, Buddhist Wisdom Books (London: George Allen and Unwin, 1958).

Hemacandra, *Yogaśāstra*, in Olle Quarnström (trans.), *The Yogaśāstra of Hemacandra: A Twelfth Century Handbook on Śvetambara Jainism* (Cambridge, MA and London: Harvard University Press, 2002).

Modern Sources and Secondary Literature

Adams, M. M., *Some Later Medieval Theories of the Eucharist* (Oxford: Oxford University Press, 2010).

Adams, Nicholas, *Habermas and Theology* (New York: Cambridge University Press, 2006).

Akbari, Suzanne Conkin, *Seeing through the Veil: Optical Theory and Medieval Allegory* (Toronto: University of Toronto Press, 2004).

Allen, Nick, 'The Category of the Person: A Reading of Mauss' Last Essay', in Michael Carrithers, Steven Collins, and Steven Lukes (eds.), *The Category of the Person: Anthropology, Philosophy, History* (Cambridge: Cambridge University Press, 1985), pp. 26–45.

Anderson, Pamela, *A Feminist Philosophy of Religion: The Rationality and Myths of Religious Belief* (Oxford: Blackwell, 1998).

Angenendt, Arnold, *Geschichte der Religiosität im Mittelalter* (Darmstadt: Wissenschaftliche Buchgesellschaft, 1997).

Ariès, Philippe, *The Hour of Our Death*, trans. Helen Weaver (Oxford: Oxford University Press, 1991 (first published 1981)).

Asad, Talal, *Genealogies of Religion: Discipline and Reasons of Power in Christianity and Islam* (Baltimore, MD and London: Johns Hopkins University Press, 1993).

Atkins, J. W. H., *English Literary Criticism: The Medieval Phase* (Cambridge: Cambridge University Press, 1934).

Badiou, Alain, *Saint Paul, the Foundation of Universalism*, trans. Ray Brassier (Stanford, CA: Stanford University Press, 2003).

Bakhtin, M., *Towards a Philosophy of the Act*, trans. Vadim Liapunov (Austin, TX: University of Texas Press, 1995).

Baldwin, J. W., *The Scholastic Culture of the Middle Ages* (Lexington, MA: Heath, 1971).

Balibar, Etienne, *Identité et différence: L'invention de la consience* (Paris: Seuil, 1998).

Bamford, N., *Converging Theologies: Comparing and Converging Terms within the Byzantine and Pratyabhijñā (Kashmir Śaivitie) Traditions within a Space for Convergence* (Delhi: ISPCK, 2011).

Banani, Amin and Vryonis, Speros (eds.), *Individualism and Conformity in Classical Islam* (Wiesbaden: Harrassowitz, 1977).

Bansat-Boudon, Lyne, *Théâtre de l'Inde ancienne* (Paris: Gallimard, 2006).

Barless, Robert, 'From Paganism to Christianity in Medieval Europe', in Nora Berend (ed.), *Christianization and the Rise of Christian Monarchy: Scandanavia, Central Europe and Russia c. 900–1200* (Cambridge and New York: Cambridge University Press, 2007), pp. 47–72.

Bartlett, R., *Trial by Fire and Water: The Medieval Judicial Ordeal* (New York: Oxford University Press, 1986).

Bayly, C., *Indian Society and the Making of the British Empire* (Cambridge: Cambridge University Press, 2002).

Bayly, Susan, *Caste, Society, and Politics in India from the Eighteenth Century to the Modern Age* (New Delhi: Replika Press, 1991).

Beaty, Nancy Lee, *The Craft of Dying: A Study in the Literary Tradition of the Ars Moriendi in England* (New Haven, CT: Harvard University Press, 1970).

Bellah, Robert, *Religion in Human Evolution: From the Paleolithic to the Axial Age* (Cambridge, MA: Belknap Press, Harvard University Press, 2012).

Benson, R. L. and Constable, G. with Lanham, C. D (eds.), *Renaissance and Renewal in the Twelfth Century* (2nd edn, London and Toronto: University of Toronto Press, 1991).

Benton, John, 'Individualism and Conformity in Medieval Western Europe', in Amin Banani and Speros Vryonis (eds.), *Individualism and Conformity in Classical Islam* (Wiesbaden: Harrassowitz, 1977), pp. 145–58.

Benton, John, *Self and Society in Medieval France: The Memoirs of Abbor Guibert of Nogent* (Toronto: University of Toronto Press, 1984).

Berreman, Gerald D., 'The Brahmanical View of Caste', *Contributions to Indian Sociology*, 5/1 (1971), 17–23.

Bharati, Agehananda, *The Tantric Tradition* (London: Rider, 1965).

Binski, Paul, *Medieval Death: Ritual and Representation* (Ithaca, NY: Cornell University Press, 1996).

Birch, Jason, 'The Meaning of Hatha in Early Hathayoga', *Journal of the American Oriental Society*, 131/4 (2011), 527–54.

Blacking, John (ed.), *The Anthropology of the Body* (London, New York, San Francisco: Scholars Press, 1977).

Boethius, *The Consolation of Philosophy*, trans V. E. Watts (London: Penguin, 1969).

Bok, Nico den, *Communicating the Most High: A Systematic Study of Person and Trinity in the Theology of Richard of St Victor (+1173)* (Paris and Turnhoult: Brepolis, 1996).

Bologar, R. R., *The Classical Heritage and its Beneficiaries* (Cambridge: Cambridge University Press, 1958).

Bornemark, Jonna and Ruis, Hans (eds.), *Phenomenology and Religion: New Frontiers* (Stockholm: Södertön University Press, 2010).

Borst, Arno, *Medieval Worlds: Barbarians, Heretics and Artists in the Middle Ages*, trans. Eric Hansen (Cambridge: Polity Press, 1991 (first published 1988)).

Bowker, John, *The Meanings of Death* (Cambridge: Cambridge University Press, 1991).

Bronkhorst, Johannes, *The Two Traditions of Meditation in Ancient India* (Delhi: MLBD, 1993).

Bronkhorst, Johannes, *Aux origines de la philosophie Indienne* (Paris: Infolio, 2008).

Brooke, C. N. L., *The Twelfth-Century Renaissance* (London: Thames & Hudson, 1969).

Brown, Bill, 'Thing Theory', *Critical Inquiry*, 28/1 (Autumn 2001), 1–22.

Brown, Norman O., *Life Against Death* (London: Routledge and Kegan Paul, 1959).

Brown, Peter, 'Society and the Supernatural: A Medieval Change', *Daedalus*, 104/2 (1975), 133–51.

Bucur, Bogdan Gabriel, *Angelomorphic Pneumatology: Clement of Alexandria and Other Early Christian Witnesses* (Leiden: Brill, 2009).

Burch, Matthew I., 'The Existential Sources of Phenomenology: Heidegger on Formal Indication', *European Journal of Philosophy*, (2011), DOI: 10.1111/j.1468-0378.2010.00446.x.

Burckhardt, Jacob, *The Civilization of Renaissance Italy*, trans S. Middlemore (London: Penguin, 1990).

Bynum, Caroline Walker, *Jesus as Mother: Studies in the Spirituality of the High Middle Ages* (Berkeley and Los Angeles, CA: University of California Press, 1982).

Cabezón, José (ed.), *Scholasticism: Cross-Cultural and Comparative Perspectives* (Albany, NY: SUNY Press, 1998).

Cadava, E., Connor, P., Nancy, Jean Luc (eds.), *Who Comes After the Subject?* (London: Routledge, 1994).

Campbell, Scott M., *The Early Heidegger's Philosophy of Life: Facticity, Being and Language* (New York: Fordham University Press, 2012).

Capps, Walter H., *Religious Studies: The Making of a Discipline* (Minneapolis, MN: Fortress Press, 1995).

Cargonja, Hrvoje, 'Ambiguous Experience: A Contribution to Understanding Experience as Discourse', *Studia Ethnogica Croatia*, 23/1 (2011), 283–308.

Carlisle, Clare, *Kierkegaard's Philosophy of Becoming: Movements and Positions* (Albany, NY: SUNY Press, 2005).

Carman, John and Marglin, Frédérique A. (eds.), *Purity and Auspiciousness in Indian Society* (Leiden: Brill, 1985).

Carozzi, Claude, *Le voyage de l'âme dans l'au-delà, d'après la literature latine (Ve-XIIe siècle)*, Collection de École Français de Rome (Paris: de Boccard, 1994).

Carrette, Jeremy, *Foucault and Religion: Spiritual Corporeality and Political Spirituality* (London: Routledge, 2000).

Carruthers, Mary, *The Book of Memory: A Study of Memory in Medieval Culture* (Cambridge and New York: Cambridge University Press, 1990).

Carruthers, Mary, *The Craft of Thought: Meditation, Rhetoric and the Making of Images, 400–1200* (Cambridge: Cambridge University Press, 1998).

Cary, Philip, *Augustine's Invention of the Inner Self* (New York: Oxford University Press, 2003).

Certeau, Michel de, *The Writing of History*, trans. Tom Conley (New York: Columbia University Press, 1988).

Certeau, Michel de, *The Mystic Fable*, vol. 1: *The Sixteenth and Seventeenth Centuries*, trans. M. B. Smith (Chicago, IL: Chicago University Press, 1992).

Certeau, Michel de, *The Possession at Loudun*, trans. M. B. Smith (Chicago, IL: University of Chicago Press, 2000).

Chalmers, David J., *The Conscious Mind: In Search of Fundamental Theory* (Oxford: Oxford University Press, 1996).

Châtillon, Jean, 'Les trois modes de la contemplation selon Richard de Saint-Victor', *Bulletin de Littérature Ecclésiastique*, 41/1 (1940), 3–26.

Châtillon, Jean and Duchet-Suchaux, Monique (eds. and French trans.), *Richard de Saint-Victor: Les Douzes Patriarches ou Beniamin Minor* (Paris: Cerf, 1997).

Chenu, M. D., *Nature, Man and* Society *in the Twelfth Century: Essays on New Theological Perspectives in the Latin West*, trans. Jerome Taylor and Lester K. Little (Chicago, IL: Chicago University Press, 1968 (first published 1957)).

Chenu, M. D., *L'éveil de la conscience* (Montreal: Institut d'Études Médiévale; Paris: Libraire Philosophique, Vrin, 1969).

Chidester, David, *Savage Systems: Colonialism and Comparative Religion in Southern Africa* (Charlottesville, VA: University Press of Virginia, 1996).

Clooney, F. *Seeing Through Texts: Doing Theology Among the Śrīvaiṣṇavas of South India* (Albany, NY: SUNY Press, 1996).

Clooney, Francis, *Hindu God, Christian God: How Reason Helps Break Down the Boundaries Between Religions* (New York: Oxford University Press, 2001).

Clooney, Francis, 'Restoring "Hindu Theology" as a Category in Indian Intellectual Discourse', in G. Flood (ed.), *The Blackwell Companion to Hinduism* (Oxford: Blackwell, 2003), pp. 447–77.

Clooney, Francis, *Comparative Theology: Deep Learning Across Religious Borders* (Oxford: Wiley-Blackwell, 2010).

Coakley, Sarah (ed.), *Religion and the Body* (Cambridge: Cambridge University Press, 1997).

Colas, G., *Viṣṇu: ses images et ses feux: Les metamorphoses du dieu chez les Vaikhānasa* (Paris: EFEO, 1996).

Connolly, Margaret (ed.), *Contemplations of the Dread and Love of God* (Oxford: Oxford University Press for the Early English Text Society, 1993).

Constable, Giles, *Three Studies in Medieval Religious and Social Thought* (Cambridge: Cambridge University Press, 1995).

Copleston, F., *A History of Philosophy*, vol. 2: *Medieval Philosophy* (London: Continuum, 1999 (first published 1950)).

Cousins, L., 'Vittaka/Vitarka and Vicāra: Stages of Samādhi in Buddhism and Yoga', *Indo-Iranian Journal*, 35 (1992), 137–57.

Cox, Collett, *Disputed Dharmas: Early Buddhist Theories on Existence* (Tokyo: International Institute for Buddhist Studies, 1995).

Cox, James, *A Guide to the Phenomenology of Religion* (London and New York: Continuum, 2006).

Critchely, Simon, *Very Little . . . Almost Nothing: Death, Philosophy, Literature* (London and New York: Routledge, 1997).

Csordas, Thomas J. (ed.), *Embodiment and Experience: The Existential Ground of Culture and Self* (Cambridge: Cambridge University Press, 1994).

Cullen, Christopher M., *Bonaventure* (New York: Oxford University Press, 2006).

Cushing, Kathleen G., *Reform and the Papacy in the Eleventh Century: Spirituality and Social Change* (Manchester: Manchester University Press, 2005).

D'Alverny, Marie-Thérèse, *Études sur le symbolisme de la sagesse et sur l'iconographie*, ed. Charles Burnett (Aldershot: Variorum, 1993).

D'Avray, D. L., *Medieval Religious Rationalities* (New York: Cambridge University Press, 2010).

D'Avray, D. L., *Rationalities in History: A Weberian Essay in Comparison* (New York: Cambridge University Press, 2010).

Dahlstrom, Daniel, '"Heidegger" Method: Philosophical Concepts as Formal Indications', *Review of Metaphysics*, 47/4 (June 1994), 775–95.

Dasgupta, S. N., *Introduction to Tantric Buddhism* (Berkeley, CA and London: Shambala, 1974).

Davidson, Ronald M., *Indian Esoteric Buddhism: A Social History of the Tantric Movement* (New York: Columbia University Press, 2002).

Davies, Oliver, *God Within: The Mystical Tradition of Northern Europe* (London: Darton, Longman and Todd, 1988).

Davies, Oliver, *The Creativity of God: World, Eucharist, Reason* (Cambridge: Cambridge University Press, 2004).

Davies, Oliver, *Love in Act: Transforming Theology* (forthcoming).

Davies, Oliver, Sedmak, Clemens, and Janz, Paul (eds.), *Transformation Theology: A New Paradigm of Christian Living* (London: T. and T. Clark, 2007).

Davis, R., *Ritual in an Oscillating Universe: Worshipping Śiva in Medieval India* (Princeton, NJ: Princeton University Press, 1991).

DeRoo, Neal and Manoussakis, John P. (eds.), *Phenomenology and Eschatology: Not Yet in the Now* (Burlington, VT: Ashgate, 2009).

Derrett, M., 'Appendix by the Translator', in R. Lingat, *The Classical Law of India*, trans. J Duncan and M. Derrett (Berkeley and Los Angeles, CA: University of California Press, 1973).

Derrida, Jacques and Vattimo, Gianni (eds.), *Religion* (Stanford, CA: Stanford University Press, 1996).

Detienne, Marcel, *Comparing the Incomparable*, trans. Janet Lloyd (Stanford, CA: Stanford University Press, 2008).

Dimock, E. and Levertov, D., *In Praise of Krishna: Songs from the Bengali* (New York: Anchor Books, 1967).

Dinzelbacher, Peter, *Vision und visionsliteratur im Mittelalter* (Stuttgart: Anton Hiersemann, 1981).

Dirks, N., *The Hollow Crown: Ethnohistory of an Indian Kingdom* (Cambridge: Cambridge University Press, 1987).

Doniger, Wendy, *The Implied Spider: Politics and Theology in Myth* (New York: Columbia University Press, 1998).

Doniger O'Flaherty, Wendy (ed.), *Karma and Rebirth in Classical Indian Traditions* (Berkeley and Los Angeles, CA: University of California Press, 1980).

Dosse, François, *History of Structuralism: The Rising Sign 1945 to 1966*, vol. 1, trans. D. Glassman (Minneapolis, MN: University of Minnesota Press, 1997).

Dravid, R. R., *The Problem of Universals in Indian Philosophy* (Delhi: Motilal, 2001).

Dronke, Peter, *Medieval Latin and the Rise of the European Love Lyric*, 2 vols (Oxford: Clarendon Press, 1966–7).

Dronke, Peter, *Poetic Individuality in the Middle Ages 1000–1150* (Oxford: Clarendon Press, 1970).

Duby, G., 'Les origines de la chevalerie', *Settimane di studio sull'alto medioevo*, 15/2 (Spoleto, 1968), 739–61.

Duby, Georges, *Le temps des cathedrals: L'art et la société 980–1420* (Paris: Gallimard, 1976).

Duffy, Eamon, *The Stripping of the Altars: Traditional Religion in England 1400–1580* (New Haven, CT and London: Yale University Press, 1992).

Duffy, Eamon, *Marking the Hours: English People and their Prayers 1240–1570* (New Haven, CT and London: Yale University Press, 2006).

Dulles, A., *Models of the Church* (Dublin: Gill and Macmillan, 1976).

Dumont, Louis, 'Le renoncement dans les religions de l'Inde', in *Homo Hierarchicus: Le system des castes et ses implications* (Paris: Gallimard, 1966), pp. 324–50; trans. Mark Sainsbury, Louis Dumont and Basia Gulati as *Homo Hierarchicus: The Caste System and its Implications* (Chicago, IL: Chicago University Press, 1970), pp. 267–86.

Dumont, Louis, 'On Putative Hierarchy and Some Allergies', in T. N. Madan et al. (eds.), 'On the Nature of Caste in India: A Review Symposium on Louis Dumont's *Homo Hierarchicus*', *Contributions to Indian Sociology*, 5/1 (1971), pp. 58–81.

Dumont, Louis, 'A Modified View of Our Origins: The Christian Beginnings of Modern Individualism', in Michael Carrithers, Steven Collins, and Steven Lukes (eds.), *The Category of the Person: Anthropology, Philosophy, History* (Cambridge: Cambridge University Press, 1985), pp. 93–122.

Dumont, Louis, *Essays on Individualism: Modern Ideology in Anthropological Perspective* (Chicago, IL: Chicago University Press, 1986).

Dupré, Louis, *Passage to Modernity* (New Haven: Yale University Press, 1993).

Dyczkowski, Mark, *The Doctrine of Vibration* (Albany, NY: SUNY Press, 1988).

Easting, Robert, *Annotated Bibliography of Old and Middle English Literature*, vol. III: *Visions of the Other World in Middle English* (New York: D. S. Brewer, 1997).

Ebner, Joseph, *Die Erkenntnislehre Richards von Sr Viktor*, Beitäge zur Geschichte der Philosophie des Mittelalters, vol. 19, pt 4 (Münster: Ashendorffschen Buchhandlung, 1917).

Eire, Carlos M. N., *From Madrid to Purgatory: The Art and Craft of Dying in Sixteenth-Century Spain* (Cambridge: Cambridge University Press, 2002).

Eliot, John H., *National and Comparative History: An Inaugural Lecture Delivered Before the University of Oxford on 10th May 1991* (Oxford: Clarendon Press, 1991).

Elvin, Mark, 'Between the Earth and Heaven: Conceptions of the Self in China', in M. Carrithers, S. Collins, and S. Lukes (eds.), *The Category of the Person: Anthropology, Philosophy, History* (Cambridge: Cambridge University Press, 1985), pp. 156–89.

Evans, Fred and Lawlor, Leonard (eds.), *Chiasms: Merleau-Ponty's Notion of Flesh* (Albany, NY: SUNY Press, 2000).

Faivre, A. and Hanegraaf, W. (eds.), *Western Esotericism and the Science of Religion* (Leeven: Peters, 1998).

Falque, Emmanuel, *Saint Bonaventure et l'entrée de dieu en théologie* (Paris: Vrin, 2000).

Faure, Bernard, *Double Exposure: Cutting Across Buddhist and Western Discourses*, trans. Janet Lloyd (Stanford, CA: Stanford University Press, 2000).

Feher, M. et al., *Fragments for a History of the Human Body*, 3 vols (New York: Urzone, 1989).

Ferreira, Jamie, *Love's Grateful Striving: A Commentary on Kierkegaard's Works of Love* (New York: Oxford University Press, 2001).

Fitzgerald, Timothy, *The Ideology of Religious Studies* (New York: Oxford University Press, 2000).

Fitzgerald, Timothy, *Discourse on Civility and Barbarity: A Critical History of Religion and Related Categories* (Oxford and New York: Oxford University Press, 2007).

Fitzpatrick, P. J., *In Breaking of Bread: The Eucharist and Ritual* (Cambridge: Cambridge University Press, 1993).

Fletcher, Richard, *The Conversion of Europe, from Paganism to Christianity 371–1386 AD* (London: Fontana, 1998).

Flood, Gavin, *Body and Cosmology in Kashmir Śaivism* (San Francisco: Mellen, 1993).

Flood, Gavin, *An Introduction to Hinduism* (Cambridge: Cambridge University Press, 1996).

Flood, Gavin, *Beyond Phenomenology: Rethinking the Study of Religion* (London and New York: Cassell, 1999).

Flood, Gavin, *The Ascetic Self: Subjectivity, Memory and Tradition* (Cambridge: Cambridge University Press, 2004).

Flood, Gavin, *The Tantric Body* (London: Tauris Press, 2006).

Flood, Gavin, *The Importance of Religion: Meaning and Action in Our Strange World* (Oxford: Wiley-Blackwell, 2012).

Flood, Gavin and Martin, Charles (trans.), *The Bhagavad Gita: A New Translation* (New York and London: Norton, 2012).

Ford, David, 'An Interfaith Wisdom: Scriptural Reasoning Between Jews, Christians and Muslims', in David F. Ford and C. C. Pecknold (eds.), *The Promise of Scriptural Reasoning* (Oxford: Blackwell, 2006), pp. 1–22.

Ford, David F., *Christian Wisdom: Desiring God and Learning in Love* (Cambridge: Cambridge University Press, 2007).

Ford, David F. and Pecknold, C. C. (eds.), *The Promise of Scriptural Reasoning* (Oxford: Blackwell, 2006).

Frassetto, Michael (ed.), *Heresy and the Persecuting Society in the Middle Ages: Essays on the Work of R. I. Moore* (Leiden: Brill, 2006).

Frazier, Jessica, *Reality, Religion, and Passion: Indian and Western Approaches in Hans-Georg Gadamer and Rūpa Gosvami* (Aldershot: Ashgate, 2008).

Freeman, Rich, 'Purity and Violence: Sacred Power in the Teyyam Worship of Malabar', PhD dissertation, University of Philadelphia, 1993.

Frei, Hans, 'The Literal Reading of Biblical Narrative in the Christian Tradition: Does it Stretch or will it Break?', in Peter Ochs (ed.), *The Return to Scripture in Judaism and Christianity: Essays in Postcritical Scriptural Interpretation* (Mahwah, NJ: Paulist Press, 1993), pp. 55–82.

Ganeri, Jonardon, *The Concealed Art of the Soul: Theories of Self and Practices of Truth in Indian Ethics and Epistemology* (Oxford and New York: Oxford University Press, 2007).

Ganeri, Jonardon, *The Lost Age of Reason: Philosophy in Early Modern India 1450–1700* (Oxford and New York: Oxford University Press, 2011).

Ganeri, R. M., *The Vedāntic Cosmology of Rāmānuja and its Western Parallels*, DPhil thesis, University of Oxford, Oxford, 2004.

Gardiner, Eileen (ed.), *Visions of Heaven and Hell Before Dante* (New York: Ithaca Press, 1989).

Garmonsway, G. M. (trans.), *The Anglo-Saxon Chronicle* (London: Dent and Sons, 1953).

Gauchet, Marcel, *The Disenchantment of the World: A Political History of Religion*, trans. Oscar Burge (Princeton, NJ and Chichester: Princeton University Press, 1997).

Gerschheimer, G., 'Les "Six doctrines de speculation" (*ṣaṭtarkī*): Sur le catégorization variable des système philosophiques dans l'Inde classique', in K. Preisendanz (ed.), *Expanding and Merging Horizons: Contributions to South Asian and Cross-Cultural Studies in Commemoration of Wilhelm Halbfass* (Wien: Verlas der Österreichischen Akademie der Wissenschaften, 2007), pp. 239–58.

Giraud, Cédric, 'Du silence à la parole: Le Latin spirituel d'Hughes de Saint-Victor dans le vanitate mundi', *Archives d'histoire doctrinale et littéraire du Moyen Âge*, 77/1 (2010), 7–27.

Golding, William, *The Spire* (London: Faber, 1964).

Gombrich, R., *Theravada Buddhism* (London: Routledge, 1988).

Gombrich, R., *What the Buddha Thought* (London: Equinox, 2009).

Goodrick-Clarke, N., *The Western Esoteric Traditions: A Historical Introduction* (New York: Oxford University Press, 2008).

Grajewski, Maurice J., *The Formal Distinction of Duns Scotus: A Study in Metaphysics Thesis*, PhD thesis, Catholic University of America, Washington, DC, 1944.

Grant, Edward, *Planets, Stars and Orbs: The Medieval Cosmos* (Cambridge: Cambridge University Press, 1996).
Grant, Edward, *God and Reason in the Middle Ages* (Cambridge: Cambridge University Press, 2001).
Greetham, D. C., *Theories of the Text* (Oxford: Oxford University Press, 1999).
Grierson, George and Barnett, L.D., *Lalavakyani or the Wise Sayings of Lalla Ded* (London: Royal Asiatic Society, 1920).
Gron, Arne, 'Heidegger's Formal Indication', paper given at Christchurch College, Oxford, September 2007.
Guenther, Herbert V., *Philosophy and Psychology in the Abhidharma* (Berkeley, CA: Shambala, 1976).
Gupta, Dipankar, *Interrogating Caste: Understanding Hierarchy and Difference in Indian Society* (New Delhi: Penguin, 2000).
Gurevish, Aaron, *The Origins of European Individualism*, trans. Katharina Judelson (Oxford: Blackwell, 1995).
Hadot, P., *Philosophy as a Way of Life*, ed. A. I. Davidson (Oxford: Blackwell, 1995).
Hadot, P., *Exercices spirituels et philosophie antique* (Paris: Albin Michel, 2010).
Hand, Seán, 'Working Out Interiority: Locations and Locutions of Ipseity', *Literature and Theology*, 17/4, (2003), 422–34.
Hannay, Alastair, *Kierkegaard: A Biography* (Cambridge: Cambridge University Press, 2001).
Hanning, Robert W., *The Individual in Twelfth-Century Romance* (New Haven, CT: Yale University Press, 1977).
Hardy, Fred, *The Religious Culture of India: Power, Love, Wisdom* (Cambridge, New York, Melbourne: Cambridge University Press, 1994).
Harper, J., *The Forms and Order of Western Liturgy from the Tenth to Eighteenth Century* (Oxford and New York: Oxford University Press, 1991).
Hart, Kevin, '"Without World": Eschatology in Michel Henry', in Neal DeRoo and John P. Manoussakis (eds.), *Phenomenology and Eschatology: Not Yet in the Now*, (Burlington, VT: Ashgate, 2009), pp. 167–92.
Hausner, Sondra, *Wandering with Sadhus: Ascetics in the Hindu Himalayas* (Bloomington, IN: Indiana University Press, 2007).
Hausner, Sondra L. and Gellner, David, 'Category and Practice as Two Aspects of Religion: The Case of Nepalis in Britain', *Journal of the American Academy of Religion*, 80/4, (2012), 971–97.
Heelas, Paul, 'Expressive Spirituality and Humanistic Expressivism: Sources of Significance Beyond Church and Chapel', in Steven Sutcliffe and Marion Bowman (eds.), *Beyond New Age* (Edinburgh: Edinburgh University Press, 2000), pp. 237–54.
Heelas, Paul, *Spiritualities of Life: New Age Romanticism and Consumptive Capitalism* (Malden, MA: Wiley-Blackwell, 2008).
Heelas, Paul and Lock, Andrew (eds.), *Indigenous Psychologies: The Anthropology of the Self* (London: Academic Press, 1981).
Heidegger, M., *Being and Time*, trans. J. Macquarrie and E. Robinson (Oxford: Blackwell, 1962).
Heidegger, M., *The Basic Problems of Phenomenology*, trans. Albert Hofstadter (2nd edn, Bloomington and Indianapolis, IN: Indiana University Press, 1988).

Heidegger, Martin, *Phänomenologie des Religiösen Lebens: Gesamtausgabe*, vol. 60 (Frankfurt: V. Klostermann, 1995); trans. Matthias Fritsch and Jennifer Anna Gosetti-Ferecei as *The Phenomenology of Religious Life* (Bloomington and Indianapolis, IN: Indiana University Press, 2004).

Heidegger, Martin, *Contributions to Philosophy (Of the Event)*, trans. Richard Rojcewicz and Daniela Vallega-Neu (Bloomington and Indianapolis, IN: Indiana University Press, 2012).

Henry, Michel, *Phénoménologie de la vie*, vol. II: *De la subjectivité* (Paris: Presses Universitaires de France, 2003).

Hiltebeitel, Alf, *Dharma: Its History in Law, Religion and Narrative* (New York: Oxford University Press, 2011).

Hirsch, John, *The Boundaries of Faith: The Development and Transmission of Medieval Spirituality* (Leiden: Brill, 1996).

Hirst, Désirée, *Hidden Riches: Traditional Symbolism from the Renaissance to Blake* (London: Eyre and Spottiswoode, 1964).

Hollis, Martin, *Models of Man: Philosophical Thoughts on Social Action* (Cambridge, New York, Melbourne: Cambridge University Press, 1977).

Hollywood, Amy, *The Soul as Virgin Wife: Mechthild of Magdeburg, Margueritte Porete, and Meister Eckhardt* (Notre Dame, IN: University of Notre Dame Press, 1995).

Hookam, S. K., *The Buddha Within: Tathāgatagarbha Doctrine According to the Shentong Interpretation of the Ratnagotravibhāga* (Albany, NY: SUNY Press, 1991).

Hopkins, Gerard Manley, *Poems of Gerard Manley Hopkins* (London, New York, Toronto: Oxford University Press, 1948).

Hoskote, Ranjit, *I, Lalla: The Poems of Lal Ded* (New Delhi: Penguin Classics, 2011).

Houlbrook, Ralph, *Death, Religion and the Family in England 1480–1750* (Oxford: Clarendon Press, 1998).

Huizinga, J., *The Waning of the Middle Ages*, trans. F. Hopman (London: Penguin, 2001 (first published 1924)).

Hunt-Overzee, A., *The Body Divine: The Symbol of the Body in the Works of Teilhard de Chardin and Rāmānuja* (Cambridge, New York, Melbourne: Cambridge University Press, 1992).

Husserl, E., *Cartesian Mediations*, trans. Dorion Cairns (Dordrecht: Kluwer, 1950).

Husserl, E., *The Phenomenology of Internal Time Consciousness*, trans. James Churchill (Bloomington, IN and London: Indiana University Press, 1966).

Husserl, E., *Ideas Pertaining to a Pure Phenomenology and to a Phenomenological Philosophy*, trans. R. Rojcewicz and A. Scuwer (Dordrecht: Kluwer, 1989).

Inden, Ronald, *Imagining India* (Oxford: Blackwell, 1990).

Inden, Ronald, Walters, Jonathan, and Ali, Daud, *Querying the Medieval: Texts and the History of Practices in South Asia* (New York: Oxford University Press, 2000).

Ingalls, D. H. H., Masson, J. M., and Patwardhan, M. V. (trans.), *The Dhvanyāloka of Ānandavardhana, with the Locana of Abhinavagupta* (Cambridge, MA: Harvard University Press, 1990).

Jackson, Michael, *Existential Anthropology: Events, Exigencies and Effects* (Oxford: Berghahn, 2005).

Jameson, Fredric, *Valences of the Dialectic* (London and New York: Verso, 2009).

Janz, Paul D., *God, the Mind's Desire: Reference, Reason and Christian Thinking* (Cambridge and New York: Cambridge University Press, 2004).

Janzen, Grace, *Power, Gender and Christian Mysticism* (Cambridge: Cambridge University Press, 1995).

Javelet, Robert, *Image et Resemblance au Douzieme Siècle de Saint Anselme à Alain de Lile*, vol. 1 (Paris: Editions Letopuizey et Ané, 1967).

Jayatilleke, K.N., *Early Buddhist Theory of Knowledge* (London: Allen and Unwin, 1963).

Jensen, J. S., *The Study of Religion in a New Key: Theoretical and Philosophical Soundings in the Comparative and General Study of Religion* (Aarhus University Press, 2003).

Joby, Christopher, 'The Extent to which the Rise in the Worship of Images in the Late Middle Ages was Influenced by Contemporary Theories of Vision', *Scottish Journal of Theology*, 60/1 (2007), 36–44.

Johnson, M., *The Body in the Mind: The Bodily Basis of Meaning, Imagination, and Reason* (Chicago, IL: Chicago University Press, 1987).

Kierkegaard, Soren, *Works of Love*, ed. and trans. Howard V. Hong and Edna Hong (Princeton, NJ: Princeton University Press, 1995).

King, Richard, *Indian Philosophy* (Edinburgh: Edinburgh University Press, 1999).

King, Richard, *Orientalism and Religion: Postcolonial Theory, India and 'The Mystic East'* (London: Routledge, 1999).

Kisiel, Theodore, *Genesis of Heidegger's Being and Time* (Berkeley and Los Angeles, CA: University of California Press, 1993).

Kockelmans, Joseph J., *Edmund Husserl's Phenomenology* (West Lafayette: Purdue University Press, 1994).

Koselleck, Reinhart, *The Practice of Conceptual History: Timing History, Spacing Concepts*, trans. T. S. Presner et al. (Stanford, CA: Stanford University Press, 2002).

Koslofsky, Craig M., *Reformation of the Dead: Death and Ritual in Early Modern Germany 1450–1700* (New York: St Martin's Press, 2000).

Koyré, Alexander, *The Astronomical Revolution*, trans. R. E. W. Maddison (London and New York: Routledge, 2009 (first published 1973)).

Kreutzer, Thomas, 'Jenseits und Gesellschaft. Zur Soziologie der "Visio Edmundi Monachi de Eynsham"', in Thomas Ehlen, Johannes Mangei, and Elisabeth Stein (eds.), *Visio Edmundi monachi de Eynsham: Interdisziplinäre Studien zur mittelalterlichen Visionsliteratur* (Tübingen: Gunter Narr Verlag, 1998), pp. 39–58.

Kristeva, Julia, *Powers of Horror: An Essay on Abjection*, trans. Leon S. Roudiez (New York: Columbia University Press, 1982).

Kristeva, Julia, *Revolution in Poetic Language*, trans. Margaret Waller (New York: Columbia University Press, 1984).

Kristeva, Julia, *Black Sun: Depression and Melancholia*, trans. Leon S. Roudiez (New York and Chichester: Columbia University Press, 1989).

Lacrosse, Joachim (ed.), *Philosophie Comparée, Grèce, Inde, Chine* (Paris: Vrin, 2005).

Larson, G., *Classical Samkhya: An Interpretation of its History and Meaning* (Delhi: MLBD, 1969).

Laruelle, François, *Philosophie et non-philosophie* (Liège: Pierre Mardaga, 1989).

Lawrence, David, *Rediscovering God with Transcendental Argument* (Albany, NY: SUNY Press, 1999).

Le Goff, Jacques, *The Birth of Purgatory*, trans. A. Goldhammer (Chicago, IL: Chicago University Press, 1986).

Le Goff, Jacques, *Medieval Civilization 400–1500*, trans. Julia Barrow (Oxford: Blackwell, 1988).

Leinhardt, Godfrey, *Divinity and Experience: The Religion of the Dinka* (Oxford: Clarendon Press, 1987 (first published 1961)).

Lerner, Robert E., *The Heresy of the Free Spirit in the Later Middle Ages* (Berkeley and Los Angeles, CA: University of California Press, 1972).

Levinson, Stephen C., *Pragmatics* (Cambridge: Cambridge University Press, 1983).

Lewis, C. S., *The Discarded Image: An Introduction to Medieval and Renaissance Literature* (Cambridge: Cambridge University Press, 1964).

Limbeck, Sven, '"Turpitudo antique passionis"—Sodomie in mittelalterlicher Visionsliteratur', in Thomas Ehlen, Johannes Mangei, and Elisabeth Stein (eds.), *Visio Edmundi monachi de Eynsham: Interdisziplinäre Studien zur mittelalterlichen Visionsliteratur* (Tübingen: Gunter Narr Verlag, 1998), pp. 165–226.

Lindbeck, George, *The Nature of Doctrine: Religion and Theology in a Postliberal Age* (Westminster: John Knox Press, 1984).

Lindberg, C. *Theories of Vision from Al-Kindi to Kepler* (Chicago, IL: Chicago University Press, 1976).

Lingat, R., *The Classical Law of India*, trans. J. Duncan and M. Derrett (Berkeley and Los Angeles, CA: University of California Press, 1973).

Lipner, Julius, *Hindus, their Religious Beliefs and Practices* (2nd edn, London: Routledge, 2012).

Lovejoy, Arthur O., *The Great Chain of Being* (Cambridge, MA: Harvard University Press, 1936).

Lukes, Steven, *Individualism* (2nd edn, Colchester: ECPR Press, 2006).

Luscombe, D. E. and Evans, G. R., 'The Twelfth-Century Renaissance', in J. H. Burns (ed.), *The Cambridge History of Medieval Political Thought c.350–c.1450* (Cambridge, New York, Melbourne: Cambridge University Press, 1988), pp. 306–40.

Lyons, William E., *Approaches to Intentionality* (Oxford: Clarendon Press, 1995).

MacCulloch, Diarmaid, *A History of Christianity* (London: Penguin, 2009).

McCutcheon, Russell T., *Manufacturing Religion: The Discourse on Sui Generis Religion and the Politics of Nostalgia* (New York and Oxford: Oxford University Press, 1997).

McEwen, Cameron, 'On Formal Indication: Discussion of the Genesis of Heidegger's "Being and Time"', *Research in Phenomenology*, 25/1 (1995), 226–39.

Macfarlane, Alan, *The Origins of English Individualism: Family, Property and Social Transition* (Oxford: Blackwell, 1979).

McGinn, Bernard, *The Flowering of Mysticism: Men and Women in the New Mysticism, 1200–1350* (New York: Crossroad Publishing, 1998).

McGrath, S. J., *The Phenomenology of Early Heidegger* (Washington, DC: Catholic University of America Press, 2006).

Machan, Tibor M., *Classical Individualism: The Supreme Importance of Each Human Being* (London: Routledge, 1998).

MacIntyre, Alastair, *After Virtue: A Study of Moral Theory* (London: Duckworth, 1985).

MacIntyre, Alastair, *Whose Justice? Which Rationality?* (Notre Dame, IN: University of Notre Dame Press, 1988).

MacIntyre, Alastair, *Three Rival Versions of Moral Inquiry* (Notre Dame, IN: University of Notre Dame Press, 1990).

McMahon, Robert, *Understanding the Medieval Meditative Ascent: Augustine, Anselm, Boethius, and Dante* (Washington, DC: Catholic University of America Press, 2006).

Madan, T. N. et al. (eds.), 'On the Nature of Caste in India: A Review Symposium on Louis Dumont's *Homo Hierarchicus*', *Contributions to Indian Sociology*, 5/1 (1971), 1–81.

Makdisi, George, *The Rise of Humanism in Classical Islam and the Christian West: With Special Reference to Scholasticism* (Edinburgh: Edinburgh University Press, 1990).

Mandair, Arvind-Pal S., *Religion and the Specter of the West: Sikhism, India, Postcoloniality, and the Politics of Translation* (New York: Columbia University Press, 2009).

Marglin, F. A., *Wives of the God-King: The Rituals of the Devadasis of Puri* (Delhi: Oxford University Press, 1985).

Mascia-Lees, F. E. (ed.), *A Companion to the Anthropology of the Body* (London: John Wiley, 2011).

Masuzawa, T., *The Invention of World Religions or How European Universalism was Preserved in the Language of Pluralism* (Chicago, IL: Chicago University Press, 2005).

Matthews, Gareth B. (ed.), *Augustine on the Trinity*, Books 8–15 (Cambridge: Cambridge University Press, 2002).

Mauss, Marcel, 'A Category of the Human Mind: The Notion of Person; the Notion of Self', trans. W. D. Halls, in Michael Carrithers, Steven Collins, and Steven Lukes (eds.), *The Category of the Person: Anthropology, Philosophy, History* (Cambridge: Cambridge University Press, 1985), pp. 1–25. [French orig., Marcel Mauss, 'Une catégorie de l'esprit humain: La notion de personne celle de "moi"', in *Sociologie et anthropologie* (Paris: PUF, 1950), pp. 331–61.]

Mauss, M., 'Les techniques du corps', in *Sociologie et anthropologie* (Paris: PUF, 1950), pp. 363–86.

Mellor, P. A. and C. Shilling, *Re-forming the Body: Religion, Community and Modernity* (London: Sage, 1997).

Meredith, Fionola, 'A Post-Metaphysical Approach', in Pamela Sue Anderson and Beverley Clack (eds.), *Feminist Philosophy of Religion* (London: Routledge, 2004), pp. 54–72.

Merleau-Ponty, M., *The Phenomenology of Perception*, trans. Colin Smith (London: Routledge, 1962).

Merleau-Ponty, M., *Le visible et l'invisible* (Paris: Gallimard, 1964); trans. Alphonso Lingis as *The Visible and the Invisible* (Evanston: Northwestern University Press, 1968).

Metzger, M., *Les Sacramentaires* (Brepolis: Turnhout, 1994).

Milbank, John, *Theology and Social Theory* (Oxford: Blackwell, 1990).

Miller, Ian, 'Deep Inner Lives, Individualism and the People of Honour', *History of Political Thought*, 16/2 (1995), 190–207.

Milner Jr., Murray, *Status and Sacredness: A General Theory of Status Relations and an Analysis of Indian Culture* (New York: Oxford University Press, 1994).

Moore, R. I., *The Origins of European Dissent* (New York: St Martin's Press, 1977).

Moore, R. I., *The First European Revolution, c. 970–1215* (Oxford and Malden, MA: Blackwell, 2000).
Morris, Colin, *The Discovery of the Individual 1050–1200* (Cambridge, MA: Medieval Academy of America, 1972).
Morris, Colin, 'Individualism in Twelfth-Century Religion. Some Further Reflections', in *The Journal of Ecclesiastical History*, 31/2 (1980), 195–206.
Morris, Richard (ed.), *An Old English Miscellany* (London: Early English Text Society, 1872).
Morsella, Ezequiel, Bargh, John A., and Gollwitzer, Peter M. (eds.), *Oxford Handbook of Human Action* (New York: Oxford University Press, 2009).
Müller, Max, 'The Science of Religion: Lecture One (1870)', in Jon R. Stone (ed.), *The Essential Max Müller: On Language, Mythology and Religion* (New York: Palgrave Macmillan, 2002), pp. 109–21.
Murty, K. Satchidananda, *Ṣaḍ-darśana samuccaya: A Compendium of Six Philosophies* (2nd edn, Delhi: Eastern Book Linkers, 1986).
Nédoncelle, Maurice, 'Intériorité', *Dictionnaire de Spiritualité: Ascétique et mystique doctrine et histoire*, ed. M. Viller, F. Cavallera, and J. de Guibert (Paris: Beauchesne, 1971), vol. 7, 1,878–903.
Nelstrop, Louise with Magill, Kevin and Onishi, Bradley B., *Christian Mysticism: An Introduction to Contemporary Theoretical Approaches* (Aldershot: Ashgate, 2009).
Nemec, John, *The Ubiquitous Śiva: Somānanda's Śivadṛṣti and his Tantric Interlocutors* (New York: Oxford University Press, 2012).
Neville, Robert C. (ed.), *Religious Truth* (Albany, NY: SUNY Press, 2001).
Neville, Robert C., *The Human Condition* (Albany, NY: SUNY Press, 2001).
Neville, Robert C., *Ultimate Realities* (Albany, NY: SUNY Press, 2001).
Newhauser, Richard G., 'Peter of Limoges, Optics, and the Science of the Senses', *Senses and Society*, 5/1 (2010), 28–44.
Newman, Barbara, 'What did it Mean to Say "I Saw?" The Clash between Theory and Practice in Medieval Visionary Culture', *Speculum*, 80/1 (2005), 1–43.
Oakley, Francis, *Natural Law, Laws of Nature, Natural Rights: Continuity and Discontinuity in the History of Ideas* (London: Continuum, 2005).
Olivelle, Patrick (ed. and trans.), *The Early Upaniṣads* (New York and Oxford: Oxford University Press, 1998).
Olivelle, Patrick (trans.), *The Law Code of Manu* (New York: Oxford University Press, 2004).
Olson, Carl, *The Allure of Decadent Thinking: Religious Studies and the Challenge of Postmodernism* (New York and Oxford: Oxford University Press, 2013).
Osborne Jr., Thomas M., 'Unibilitas: The Key to Bonaventure's Understanding of Human Nature', *Journal of the History of Philosophy*, 37/2 (1999), 227–50.
Overfield, James H., *Humanism and Scholasticism in Late Medieval Germany* (Princeton, NJ: Princeton University Press, 1984).
Paden, William, 'Elements of a New Comparativism', in Kimberley C. Patton and Benjamin C. Ray (eds.), *A Magic Still Dwells: Comparative Religion in the Postmodern Age* (Berkeley, CA: California University Press, 2000), pp. 182–92.
Padoux, André, *Vāc*, trans. J. Gontier (Albany, NY: SUNY Press, 1990).
Padoux, André, *Comprendre le tantrisme: Les soures Hindous* (Paris: Albin Michel, 2010).
Palazzo, Éric, *Le Moyen Âge: Des origines au XIII siècle* (Paris: Beauchesne, 1993).

Palazzo, Éric, *Liturgie et société au Moyen Age* (Paris: Aubier, 2000).

Pandey, K. C., *Abhinavagupta: An Historical and Philosophical Study* (Varanasi: Chowkhamba Sanskrit Series, 1963 (first published 1936)).

Panofsky, E., *Abbot Suger on the Abbey Church of Saint Denis and its Art Treasures* (2nd edn, Princeton, NJ: Princeton University Press, 1979 (first published 1946)).

Parimoo, B. N., *The Ascent of the Self* (Delhi: MLBD, 1978).

Parkin, Robert, *Louis Dumont and Hierarchical Opposition* (New York and Oxford: Berghahn Books, 2002).

Parry, Jonathan, *Caste and Kinship in Kangra* (London: Routledge and Kegan Paul, 1979).

Parry, Jonathan, *Death in Banaras* (Cambridge, New York, Victoria: Cambridge University Press, 1994).

Patil, Parimal, 'A Hindu Theologian's Response', in Francis Clooney (ed.), *Hindu God, Christian God: How Reason Helps Break Down the Boundaries Between Religions* (New York: Oxford University Press, 2001), pp. 185–95.

Pattison, George, *Kierkegaard's Upbuilding Discourses: Philosophy, Theology, Literature* (London: Routledge, 2002).

Pattison, George, *The Philosophy of Kierkegaard* (Montreal and Kingston; Ithaca, NY: McGill Queens University Press, 2005).

Pattison, George, *God and Being: An Enquiry* (Oxford: Oxford University Press, 2012).

Patton, Kimberley C. and Ray, Benjamin C. (eds.), *A Magic Still Dwells: Comparative Religion in the Postmodern Age* (Berkeley, CA: California University Press, 2000).

Peirce, C., 'Prolegomena to An Apology for Pragmatism', 4.538, *The Monist*, 16/4 (1906), 492–546.

Pepin, Jean, 'La notion d'allegorie', in *Dante et la tradition d'allegorie* (Paris: Vrin, 1970), pp. 11–51.

Persson, Per Erik, *Sacra Doctrina: Reason and Revelation in Aquinas*, trans. Ross Mackenzie (Oxford: Basil Blackwell, 1970 (first published 1957)).

Polhemus, Ted (ed.), *Social Aspects of the Human Body: A Reader of Key Texts* (London: Penguin, 1978).

Pollock, S., *The Language of the Gods in the World of Men: Sanskrit, Culture and Power in Premodern India* (Chicago, IL: Chicago University Press, 2006).

Preus, J. S., *Explaining Religion: Criticism and Theory from Bodin to Freud* (Atlanta, GA: Scholars Press, 1996).

Quigley, D., *The Interpretation of Caste* (Oxford: Clarendon Press, 1993).

Raheja, Gloria, *The Poison in the Gift* (Chicago, IL: Chicago University Press, 1988).

Ram-Prasad, C., *Knowledge and Liberation in Classical Indian Thought* (London: Palgrave, 2001).

Ram-Prasad, C., *Advaita Epistemology and Metaphysics: An Outline of Indian Non-Realism* (London: Routledge-Curzon, 2002).

Ram-Prasad, C., *Indian Philosophy and the Consequences of Knowledge* (Aldershot: Ashgate, 2007).

Ram-Prasad, C., 'Finding God with—and Through—the Other', *Harvard Theological Review*, 105/2 (2012), 247–55.

Rappaport, Roy A., *Ecology, Meaning and Religion* (Berkeley, CA: North Atlantic Books, 1979).

Ratié, Isabelle, *Le soi et l'autre: Identité, difference et altérité dans la philosophie de la Pratyabhijñā* (Leiden: Brill, 2011).

Rawlinson, Andrew, 'Nāgas and the Magical Cosmology of Buddhism', *Religion*, 16/2 (1986), 135–52.

Rawlinson, Andrew, 'Visions and Symbols in the Mahāyāna', in P. Connolly (ed.), *Perspectives on Indian Religion: Papers in Honour of Karel Werner* (Delhi: Sri Satguru, 1986), pp. 191–214.

Reid, Charles J., *Power over the Body, Equity in the Family: Rights and Domestic Relations in Medieval Canon Law* (Grand Rapids, MI and Cambridge: Eerdmans, 2004).

Reinis, Austra, *Reforming the Art of Dying: The Ars Moriendi in the German Reformation (1519–1528)* (Aldershot: Ashgate, 2007).

Ricoeur, Paul, 'The Model of the Text: Meaningful Action Considered as a Text', in Ricoeur, *Hermeneutics and the Human Sciences*, trans. J. B. Thompson (Cambridge: Cambridge University Press, 1981), pp. 197–221.

Ricoeur, Paul, *Temps et récit*, tome 1: *L'intrique et le récit historique* (Paris: Seuil, 1983); trans. Kathleen McLaughlin and David Pellauer as *Time and Narrative*, vol. 1 (Chicago, IL: Chicago University Press, 1983).

Ricoeur, Paul, *Du texte à l'action: Essais d'herméneutique II* (Paris: Éditions du Seuil, 1986).

Ricoeur, Paul, *Temps et récit*, tome 3: *Le temps raconté* (Paris: Seuil, 1983); trans. Kathleen Blamey and David Pellauer as *Time and Narrative*, vol. 3 (Chicago, IL: Chicago University Press, 1988).

Ricoeur, Paul, *Oneself as Another*, trans. Kathleen Blamey (Chicago, IL: Chicago University Press, 1992).

Ricoeur, Paul, 'The Bible and the Imagination', in *Figuring the Sacred: Religion, Narrative and Imagination* (Mineapolis, MN: Fortress Press, 1995), pp. 144–66.

Ricoeur, Paul, *Memory, History, Forgetting*, trans. Kathleen Blamey and David Pellauer (Chicago, IL: Chicago University Press, 2004).

Ricoeur, Paul, 'Méthode et tâches d'une phenomenology de la volonté', in *A l'école de la phenomenologie* (Paris: Vrin, 2004 (first published 1986)), pp. 65–92.

Rilke, Rainer Maria, *Duino Elegies*, trans. J. B. Leishmann and Stephen Spender (London: Hogarth Press, 1939).

Rivera, Joseph M., 'Generation, Interiority and the Phenomenology of Christianity in Michel Henry', *Continental Philosophy Review*, 44/2 (2011), 205–35.

Robertson, A. W., *The Service Books of the Royal Abbey of Saint Denis: Images of Ritual and Music in the Middle Ages* (Oxford: Oxford University Press, 1991).

Robinson, Rowena, *Sociology of Religion in India* (New Delhi: Sage, 2004).

Rose, E., *Ritual Memory: The Apocryphal Acts and Liturgical Commemoration in the Early Medieval West (c. 500–1215)* (Leiden: Brill, 2009).

Rose, Gillian, *Hegel Contra Sociology* (London and New York: Verso, 2009 (first published 1981)).

Ruegg, D. S., *La Théorie du Tathāgatagarbha et du Gotra* (Paris: École Française d'Extrême Orient, 1969).

Salmón, Fernando, 'Medieval Theories of Vision in the Medical Classroom', *Endeavour*, 22/3 (1998), 125–8.

Sanderson, Alexis, 'Review of Lilian Silburn's *Śivasūtra et Vimarśinī de Kṣemarāja. (Études sur le Śivaïsme du Cachemire, École Spanda.) Traduction et introduction*, Publications de l'Institut de Civilisation Indienne 47, Paris, 1980.', *Bulletin of the School of Oriental and African Studies*, 46/1 (1983), pp. 160–1.

Sanderson, Alexis, 'Purity and Power Among the Brahmans of Kashmir', in M. Carrithers, S. Collins, and S. Lukes (eds.), *The Category of the Person: Anthropology, Philosophy, History* (Cambridge: Cambridge University Press, 1985), pp. 190–216.

Sanderson, Alexis, 'Maṇḍala and Āgamic Identity in the Trika of Kashmir', in André Padoux (ed.), *Mantras et Diagrammes Rituelles dans l'Hindouisme*, Équipe no. 249: L'Hindouisme: Textes, doctrines, pratiques (Paris: Éditions du Centre National de la Recherche Scientifique, 1986), pp. 169–214.

Sanderson, Alexis, 'Abhinavagupta', in Mircea Eliade (ed.), *The Encyclopedia of Religion* (New York: Macmillan, 1987), vol. 1, pp. 8–9.

Sanderson, Alexis, 'The Śaiva and Tantric Traditions', in F. Hardy et al. (eds.), *The World's Religions* (London: Routledge, 1988), pp. 190–216.

Sanderson, Alexis, 'The Visualisation of the Deities of the Trika', in A. Padoux (ed.), *L'image divine: Culte et méditation dans l'Hindouisme* (Paris: Éditions du Centre National de la Recherche Scientifique, 1990), pp. 31–88.

Sanderson, Alexis, 'The Doctrine of the *Mālinīvijayottaratantra*', in T. Goudriaan (ed.), *Ritual and Speculation in Early Tantrism: Studies in Honour of André Padoux* (Albany: SUNY Press, 1992), pp. 281–312.

Sanderson, Alexis, 'Meaning in Tantric Ritual', in Ann-Marie Blondeau and Kristopher Schipper (eds.), *Essais sur le rituel III* (Louvain, Paris: Peeters, 1995), pp. 15–95.

Sanderson, Alexis, 'Vajrayāna, Origin and Function', in *Buddhism into the Year 2000: International Conference Proceedings* (Bangkok and Los Angeles, CA: Dhammakāya Foundation, 1995), pp. 89–102.

Sanderson, Alexis, 'History Through Textual Criticism in the Study of Śaivism, the Pañcarātra and the Buddhist Yoginītantras', in François Grimal (ed.), *Les Sources et le temps. Sources and Time: A Colloquium, Pondicherry, 11–13 January 1997*, Publications du département d'Indologie 91. (Pondichéry: Institut Français de Pondichéry/École Française d'Extrême-Orient, 2001), pp. 1–47.

Sanderson, Alexis, 'The Śaiva Religion among the Khmers of Kashmir, Part 1', *Bulletin de l'Ecole française d'Extrême-Orient*, 90–1 (2003–4), pp. 349–463.

Sanderson, Alexis, 'A Commentary on the Opening Verses of the Tantrasāra of Abhinavagupta', in Ernst Fürlinger (ed.), *Sāmarasya: Studies in Indian Arts, Philosophy, and Interreligious Dialogue* (New Delhi: D. K. Printworld, 2005), pp. 89–147.

Sanderson, Alexis, 'Śaivism and Brahmanism in the Early Medieval Period', Gonda Lecture 2006 <http://www.alexissanderson.com/uploads/6/2/7/6/6276908/gondalecture2.pdf> (accessed 28 May 2013).

Sanderson, Alexis, 'The Śaiva Exegesis of Kashmir', in Dominic Goodall and André Padoux (eds.), *Mélanges tantriques à mémoire d'Hélène Brunner* (Pondichéry: Institut Français de Pondichéry, 2007), pp. 231–442.

Sanderson, Alexis, 'The Śaiva Age: The Rise and Dominance of Śaivism during the Early Medieval Period', in Shingo Einoo (ed.), *Genesis and Development of Tantrism* (Tokyo: Institute of Oriental Culture, 2009), pp. 41–350.

Schalow, Frank and Denker, Alfred, *Historical Dictionary of Heidegger's Philosophy* (Lanham, MD: Scarecrow Press, 2010).

Seagrave, S. Adam, 'How Old are Modern Rights? On the Lockean Roots of Contemporary Human Rights Discourse', *Journal of the History of Ideas*, 72/2 (April 2011), 305–27.

Searle-Chatterji, M. and Sharma, Urshula (eds.), *Contextualising Caste: Post-Dumontian Approaches* (New Delhi: Rawat, 2003).

Seigel, Jerrold, *The Idea of the Self: Thought and Experience in Western Europe Since the Seventeenth Century* (Cambridge and New York: Cambridge University Press, 2005).

Sharpe, Eric, *Comparative Religion: A History* (London: Duckworth, 1975).

Shaw, Sarah, *Buddhist Meditation* (London: Routledge, 2010).

Silburn, L., *Kuṇḍalinī: The Energy from the Depths*, trans. Jacques Gontier (Albany, NY: SUNY Press, 1990).

Singh, Sawan and Maharaj, Huzur, *Philosophy of the Masters* series 1, anonymous English trans. (Punjab, India: Radha Soami Satsang Beas, 1963).

Sjoholm, Cecelia, 'Crossing Lovers: Luce Irigaray's Elemental Passions', *Hypatia*, 15/3 (2000), 92–112.

Smart, Ninian, *Dimensions of the Sacred: An Anatomy of the World's Beliefs* (London: Harper Collins, 1996).

Smith, Frederick M., *The Self Possessed: Deity and Spirit Possession in South Asian Literature and Civilization* (New York and Chichester: Columbia University Press, 2006).

Smith, J. Z., 'In Comparison a Magic Dwells', in J. Z. Smith, *Imagining Religion: From Babylon to Jonestown* (Chicago, IL: University of Chicago Press, 1982), pp. 19–35.

Snellgrove, David, *Indo-Tibetan Buddhism: Indian Buddhists and Their Tibetan Successors* (London: Serindia Publications, 1987).

Southern, Richard W., *Medieval Humanism and Other Studies* (Oxford: Blackwell, 1970).

Spence, Sarah, *Texts and the Self in the Twelfth Century* (Cambridge, New York, Melbourne: Cambridge University Press, 1996).

Spijker, Ineke van, *Fictions of the Inner Life: Religious Literature and Formation of the Self in the Eleventh and Twelfth Centuries* (Turnhout: Brepols, 2004).

Steinbock, Anthony, *Home and Beyond: Generative Phenomenology After Husserl* (Evanston, IL: Northwestern University Press, 1995).

Steinbock, Anthony J., *Phenomenology and Mysticism: The Verticality of Religious Experience* (Bloomington, IN: Indiana University Press, 2007).

Stevens, Wallace, 'Re-statement of Romance', *Collected Poems* (London and Boston, MA: Faber and Faber, 1954).

Stone, Jon R. (ed.), *The Essential Max Müller: On Language, Mythology and Religion* (New York: Palgrave Macmillan, 2002).

Strauss, Leo, *Natural Right and History* (Chicago, IL: University of Chicago Press, 1953).

Stroumsa, Guy, *A New Science: The Discovery of Religion in the Age of Reason* (Cambridge, MA: Harvard University Press, 2010).

Suarez-Nani, Tiziana, *Les anges et la philosophie: Subjectivité et fonction cosmologique des substances séparées au XIIIe siècle* (Paris: Vrin, 2002).

Suarez-Nani, Tiziana, *Connaissance et langage des anges selon Thomas d'Aquin et Gilles de Rome* (Paris: Vrin, 2003).

Suarez-Nani, Tiziana, 'Pierre de Jean Olivi et la subjectivité angélique', *Archives d'histoire doctrinale et littéraire du Moyen Âge*, 2003/1 (Tome 70), pp. 233–316.

Suzuki, D. T., *Essays in Zen Buddhism*, vol. 3 (London: Rider, 1953).

Swanson, R. F., *The Twelfth Century Renaissance* (Manchester: Manchester University Press, 1999).

Synor, J. P., *Ramanuja and Schliermacher: Toward a Constructive Comparative Theology* (Cambridge: James Clarke and Co., 2012).

Taylor, Charles, *Sources of the Self* (Cambridge and New York: Cambridge University Press, 1989).

Taylor, Charles, *The Secular Age* (Cambridge, MA: The Belknap Press of Harvard University, 2007).

Taylor, Charles, 'What is Secularity?', in Kevin Vanhoover and Martin Warner (eds.), *Transcending Boundaries in Philosophy and Theology* (Aldershot: Ashgate, 2007), pp. 57–76.

Thapar, Romila, *Interpreting Early India* (Delhi: Oxford University Press, 1993).

Thompson, Kevin, 'Forms of Resistance: Foucault on Tactical Reversal and Self-Formation', *Continental Philosophy Review*, 36/2 (2003), 113–38.

Throop, J. C. 'Minding Experience: An Exploration of the Concept of "Experience" in the Early French Anthropology of Durkheim, Lévy-Bruhl, and Lévi-Strauss', *Journal of the History of the Behavioural Sciences*, 39/4 (2003), 365–82.

Tierney, Brian, *The Idea of Natural Rights: Studies on Natural Rights, Natural Law and Church Law 1150–1625* (Atlanta, GA: Scholars Press, 1997).

Tierney, Brian, 'Natural Law and Natural Rights: Old Problems and Recent Approaches', *The Review of Politics*, 64/3 (2002), 389–406.

Tierney, Brian, 'Historical Roots of Modern Rights: Before Locke and After', *Ave Maria Law Review*, 3/1 (2005): 23–43, 25.

Tollefsen, Torstein Theodor, *Activity and Participation in Late Antique and Early Christian Thought* (Oxford and New York: Oxford University Press, 2012).

Tripathi, C. Lal, *The Problem of Knowledge in Yogacara Buddhism* (Varanasi: Bharat-Bharati, 1972).

Turner, Brian, 'The Body in Western Society: Social Theory and its Perspectives', in Sarah Coakley (ed.), *Religion and the Body* (Cambridge: Cambridge University Press, 1997), pp. 15–41.

Turner, Brian, 'What is the Sociology of the Body?', *Body and Society*, 3/1 (1997), pp. 103–7.

Turner, Denys, *The Darkness of God: Negativity in Christian Mysticism* (Cambridge: Cambridge University Press, 1995).

Ullman, Walter, *Individual and Society in the Middle Ages* (London: Methuen, 1967).

Ullman, Walter, *Medieval Foundations of Renaissance Humanism* (London: Elek, 1977).

Urban, Greg, 'The I of Discourse', in Benjamin Lee and Greg Urban (eds.), *Semiotics, Self and Society* (Berlin and New York: Mouton de Gruyter, 1989), pp. 27–51.

Vasquez, Manuel A., *More than Belief: A Materialist Theory of Religion* (Oxford and New York: Oxford University Press, 2011).

Vasudeva, Somadeva, *The Yoga of the Mālinīvijayottara-tantra* (Pondichéry: École Française d'Extrême-Orient, 2004).

Villey, Michel, *La formation de la pensée juridique moderne: Cours d'histoire de la philosophie du droit* (4th edn, Paris: Montchrestien, 1975).

Vogel, C., *Medieval Liturgy: An Introduction to the Sources*, trans. W. G. Storey and N. K. Rasmussen (Washington, DC: Pastoral Press, 1986).

Vološinov, V. N., *Marxism and the Philosophy of Language*, trans. L. Matejka and I. R. Titunik (Cambridge, MA: Harvard University Press, 1973).

Vos, Antonie, *The Philosophy of John Duns Scotus* (Edinburgh: Edinburgh University Press, 2006).

Vovelle, Michel, *La mort et l'Occident de 1300 à nos jours* (Paris: Gallimard, 2001 (first published 1983)).

Vries, Hent de, *Philosophy and the Turn to Religion* (Baltimore, MD and London: Johns Hopkins University Press, 1999).

Wade Giles, *Travels of Fa-hsien (399–414 AD) or Record of the Buddhist Kingdoms* (Cambridge: Cambridge University Press, 1923).

Wallace, Vesna, *The Inner Kalacakratantra: A Buddhist Tantric View of the Individual* (New York: Oxford University Press, 2001).

Wallace, Vesna, *Kālacakra Tantra, The Chapter on Sādhanā, Together with the Vimalaprabhā Commentary: A Study and Annotated Translation* (New York: American Institute of Buddhist Studies, 2010).

Wallis, Christopher, 'The Descent of Power: Possession, Mysticism, and Initiation in the Śaiva Theology of Abhinavagupta', *Journal of Indian Philosophy*, 36/2 (2008), pp. 247–95.

Warder, A. K., *Indian Buddhism* (Delhi: MLBD, 1970), p. 83.

Webb, D., *Medieval European Pilgrimage, c.700–c.1500* (Basingstoke: Ashgate, 2002).

Welton, Donn, *The Other Husserl: The Horizons of Transcendental Phenomenology* (Bloomington and Indianapolis, IN: Indiana University Press, 2000).

White, David, *The Kiss of the Yoginī: Tantric Sex in its South Asian Contexts* (Chicago, IL: Chicago University Press, 2003).

Wiebe, Donald, *The Politics of Religious Studies* (New York: St Martin's Press, 1999).

Wiercinski, Andrzej (ed.), *Between Description and Interpretation: The Hermeneutic Turn in Phenomenology* (Toronto: Hermeneutic Press, 2005).

Wierzbicka, A., *Semantics: Primes and Universals* (Oxford and New York: Oxford University Press, 1996).

Williams, Paul, *Mahāyāna Buddhism: The Doctrinal Foundations* (2nd edn, London: Routledge, 2009).

Williams, Rowan, *Lost Icons: Reflections on Cultural Bereavement* (Edinburgh: T. and T. Clark, 2000).

Williams, Rowan, *Dostoyevsky: Language, Faith and Fiction* (London and New York: Continuum, 2008).

Wilmart, Dom A., *Auteurs Spirituels et textes dévots du Moyen Age latin* (Paris: Librarie Bloud et Gay, 1932).

Witzel, E. J. Michael, *The Origins of the World's Mythologies* (New York: Oxford University Press, 2012).

Yates, Frances, *Giordano Bruno and the Hermetic Tradition* (London: Routledge, 2002 (first published 1964)).

Zaehner, R. C., *Our Savage God* (London: Collins, 1974).

Zahavi, Dan, *Subjectivity and Selfhood: Investigating the First Person Perspective* (Cambridge, MA: MIT, 2005).
Zaner, Richard M., *The Problem of Embodiment: Some Contributions to a Phenomenology of the Body* (The Hague: Nijhoff, 1971).

Online References

Casati, Roberto and Varzi, Achille, 'Events', *The Stanford Encyclopedia of Philosophy* (Spring 2010 edition), ed. Edward N. Zalta, <http://plato.stanford.edu/archives/spr2010/entries/events/>.
Casati, Roberto and Varzi, Achille (eds.), *50 Years of Events: An Annotated Bibliography 1947 to 1997*, Philosophy Documentation Center, <http://www.pdcnet.org/pages/Products/electronic/events.htm>.
Davies, Oliver, 'Transformation Theology in its Historical Context', Transformation Theology, <http://www.transformationtheology.com/tt-in-its-historical-context.html>.
Milbank, John, *Against Human Rights* [document], Centre for Philosophy and Theology, University of Nottingham, <http://www.theologyphilosophycentre.co.uk/papers/Milbank_AgainstHumanRights.pdf>.
Simmel, Georg, 'Individualism', *Theory, Culture and Society*, 24/7–8 (2007), 66–71. Also in Klaus Latzel (ed.), *Georg Simmel Gesamtausgabe*, vol. 13, trans. Austin Harrington (Frankfurt: Suhrkamp, 2000), pp. 299–306. Online version at: <http://tcs.sagepub.com/content/24/7-8/66.citation>.

Index

Abelard, Peter 36, 38
Abhidharma 173
Abhinavagupta 18, 118, 130, 141–66, 181, 194–9, 201, 216, 220, 232, 240, 244, 264
abjection 14, 219, 220
act theory 192, 256, 262–7
action 9, 20, 48, 92, 103, 111, 140, 144, 154, 155, 161, 183, 199, 200, 208, 213, 218, 239, 243, 247, 262, 264, 266; speech act 266
Adams, M. 48
Adams, Nick 254n23
agency 13, 132
  supernatural 69
Aghoraśiva 123, 140, 141
Akbari, S.C. 94n85
ālayavijñāna 180
alchemy 99
alienation 8, 70, 89, 93, 191, 216, 222
allegory 83, 90
Allen, Nick 203
Amitābha 176, 177, 179
Ānandavardhana 141
Anderson, Pamela 234, 235
angel/s 6–7, 29, 43, 44, 46, 58, 59, 60, 67, 76, 78, 79, 94, 197, 210; wicked angel 50
Angenendt, A. 43n49, 45n58
Annales School 20
annunciation 43
Anselm 35, 70
antarātman 4, 23, 28, 103, 114, 119, 200–1, 211
Anthropology 19
Apocalypse of Paul 54
Apulius 42
Aquinas, Thomas 32, 35, 43, 44, 47, 48, 70, 71–2, 78, 81
architecture 48
Ariès, P. 52n83
Aristotle 32, 71, 72, 93
Aristotelianism 74
Ars Moriendi 31, 52, 53
artha 106
Aryadeva 181
Asad, Talal 22n39, 251
asceticism 4, 7, 10, 14, 23, 24, 30, 34, 40, 46, 64, 69, 112, 168, 205, 210, 214, 233, 242, 267
Asia 168; South Asia 6, 12, 14, 24, 27, 28, 106, 108, 110, 164, 165, 213–14, 269; South-East Asia 170
Aśoka 113
ātmā/ātman 103, 147, 164, 182
Atkins, J.W.H. 33n9
atonement 79
Augustine 18, 36, 44, 70, 74, 84–5, 93, 97, 227
authority 28, 73, 89, 141
autonomy 40, 98, 128, 157, 207
axial age 12, 268

Bacon, Roger 98, 165
Badiou, Alain 14, 192, 264, 265
Bakhtin, M.M. 15n21, 191
Baldwin, J.W. 33n9
Balibar, E. 214n34
Bamford, N. 255n24
Bansat-Boudon, L. 115n42
Barnes, Dick 71n2, 88n66
Barnett, L.D. 212n32
Bayly, C. 107n8
Bayly, S. 107n8
beatitude 75
Beatrice of Nazareth 38
Beaty, N.L. 53n84
Bede 54
Beguines 54, 62, 212
being 16, 76, 181, 229, 259; hierarchy of being 44, 59, 79, 111, 171; meaning of being 11, 257; philosophy of being 99; scale of being 43
belief 63
Bellah, Robert 13n15, 268n46
Benson, R.L. 34n13
Benton, John 38, 39
Bernard of Clairvaux 73, 81, 97
Bhagavad Gītā 114, 115
Bhairava 117, 124, 128, 130, 133, 156, 161, 244
bhakti 114, 116, 132
Bharati, A. 186n49
Bhaṭṭanārāyaṇa 115
Bhaṭṭarāmakaṇṭha 140
Bhojadeva 140
Bible 82, 201
Binski, Paul 53n84
Birch, Jason 131n86
Blacking, John 19n30

Blake, William 100
Bock, Nico den 86n56
bodhicitta 175, 179, 180
body 4, 9, 19, 24, 30, 48, 50, 53, 54, 59, 60, 62, 65, 67, 72, 77, 78, 84, 93, 98, 100, 109, 110, 112, 114, 118, 120, 125, 128, 130, 131, 132, 136, 140, 149, 150, 151, 152, 162, 163, 169, 170, 171, 183, 185, 201, 109, 134, 135, 239, 243, 261; purification of the body 119, 125, 199; soul and body 77–9; subtle body 162; techniques of the body 208
Boehme, Jacob 83, 100
Boethius 78, 92
Bologar, R.R. 33nn9, 10
Bonaventure 46, 70, 71, 72–83, 84, 85, 86, 94, 95, 96, 97, 98, 194, 195, 196, 197, 198, 199, 200, 216, 217, 220, 232, 240, 244
Bornemark, J. 247n1
Borst, A. 45n57
Bowker, John 257, 267
Brahman 113
Brahmans 115–16
breath 131, 162, 163, 170, 173, 183
breathing 169, 171
Bṛhadāranyaka Upaniṣad 112, 164
Bronkhorst, Johannes 139n1, 168n2
Brooke, C.N.I. 34n15
Brown, Bill 262n36
Brown, Norman 100n107
Brown, Peter 32n7
Brunner, H. 121n60, 163n67
Bruno, Giordanno 99, 96
Buddha 2, 167, 168, 170, 171, 172, 173, 174, 175, 176, 177, 179, 180, 181, 182, 184, 186, 190, 195, 213, 264, 265, 268; dhyāni Buddhas/jinas 183–5
Buddhahood 2, 186, 199
Buddhism 2, 3, 4, 12, 24, 25, 40, 104, 105, 111, 116, 118, 140, 142, 160, 166, 167–90, 193, 195, 200, 209, 220, 261, 267, 268, 271; Hīnayāna/Theravāda/Nikāya Buddhism 168, 173, 175, 176186, 190; Mahāyāna 119, 167, 168, 173, 175, 176, 179, 180, 186, 188, 190, 195; Vajrayāna/ tantric 119, 175, 182–5, 187, 188, 190
Bunyan, John 65, 240
Burch, M. 16
Burghardt, Jacob 38
Bynum, Caroline Walker 39

Cabezon, J. 71n3
Cambridge 71
Campanella, T. 96
Caṇḍamahārośana-tantra 187
capitalism 268
Capps, Walter 247n1
care 219
Cargonja, H. 19n30
Carlisle, C. 218n47
Carman, John 107n9
Carmelites 98
Carozzi, Claude 53
Carruthers, Mary 92
Casati, R. 265
Cassiodorus 203
caste 106, 108, 116
Catholicism 21, 98
causation/causality 16, 149, 153, 198, 249
celibacy 186
Certeau, Michel de 30, 36n22, 45n55, 81n38, 82, 99, 100n106, 202n12
Chalmers, David J. 225, 233
Chāndogya-upaniṣad 113, 164
charity 49, 50, 66
Charlemagne 30
Châtillon, Jean 89n73
Chenu, M.D. 59n102, 63n110, 86, 93
Chidester, D. 22n38, 251
China 176, 203, 204, 205
Chinese 213
Christ, Jesus 30, 44, 45, 46, 49, 51, 52, 53, 58, 59–60, 65, 66, 67, 74, 79, 80, 86, 196, 197, 199, 200, 201, 202, 268; Cosmic Christ 64
Christianity 1, 2, 4, 5, 7, 8, 12, 24, 25, 27, 29, 33, 34, 42, 43, 46, 99, 135, 191, 193, 200, 202, 203, 204, 209, 210, 211, 217, 219, 220, 251, 252, 253, 256, 261, 267, 268, 271
Church 30, 34, 36, 39, 40, 43, 46, 47, 49, 56, 64, 70, 79, 95, 96, 99, 100, 213; Church expectant, triumphant and militant 45
Citeaux 65
citizen 38, 69, 70, 202
Clement of Alexandria 74
Clooney, Francis 22–3, 71n3, 132, 135, 139n1, 254–25
Cloud of Unknowing, The 49, 83, 95
Cluny 34, 65
Coakley, Sarah 19n30
cognition 70, 128, 145, 146, 154, 155, 158, 159, 160, 161, 162, 164, 165
Colas, G. 118n56
colonialism 21, 22, 108, 165, 202; post-colonialism 251–2, 253
communism 8
comparative religion 11, 20–2, 27, 192, 247, 249–53; comparative religion and phenomenology 256–62
compassion 3, 20, 21–4, 40, 175, 186, 188
Compte, Auguste 13
confession 66

conformity 40, 46, 66, 70
Confucius 268
conscience 63–6, 98, 189, 202, 203, 217, 218
consciousness 10, 13, 98, 114, 118, 124, 131, 144, 154, 155, 156, 157, 158, 161, 162, 168, 171, 174, 176, 192, 195, 201, 203, 210, 216, 224–9, 230, 231, 238, 241, 257, 258, 266; absolute consciousness 128, 129, 130, 140–1, 143; consciousness only 180, 190; intentional 225, 233; phenomenal and psychological 225, 233; philosophy of consciousness 10, 14, 99, 191, 264
Constable, G. 34n13
constructivism 8
contemplation 39, 40, 46, 55, 64, 69, 70, 79, 80, 83, 86, 87, 88, 89, 91, 93, 97, 127, 133, 135, 136, 194, 197
Contemplations of the Dread Love of God 49–51, 198
conversion 21
Copernicus 96
Copleston, F. 71n5, 207n26
cosmical hierarchy 122, 143
cosmology 8, 10, 28, 30, 42–5, 53, 60, 62, 63, 64, 69, 96, 98, 99, 101, 153, 168, 179, 183, 194, 218, 232; cosmology and morality 189
cosmos 12, 24, 28, 29, 36, 42–5, 46, 47, 51, 63, 64, 70, 75, 78, 82, 91, 95, 96, 99, 100, 101, 111, 120, 128, 136, 140, 143, 144, 152, 153, 156, 158, 162, 166, 169, 171, 174, 183, 184, 185, 188, 194, 199, 201, 205, 206, 214, 216, 220
Cousins, Ewart 73n8
Cousins, Lance 168n2
Cox, C. 171n10, 247n1
craft of dying, *see* Ars Moriendi
Crane, Hart 100
Critchley, Simon 138n2
critical theory 250
Crowe, S. 15
Csordas, T.J. 192
Cudworth, Ralph 98
Cullen, C.M. 79n32, 82n43
cult of relics 36
culture 5, 11, 13, 19, 20, 40, 104, 132, 135, 194, 208, 209, 224, 225, 234, 235, 239, 242, 243, 244, 259; cultural identity 29; literary culture 113, 114
curiosity 82, 87, 85
Cushing, K.G. 33n8

D'Alverny, M.T. 59n102
D'Avray, D.L. 22n37, 53n86, 54nn88, 90
Dahlstrom, D. 17n26
Damian, Peter 49
Dante 44, 53, 62, 71, 210
Dārā Shukoh 165
Dasein 16, 226, 229–30, 239, 257
Dasgupta, S.N. 184n46
Davidson, R. 182n39
Davies, Oliver 11n14, 44n54, 95, 254, 262
Davis, R. 121n60, 163n67
death 5, 24, 35, 52, 63, 64, 65, 66, 72, 74, 75, 96, 110, 143, 168, 174, 187, 189, 209, 224, 240, 266, 272; mindfulness of death 171; training for death 210
Dee, John 99
deixis 223
democracy 69
demons 46, 56, 65, 67, 110
Denker, A. 16–17
Denys the Carthusian 97
Denys, Pseudo- 36, 43, 44, 73–4, 80, 82, 95, 97
Derrida, J. 3
Descartes, R. 13, 98, 165, 191, 214, 215, 227
description 257, 258–60
desire/s 24, 42, 50, 60, 72, 78, 85, 151, 172, 198, 206, 213, 218, 219, 271, 272
detachment 115, 129, 169, 210, 264
Detienne, Marcel 268n47
Devil, the 45, 100
devotion 36, 51, 95, 104
Dezso, Csaba 115n43
dharma 106, 113, 114, 140, 171, 205
Dharmakīrti 139
dhyāna 120, 160; Buddhist *dhyāna*/*jhāna* 119, 167, 168, 172–4, 176, 177, 188
dignity 79
Dimock, E. 113n38
Dinzelbacher, Peter 52n79
Dionysius the Pseudo Areopagite, *see* Denys, Pseudo-
Dirks, N. 107n6
discourse 6, 194, 196, 209
disgust 187
divine darkness 80
Dombart, B. 85n54
Dominicans 66
Doniger, Wendy 111n28, 257n26
Dosse, F. 20n34
Douie, Decima L. 55n94
Dravid, R.R. 150n29
dream 93
Dronke, Peter 38, 94n88
Dryhthelm, Visions of 54
dualism 85
Duby, G. 34n12, 36n21
Duffy, E. 35n19, 52n83
Dulles, A. 64n111

Dumont, Louis 38n28, 106–9, 115, 134, 192, 194, 202, 204–5, 206, 268
Duns Scotus 97, 207–8
Durkheim, Emile 13, 192, 202, 248
Dyczkowski, Mark 142n11

East–West schism 32
Easting, Robert 53n86
Ebner, Joseph 88n65, 89n68, 92n80
Eckhart, Meister 2, 70, 213
ecstasy 74, 80, 81, 82, 89, 91
eden 45
Edmund Leversedge 60–1, 63
Edmund monk of Eynsham 54–60, 64, 200, 202, 208, 232, 240, 243, 245, 264
Eire, C.M.N. 53n84
Eliade, Mircea 250
Eliot, J.H. 268n47
Elvin, Mark 204
Ely 54
emanationism 44, 134
emotions 113
empathy 17, 18, 232
empiricism 96, 216
emptiness 133, 134, 149, 176, 179, 182, 185, 186, 188, 189, 190
enlightenment 153, 156, 157, 159, 160, 164, 167, 168, 171, 174, 183, 184, 186, 187, 188, 189, 190, 198, 201, 240, 264, 265
Enlightenment, the 21, 34, 214, 248
Epicureans 210
epoché 17, 133, 227, 228, 249, 258
Er, myth of 54
eschatology 66
essence 72, 80, 129, 150, 159, 197, 227
Eucharist 35, 47, 48
Europe 6, 14, 24, 28, 40, 64, 71, 106, 165, 166, 194, 198, 205, 212, 213, 240, 242
Evagrius 43
Evans, G.R. 34n13
event 20, 51, 245, 262, 263, 264, 265
evil 85, 272
exegesis 70
exessus mentis 80, 81, 89, 93
existence 72, 217, 218, 219, 230, 234, 235, 239
existentialism 216
experience 2, 3, 8, 24, 57, 69, 70, 73, 80, 82, 97, 99, 114, 118, 133, 134, 135, 137, 144–7, 152, 160, 190, 196, 198, 212, 215, 217, 225, 227, 233, 234, 240, 241, 243, 245, 249, 259, 264; communal experience 40; flow of experience 149–54; mystical experience 46, 60, 141; religious experience 9, 36, 154, 244, 250; somatic experience 244, 245
expressivism 100
exteriority 76
extramission 93–4

face-to-face, the 222
Fa-hsien 108
faith 29, 65, 66, 72, 86, 95, 99, 217, 219
Faivre, A. 99n104
Fall, The 45, 66, 75, 86, 264
Falque, E. 83nn45, 46
Farmer, Dom H. 55n94
fasting 4, 39, 208
Faure, B. 167n1
Ferreira, Jamie 218nn45, 46
feudal system 34
Fichte, J.G. 203
Ficino, Marsilio 96, 99
fiction 239
Fitzgerald, T. 22n39, 251
Fitzpatrick, P.J. 47n63, 48n64
Fletcher, R. 34n13
Flood, Gavin 11n13, 109n19, 116n44, 243n56
Fludd, R. 96, 99
Ford, David 254
formal indication 15–18, 136, 202, 208, 232, 257
Foucault, M. 13, 213
France 33, 100
Francis, St. 73, 74, 80
Frank, Manfred 14
Frankfurt School 191
Frazier, Jessica 255n24
Free Spirit 46
freedom 148, 150, 153, 156, 158, 199, 263
Freeman, Rich 109n20, 110n24
Frei, Hans 253n18
Freud, S. 14, 191, 216, 218, 259
Frome 61, 62

Galileo Galilei 96
Gallus, Thomas 97
Ganeri, Jonardon 113, 165
Ganeri, R.M. 254n24
Gauchet, Marcel 98
Gellner, David 251
gender 62, 110, 219
Geoffrey of Monmouth 42
Gershheimer, G. 140n3
Gichtel, J.G. 100
Giles, C. 30n4
Giles, Wade 108n13
Giraud, C. 92n77
globalization 194, 252
God 2, 3, 4, 30, 31, 35, 39, 42, 43, 44, 45, 46, 48, 49, 50, 51, 58, 60, 64, 65, 67, 70, 71, 72, 73, 74, 75, 76, 77, 79, 80, 81, 82, 83, 84, 85,

86, 87, 89, 91, 92, 93, 94, 98, 99, 100, 103, 113, 114, 129, 139, 144, 165, 167, 188, 195, 196, 199, 201, 209, 217, 218, 219, 243, 264; death of God 223
Goddess 115, 116, 118, 125, 129, 155, 160, 162
Goff, J. Le 43n51, 45n56
Golding, William 29, 56, 67
Gombrich, R. 115n41, 168n4
good, human 21; good versus evil 41; higher good 134, 139; highest good 143
Goodall, Dominic 120, 123, 158n51
Goodrick-Clarke, N. 99n104
grace 30, 43, 48, 49, 65, 78, 80, 81, 83, 86, 89, 96, 100, 195, 220
grammar 92
Grant, E. 34n15, 96n94
Greek 213
Greetham, D.C. 259n32
Gregory of Nyssa 110
Gregory, Saint 50
Gregory of Tours 54
Grierson, G. 212n32
Gron, Arne 16n22
Guenther, H.V. 170, 173nn11, 13
Guhyasamāja-tantra 173, 243
Guillaumont, A. 43n51
Gupta, D. 107n8
Gurevish, A. 38n28
guru 117
Guyon, Madame 100

Habermas, Jürgen 14
habit 171, 217
habitus 9, 72, 85, 90, 91, 92, 135, 208–9, 233, 271
Hadot, P. 141, 210
haecicity 97
Hanegraaf, W. 99n104
Hannay, A. 217nn39, 42
Hanning, Robert W. 38
Hardy, Dan 254
Hardy, F. 110
Harmless, W. 82
Harrison, P. 175, 177
Hart, Kevin 235n38
Hausner, Sondra 112n30, 134n90, 251
heart 103, 104, 113, 120, 121, 125, 127, 131, 195, 243; purity of heart 218
heaven 53, 55, 58, 59, 60, 64, 66, 78, 81, 92, 197
Hebrew 213
Heelas, Paul 24n42, 109n19
Hegel, G. 191, 249, 250, 252
Heidegger, Martin 13, 15, 16, 17, 18, 19, 207n25, 208, 226, 229–31, 232, 238, 239, 257, 260, 264, 266n43
Heidelberg School 248
hell 52, 53, 55
Hemacandra 114
Henrich, Dieter 14
Henry, Michel 235n38
Henry of Sawtry 54
Hercules 53
heresy 70
hermeneutics 11, 18, 254
Hermes Trismegistus 99
Hertz, R. 192
Hevajra-tantra 187
hierarchy 43, 76, 79, 196, 198; cosmic hierarchy 44; ecclesiastical hierarchy 36; interiorized hierarchy 74
Hildegard of Bingen 211
Hiltebeitel, Alf 168n5, 171n10
Hinduism 3, 4, 5, 12, 24, 25, 33, 103, 104, 112–19, 185, 193, 209, 220, 255, 256, 261, 267, 268, 271
Hirsch, John 49n71
Hirst, D. 99n104
historiography 10, 45, 211
history 2, 8, 11, 12, 13, 15–21, 23, 28, 30, 45, 67, 103, 108, 136, 191, 192, 193, 202, 208, 211, 213, 214, 224, 226, 239, 241, 242, 248, 251, 253, 257, 262, 264, 266–76, 271; cultural history 6; comparative history 121, 122; global history 267–8; macro history 5, 20, 247
Hobbes, T. 41, 69
Hollis, Martin 109n19
Hollywood, Amy 62n108
holy spirit 65
homo interior 4, 23, 35, 39, 86, 200, 211, 217, 233, 234
homosexuality 56
Hookham, S.K. 179n28
Hopkins, G.M. 1, 4, 6, 272
Houlbrook, R. 53n84
Hugh of St Victor 48, 85, 91, 92, 97
Huizinga, J. 40n42, 53n84
human nature 6, 48, 215, 252, 261; human condition 136, 233, 261
humanity 40, 43, 44, 246
Hume, David 216
Hunt-Overzee, A. 255n24
Husserl, E. 11, 15, 17, 133, 191, 226–9, 233, 236, 237, 238, 241, 245, 249, 256, 258, 260

I, the 2, 16, 17, 18, 19, 20, 151, 170, 171, 189, 193–4, 195, 196, 199–202, 214, 222, 228–9, 232, 234, 236, 242; I-consciousness 151–53; indexical I 259; I-ness 143; Ichlikchkeit 18
idealism 12, 142, 229

ideology 13, 136, 220, 263, 264
Ignatius Loyola 49
ignorance 155, 196
image 75, 76, 77, 79, 82, 119, 121, 127, 129, 133, 157, 179
imagination 31, 32, 50, 51, 53, 73, 75, 77, 83, 87, 89, 90, 91, 92, 94, 105, 118, 120, 125, 127, 132–3, 137, 187, 188, 209, 210, 214, 222, 239, 257, 262, 263; collective imagination 70, 192, 198; corporate imagination 1, 194, 210
Inden, R. 108n11, 112n31
indexicals 16, 17; indexicality 81, 82, 83, 192, 199, 200, 207
India 21, 39, 45, 94, 104, 106, 139, 194, 198, 202, 203, 204, 205, 210, 212, 242; intellectual history of India 164–5
individual 2, 8, 37–42, 46, 105, 106, 111, 134, 183, 185, 204, 205, 217, 218
individualism 2, 4, 6, 7, 8, 24, 28, 37–42, 101, 133, 134, 193, 194, 202–6, 207, 210, 214, 215, 216, 218, 271; as a value 205
individuality 7, 30, 39, 40, 42, 51, 66, 69, 106, 112, 132, 174, 193, 194, 206–8
Ingalls, D.H.H. 141n7
initiation 109, 116, 117, 184, 186
inner flight 4
inner man, *see homo interior*
inner self, *see antarātman*
intellect 72, 77, 91, 92, 100
intelligence 78, 90, 91
intentionality 157, 225, 226, 227, 229–30, 236, 238, 239, 241, 257, 260, 265, 266
interiority 6, 8, 12, 13, 19, 23, 70 *passim*
intromission 93–4
invisible, the 16
inwardness 1, 3, 4, 5, 6, 8 *passim*; as metaphor 3; as mystical ascent 69–101; bare inwardness 169–72; cosmological inwardness 42–5, 96; ritual and inwardness 46–63, 127–31; romantic inwardness 97, 100; time and inwardness 236, 237
Irigaray, L. 216
Iśānaśivagurudeva-paddhati 110, 121, 123
Islam 71, 165
Israel 87

Jackson, M. 19n30
Jainism 111, 116, 119
Jameson, F. 10, 191
Janz, Paul 269n49
Janzen, Grace 62n108
Jaspers, Karl 268
Javelet, Robert 45n39, 47n61
Jayākhya-saṃhitā 125–7, 199, 201
Jean des Anges 100
Jensen, J.S. 248n1
Jerusalem 45
Joby, C. 94n86
John of Salisbury 33
Johnson, Mark 201
Joseph de Maistre 38
journey to God 70, 73–6, 77, 78, 80, 240; inner journey 83, 96, 224; life as journey 240; otherworld journey 62; spiritual journey 94
Judaism 29, 40
judgment 17, 63, 66, 87, 160, 248, 249, 262, 263, 264, 265, 266; Final/Last Judgment 44, 45, 56, 66, 96, 199
Julian of Norwich 212
Jung, C.G. 14, 202, 216
justice 21, 41–2, 69; *ius* 41

Kālacakra-tantra 176
Kālī 117, 158; as Kālasaṃkārṣinī 159; twelve Kālīs 159–60, 163
Kālidāsa 115
kāma 106, 113
Kāma-sūtra 113, 115
Kant, I. 37, 133, 191, 216, 248, 249
Kāpālikas 117
karma 103
Kashmir 105, 121, 124, 135, 140, 142, 166, 212
Katz, S. 244
Kerala 110
Kierkegaard, S. 4, 100, 216–18, 219, 220
kinesis 218–19
King, R. 22n39, 112n32, 251
kingship 55
kinship 108
Kisiel, T. 15
knighthood 31
Kook, I. 3
Koselleck, R. 265n4
Koslofsky, C.M. 53n84, 66n118
Koyré, A. 96n94
Krama 158, 159, 163
Kreuzer, T. 56n97
Kristeva, Julia 13, 14, 191, 216, 218–19, 220, 235, 258–9
Kṛṣṇa 113
Kṣemarāja 128, 130, 131, 132, 133, 137, 141, 154
Kula 158
Kuṇḍalinī 162, 185; as Caṇḍalī 185

Lacan, Jacques 14, 191, 216, 218, 259
Lacrosse, J. 255n24
ladder 75, 76, 79, 80, 196, 198, 217; Jacob's ladder 76

Lala Ded 212
Lamotte, E. 176n22
language 4, 8, 13, 16, 32, 143, 144, 145, 153, 155, 170, 191, 192, 200, 219, 223, 224, 233, 234, 235, 244, 245, 258, 259; paradoxical language 81
Laṅkāvatāra-sūtra 167, 180
Larson, G. 123n62
Laruelle, F. 5n5
Latin 6, 12, 28, 31, 33, 52, 53, 54, 60, 61, 62, 174, 195, 200, 208, 212
law 3, 4, 9, 32, 39, 69, 70, 208; canon law 70; moral law 37; roman law 41
Lazamon 42
lectio 91–2
Leinhardt, G. 109n19
Lerner, R.E. 46n60
Levinas, E. 241, 261
Levinson, S. 223n3
Lewes 35
Lewis, C.S. 42–3
liberation (*mokṣa*) 103, 104, 106, 111, 112, 113, 114, 115, 116, 117, 118, 119, 128, 129, 132, 134, 139, 140, 141, 144, 162, 168, 199, 205, 264; paths to *mokṣa* 154–64
liberty 38
life 3, 17, 24, 78, 80, 84, 92, 108, 110, 137, 164, 172, 174, 194, 208, 214, 219, 234, 239; as suffering 168; goal of life 81, 104, 111, 113; horrors of life 188; inner life 203; ways of life 209
lifeworld 11, 19, 238, 258
light, inner 131
Limbeck, Sven 56n96
Lindbeck, George 253
Lindberg, C. 94n85
Ling, Trevor 174n16
liṅga 117, 119, 121
Lingat, R. 108n15
linguistics, comparative 21, 22
Lipner, Julius 114n39
literature, genres of 31, 32, 36, 40, 104, 136, 208; pre-philosophical literature 65, 67, 166; mystical literature 62; soteriological literature 114; theological literature 64
liturgy 2, 14, 31, 35, 46, 47–9, 67, 208, 210, 231, 267; liturgy of the hours 35
Locke, John 98, 99, 191, 214–15
logic 33, 139
Lokakṣema 177
Lombard, Peter 48
Longère, Jean 81n35, 86n55, 89n68
longing 216
love 3, 4, 42, 50, 86, 87, 113, 114, 115, 217, 272; love of God 81, 94–5; romantic love 41
Lovejoy, Arthur O. 44
Lukács, Georg 191
Lukes, Steven 28, 38n35, 39n36
Luscombe, D.E. 34n15
Luther, Martin 66, 218
Lyons, W.E. 229n21

MacCulloch, D. 33, 34nn11, 17
McCutcheon, R. 22n39, 251
McEwen, Cameron 16n23
Macfarlane, Alan 38
McGinn, Bernard 62n108, 73n9
McGrath, S.J. 17
MacIntyre, A. 21, 239n49, 240
McMahon, Robert 76
Macrobius 43–4
macrocosm and microcosm 28, 43, 125, 183
Madan, T.N. 107n8
Madhva 140
Madhyamaka 176, 180
magic 99
Magna Carta 69
Mahābhārata 104, 113
Mahāyāna 119
Makdisi, George 71n3
Mālinivijayottara-tantra 111, 142, 153, 156, 162, 163
Mallinson, J. 131n86
Mandair, A.P. 22n39, 251–2
maṇḍala 2, 118, 119, 134, 184, 188
Mañjuśrimūlakalpa 180, 183
mantra 120, 128, 161, 162, 201, 243; path of mantras 116–17
Manusmṛti 108
Marburg School 248
Marglin, F.A. 107n9
Marx, Karl 13, 191, 216
Mascia-Lees, F.E. 19n30
master 39, 159, 171, 175
Masuzawa, T. 22n39, 251
material reality/world 48, 76, 98, 272; material causation 137; material power 131; material/spiritual distinction 196
matter 103, 104, 134, 258
Mauss, Marcel 105, 106, 192, 202–4, 205, 206, 208
māyā 151–2
meaning 8, 10, 16, 24, 47, 83, 84, 137, 194, 230, 239, 242; meaning of life 214; web of meaning 243
Mechtild of Magdeburg 54, 62

medicine 12, 33
meditation 10, 12, 14, 24, 36, 49, 50, 51, 89, 91, 92, 96, 119, 129, 130, 131, 133, 134, 155, 158, 159, 160, 161, 162–3, 167, 169–74, 175–7, 183, 186, 188, 190, 195, 197, 198, 199, 205, 208, 210, 214, 216, 242, 243, 244, 264; meditation on death 171
Mellor, P.A. 19n30
memory 20, 65, 77, 84, 145–50, 159, 238, 241–2
Meredeth, Fiona 234, 235
Merleau-Ponty, M. 19, 228, 234, 235, 241, 243
metaphor 4, 8, 9, 133, 145, 201
method 10–15
Metzger, M. 35n18
middle ages 30, 32–42, 54, 62, 65, 66, 67, 89, 95, 101, 202, 211, 267
Middle English 32, 53, 54, 55, 60, 200; literature 63
Milbank, John 41, 253, 254n20
Miller, W.I. 32n6, 38n28
Milner, M. 107n8
Mīmāṃsā/Mīmāṃsakas 139, 140
mind 79, 81, 88, 91, 92, 93, 94, 128, 129, 135, 159, 167, 169, 172, 173, 174, 179, 180, 190, 191, 196, 197, 198, 272; absorbed states of mind 84; wholesome and unwholesome mind 170
mindfulness 169–72, 188, 190
Mirandola, Picco dela 96
modernity 6, 7, 14, 24, 28, 36, 37, 39, 40, 41, 66, 70, 96, 97, 100, 101, 166, 193, 194, 202, 205, 213–16, 232, 233, 245, 246, 268, 271; modernism 166
Mohammed 268
momentariness 164
monastery 36, 46
monasticism 34, 112
monks 172, 174, 206
Moore, R.I. 34n15, 39n40
morality 21, 53, 63, 64, 98, 129, 187, 189, 190; moral space 3, 231, 232, 133, 140
Morris, Colin 38, 39, 40n41
Morsella, E. 262n37
Moses 268
Müller, Max 249
multiculturalism 252
music 8, 14, 226, 231, 233, 234, 243
mysticism 9, 36, 46, 70, 83–5, 95, 97, 98, 99, 101, 213; mystical ascent 70, 83–93, 95, 98
myth 98

Nāgārjuna 182, 187, 190
nāgas 110
Nārāyaṇa 125, 127, 134, 197
narratability 6, 8, 19, 219, 238, 244
narration 214, 245, 253
narrative 19, 171, 192, 200, 224, 238–42, 245, 246, 261
nature 83, 222
Nédoncelle, Maurice 76n17
Nelstrop, Louise 9n8
Nemec, John 141n5
Neoplatonism 29, 43, 44, 70, 72, 74, 99, 214
Nepal 105, 135
Netra-tantra 124, 125, 128, 132, 133, 137
Neville, Robert C. 253
New Testament 51, 87
Newhauser, R.G. 94n87
Newman, Barbara 80, 81nn35, 37, 84
Nicholas, Saint 56, 58, 60, 63
Nietzsche, F. 13, 216, 218, 223
nimitta 24, 172, 173
nirvāṇa 167, 168, 179, 186, 198; *nibbāna* 173
noesis/noema 133, 258
Nogent, Guibert de 36, 38
nominalism 43, 97
nostalgia 219, 269
Novalis 100, 210
Nyāya 165

Oakley, Francis 41n43
objective validity 248–9
objectivity 10
Ochs, Peter 254
Ockham, William of 98
Odysseus 53
Oliivelle, P. 108n12, 113nn34, 35, 173n12
ontology of process 132, 136, 200
ordeal, trial by 69
Origen 43
Orm, Monk of 54
Orpheus 53
Osborne, T.M. 78n26
Overfield, J. 71n2
Oxford 61, 71, 211

Paden, William 252
Padoux, André 116n44, 144n14, 155n42
Palazzo, Eric 47, 48n66
Pāñcarātra 118, 120, 125, 132
Panofsky, E. 48n69
paradise 264
Paris 71, 72, 73, 85, 211
Parkin, Robert 107n8
Parry, J. 108n14, 110n24
participation 63–7, 70, 171, 189, 193, 194, 197, 198, 199, 200, 202, 217, 236, 271
passion 50
Patañjali 167, 198; the grammarian 168
Patil, Parimal 255n25

Pattison, George 217nn39, 41, 235n38
Patton, K.C. 252
Paul, Saint 15, 17–18, 81
peace 74
peace of God 33
Peirce, C. 23, 253
penance 31, 46, 65
Peppin, Jean 201n10
perception 19, 70, 78, 93–4, 129, 130, 131, 144, 147, 150, 156, 159, 189, 234, 242, 249; erroneous perception 3; hierarchy of perception 84; purity of perception 59, 60
perfection 59, 78, 85, 87, 114, 136, 198
person 1, 5, 8, 9, 12, 13, 14, 20 *passim*; personalism 40–1; theories of the person 5, 6, 77, 78, 96, 105–12, 143–8, 163; sacrality of the person 70, 211, 271
Persson, Per Erik 71n4, 82n39
Peter Lombard 72, 73, 77
phemic sheet 23–4
phenomenology 10, 13, 15, 16, 17, 20, 27, 133, 136, 137, 157, 191, 193, 208, 209, 216, 218, 220, 249, 254, 256, 258; first level phenomenology 211, 257; hermeneutical phenomenology 8, 10, 11, 12, 14, 25, 133, 247, 261; phenomenology of inwardness 231–46; phenomenology of religion 11, 15, 248, 250, 258
philology 137, 256, 259
philosophy 6, 9, 16, 28, 31, 33, 39, 72, 104, 137, 139, 141, 215, 244; analytic philosophy 214; as a way of life 210; history of philosophy 191; philosophy of mind 225; philosophy of sign 261; philosophy of religion 257; post-foundational philosophy 13; pre-philosophy and inwardness 298–310, 261
piety 31, 35, 63, 93
pilgrimage 31, 34, 46, 65
Pilgrimage of Human Life 65
Plato 42, 54, 84
Platonism 74, 99
Plotinus 43, 99
Plutarch 54
Polhemus, Ted 19n30
politics 61, 103, 209; politics of inwardness 211–13; politics of representation 21, 209
Pollock, S. 6, 109, 113, 115nn41, 42
pollution 107
Porete, Marguerite 2, 62, 70
possession 106, 109, 110, 156
postmodernity 11, 13; postmodernism 191
Pound, Ezra 71, 105
power 21, 31, 33, 34, 39, 62, 78, 86, 104, 107, 115, 117, 119, 131, 134, 155, 159, 209, 213, 248, 252; inner power 160; power and status 108
prāṇa 128
Pratyabhijñā 118, 140, 152, 158, 166
pratyātmavedya 181, 188, 211
Pratyutpanna-sūtra 177–9, 180, 197
prayer 2, 4, 10, 14, 24, 31, 34, 35, 39, 46, 49–51, 64, 67, 84, 86, 96, 106, 112, 120, 135, 136, 199, 208, 217, 233, 243, 267
Preus, J.S. 247n1
Pricke of Conscience 52
Proclus 99
pronouns 222–3
Protestantism 13, 30, 38, 98, 100, 202
Proust, M. 225
psychoanalysis 13, 14, 216
psychology 194; cosmological psychology 70, 97, 98, 100, 198, 206, 210, 212, 232; meditational psychology 174
Purāṇas 115
pure land 179
purgation 84
purgatory 53, 55, 56, 57, 60, 63, 64, 65, 66, 197, 264
purity 60, 94, 106; ritual purity 117; purification 84, 86, 125, 159, 60, 161, 162, 179, 218

Quarnström, Olle 114n40
Quigley, D. 107n8, 108

Raheja, Gloria 107n9, 108n10
Ram Prasad, C. 104n1, 149n4, 255n25
Rāmānuja 112, 139, 140
Rāmāyana 113
Rappaport, Roy 135
rapture 81
Ratié, I. 141, 144n15, 146, 147, 148nn23, 24, 149n27, 201n8
rationalism 96
rationality 21, 22, 233, 254
Ratnagotravibhāga 181
Rawlinson, Andrew 176
Ray, B.C. 252
reading 35, 40, 69, 83, 86, 87, 92, 208, 210, 214, 217, 233, 242, 267
realism 43
reason 31, 32, 40, 71, 72, 77, 81, 87, 89, 92, 95, 98, 165, 232
recognition 129, 140, 154
redemption 40, 42, 44, 264
reflectivity 214, 224, 240
Reformation 63, 64, 66, 96
Reid, C.J. 41n43

reincarnation 103, 106, 110, 119, 159, 199, 264
Reinis, A. 53n84
relativism 161, 267
religion 2, 3, 4, 9, 10, 11, 13, 17, 20–4, 27, 31, 35, 38, 57, 60, 63, 65, 67, 71, 96, 115, 116, 135, 142, 167, 214, 235, 248, 249, 251, 252, 253, 255; critique of religion 250; history of religions 2, 5, 7, 8, 9, 13, 14, 249; scriptural religions 1, 4, 213
Renaissance 7, 35, 37, 38, 63, 96, 99, 165, 211
renunciation 30, 104, 112, 115, 134
repentance 49
reportability 220, 224, 233–5, 238, 245, 246
resurrection 34, 65, 100
revelation 71, 72, 82, 90, 96, 117, 128, 236, 139, 140, 145, 230, 253
reversibility 234
Rg-veda 110
Richard of St. Victor 70, 85, 86–96, 97, 195, 197, 198, 201, 240
Ricoeur, Paul 10, 11, 19–20, 85n52, 99, 133, 200, 226, 231, 238–9, 240, 241, 257, 258, 266, 267
rights 8, 41–2, 70, 99, 202, 214, 271; human rights 37, 41; rights discourse 69
Rilke, R. M. 6–7, 100
risibility 79
rites of passage 31
ritual 7, 14, 23, 35, 46–9, 105, 108, 112, 119, 134, 141, 142, 143, 154, 161, 183, 208, 231, 236, 245; ritual thinking 132, 135
Rivera, J.M. 235n38
Robert of Brunne 63, 64
Robertson, A.W. 48n69
Robinson, R. 107n8
romanticism 2, 6, 101, 216
Rorty, R. 265
Rose, E. 25nn18, 19
Rose, Gillian 248–50
Ruegg, D.S. 179n28
Rufinus 41
Ruusbroec, Jan Van 97

sacramentarium 35
sacraments 35, 48–9, 65
sacred-profane 32, 250
sacrifice 47; mental sacrifice 120
Sadāśiva 117, 121, 122, 123, 125
Sādhanamālā 199
sadhu 206
Śaiva Siddhānta 110, 117, 119, 120, 121, 122, 124, 125, 128, 133, 140, 163
Śaivism 116–21, 131, 133, 142, 154, 166, 183, 184
salvation 30, 31, 44, 45, 55, 64, 67, 87, 158, 164, 166, 199, 211
samādhi 176–7, 188
Sāṃkhya 104, 105, 106, 147, 164
Sanderson, Alexis 105, 106n3, 109nn17, 18, 116, 118, 125, 127, 142nn9, 12, 143, 154, 159n55, 183n40, 204
Śaṅkara 112, 140
Sanskrit 6, 12, 28, 104, 139, 158, 194, 200213
Santiego de Compostela 34
Schalow, F. 16–17
Scholasticism 69, 71–3, 116, 207
science 12, 33, 63, 96, 101, 218, 227, 260; science of religion 247, 249, 253
scriptural reasoning 248, 254, 256
scripture 83, 90, 140, 160, 168, 244, 253
Seagrave, S.A. 41n43
Searle-Chatterji, M. 107n8
secularization 8, 69
Seigel, J. 215, 224
self 1, 2, 3, 5, 8, 13, 14, 15, 18, 19, 23, 24, 42, 48, 67, 70, 80, 81, 83, 86, 92, 94, 98, 100, 101, 103–4, 105, 106, 110, 112–13, 114, 119, 127, 128, 134, 140, 144, 145, 146, 147, 149, 150, 151, 153, 163, 164, 165, 166, 182, 188, 190, 192, 195, 196, 197, 198, 200, 202, 203, 208, 209, 210, 213, 215, 216, 221, 222, 224, 226, 228, 231, 232, 233, 236, 245, 249, 256, 265, 268, 271; not-self 160, 167, 179, 182, 186, 190, 216; porous and buffered self 14, 109; search for self 39; self-assertion 8, 207, 219; self-control 215; self-disclosure 230; self-forgetting 82; self-identity (*idem* and *ipse*) 19, 20, 200; universal self 195
self-reflection 6, 8, 20, 219, 220, 224–33, 235, 242, 244, 245, 246
semiotics 13, 14, 20, 193, 254; semiosis 244
sex, ritual 117, 118, 143, 186–8
Sharma, U. 107n8
Sharpe, Eric 247n1
Shaw, S. 119n57, 170
sign 11, 31, 48, 82, 129, 133, 172, 192, 200, 224, 234; material nature of the sign 11, 20; mediation/disclosing by signs 242–5; philosophy of the sign 191
Silburn L. 128n73
silence 83, 243
Sikhism 252
Simmel, Georg 37, 41, 202
sin 31, 45, 49, 52, 55, 57, 60, 61, 64, 65, 66, 85, 94, 199, 219
Śiva 115, 116, 117, 119, 120, 122, 123, 124, 125, 129, 130, 134, 144, 153, 154, 155, 156, 157, 158, 159, 162, 166, 197, 200, 212

six paths 163
Sjoholm, C. 234n35
Smart, Ninian 250n7
Smārtas 115
Smith, F.M. 109n20
Snellgrove, David 186n49, 187nn53, 54
social imaginary 135–7
social science 13, 19, 256
society 12, 13, 24, 30, 31, 38, 39, 46, 53, 79, 103, 106, 108, 109, 111, 117, 203, 213, 214, 242
sociology 9, 12, 13, 20, 191, 192, 193, 248, 256, 257; sociology of religion 250
Somānanda 140
Somaśambhu 121, 123
somnium 93, 197
soteriology 164
soul 39, 44, 45, 48, 58, 59, 60, 61, 65, 66, 72, 77, 79, 81, 83, 84, 85, 89, 91, 93, 100, 110, 140, 161, 195, 196, 206; pure soul 64; voyage of the soul 33, 54
sound, inner 129, 130
Southern, Richard 38
Spence, Sarah 40n42
Spijker, I. van 69n1, 92nn77, 78, 94n89
spiritual practice/s 1, 3, 4, 5, 6, 24, 27, 40, 42, 46, 47, 104, 119, 120, 133, 193, 198, 206, 208, 214, 217, 271; spiritual exercises 39, 40, 132, 198, 208, 209, 210, 242
spirituality 9, 86; Franciscan spirituality 212; women's spirituality 212
state 69, 70, 202
Steinboch, A. J. 226, 241n53, 244
Stevens, Wallace 100, 220, 221, 222, 223, 228, 231, 232, 245, 246
Stoics 203, 210
Strauss, Leo 41
Stroumsa, Guy 247n1
Suarez-Nani, T. 78n27
subjectivity 1, 6, 7, 8, 9, 11, 12, 13, 14, 18, 19, 20, 23, 28, 31, 40, 46, 48, 49, 51, 62, 66, 69, 70, 96, 98, 101, 112, 127, 133, 136, 137, 154, 185, 191, 192, 193, 195, 205, 206, 208, 211, 214, 215, 217, 219, 221, 222, 223, 224, 226, 228, 231, 234, 235, 236, 238, 239, 241, 245, 247, 256, 257, 258–59, 262, 263, 265, 267, 271, 272; absolute subjectivity 149, 152, 153, 166, 237; collective/shared subjectivity 1, 6, 8, 28, 49, 51, 63, 70, 100, 101, 132, 133, 134, 135137, 192, 194, 202, 207, 214, 216, 224, 236, 242, 243, 261, 268
Suger, Abbot 48
Sukhavativyūha 176
sun 116, 122, 123
superstition 109
Surin, Jean J. 99–100
Śūraṃgamasamādhi-sūtra 176
suṣumnā 130, 162
Suzuki, D.T. 176n23
Svacchandabhairava-tantra 124, 128, 132, 133, 137
Śvetāśvatara-upaniṣad 111, 113
Swanson, R.F. 33n9
symbol 74, 201; symbolic system/order 30, 31, 83, 134, 225, 239; symbolic universe 69, 72, 74, 82, 186, 200, 201
symbolism 47, 82
Synor, J.P. 254n24

Takasaki, J. 181
Tantras 105, 116, 121, 136, 141, 183, 244
Tantrism 185
tathāgatagarbha 179, 180, 181, 199
tattva 122, 143, 144
Taylor, Charles 14, 84n50, 98n100, 100, 101, 109, 214, 232–3, 240, 268
teleology 99
temptation 65
text 1, 5, 9, 51, 72, 82, 104, 120, 127, 136, 209, 211, 224, 225, 230, 231, 232, 236, 239, 240, 243, 264; textuality 209, 261; universe as text 201
Thapar, Romila 168n3
theology 6, 9, 17, 32, 35, 47, 48, 52, 61, 71, 72, 73, 82, 83, 96, 97, 98, 100, 101, 128, 137, 141, 184, 197, 247, 253; comparative theology 22–3, 248, 249, 254, 256, 260; Hindu theology 139; mystical theology 3, 36, 46, 69, 81, 95, 97, 101; scholastic theology 70, 79; systematic theology 31; Victorine theology 90
theoria 92, 94
theory 256, 260, 261; theory of inwardness 193–220
theosis 49
Thompson, K. 213n33
Thripathi, C. Lal 150n29
throne 58, 59, 60, 120, 121–7, 128, 133, 201
Tierney, Brian 41
time 144, 149, 151, 164, 189, 200, 224, 237, 238, 239, 240, 241, 263; temporality 16, 218, 220, 236–8, 245
Tiruvāymoli 132
Tollefsen, T.T. 45n59
tonsure 30
tradition 2, 3, 4, 5, 9, 11, 24, 40, 42, 112, 120, 127, 133, 134, 135, 136, 171, 181, 187, 190, 194, 200, 205, 208, 213, 214, 231, 232, 241, 243, 254, 267, 268
traducionism 78
trance 55, 208, 245

transcendence 1, 3, 6, 8, 12, 31, 67, 79, 81, 94, 103, 114, 115, 120, 181, 189, 195, 197, 206, 230, 256
Trika 117–18, 125, 128, 154, 163
trinity 79, 84, 86, 89
truth 1, 3, 5, 9, 27, 48, 84, 90, 91, 103, 119, 137, 149, 159, 164, 167, 168, 171, 180, 188, 189, 197, 209, 216, 217, 218, 259, 264; inner/internal truth 3, 5, 6, 7, 10, 23, 32, 36, 67, 104, 105, 118, 128, 166, 176, 182, 293, 195, 212, 213, 232; principle of truth 180–1; ultimate truth 160
Tundale, The Vision of 54
Turner, Brian 19n30
Turner, Denys 36n20, 73, 74n12, 77, 95, 97

Ulman, Walter 38
unibilitas 78
universals 32, 207
unknowing 82
Upaniṣads 103, 110–11, 112, 140, 164, 165
Urban, Greg 222
Utpaladeva 141, 144, 145, 146, 150, 151, 153, 166

values 63, 103, 115, 192, 213, 242, 259, 271
vāsanā 151
Vaśeṣika 147, 165
Varsi, A. 265
Vasudeva, Somadeva 153n37, 160n87, 162n62
Vasugupta 156
Veda 117, 124, 140
Vedānta 104, 105, 106, 112, 115, 140, 147, 163, 165
vestige 76–7, 82
Victorines 85, 98
Vijñānabhairava-tantra 117, 128, 133
Villey, Michel 41
virgin 53
virtue/s 35, 42, 63, 65, 66, 87, 92, 106, 113, 114, 186, 235, 240; love of virtue 50
vision 29, 31, 35, 36, 47, 51, 52–64, 67, 70, 74, 79, 80, 81, 83–5, 94, 96, 176, 177, 198, 200, 212, 242, 243, 245; beatific vision 95, 198, 205; inner vision 12, 69, 70; ecstatic vision 74; vision of Buddhas 179; vision of God 76; visual contemplation 119–31, 200; visualization 12, 23, 49, 50, 51, 83, 84, 173, 184, 188, 200, 201
vision literature 7, 49, 52, 53, 54, 61, 62, 64, 66, 72, 194, 197, 235, 240
Viṣṇu 115, 116, 118, 125, 126, 140
vitalism 19
Vogel, C. 35n18, 47n62
Voloshinov, V.N. 11n14, 191
Vos, A. 207n26
Vovelle, Michel 52n84
Vries, Hent de 17n26
Vulgate 81

Wach, J. 250
Wallace, Vesna 183nn43, 44, 45, 187n51
Wallis, C. 155n45
Warder, A.K. 170
wealth 33
Webb, D. 34n16
Weber, Max 13, 23, 30, 98, 192, 248, 250, 256
Welton, Donn 228, 230n25, 236
Wenlock, The Monk of 54
West, the 8, 12, 27, 41, 84, 105, 106, 113, 139, 170, 202, 223, 251, 252, 266
Wetti, vision of 54
White, David 117n49
Wiebe, D. 248n1
will 20, 29, 51, 72, 77, 81, 82, 84, 100, 154, 155, 156, 217, 218; divine will 29, 51, 81, 83
William of Ockham 41
Williams, Paul 175n18, 177, 179n28
Williams, Rowan 1n2, 269n48
Wilmart, Dom A. 55n94
wisdom 50, 74, 82, 83, 88, 90, 91, 184, 186, 188, 209
world 4, 7, 8, 10, 14, 16, 30, 46, 49, 62, 64, 74, 75, 78, 79, 82, 83, 96, 97, 98, 101, 105, 111113, 127, 128, 132, 133, 134, 135, 136, 140, 143, 145, 150, 156, 164, 165, 176, 188, 198, 199, 209, 214, 215, 221, 222, 226, 230, 233, 234, 237, 239, 261, 262, 263, 264, 265, 266; disenchantment with the world 6, 67, 98; inner world 240; invisible world 91, 144; material world 49, 76, 152, 164; other/next world 53, 54, 57, 61, 65, 87, 110; real world 104; spiritual world 48, 49; symbolic world 31; visible world 94, 144; world of experience 60, 174

Yajñavalkya 110, 268
Yale School 253
Yates, Frances 96n93
Yeats, W.B. 100
yoga 114, 130, 160, 198; sixfold yoga 160, 183
Yogācāra 176, 177, 180, 182, 188, 190
Yudhiṣṭhīra 104

Zaehner, R.C. 189n56
Zahavi, Dan 237n45
Zaner, R.M. 19n30
Zinn, Grover 86n55

Printed in Great Britain
by Amazon